Hospital Patient Feeding Systems

Proceedings of a Symposium
Held at Radisson South Hotel
Minneapolis, Minnesota
October 19-21, 1981

Advisory Board on Military Personnel Supplies
Commission on Engineering and Technical Systems
National Research Council

Sponsored by

U.S. Army Natick Research and Development
    Laboratories
Advisory Board on Military Personnel Supplies of the
    National Research Council
The Office of the Surgeon General of the Department
    of the Army
The American Society of Hospital Food Administrators
    of the American Hospital Association
The American Dietetic Association

NATIONAL ACADEMY PRESS
Washington, D.C. 1982

The National Research Council was established by the
National Academy of Sciences in 1916 to associate the
broad community of science and technology with the
Academy's purposes of furthering knowledge and of
advising the federal government. The Council operates in
accordance with general policies determined by the
Academy under the authority of its congressional charter
of 1863, which establishes the Academy as a private,
nonprofit, self-governing membership corporation. The
Council has become the principal operating agency of both
the National Academy of Sciences and the National Academy
of Engineering in the conduct of their services to the
government, the public, and the scientific and
engineering communities. It is administered jointly by
both Academies and the Institute of Medicine. The
National Academy of Engineering and the Institute of
Medicine were established in 1964 and 1970, respectively,
under the charter of the National Academy of Sciences.

Library of Congress Catalog Card Number 82-61132

International Standard Book Number 0-309-03296-2

Available from

NATIONAL ACADEMY PRESS
2101 Constitution Avenue, N.W.
Washington, D.C. 20418

Printed in the United States of America

Preface

Alternatives to the conventional cook-serve food production system have been developed and implemented in
hospitals throughout the United States since the early
1960s. These alternative methods include cook-chill,
cook-freeze, and assembly-serve or convenience systems.
Such changes in food production methods necessitated
changes in hospital patient feeding systems, meal assembly, meal distribution, and meal service.

What is the state of the art today in equipment and
systems for meal assembly, distribution, and service in
hospitals? What is known about the effects of these
processes on the sensory, microbiological, and nutrient
qualities of menu items served to patients? How are the
qualities of menu items measured and managed throughout
the meal assembly, distribution, and service processes in
conventional, cook-chill, and cook-freeze food service
systems? How acceptable are hospital meals to patients?
What are the future needs for research in hospital patient
feeding systems? To answer these questions, planners of
the symposium brought together speakers with experience
in studying hospital food service. The speakers brought
diverse educational backgrounds--food service directors,
dietitians, educators, food scientists and technologists,
nutritional and medical researchers, a behavioral scientist, a food service facility consultant, and an operations research and systems analyst.

The symposium consisted of five half-day sessions.
The first session was designed to identify key issues and
emerging trends that will affect hospital food services
in the near future. Patients' perceptions of meal acceptability and food service managers' perceptions of meal
quality were described to provide a context for thinking
about systems used for hospital patient tray services.

iii

The next three sessions provided information on the alternatives for menu item flow in hospital patient feeding systems. Recent innovations in the production of modified diet meals for patients were described. Technological opportunities available to food service managers for meal assembly, distribution, and service processes were illustrated in multimedia presentations. A panel of sensory, microbiological, and nutritional scientists reviewed the effects of these three meal processes on the quality of menu items in hospital patient feeding systems.

The final session focused on decision criteria and methods of measuring and evaluating equipment, systems, and the quality of meals from the research project on patient feeding systems at Moncrief Army Hospital in Fort Jackson, South Carolina.

Funding for this symposium was provided by Natick Laboratories under the Herbert A. Hollender Workshop Series in Food Engineering and Food Sciences, a program honoring Dr. Hollender for his many contributions, over 30 years, to military food programs.

This volume contains papers, references, and illustrations from speakers, as well as transcripts of discussions by panels who explored questions asked by participants. It should be a valuable reference book for those with present and future concerns for the health and morale of patients and the management of food service systems in hospitals.

M. Eileen Matthews
Chair, Program Planning Committee

Charnette Norton
Chair, Steering Committee

Contents

Hospital Patient Feeding Systems

Overview

M. Eileen Matthews

HISTORICAL BACKGROUND

During the 1960s and 1970s, hospital food service facilities experienced revolutionary changes in methods of processing and delivering meals to patients. These technological changes occurred in equipment, food products, and
food production systems as conventional or cook-serve
methods gave way to cook-chill, cook-freeze, and convenience or assembly-serve methods. The alternative food
service systems were developed in response to the rising
costs of labor, food, and energy; low productivity; a
lack of skilled labor for food production; inefficient
use of equipment; and poor temperature quality of menu
items at the point of service to patients (Matthews,
1980). Efforts to alleviate these problems in individual
hospitals resulted in changing the entire system of menu
item flow in meal production, assembly, distribution, and
service.

MAJOR PROBLEMS

Lack of Research Data

Despite the obvious importance of providing hospitalized
patients menu items that are of adequate sensory, micro-

M. Eileen Matthews, Ph.D., R.D., is Professor of Foodservice Administration, Department of Foodservice,
University of Wisconsin-Madison.

1

biological, and nutritive quality, scientific data on the
quality and safety of menu items prepared and served in
hospital food service systems are limited. No systematic,
controlled research of significance has been done on
nutrient retention and on sensory and microbiological
qualities of menu items to determine how quality of food
is affected by the processes of meal assembly, distribution, and service. What little research that has been
done is fragmented, perhaps because investigators have
lacked the motivation or resources to continue working in
the area. Hence, a body of knowledge about the quality
of menu items during processing stages in food services
has not been developed for practitioners to use in
decision-making.

State of the Art

Because the ultimate effects of the meal assembly,
distribution, and service processes on the quality of
menu items are largely unknown, hospital food services
seem to be operating as if they were experimental
laboratories in which patients--the population at high
risk--were being fed something of undetermined nature.
Most of the literature about the effects of food
preparation and service methods on the quality of menu
items appears to be unrelated to equipment and systems
used in hospital food service facilities today. Although
new equipment has become available for meal assembly,
distribution, and service in hospital food services,
performance data for this equipment under actual use
conditions are not usually available from manufacturers.
Also, because of the bewildering array of equipment and
systems available, considerable effort has been spent in
individual hospitals during the past decade in determining
the feasibilities of these alternative systems for meal
production, assembly, distribution, and service.
Most hospitals do not have the technical staffs or
financial resources needed to design and conduct studies
that evaluate the interrelationships of food quality,
equipment, and systems under actual operating conditions.
Research for the hospital food service industry is done
either by large food service management companies (who do
not publish their results) or in those universities where
doctoral programs in food service administration have
been established (such programs number fewer than 10 in
the United States). Thus little research effort is spent

on solving the problems of the hospital food service industry.

Reports on implementing new patient feeding systems in hospitals have stressed the development of processes and the workability of the system in terms of equipment costs and personnel requirements. Such reports provide few criteria for evaluating the quality of menu items, and in general little attention has been given to developing and implementing food quality management programs in hospital food service facilities.

Hospital patient feeding systems are complex systems requiring sophisticated technical design and evaluation. What kind of food service equipment, if any, is on the drawing board for the future? Who is doing the design of this new food service equipment? Why is there a lack of communication between the food service equipment industry and the hospital food service industry?

Most hospitals in the United States are small, with fewer than 200 beds, and are not staffed to do research. Most food service equipment manufacturers are small businesses; neither do they do much research and development for the hospital food service industry.

The design of alternatives for food service equipment and the implementation of the new technology involves economic constraints, technical developments, policy decisions, and social improvements. Communication among food service equipment manufacturers, food service facility consultants, and hospital food service directors needs to be improved.

Research Needs

Few of the research efforts in food service systems have gone into model formulation. But knowledge of food service systems cannot be acquired through a mere accumulation of data. A systematic analysis of the existing pattern of relationships in the food service system is necessary. Such an analysis can only be done through the development of models.

Several speakers pointed out the lack of money available for food service research. Who pays for research in hospital food service systems? Who does the needed research? What are the roles of research for government agencies, universities, professional organizations, and hospital food service directors and staffs? What are the research opportunities for the vendors who sell food products, food service equipment, nonfood supplies, and technical or management services to the hospital food service industry?

A continuing, long-term, well-coordinated research program addressing the major problems facing the military and civilian hospital food service industry in the United States needs to be planned and implemented. Without such an approach, coordinating leadership and funding at the national level, little or no change can occur in hospital food services.

DIRECTIONS FOR THE FUTURE

One speaker pointed out that the difference between mediocre and superior food is management or supervision. Studies made under actual operating conditions and in laboratory controlled simulations of food product flow in hospital food services have also identified the need for management control of food quality.

The five components of the management control system illustrate how the control process works: activity, measurements, standards, analysis, and corrective action. Activity is the actual performance, something that is occurring. An activity, for example, might be that of determining the quality of a hot entree at the point of service to patients. Measurements of the activity must be made; for example, to control the temperature quality of food, a thermometer would be used to measure the temperature of the menu item. Standards are the desired performance. For example, a standard for the hot entree at the bedside of the patient could be a minimum temperature of 140°F (60°C). The control process cannot be accomplished without standards and methods of measurement. Analysis is the comparison of actual or existing conditions with the ideal, expected, or desired standards. Standards, by themselves, are not controls. Analysis is necessary to identify deviations from predetermined standards. The results of the analysis must be reported to the food service supervisor. Corrective action must be taken when activities are not leading to the desired results. The aim of the management control process is to ensure that the results of operations conform as closely as possible to established objectives.

The nature of any system, including a food service system, is that every component is connected to every other. A change in any part of the system will have a "ripple effect," because that change will affect other parts of the system. Loss of control of food quality in one subsystem of the food service may result in a loss of control in other subsystems. Thus, control of the quality of menu items throughout all the subsystems of production, assembly, distribution, and service is a primary objective of managers. Because the dietary or food service department of a hospital produces and serves many different types of menu items daily, often in very small quantities for the special diets of patients, a food quality control program needs to be implemented by managers in every hospital facility. For instance, time-temperature histories of menu items as they are transported through a food service system, beginning with receipt of ingredients and ending with service of menu items to patients, have assisted in identifying critical process steps where monitoring techniques should be used to ensure quality. As part of the Hazard Analysis-Critical Control Point models, Bobeng and David (1977) developed time-temperature standards to control food quality at critical process steps in conventional cook-chill, and cook-freeze food service systems (Tables 1, 2, and 3).

TABLE 1 Time-Temperature Critical Control Points at Control Points During Entree Production in a Conventional Food Service System

| Control Point | Critical Control Point | |
	Time	Temperature[a]
Preparation	Minimal	7-60 C
Heating	[b]	$\geq$ 60 C[c]
Hot holding	[b]	$\geq$ 60 C
Portioning, assembly, and distribution	Minimal	$\geq$ 60 C
Service	Minimal	$\geq$ 60 C

[a]Internal temperature of entree at completion of control point activity.
[b]Time will vary with entree, equipment, and/or system.
[c]Minimum temperature; will vary with entree.

SOURCE: Reprinted with permission of Journal of Food Protection; from Bobeng and David (1977), p. 636.

TABLE 2 Time-Temperature Critical Control Points at
Control Points During Entree Production in a Cook-Chill
Food Service System

Control Point	Critical Control Point	
	Time	Temperature[a]
Preparation	Minimal	7-60 C
Heating	[b]	≥ 60 C[c]
Chilling	≤ 4h[d]	≤ 7 C
Chilled storage	≤ 20h[d]	≤ 7 C
Portioning and assembly	Minimal	≤ 7 C
Cold holding and distribution	[b]	< 7 C
Heating	[b]	74-77 C
Service	Minimal	≥ 60 C

[a]Internal temperature of entree at completion of
control point activity.
[b]Time will vary with entree, equipment, and/or system.
[c]Minimum temperature; will vary with entree.
[d]Combined time of chilling and chilled storage should
be ≤ 24 h.

SOURCE: Reprinted with permission of Journal of Food
Protection; from Bobeng and David (1977), p. 636.

The Hazard Analysis-Critical Control Point concept is
a preventive approach to quality control, emphasizing
microbiological control and identifying process stages at
which loss of control could present a food safety risk.
The basis for the standards was to minimize the time that
the temperature of entrees was in the zone of growth for
microorganisms, 45°-140°F (7°-60°C). Bobeng and David
recommended establishing time-temperature standards as a
practical method for monitoring entree production in
hospital food service systems. If continuous time-
temperature surveillance is implemented, data can be
available for immediate corrective action. And adherence
to minimum temperature standards during heat processing
also conserves the nutritional and sensory qualities of
the entree.
    Research on quality of food in alternative systems of
meal production, assembly, distribution, and service

requires a multidisciplinary team of food-related professionals: food scientists, food microbiologists, food engineers, food technologists, nutritional scientists, and others. In 1977, members of the North Central Regional Research Committee on the Quality of Safety of Food in Foodservice Systems (Unklesbay et al., 1977) indicated the need to direct future regional research toward the following areas:

1. Investigating the effects of alternate methods of food procurement, storage, preparation, and service upon the microbial, nutritional, and sensory qualities of selected menu items in food service operations.
2. Determining the effects of innovative materials handling techniques and/or food

TABLE 3   Time-Temperature Critical Control Points at Control Points During Entree Production in a Cook-Freeze Food Service System

Control Point	Critical Control Point	
	Time	Temperature[a]
Preparation	Minimal	7-60 C
Heating	[b]	$\geq$ 60 C[c]
Freezing	$\leq$ 1.5 h	$\leq$-20 C
Frozen storage	< 8 weeks	$\leq$-18 C
Portioning and assembly	Minimal	$\leq$ 7 C
Cold holding and distribution	[b]	< 7 C
Heating	[b]	74-77 C
Service	Minimal	$\geq$ 60 C

[a]Internal temperature of entree at completion of control point activity.
[b]Time will vary with entree, equipment, and/or system.
[c]Minimum temperature; will vary with entree.

SOURCE: Reprinted with permission of Journal of Food Protection; from Bobeng and David (1977), p. 636.

service equipment in each type of food
service system upon the growth and survival
of pathogenic microorganisms of public health
significance.

3. Formulating procedures to be used as
    managerial tools for decision-making about
    preparing and serving quality menu items
    within each of the food systems.

4. Identifying factors within the physical
    environment of the food service system that
    directly affect food quality and safety, and
    correlating the effect of the interrelation-
    ships among these influential factors with
    food quality.

5. Determining methods through which the
    systematic control of food quality and safety
    can be achieved by automated and computerized
    methods.

Research emphasis on identifying and defining information needs within hospital food service systems is also
recommended. Model formulation may uncover hidden
information gaps and consequently may suggest improvements. For example, models need to be developed for
predicting nutrient retention in menu items that have
been heated by conduction, convection, or radiation and
are then subjected to hot or cold storage in the meal
assembly and distribution processes. In addition, the
use of input/output models for analyzing food service
systems could help managers become more accountable for
assigning the costs of food, labor, and other resources
(food service inputs) to menu items (food service out-
puts). Through the use of computer simulation, more
complex models of food service systems could be constructed to study operating adjustments to a variety of
management policies. Data from these models could
provide managers with a decision-making technique by
forecasting the effects of contemplated changes in food
service operations.
  It is only by conducting research that we will derive
new knowledge to advance our understanding of the interrelationships among food, equipment, employees, systems,
costs, and management in hospital food service systems.
Coordination of research efforts by government agencies,
universities, and professional organizations, as well as
the industries that sell food service equipment, food
products, nonfood supplies, and technical or management

services to hospital food service systems, is essential.
We need to learn how to communicate with these agencies
and organizations, which have different mission statements
and goals, and to find ways to share resources. Methods
must be found to improve communications and start coordinating research activities for the betterment of hospital
food service systems. A number of suggestions present
themselves:

* Identify areas in hospital food services that
need research, and identify disciplines that can
contribute knowledge to solve problems.
* Determine problem areas and priorities with which
the problems should be approached. The establishment of
agreements about priorities is an essential step in
coordination.
* Delineate research needs and methods. Methodology for research work in food service administration is
needed to establish some uniformity of procedures and
techniques, as well as methods of testing. This would
provide a basis for valid comparisons of results.
* Identify groups (government agencies, universities, professional organizations, and industry) that
can best cooperate to do the needed research.
* Develop mechanisms to get the groups together,
such as research and development committees, advisory
councils, and peer review systems.
* Design and use mechanisms to evaluate the
effectiveness and efficiency of research efforts. This
evaluation should include both scientific and business
relevance to hospital food service. For example,
questions to ask may be: "How does one measure and
evaluate a successful hospital food service system? What
are the criteria for success?"
* Develop international communications and research
efforts for hospital food services with other
industrialized nations of the world, and share expertise
with developing countries.

In the future, more applications of food science and
business administration will be needed in hospital food
service systems. Areas of knowledge in these two
disciplines include the following:

Food Science   Business Administration

Food Analysis   Decision-Making and Systems

Food Chemistry	Analysis
Food Microbiology	Managerial Accounting and
Food Processing/Food	Computer Processing
Engineering	Marketing and Consumer
Nutritional Sciences	Information
Sensory Sciences	Organizational Administration
	and Management Processes
	Industrial or Engineering
	Management
	Personnel Management

Education of professional personnel involved in managing hospital food services must be equally future-oriented. Undergraduate educational programs should meet requirements for scientific competence as well as relevance to business management and economic realities.

Some of the first speakers told us that hospitals are entering an era of new economic realities as we move toward the 1990s. The hospital food service industry has a long history of responding to pressures and developments imposed by the technological, economic, political, and social environment in which it exists. Isn't it about time that we took the initiative to design some alternative futures for the hospital food service industry in the 21st century? We need to look imaginatively into the future, now more than ever.

REFERENCES

Bobeng, B. J., and B. D. David. 1977. HACCP models for quality control of entree production in foodservice systems. J. Food Prod. 40(9):632-638.

Matthews, M. E. 1980. Serving meals with fiscal responsibility. Hospitals 54(7):77-78, 80, 82.

Unklesbay, N. F., R. B. Maxcy, M. E. Knickrehem, K. E. Stevenson, M. L. Cremer, and M. E. Matthews. 1977. North Central Regional Research Pub. No. 245. M. Agric. Exp. Stn., Columbia. 36 pp.

Population Trends and Implications for Health Care Facilities

James A. Rice

This environmental assessment describes the main trends expected to influence the hospital industry and in turn the role of food service managers in upcoming years. These trends are discussed within eight categories:

1. General Background
2. The Patient
3. Industry Composition and Structure
4. Financing
5. Regulation, Legislation, and Litigation
6. Human Resources
7. Patient Services
8. Hospital Organization

GENERAL BACKGROUND

Trends relating to general economic social factors and public opinion include the causes of inflation, the relationship between health care utilization and the business cycle, and public feelings about experiences with the health care system.

Consumer Prices: 1965-1980

The health care industry experiences a higher rate of inflation than the economy as a whole. Generally, over the last 15 years both the Medicare care component and

James A. Rice is Vice President, Corporate Planning and Development, Health Central, Inc., Minneapolis, Minnesota.

11

hospital room components of the consumer price index (CPI) have been increasing at a higher rate than the CPI for all items. Wages, in particular, have contributed to the increase in health care prices. However, energy costs, interest rates, and drug costs are also responsible for this trend.

Public Opinion: 1973-1978

The public is generally satisfied with the availability and quality of health care services. However, there is concern regarding hospital costs. Over the last 5 years individuals surveyed by the National Opinion Research Center were most satisfied with the status of their own health and the caliber of health care leaders, such as physicians, dentists, and government officials. These same individuals were least satisfied with the cost of health care services.

General Background--Summary

In summary, these trends indicate that: Hospital utilization is affected by the business cycle; and the public is satisfied with the health care system after a personal encounter, yet concerned about health care costs.

THE PATIENT

Major trends have been identified with respect to population growth, regional population shifts, changes in service utilization, and changes in attitudes about health.

Population Growth

Growth of U.S. Population: 1980-2030

Between 1980 and 2010 growth will be concentrated in the 25-64 age group. After that time the most rapidly growing segment of the population will be the over-65 and over-75 age group.

As a whole the age structure of the population will continue to shift upward, the median age will continue to increase, and a larger proportion of the population will be concentrated in the over-65 age group. Clearly there will be more older patients with unique nutritional needs during the 1980s.

Population Over 65: 1980-2030

The over-65 age group will continue to expand in the 1980s. It is estimated that by the year 2000, 11.7 percent of the population will be over 65 and 5 percent will be over 75.

This is particularly important for hospitals. While the over-65 group is much smaller than other age groups, it consumes a larger share of health care services. For example, people over 65 are admitted to health care facilities 3 times more often, their average length of stay is 5 days longer, and the cost of care is 3 1/2 times greater for them than for those who are younger. Moreover, 90 percent of the hospital expenditures on health care services for the elderly are paid from public funds, and there is mounting pressure for curtailment of those funds.

Food service managers can therefore expect to face the challenge of doing more for an older client base with fewer resources.

Estimated and Projected Growth of U.S. Population by Region: 1970-1990

All regions except the Mid-Atlantic experienced a population increase between 1970 and 1980. Over the last 10 years, those areas that traditionally have accounted for the largest share of the total U.S. population—New England, the Mid-Atlantic states, and the North Central states—showed increases substantially below the U.S. average. These trends indicate that the demand for hospital services has shifted from the Northeast, which used to be the nation's most populous area, to the Southwest and Far West, regions with historically more limited availability of resources. In the next 10 years it is projected that the South Atlantic, Mountain, and Pacific regions will experience the greatest population growth.

In response to these trends, hospitals will have to monitor and carefully assess the changes in their communities and plan how best to meet new needs. Hospitals in areas of declining population may struggle to maintain occupancy rates; hospitals in areas of increasing population will be expected to provide services to meet community needs and may be required to do so within severe capital limitations.

Regional Growth of Population Over 65: 1970-1979

There are also regional variations in the increase of the over-65 population, particularly in the warm-weather areas of the Western Mountain and South Atlantic regions. As a group, most of the elderly in the Western Mountain and South Atlantic regions will be less economically dependent than their counterparts in other urban areas. But hospitals in areas with growing elderly populations will be faced with the challenge of developing new services to satisfy their health care needs. Examples of such services include health education, social service, and outreach programs, as well as long-term care and hospice programs for the terminally ill.

Service Utilization

In addition to population trends, hospitals will need to consider utilization trends in their service areas--for example, the trends in hospital admissions by age groups.

Hospital Admissions: 1967-1980

Total hospital admissions have increased steadily over the last 13 years for both the under-65 and the over-65 age groups. This increase has been caused by the growth of total U.S. population, the increased incidence of disease, and broadened insurance coverage. The growth of hospital admissions rates emphasizes the increased use by the over-65 age group.

Hospital Admission Rates: 1967-1980

The growth in the over-65 population accounted for an admissions increase of over 40 percent between 1967 and

1980. Utilization rates of the over-65 population alone
have increased from 279 per 1,000 to 422 per 1,000 between
1967 and 1980. In contrast, hospital admission rates for
the under-65 population have remained constant from 1967
to 1980 at approximately 138 per 1,000. This means that
only 11 percent of the population uses over one-third of
the hospital resources. By 2015 it is estimated that
those over 65 will use 50 percent of the resources.

Admission Rates for Selected Diagnostic Conditions

There are several reasons why the older population uses
hospital services more frequently and intensely than other
age groups. First, the over-65 population experiences an
extremely high incidence of chronic conditions that
require continuous treatment over an extended time.
Second, the incidence of acute care conditions tends to
rise with age, although the increase is less pronounced
than it is for chronic conditions. Acute care has
historically been the mainstay of hospital services, but
as the percentage of the population over 65 rises,
hospitals will increasingly be called upon to provide
treatment for chronic and debilitating diseases.
  Food service managers will need to be prepared to meet
needs of chronically ill rather than younger acute-care
patients. Different diets and different ways of pre-
senting the food will be required.

Control Over Future Health

Public interest in personal health and health care
activities will increase. A national survey on Personal
Health Practices conducted in 1979 by the National Center
for Health Statistics revealed that 50 percent of both
men and women felt they exert a great deal of control
over their own health through physical fitness, good
diet, and other preventive practices. As interest in and
knowledge of health care issues increase, consumers are
likely to become more assertive and will seek more
complete information about their own illnesses. This may
warrant a greater degree of participation in provider
decisions that affect an individual's health. There is
likely to be need for nutritional counseling outside the
hospital.

The Patient--Summary

We can identify five significant factors related to the patient that will have great impact on the hospital industry in the 1980s:

- an increasing and aging population;
- regional differences in population growth and aging;
- increased hospital use by the older population;
- different health problems for the older population; and
- more public concern about health promotion.

INDUSTRY COMPOSITION AND STRUCTURE

System Capacity

The total number of community hospital beds doubled between 1950 and 1979, increasing from approximately 500,000 to 1 million in that 29-year period. Beds per 1,000 population have increased 14.8 percent from 1950 to 1979 and have remained constant at 3.1 per 1,000 over the last 5 years.

Competition

In the next several years it is likely that competition will become more prevalent among hospital and nonhospital providers. Competition is likely to develop on two levels: for specific services at the point of delivery and for certain population groups. For example, in the provision of laboratory tests, hospitals will compete with other hospitals, free-standing ambulatory care centers, and independent laboratory services in physician office buildings. In a competitive climate, food service quality will be an important element of consumer choice.

Multihospital Systems

Although the presumption is empirically untested, it is thought that multihospital systems have grown due to:

- the need to develop critical mass to manage, operate, and control efficiently;
- the increased cost of medical technology;
- the added regulations and other constraints placed upon hospitals; and
- the increased competition within the health care industry.

Currently, there are no consistent definitions of multihospital sytems. The AHA defines such a system as two or more short-term care hospitals that are owned, leased, or contract-managed by a single entity. This definition excludes any psychiatric long-term care or nursing home facilities, as well as all consortia. Modern Healthcare, in its annual survey of multihospital systems, defines them only as systems that act like centrally managed entities. It thus excludes the Catholic systems. For the purposes of this discussion, the AHA's definition will be used. The data were collected by the AHA's Center for Multi-Institutional Arrangements in 1981.

Growth of Hospitals in Multihospital Systems: 1940-1979

As of 1981 there were 256 multihospital systems control- ling 32 percent of all hospitals (1,884) and 36 percent of hospital beds (353,000). In a survey conducted by the Center, 189 respondees represented 1,500, or 80 percent, of the hospitals in multihospital systems. The number of hospitals in multihospital systems increased 580 percent between 1940 and 1981, from 218 to 1,500. Investor-owned sytems have the greatest number of hospitals (661), followed by the not-for-profit (354), Catholic (351), and other religious groups (126).

Multihospital Systems by Control Category: 1970-1981

According to AHA data, investor-owned systems represent approximately 40 percent of multihospital systems. Catholic systems are the second largest group, accounting for 28 percent. Voluntary systems make up approximately 25 percent, and other religious groups control 8 percent of all multihospital systems. Since 1970 the most rapid rate of growth has occurred in the investor-owned and other-religious ownership categories.

Hospitals in Multihospital Systems: 1981

As of 1981, 86 percent of not-for-profit hospitals are
owned or leased and 14 percent are contract-managed.
Sixty percent of the investor-owned are owned or leased
and 40 percent are contract-managed. In the future,
multihospital systems are expected to:

   •   increase standardization of management and
operating procedures and practices throughout the
hospital industry;
   •   include specialized hospitals, nursing homes, and
extended care facilities; and
   •   compete for members and provide services to
members.

   Expansion of multihospital systems will be seen as a
key strategy for the formation of new capital in the
health care industry. In particular, affiliation with
the proprietary multihospital system will be perceived as
a source of modernization funds and improved compensation
packages. It can be expected that antitrust issues will
increasingly be raised as multihospital systems
predominate.

Industry Composition and Structure--Summary

Trends in the industry composition and structure over the
past two decades indicate the following:

   •   The number of community hospitals has remained
stable since 1974.
   •   Community hospital beds are increasing.
   •   There will be increasing competition among
hospitals.
   •   There will be more multiinstitutional arrangements.

   Food services managers will need to be prepared to
work within hospital systems--i.e., they will have to tap
a broader pool of resources.

Benefits

Private Health Insurance Benefits: 1940-1979

It is likely that the scope of health care benefits will
continue to expand as prepayment and commercial insurance

firms compete for new and existing markets. Emphasis
will be placed on expansion of benefits that reduce use
of inpatient care. In addition, business purchasers of
health care insurance will seek to provide their employees
with a broader, more tailored package of benefits. For
their part, employees will have the opportunity to select
the type and scope of benefits that best suit their needs.

Currently, 83 percent of the population has hospital
coverage, 79 percent has surgical coverage, 74 percent
has physician coverage, 67 percent has major medical
coverage, and 32 percent has dental coverage.

Health Care Expenditures and Hospital Payment

It is important for hospitals to understand trends in
health expenditures and the pressures exerted on carriers
and/or government agencies providing reimbursement for
health care services.

Sources of Federal Government Revenue: 1950-1984

As a percentage of total federal government revenues,
social insurance taxes and contributions have increased
consistently since 1950. The relative percentage of
personal income tax has increased, while percentages of
the corporate income tax and other revenue sources have
remained approxiately the same. Much of the increase in
the share of payroll deductions in current sources of
federal government revenues can be attributed to the
Social Security and Medicare programs. As a result the
federal government increasingly focuses on medical care
cost containment in an effort to control rising taxes.
Through 1984 all sources of federal revenue are expected
to increase, but at a decreasing rate. Cost containment
pressures will rise. There will be less capital available
for operating and less capital for budgets of food service
managers.

Federal Budget Outlays: 1960-1980

The federal budget increased from $92.2 billion in 1960
to $563.6 billion in 1980. Outlays for health grew 12
percent compared to income security, which increased 14
percent, and defense, which decreased 26 percent.
Currently, health care expenditures account for 12 percent

of the federal budget, income security 34 percent, defense
23 percent, and education 5 percent.

Health Expenditures as a Percentage of Government Expenditures: 1950-1979

In 1979, 12 percent of the federal budget and 9 percent
of state and local budgets were devoted to health care.
Since 1965 the percentage of federal expenditures devoted
to health care has quadrupled (3.4 percent to 12 percent).
Since 1965-1970 the federal government has spent a greater
portion of its budget on health care than have state and
local governments. It is the intent of the Reagan Administration to shift a greater portion of health expenditures to state and local governments.

Projections of Health and Defense Portions of Federal Budget: 1960-1984

The Office of Management and Budget has projected that
the portion of the federal budget devoted to health care
will remain stable at 10-12 percent in order to accommodate increases in such other areas as defense. This
reflects changing priorities of the new administration.

Distribution of Public and Private Health Expenditures: 1950-1979

From 1950 to 1979, total health expenditures increased 16
times, from $12.6 billion to $213 billion. The private
sector has financed most health care expenditures. In
1979 it provided $121 billion of support compared to $92
billion from the public sector. However, the public
sector has provided an increasingly greater proportion of
health expenditures over the last 20 years. In 1950
public support accounted for 25 percent of health
expenditures, compared to 37 percent in 1970 and 43
percent in 1979.

Hospital Care Expenditures by Third-Party Payors: 1979

Private health insurance is the single largest source for
hospital care expenditures, 35 percent. Medicare con-

stitutes 25 percent, Medicaid 9 percent, and other government programs 21 percent. Finally, direct payments
account for 8 percent and private donations 1 percent.

Hospital Expenses

Total Community Hospital Expenses: 1979

In 1979, labor expenses constituted 57 percent of total
community hospital expenses. Of nonlabor expenses, house-
keeping, food, insurance, and supplies were the most
significant. In addition to the operational expenses,
hospitals have capital requirements for modernization and
replacement of facilities, equipment, and technology.

Sources of Funds

Trends in Financing for Community Hospital Construction:
1973-1979

Since 1977, tax exempt debt has become the major source
of capital for hospitals. Taxable debt and private
contributions have declined as sources of funds, while
government grants and internally generated funds
(operating margin, funded depreciation) have increased.
 In 1979, tax exempt debt provided 50 percent of
financing for hospitals, followed by internally generated
funds (25 percent), taxable debt (15 percent), private
contributions (6 percent), and government grants (4
percent).

Financing--Summary

The major factors affecting financing may be summarized
as follows:

- reduced federal expenditures and increased state
expenditures for health care
- anticipated increases in hospital expenses and
expenditures
- availability of funds for modernization and
replacement of facilities
- limited sources of funds
- changing financial options

Food service managers will have to do more with less. Financial management skills will need to be strengthened, as will the clinical role of nutrition.

REGULATION AND LEGISLATION

Role of the Federal Government

The major priorities of the Reagan Administration with respect to U.S. expenditures include:

* balancing the federal budget
* increasing defense spending
* modifying the approach to cost containment
* decreasing interference in how health care costs are contained, as long as they are successfully contained

Regulation

Regarding regulation, it is expected there will be:

* less government interference
* less federal regulation
* more pressure on private sector to establish and maintain voluntary solutions (especially with regard to regulation and financing)
* reduced federal expenditures for Medicare/Medicaid and no federal standards for states

The shift of responsibilities from the federal to the state level, expected earlier in the Reagan Administration, will not occur.

Legislation

Although new legislative initiatives are not anticipated, we do expect:

* reform of the regulatory process
* reform of social security
* improvement of delivery system cost-effectiveness

We may also see legislation regarding:

- provision of coverage of catastrophic and chronic illness
- encouragement of competition/consumer choice
- repeal or modification of HMOs, PSROs, and health planning, health professions, and health education laws

A cost containment bill is unlikely unless voluntary measures prove ineffective.

HUMAN RESOURCES

Human resources refers to supply, specialization, and geographic distribution of health care professionals.

Physician Supply

Expansion of Physician Supply and Growth of Population: 1960-1990

By 1990 the total number of physicians practicing in the United States is expected to reach 525,000, an increase of 60 percent since 1975. According to the Graduate Medical Education National Advisory Committee (GMENAC), this will represent an excess of 35,000-85,000 physicians by 1990. If the increasing supply of M.D.s remains constant, GMENAC projects an excess of 145,000 physicians by the year 2000.

Except for psychiatry, emergency medicine, and pediatric subspecialties, where shortages are expected, GMENAC predicted an oversupply of physicians in 1990 for all other primary care and specialty groups. Surpluses will be especially prominent in obstetrics/gynecology and general surgery.

To alleviate this oversupply GMENAC recommended that:

- no new medical schools be opened in the United States
- medical school enrollment be reduced by at least 10 percent by 1984
- opportunities for foreign medical school graduates to practice medicine in the United States be decreased
- fewer foreign students be accepted in U.S. medical schools, and financial aid to U.S. students studying abroad be denied

• the use of paraprofessionals as substitutes for M.D.s be discontinued
• levels be delegated for primary care and specialty M.D.s

Since population growth is expected to remain stable over this period, the growth of the physician supply will increase physician-to-population ratios 220 M.D.s per 100,000 population in 1990 and 247 M.D.s per 100,000 population in the year 2000 (compared to 171 M.D.s per 100,000 population in 1978). Consequently, physicians will have the opportunity to reduce workload and will face greater competitive pressures as they look for patients.

Physicians will practice in groups more than ever. Food service managers may need to take different approaches to the education and orientation of clinics as to their role in counseling patients on nutrition. There will be more out-of-hospital roles for food service managers.

Human Resources--Summary

In the upcoming years it is expected that:

• the supply of nurses will decrease
• the supply of M.D.s will increase but there will be regional and local shortages
• there will be increasing needs for allied professionals

Several results can be anticipated:

• hospitals are likely to experience higher labor costs
• the supply of health professionals is not expected to affect favorably the maldistribution problem
• it is likely that underserved areas will continue to be underserved.

PATIENT SERVICES

Alternative Modes of Delivery

Hospital Services: 1950-1980

Presently, technology-based services are more widespread than services representing alternative modes of delivery.

However, hospitals are increasingly expanding services
that are not technology intensive. Alternatives to
in-patient care, such as ambulatory care, hospice care,
home care, long-term care, and substance abuse programs,
are reported with greater frequency by community hospitals. In 1980, 80 percent of these hospitals offered
ambulatory surgery, 20 percent offered hospice care, 16
percent offered long-term care, 9 percent offered
alcoholism programs, and 8 percent offered home care.

HMO Enrollment: 1974-1980

Health Maintenance Organizations (HMOs) represent still
another alternative to acute in-patient hospital care.
Enrollment in HMOs has increased from 5.3 million in 1974
to 8.2 million in 1980, covering about 4 percent of the
total U.S. population. Overall, HMOs constitute a
relatively small share of the total market for health
insurance, but in some areas their market share is up to
7 times the national average.
   The long-range significance of HMOs is their ability
to provide to health care consumers a full range of
health services for a uniform per capita payment. Consumers will be able to compare such a system with more
traditional delivery systems. HMOs reporting lower in-
patient hospitalization rates will be used by regulators
to set an industry standard for utilization patterns.
The continued growth of HMO enrollments raises the possibility of a reduction in overall hospital utilization
rates and an increase in the importance of HMOs as a form
of health insurance and a source of reimbursement. As
the number of HMOs increases, hospitals will have to
reassess the capabilities of their programs in terms of
meeting new service needs to compete with this new
delivery system. Local hospitals will have to exercise
organizational creativity in determining the nature and
scope of their involvements with the HMOs emerging in
their areas.

Health Promotion

The role of the health care delivery system will be
defined increasingly in terms of preventing illness and
maximizing the ability of the individual to maintain or
improve his own health. This trend will include

increased emphasis on less intrusive and less costly
therapies.

Number of Hospitals offering Health Promotion Programs:
1979

According to a 1979 survey conducted by AHA's Center for
Health Promotion, 55 percent of community hospitals
offered nonpatient community health programs.

Patient Services--Summary

In the 1980s, the hospital industry may see:

  • changes in utilization patterns and service
demands, including prevention services
  • more cooperative arrangements to share expensive
technologies
  • a variety of models for medical practice and
delivery of services

  Food service managers will increasingly be expected to
direct nutrition counseling to in- and out-patient
populations to stress health promotion.

HOSPITAL ORGANIZATION

Governance

Governing boards will retain legal liability for everything that occurs in the hospital and may become directly
accountable to the public or community served by the
hospital. Governance and management will continue to be
reorganized along corporate lines, with hospital governing
boards reviewing management decisions for compliance with
board-developed policies and strategies. Multihospital
arrangements will pose challenges to traditional notions
of governance. In arrangements where strong central
control is exerted, significant governance activity will
shift from the boards of individual institutions to the
central governing board.

Traditional Corporate Structure and Key Characteristics--
New Corporate Structure and Key Characteristics

Traditional structure is characterized by a single governing board and a centralized management structure and
is organized by function. The new corporate structure is
characterized by a multilevel governance structure and a
decentralized management structure and is organized by
line of business. As pressures on hospitals increase,
they will develop new methods of facilitating the performance of board functions. It may become necessary for a
hospital's management team and board of trustees to
formalize their expectations and relationships. Some
hospitals, for example, may consider compensating board
members for their service.

Management

The role and responsibilities of the chief executive
officer will continue to develop along patterns found in
business organizations. That is, the chief executive
officer will become responsible for the development and
evaluation of policy and program alternatives for board
consideration and will be identified as the single point
of accountability for the execution of board policy.

The management staffs of hospitals will continue to
become more specialized and sophisticated as they apply
marketing principles within hospitals and make use of
more sophisticated management, financial, and clinical
information systems. Formal planning on an institutional
basis will be undertaken more frequently. To manage a
more highly specialized management and professional
staff, hospitals will need to develop more sophisticated
mechanisms for integrating clinical, administrative, and
financial decision-making. Food service managers must
become more productive and effective as members of the
management team.

Finally, the traditional prerogatives and organizational practice preferences of physicians within hospitals
are likely to be altered by regulatory mechanisms,
increases in the supply of physicians, and changes in
payment systems. In particular, cost constraints will
provide hospital managers with a vehicle for greater
influence in medical decision-making. As a corollary,
this situation will require the greater involvement of
physicians in the management and administration of the

CONCLUSIONS

1. Food service managers will be expected to do more with less.
2. The role of food services in a hospital's marketing strategies will become even more evident in the competitive environment of the future.
3. Interpersonal skills will become more important as "on the floor" interaction with patients and their families increases.
4. The role of nutrition counseling for elderly persons with chronic diseases will become much expanded.
5. Nutrition's role in health promotion initiatives will be stressed--from within, but increasingly from outside, the traditional hospital's four walls.
6. Food service managers will need to be prepared to work as stronger members of the hospital's management team through knowledge and skill development in management areas outside those of clinical nutrition. This management role will increasingly be performed in multihospital systems.
7. Additional research into the role of nutrition for sufferers of chronic diseases will be necessary.

DISCUSSION

QUESTION: What is the impact of the data you presented or your opinion on hospitals that seem to be operated on behalf of the medical staff?

RICE: There exist some interesting trends in the number of doctors and their market competiveness; that is true. The first part of the question: Most of the information we have suggests that it will be increasingly difficult for most hospitals, even hospitals that are 300 to 400 beds, to stand in isolation from one another. The prognosticators vary on what is likely to happen in the growth of hospital systems. A recent forum article suggested that as we move into the 1990s there will be a coalescing from the 5,500 ownership entities that we have now to maybe only 25, of which 5 would be for-profit. We are not going to see that type of consolidation in the industry, but we are certainly going to see more; and I would suspect that the freestanding institutions are going to be very few and far between. They will at least share some services with others, even if they are not joined together. And so, if you are in a hospital that industry, but we are certainly going to see more; and I would suspect that the freestanding institutions are going to be very few and far between. They will at least share some services with others, even if they are not joined together. And so, if you are in a hospital that remains isolated, it will be a less simulating and interesting place to work during the 1980s.

The comment on doctors is clearly true. More doctors will be forming more groups. Those groups will be hiring more talented clinic administrators. Those administrators will be helping groups of doctors diversify, and doctor groups are going to diversify into areas that used to be the hospitals'. Hospitals will diversify into areas that used to be the doctors'. We will have a collision about July 1985.

QUESTION: To what degree will food service be expected to move away from cost centers to profit centers?

RICE: In most hospitals they will continue to be a cost center in support of some of the other principle service initiatives. However, there are some hosptals that have a sufficient resource base and enough talent in their food service management that they can secure nonpatient revenues either through consulting or selling services outside, particularly in some of the health promotion activities.

QUESTION: Why is the dietary department the first to go to contact management within the hospital? What can we, as dietitians, do to match their strength?

RICE: You bear the brunt of a lot of complaints because your function has a lot of direct contact with the public, the patients, and their families. I am not sure what a rigorous research study would show, but I suspect the complaints are divided fairly equally between patients and their families. Somtimes the patients are pretty comfortable and the families are complaining about the way it looks or the way they think it feels or tastes.

QUESTION: If hospitals become more active in the nursing home business, how will that change the quality of care in nursing homes, and what will happen to present nursing home owners and operators? Will quality improve?

RICE: Some of my friends in the nursing homes feel that quality will be jeopardized. I believe the response is going to vary between the hospital operators and nursing homes. There are a large number of nursing homes that are exemplary in the approach they take to all aspects of patient care. There is a possibility that in some nursing homes quality can improve with access to a

QUESTION: What is going to happen to nursing home owners and operators?

RICE: Some of them will contract out for more management help and support with shared services. Some will become employees of the multiinstitutional systems that are developing, and some will retire and become residents.

Patients' Perceptions of Meal Acceptability

Armand Cardello

INTRODUCTION

The quality of hospital food and food services can be
evaluated by a variety of objective indexes. These
include the chemical composition, nutritional adequacy,
and microbiological safety of the food, as well as the
energy, labor, and cost efficiencies of the system.
However, there is also an important subjective index of
the quality of these products and services--namely, the
quality as it is perceived by the hospitalized patient.

Although the phrase "patient perception" connotes a
lack of objectivity, this is true only in the philo-
sophical sense of physical objectivity. It does not mean
that perceptions do not exist or that they cannot be
measured. In fact, there is an entire subdiscipline of
psychology, known as psychophysics, that is devoted to
the problem of quantifying human perception. As a psycho-
physicist who is working in food acceptance, I would like
to discuss the variety of techniques available to measure
patients' perceptions of meal acceptability and certain
factors that must be taken into account when conducting
food-related sensory tests in the hospital setting.

In approaching this problem, I will address the
following questions:

Armand Cardello, Ph.D., is Research Psychologist, Science
and Advanced Technology Laboratory, U.S. Army Natick
Research and Development Laboratories, Natick,
Massachusetts.

31

1. What are the basic concepts that must be understood
when evaluating patients' perceptions of hospital food?
2. What tools and techniques are available for measuring patients' perceptions of food and meal acceptability?
3. What food and nonfood factors will affect patients'
perceptions of meal acceptability?
4. How do you conduct a food acceptance or food
preference test in a hospital setting?
5. What special problems are encountered when working
with hospitalized patients?

In addition, examples of methods and survey instruments
will be provided; and data collected from previous patient
and staff surveys at U.S. Army medical facilities will be
presented to highlight the discussion.

The Problem of Hospital Food

Historically, concern with the role that food may play in
the recovery of patients from illness can be traced back
to one of the earliest medical works, the Hwang Ti Nei-
Chang Su Wen (the Yellow Emperor's Classic of Internal
Medicine (722-721 B.C.), in which it is stated that,
"Curing and nurturing come from the same source." Two
thousand years later, in 1859, Florence Nightingale
underscored the importance of hospital food preparation
in her Notes on Nursing when she admonished that "Sick
cookery should half do the work of your patient's weak
digestion." In its 1980 edition the Accreditation Manual
for Hospitals states that, for hospital food, "maximum
effort should be made to assure the appetizing appearance,
palatability, proper serving temperature, and nutrient
value of food." Yet, in spite of over 2,000 years of
awareness of the important role that food plays in the
recovery of patients from illness, one still frequently
encounters the opinion, best expressed in the title of a
recent newspaper column, that "Hospital Food is
Chronically Sick" (Beard, 1977).
Whether this poor opinion of hospital food is based on
fact or merely reflects an outdated stereotype is a
question of concern to hospital administrators and
dietitians. As Feldman (1962) points out, most professionals in the field of hospital patient feeding feel
that patients are quite satisfied with their meals; and
several studies of hospitalized patients have shown
favorable attitudes toward hospital food (Opinion

Research, 1955; Friedson and Feldman, 1958; Roper, 1958; Sheatsley, 1965; Herz et al., 1978).

One obvious reason for conflicting opinions about the quality of hospital food arises from the discrepancy between patients' and dietitians' opinions of what characterizes quality food. To the dietitian the definition of quality food is based largely on nutritional (objective) criteria, whereas for the patient it is based largely on sensory (subjective) criteria (McCune, 1962). The latter include such attributes as the appearance, texture, flavor, and temperature of the food.

In some sense the problem with hospital food is similar to the problem with military food. Military food has long suffered from a negative stereotype originating from the experiences of soldiers in World War II, World War I, and earlier. Although the quality of military food has improved greatly during the past several decades, the disparaging stereotype still remains. Thus, one purpose of this symposium is to break through the stereotypes surrounding hospital food, objectively state the problems, and identify those state-of-the-art methods that may assist in the reduction or elimination of problems within this important area of patient care.

General Considerations

I would like to raise two conceptual issues. The first is the issue of situational versus general problems in patient feeding and the second is the role of the food versus that of the system. Concerning the first, although one goal of the behavioral scientist in evaluating patients' perceptions of hospital food is to uncover general problems and, correspondingly, general solutions to these problems, this approach will lead to failure unless sufficient data have been accumulated in a large number of hospitals to support the generality of the problem and its solution. Although certain state-of-the-art methods of food preparation, cooking, storage, transport, and distribution may work well in some hospitals, these same methods may not work at all in other hospitals. In fact, Sheatsley (1965) has shown that the greatest differences in attitudes toward hospital food are found not among patients of varying characteristics but among the patients residing in hospitals of varying characteristics. The size of the hospital, physical layout, location, staffing, financial resources,

and other similar factors will determine the success of
any particular method. Thus, before deciding upon a
course of action to improve hospital food service operations, the food service manager must be able to assess
adequately the problems, both from an operational perspective and from the patients' perspective. Only then
can a system be chosen to reduce or eliminate these
problems.

The second issue concerns two interacting factors that
must be considered when analyzing problems in hospital
feeding. The first is the food itself, i.e., the recipes
and ingredients. The second is the food service system,
i.e., the cooking methods, delivery methods, menus, dining
atmosphere, etc. The latter factors, while frequently
categorized independently of the food, will nevertheless
affect the patient's perception of the system and his
perception of the food. A poor tray delivery system will
result in cold food reaching the patient, which will
affect not only his perception of the system that
delivered that food but also his perception of the food
itself. Thus, the cause of patient dissatisfaction with
hospital food is frequently related to problems with the
system, and the food service manager/administrator should
be prepared to assess patients' opinions of both the food
and the system, so that the true cause of the problem can
be identified.

Although the food and the system are the two factors
that are under the control of the food service adminis-
trator, they are by no means the only factors affecting
patients' perceptions of food. Numerous physiological,
psychological, socioeconomic, and other factors contribute
to a patient's perceptions. Some of these will be discussed later. At the outset, we will consider the various
methods and techniques available for assessing patients'
perceptions of food. This will be followed by a discussion of some simple principles for collecting valid
patient/consumer data in a hospital setting and then by a
discussion of system factors that affect the perception
of hospital food.

HOSPITAL FOOD: MEASURES OF LIKING

Terminology

A number of techniques have been developed over the years
to measure consumer likes and dislikes for food and other

hedonic (pleasant instead of unpleasant) stimuli. Unfortunately, many of the techniques and approaches have become confounded within the literature and subsequently within the minds of food service practitioners. This confusion has resulted from a failure to define adequately the terminology. Terms such as consumer "preference," "acceptance," "consumption," and "satisfaction" have been used interchangeably in the literature. However, each refers to a specific measurement process and each has a specific definition. The first three can be defined as follows:

1. Consumption--the number and/or amount of a food or food item that is actually ingested by the individual.
2. Preference--the expressed degree of liking or disliking for a food when obtained in response to a food name. The name serves as a representation of the food, independent of particular preparation factors. Note that an alternative definition of preference is "choice of one food over another." However, the present definition is more consistent with prior usage in the area of food attitude assessment (Branch, 1973; Meiselman and Waterman, 1978).
3. Acceptance--the expressed degree of liking or disliking for a food when obtained in response to an actual preparation of the food item.

Although the term "satisfaction" is sometimes used, it is very ambiguous. Thus, I will use it only loosely here to refer to consumer evaluations of system factors and will define it as follows:

4. Satisfaction--the expressed degree of liking or disliking for nonfood-related aspects of food service systems.

Sensory Factors Determining the
Affective Response to Foods

When considering likes and dislikes for food, we must remember that the major factors determining the affective response are the sensory attributes of the food. These include its appearance, flavor, texture, and temperature. Appearance refers to those aspects of the food that are appreciated by the sense of sight. These include the color, light reflectance, size, shape, and microgeometry

of the food. <u>Flavor</u> refers to the combined sensations of
taste and smell, where taste is defined as the sensations
resulting from stimulation of receptors on the tongue,
palate, and pharnyx--which results in the salty, sweet,
sour, and bitter qualities--and where smell is defined as
the sensations resulting from volatile compounds stimulating the receptors in the olfactory mucosa via the
nares or through the back of the mouth. <u>Texture</u> refers
to the oral tactile sense and the perception of the
mechanical, geometrical, and moisture properties of food
in the mouth. Lastly, <u>temperature</u> refers to oral-thermal
sensations resulting from food that differs in temperature from that of the oral mucosa.

Although each of the above factors can be appreciated
independently in foods, all interact in complex ways to
determine the acceptability of a particular product.
Moreover, the relative importance of any one attribute is
dependent on the particular food item. For example, for
chicken soup flavor may be the predominant factor determining acceptance, whereas for bread texture may be the
most important factor. As we shall see, many of the
methods used to assess overall liking or disliking for a
food can also be used to assess liking or disliking for
specific aspects of the sensory quality of the food.
This will be useful for investigating the reasons for a
decline in the acceptance of a menu item, since it will
be possible to isolate the specific sensory attribute
that is failing and, in turn, the specific ingredient or
process that is failing.

Consumption: The Ultimate Criterion of Liking

Obviously, one important index of whether a patient likes
or dislikes a food item is whether he eats it. This
index is particularly important in a hospital setting,
where adequate food intake is essential to rapid recovery
from certain disease states. The nutritional quality of
food becomes secondary when the food is not consumed.
Consumption measures are also important from an economic
point of view, since food waste can be a major source of
lost revenues in food service departments. Unfortunately,
consumption is a difficult, time-consuming, and costly
measure of liking or disliking. Direct measures of individual consumption (or its inverse, plate waste) require
weighing the amount of each food item that is served to a
patient and then weighing the uneaten portions. For even

a small hospital, this procedure is time-consuming and labor-intensive. Other less complicated methods, such as visual estimation of food intake or aggregate measures of consumption, suffer from loss of accuracy and/or loss of information about an individual patient's intake. These difficulties have led most researchers toward the development and use of simpler methods of assessing liking, such as preference and acceptance techniques.

While the major focus of this paper will be on the methods and techniques for collecting preference and acceptance data, for those interested in consumption and plate waste measurement, the reports by Burk and Pao (1976), Comstock et al. (1979), and Croughan et al. (1981) provide the necessary literature reviews.

Acceptance and Preference Measures

In food acceptance and food preference testing, a variety of measurement techniques are available. The decision to examine food preference or acceptance will depend on the problem at hand and the information required. In general, preference techniques (likes/dislikes in response to food names) are used to obtain information for menu planning purposes or to assess the potential for new food items. Acceptance techniques (likes/dislikes in response to the actual food item) are used to obtain information about different brands or recipes for the same item, where a food name would not serve to define adequately the differences between the products. For example, if a food service manager wishes to determine which of a variety of different soups should be included on patient menus, he would conduct a preference test, asking patients to rate their liking/disliking for a variety of soups by giving them the names of the soups--chicken noodle, cream of tomato, and so on. However, if the manager is considering one of two different brands or one of two different recipes for bean soup, then an acceptance test would be needed, with patients rating their liking/disliking for actual test samples of the two brands or recipes of soup.

Much of the early research and development in the area of food preference and food acceptance testing was carried out at the Quartermaster Food and Container Institute in Chicago. This work has since been continued at the U.S. Army Natick Research and Development Laboratories in Natick, Massachusetts. The emphasis of much of the early research was on the development of preference and accep-

tance measures that would predict consumption. Most of
these measures, as well as more recently developed
methods, are based on the assignment of numerical ratings
to foods in order to index the degree of liking or disliking for them. The most common measures (or scales)
can be classified into three types: (1) category scales,
(2) ratio scales, and (3) frequency scales.

Category Scales

Category scales are the most commonly used methods for
assessing food likes and dislikes. They are characterized by a series of labeled points or categories, and a
food item is rated by assigning it to one of several
(usually 3-10) available descriptive categories. One of
the earliest and still most commonly used scales of food
preference and food acceptance is based on the category
method. This is the "9-point hedonic scale" (Peryam and
Girardot, 1952; Peryam and Pilgrim, 1957) developed in
the early 1950s at the Quartermaster Institute. Figure 1
shows this scale.
     The hedonic scale consists of nine points or cate-
gories, ranging from "dislike extremely" to "like
extremely." There is also a neutral category that is
labeled "neither like nor dislike." While it is generally assumed that the points on the scale represent equal
subjective intervals--that is, that the difference in
acceptability between two products rating 1 and 2 on the
scale is the same as the difference between two products
rating 8 and 9 on the scale--much evidence indicates
otherwise. For example, in an early paper by Jones et
al. (1955), a variety of different category labels were
scaled for their meaning on an independent like-dislike
scale. These data, shown in Table 1, reveal that the
intervals between category labels for the 9-point hedonic
scale are unequal. As can be seen, the interval between
"like extremely" and "like very much" is larger than the
interval between "like moderately" and "like slightly."
More recently, Moskowitz and Sidel (1971) and Moskowitz
(1977) have also demonstrated nonequivalence of hedonic
scale intervals using magnitude estimates of liking (to
be discussed in the next section).
     Another problem with category scales is that respon-
dents tend not to use the extreme category because they
fear that if they use it to rate a food item, and another
food item is presented that they like even better, then

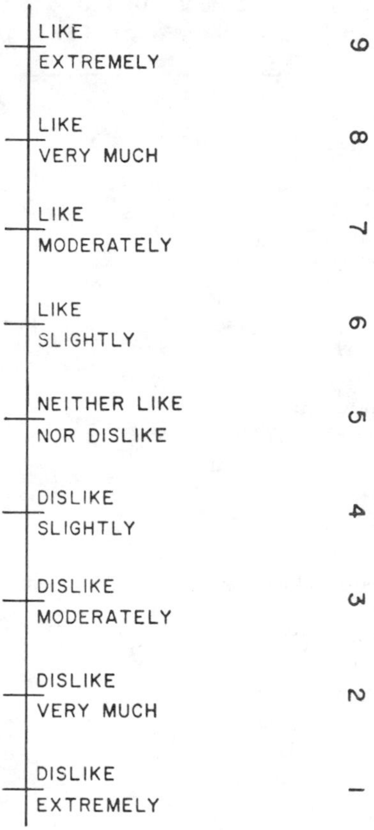

```
          ┬ LIKE
          ┼ EXTREMELY        9

          ┬ LIKE
          ┼ VERY MUCH        8

          ┬ LIKE
          ┼ MODERATELY       7

          ┬ LIKE
          ┼ SLIGHTLY         6

          ┬ NEITHER LIKE
          ┼ NOR DISLIKE      5

          ┬ DISLIKE
          ┼ SLIGHTLY         4

          ┬ DISLIKE
          ┼ MODERATELY       3

          ┬ DISLIKE
          ┼ VERY MUCH        2

          ┬ DISLIKE
          ┼ EXTREMELY        1
```

FIGURE 1 The Quartermaster
9-point hedonic scale.

they have no category available to assign it to. As such,
the 9-point hedonic scale is effectively a 7-point scale
of liking or disliking. Also, many category scales (such
as the 9-point hedonic scale) have a neutral point. There
is some evidence that eliminating this neutral point may
increase the efficiency of the scale (Jones et al., 1955)
and may discourage the complacency in judgment that is
provided by this "safe" category (Gridgeman, 1961).
   In spite of these problems, many studies adopted the
9-point hedonic scale for studying both food preference
and food acceptance, primarily because of its simplicity,
its applicability to both preference and acceptance data,
and its good reliability, reported to be .94 to .99
(Schutz, 1957; Peryam et al., 1960; Waterman et al.,
1974; Wyant et al., 1979) for groups and .74 (Smutz et
al., 1974) and .60 (Waterman et al., 1974) for
individuals.

TABLE 1 Scale Values and Standard Deviations for 51
Descriptive Phases of Liking/Disliking[a]

Phrase	Scale Value	Standard Deviation
Best of All	6.15	2.48
Favorite	4.68	2.18
Like extremely	4.16	1.62
Like intensely	4.05	1.59
Excellent	3.71	1.01
Wonderful	3.51	0.97
Strongly like	2.96	0.69
Like very much	2.91	0.60
Mighty fine	2.88	0.67
Especially good	2.86	0.82
Highly favorable	2.81	0.66
Like very well	2.60	0.78
Very good	2.56	0.87
Like quite a bit	2.32	0.52
Enjoy	2.21	0.86
Preferred	1.98	1.17
Good	1.91	0.76
Welcome	1.77	1.18
Tasty	1.76	0.92
Pleasing	1.58	0.65
Like fairly well	1.51	0.59
Like	1.35	0.77
Like moderately	1.12	0.61
OK	0.87	1.24
Average	0.86	1.08
Mildly like	0.85	0.47
Fair	0.78	0.85
Acceptable	0.73	0.66
Only fair	0.71	0.64
Like slightly	0.69	0.32
Neutral	0.02	0.18
Like not so well	−0.30	1.07
Like not so much	−0.41	0.94

TABLE 1 (continued)

Dislike slightly	-0.59	0.27
Mildly dislike	-0.74	0.35
Not pleasing	-0.83	0.67
Don't care for it	-1.10	0.81
Dislike moderately	-1.20	0.41
Poor	-1.55	0.87
Dislike	-1.58	0.94
Don't like	-1.81	0.97
Bad	-2.02	0.80
Highly unfavorable	-2.16	1.37
Strongly dislike	-2.37	0.53
Dislike very much	-2.49	0.64
Very bad	-2.53	0.64
Terrible	-3.09	0.98
Dislike intensely	-3.33	1.89
Loathe	-3.76	3.54
Dislike extremely	-4.32	1.86
Despise	-6.44	3.62

[a]Scale values are interpreted as the average meaning of the phrase on a like (positive)/dislike (negative) dimension. The standard deviations are interpreted as ambiguity measures for the phrases (taken from Jones et al., 1955).

While Figure 1 shows the typical format of the scale when used for food acceptance testing, i.e., where a patient actually tastes a particular food item, Figure 2, taken from the U.S. Army Food Preference Survey (Wyant et al., 1979), shows the application of this scale to preference testing (top and left side), in which only food names are judged. As can be seen, the scale can be used to collect data on large numbers of food items in a short time, and preference data collected in this way can be especially useful for planning hospital menus and for assessing the desirability of new items for use in both ward and cafeteria dining situations. The complete questionnaire with general instructions for the use of this type of preference survey is found in Appendix A.

1	2	3	4	5	6	7	8	9
dislike extremely	dislike very much	dislike moderately	dislike slightly	neither like nor dislike	like slightly	like moderately	like very much	like extremely

	NEVER TRIED	HOW MUCH you like or dislike the food (1-9)		HOW OFTEN you want to eat the food in days per month (01-30)
001 Tea				
002 Roast Turkey				
003 Strawberry Shortcake				
004 Celery & Carrot Sticks				
005 Boiled Pigs' Feet				
006 Hot Turkey Sandwich with Gravy				
007 Sliced Tomato Salad				
008 Braised Liver with Onions				
009 Tomato Juice				
010 Peas				
011 Cooked Turnips				
012 Fried Rice				
013 Corned Beef				
014 Jellied Fruit Salad				
015 Apricot Pie				
016 Cheeseburger				
017 Sausage Links				
018 Banana Cake				
019 Lima Beans				
020 Skimmed Milk				
021 Pizza				
022 Split Pea Soup				
023 Ice Cream				
024 Simmered Sauerkraut				
025 Steamed Rice				
026 Buttered Noodles				
027 Swiss Steak				
028 Hot Fudge Sundae				
029 Green Beans				
030 Chitterlings				
031 Pork Chop Suey				
032 Lasagna				
033 Hamburger				
034 Fish Chowder				
035 Corned Beef Hash				
036 Hot Pastrami Sandwich				
037 Rice Pudding				
038 Apple Crisp				
039 Tossed Green Salad				
040 Baked Tuna & Noodles				

FIGURE 2 Response form from the U.S. Army Food Preference Survey, showing the application of the 9-point hedonic scale (top and left) and an absolute frequency scale (right) for preference testing of foods (from Wyant et al., 1979).

Since the 9-point hedonic scale can be used for both preference and acceptance testing, several published studies have used this scale to examine the relationships between preference, acceptance, and consumption. A series of studies (Kamenetzky et al., 1957; Peryam and Pilgrim, 1957; Schutz, 1957; Kamenetzky and Pilgrim, 1958; Peryam et al., 1960; Pilgrim, 1961; Kamen, 1962), found food preference and/or acceptance ratings obtained by the hedonic scale technique were correlated with measures of consumption, consisting of either the proportion of servings eaten or the proportion of subjects selecting a particular food item. The combined results of these studies indicated that about 25-50 percent of the variability in consumption measures could be accounted for by the preference or acceptance measures. More recent studies have supported this early research, finding correlation coefficients with consumption of .35-.50 for preference (Smutz et al., 1974; Sullins et al., 1977; Wyant et al., 1979) and .81 for acceptance (Sidel et al., 1972).

On the basis of the above studies, it can be concluded that labeled category scales, such as the 9-point hedonic scale, provide reliable measures for both preference and acceptance testing and are valid predictors of the relative consumption of food items. However, in addition to being reliable and valid, a good scale should be easy to administer, easy to understand, and easy to analyze. While the hedonic scale is easy to administer and simple to use with adult populations, the verbal labels often pose problems for children, the visually impaired, or those with reading difficulties. Thus, its use in pediatric or geriatric wards is limited. However, a variety of facial and/or pictorial scales have been developed under these conditions (Schmalz, 1963; Ellis, 1964; Twedt, 1966; LaChance, 1976). Scales such as these have been shown to work particularly well with children (Wells, 1965), and they avoid problems of confusion in terminology. Figure 3 shows a 5-point facial scale that was developed in our laboratory for evaluating food acceptance in children eating in the school lunch program. When such pictorial scales are used, the data are statistically analyzed by assigning an ordinal series of numbers to the categories and using these numbers as the response measures.

As is evident, category scales, whether labeled or pictorial, are extremely versatile. They can also be easily adapted to obtain information on the acceptability of specific sensory aspects of the food. By simply indicating what sensory attribute is to be evaluated, the researchers can obtain information on the acceptability of the flavor, appearance, texture, etc. using the same scale structure. Figure 4 shows a response card used in recent studies at Moncrief Army Hospital, Fort Jackson, Columbia, South Carolina that uses 7-point scales to obtain information on the acceptability of appearance,

TOMATOES

 AGE

 SEX

**PUT AN X ON THE FACE THAT
TELLS US HOW IT TASTES.**

FIGURE 3 Facial hedonic scale rating card developed at
the U.S. Army Natick Research and Development
Laboratories for use with children and the elderly.

flavor, texture, and temperature, as well as the overall
acceptability of a food item. The patient simply darkens
the box corresponding to his response choice. The data
can then be easily key-punched for computer analysis by
using the column coding numbers shown in parentheses. A
space for open-ended comments is also available.

In all category scale methods, standard parametric
statistical tests (t-tests, ANOVAs, etc.) can be applied
to the data to determine whether statistically significant
differences exist between ratings assigned to different
samples, products, etc.

Ratio Scales

One disadvantage of category scales is that they are only
interval in nature (S. S. Stevens, 1971); that is, they
only provide information about the degree of difference
between two food items. They do not provide information
about the ratios of acceptabilities among items--e.g.,
"this beef stew is liked twice as much as that one." To
be able to make such ratio statements, one must use ratio
scales.

CONSUMER OPINION CARD

FOOD ITEM: ______________________________ (11–20)

After you have eaten this item, rate it on the following characteristics. Select the ONE phrase that best describes your opinion of each and darken the box beside it.

Appearance (21)		Temperature (22)		Flavor (23)		Texture (24)	
Very Bad Appearance	7	Much Too Hot	7	Very Good Flavor	7	Very Bad Texture	7
Bad Appearance	6	Too Hot	6	Good Flavor	6	Bad Texture	6
Slightly Bad Appearance	5	Slightly Too Hot	5	Slightly Good Flavor	5	Slightly Bad Texture	5
Neutral Appearance	4	Just Right	4	Neutral Flavor	4	Neutral Texture	4
Slightly Good Appearance	3	Slightly Too Cold	3	Slightly Bad Flavor	3	Slightly Good Texture	3
Good Appearance	2	Too Cold	2	Bad Flavor	2	Good Texture	2
Very Good Appearance	1	Much Too Cold	1	Very Bad Flavor	1	Very Good Texture	1

What is your OVERALL OPINION of this item? (25)

7	6	5	4	3	2	1
Very Good	Good	Slightly Good	Neutral	Slightly Bad	Bad	Very Bad

COMMENTS:

Please drop this card in the box as you leave.
Thank you.

FIGURE 4 Consumer response card developed at the U.S. Army Natick Research and Development Laboratories to assess patient and staff acceptance for food items served at military hospitals.

Although several ratio scale methods have been developed and described (S. S. Stevens, 1971), the one most
commonly used for judging the sensory properties of food
is magnitude estimation. In magnitude estimation the
subject (or patient, in this case) is asked to judge
foods relative to one another by assigning a number to
each food to reflect the perceived ratio of their acceptabilities. For example, in a test involving three brands
of applesauce, raters (patients or in-house test panelists) would be told that the acceptability of sample B
has an arbitrary value (called a modulus) of, say 100,
and that samples A and C are to be rated on acceptability
by assigning numbers to them such that the ratio of the
numbers assigned to each, relative to 100, is the same as
the ratios of the perceived acceptability of each to B.
Thus, if sample A is one-third as acceptable as B, it
would be assigned the number 33.3; if sample C is
one-and-a-half times as acceptable as B, it would be
assigned the number 150. Alternatively, a modulus need
not be assigned to sample B, and subjects would then be
free to assign any arbitrary number they wish to this
"standard" sample. For such "nonmodulus" methods, a
variety of post hoc techniques for equating all individual moduli to a common value have been developed
(S. S. Stevens, 1971, 1975). In addition, as with
category scales, all parametric statistics can be applied
to magnitude estimation data as long as the data have
been "normalized" to account for the fact that they are
log-normally distributed (J. C. Stevens, 1957).

One disadvantage with magnitude estimation is that
when data are to be collected over several days, weeks,
or months, there must be some way to equilabrate the
number of scales being used on different days. Approaches
for doing this include use of a common sample (or samples)
on different days (Moskowitz, 1970; Murphy et al., 1981)
or equilibration to a common verbal label (Moskowitz,
1977; Moskowitz et al., 1979). Another disadvantage is
that the method requires detailed instruction to ensure
that the scale is used properly, although practice per se
is not necessary. The advantages of the scale are: (1)
the ratio nature of the data it provides, and (2) its
greater sensitivity than the 9-point category scale
(McDaniel and Sawyer, 1981; Moskowitz, 1980).

An alternative ratio scale method that has achieved
popularity uses an unstructured line scale, such as shown
in Figure 5. Using this type of scale, the subject
merely places a hash mark on the line to indicate the

LIKE	DISLIKE
EXTREMELY	EXTREMELY

FIGURE 5 A line scale (form or ratio scaling) for
assessing the acceptability of food items.

acceptability of the item. The measured distance of the
hash mark from the end of the line is taken as the
acceptability (or preference) value for that food.

Frequency Scales

The need for frequency scales arose from the fact that,
although a food item may score high on a category or
magnitude estimation scale this does not reflect the
frequency with which an individual would want to eat the
item. For example, cheesecake may receive a rating of 8
on a 9-point hedonic scale, whereas milk may receive a
rating of 7. This does not mean, however, that the
patient would want to eat cheesecake more often that he
wants to drink milk. Thus, hedonic judgments of the
acceptability of foods are not as useful for menu
planning as are judgments of the desired frequency of
serving.
    The first form of frequency scale was developed by
Schutz (1965) as a supplement to the 9-point hedonic
scale. As shown below, this scale, known as the FACT
(Food Action) scale, consists of a series of statements
concerning the frequency with which a food item is desired
to be eaten, ranging from "eat every opportunity" to "eat
if forced." By combining hedonic scale data with FACT
scale data, information can be obtained about both the
acceptability of a food item and the relative frequency
that it is desired. Moreover, the FACT scale has been
shown to be quite reliable, with group reliability
coefficients reported to be .97 (Schutz, 1965):

FACT SCALE
_____

    Eat Every Opportunity
    Eat Very Often
    Frequently Eat
    Eat Now and Then

Don't Like, Eat on Occasion
Hardly Ever Eat
Eat If No Other Choices
Eat If Forced

While the FACT scale provides only relative frequency estimates, other frequency techniques can be used to provide absolute frequency measures. The right side of Figure 2 shows such a frequency scale used to assess food preferences of military men (Meiselman et al., 1974). As can be seen, the respondent indicates the number of times during a 30-day period that he would like to have the item served. The group reliability for such frequency scales has been reported to be .98 (Waterman et al., 1974), and individual reliability coefficients have been reported to be .69 (Smutz et al., 1974) and .58 (Waterman et al., 1974). Moreover, the correlation with consumption has been reported to be .59-.66 (Sullins et al., 1977).

One word of caution should be said about using frequency scale data. Care should be taken when using frequency judgments for menu planning because hospitals with a rapid patient turnover rate may be able to serve certain low-cost items more frequently, without loss of acceptability, than would be predicted by patient frequency judgments (Schuh et al., 1967).

Choice of Methods

The decision to use a verbal category scale, pictorial scale, line scale, frequency scale, magnitude estimation, etc. should be based on the nature of the information that is needed and the restraints of time and labor. If simple preference data are needed for menu planning, a hedonic category scale can be used, and the number of categories can be left to the discretion of the test coordinator. Verbal labels can be chosen from those listed in Table 1, although for purposes of cross-comparing data the verbal labels assigned to the 9-point hedonic scale are preferable. Alternatively, a line scale or magnitude estimation may be used to rate preferences for food items. However, the data analysis will be complicated by the need to measure distances along the line scale or to normalize the magnitude estimates. Because preference data are frequently used only

to decide which of two or more starches, entrees, etc.,
is preferred, there is no special need to know the exact
magnitude of difference in preference among the items.
Under these circumstances the simplicity of the category
scale makes it more desirable than the more sensitive but
less convenient ratio scales. Moreover, if pediatric,
geriatric, or visually impaired patients constitute a
large portion of the hospital census, then a pictorial or
facial scale may be needed. In addition, when preference
data are collected for menu planning, information should
also be obtained about desired serving frequency. For
this purpose, either the FACT scale or an absolute
frequency scale should be used in combination with a
hedonic scale of choice.

  If, in contrast to preference data, acceptance data
are needed, then either the category scale, the pictorial
scale, or one of the ratio scales should be used, with
the same considerations applying as for preference data.
The frequency scales are less appropriate here; for
example, two brands of coffee may differ noticeably in
acceptability, yet both may be desired equally often due
to other motivational factors that determine coffee-
drinking behavior. Also, as will be discussed, it is
frequently desirable for quality control purposes to
conduct acceptance tests with small in-house panels made
up of dietary staff members. Here, because of the limited
number of panelists used and because only subtle differences in acceptability may be present, use of ratio
scales is recommended.

Relationships Among the Different Methods

Although the choice of a scale for measuring preference
or acceptance is primarily determined by the nature of
the data that are desired and the personal preference of
the users of the data, there is nevertheless considerable
evidence showing that the data obtained by the different
methods is nonlinearly related. For example, if one plots
judgments of sensory intensity obtained using a category
scale against judgments of sensory intensity obtained
using a ratio scale, the category scale data will be con-
cave downward relative to the ratio scale data (Stevens
and Galanter, 1957). For judgments of acceptability, the
relationship between category and ratio scales will
primarily be determined by the verbal labels assigned to
the category scale points. Table 2 shows magnitude

TABLE 2 A Comparison of the 9-Point Hedonic Scale Values
and Magnitude Estimation Values for the Verbal Labels of
the Hedonic Scale

Hedonic Scale Label	Hedonic Scale Value	Magnitude Estimate
Like extremely	9	+185.1
Like very much	8	+137.5
Like moderately	7	+103.4
Like slightly	6	+ 59.3
Neither like nor dislike	5	0
Dislike slightly	4	− 54.0
Dislike moderately	3	− 85.8
Dislike very much	2	−101.5
Dislike extremely	1	−137.2

SOURCE: Moskowitz, 1977.

estimation values corresponding to the different verbal
categories of the 9-point hedonic scale (Moskowitz, 1977).
As can be seen, although the labels "like moderately" and
"like slightly" have hedonic scale values of 7 and 6,
respectively, "like moderately" is almost twice as acceptable as "like slightly" in terms of their magnitude
estimates.

The relationship between hedonic scale data and
frequency scale data can be seen in Table 3 for selected
items of the Armed Forces Food Preference Survey (Waterman
et al., 1974). Here it should be noted that certain items
may have approximately equivalent acceptabilities--e.g.,
lobster, pizza, and roast turkey--yet one (roast turkey)
may be desired much less frequently. In fact, in these
data roast turkey is desired less frequently than a hot
turkey sandwich or even roast lamb, both of which have
much lower hedonic scale ratings. In contrast, fresh
coffee (and certain other breakfast items) are desired
more frequently than would be predicted by their hedonic
scale value alone.

TABLE 3 Mean Hedonic Ratings (Obtained via the 9-Point Hedonic Scale) and Mean Desired Frequencies of Serving per Month (30 Days) for Selected Food Items

Food Name	Mean Hedonic Rating	Mean Desired Frequency per Month
Milk	7.85	23.64
Grilled steak	7.67	14.23
Eggs to order	7.32	19.44
Ice cream	7.27	17.74
Lobster	7.04	11.23
Pizza	7.04	11.85
Roast turkey	7.02	8.72
Hot turkey sandwich with gravy	6.90	10.21
Beer	6.89	18.02
Hamburger	6.83	12.63
Baked potatoes	6.78	11.16
Doughnuts	6.72	12.78
Baked chicken	6.65	10.22
Soft serve ice cream	6.60	12.50
Lasagna	6.56	9.78
Pepper steak	6.50	9.34
French toast	6.47	12.78
Mixed fruit salad	6.43	10.47
Fresh coffee	6.36	18.89
Cherry pie	6.32	9.42
Fried fish	6.26	9.10
Roast veal	6.15	8.57
Egg salad sandwich	6.08	8.62
Roast lamb	5.98	9.06
Buttered mixed vegetables	5.96	10.72
Cold cereal	5.87	11.35
Tomato soup	5.83	8.63
Gingerale	5.81	10.05
Tomato juice	5.63	11.77
Buttered peas and carrots	5.53	7.99
Salami sandwich	5.50	7.58
Minestrone soup	5.42	6.83
Brussel sprouts	5.10	6.83
Braised liver with onions	4.61	5.66
Boiled pigs' feet	4.34	4.78
Skimmed milk	3.95	7.46
Low-calorie soda	3.93	6.78

SOURCE: Waterman et al., 1974.

Point-of-Service Versus On-Line Evaluations

Up to this point, we have discussed point-of-service
evaluations made by patients. However, for many purposes
this type of evaluation comes too late to take corrective
action. What are needed for good quality control are
"on-line" evaluations. In a conventional cook-serve
system, such on-line evaluations could be made at the
point of tray assembly by dietary staff members. In
cook-chill or cook-freeze systems, formal taste panels
could be arranged between meals to evaluate prepared
products. Such taste tests, utilizing the acceptance
testing techniques outlined in previous sections, could
be carried out by a panel of six to ten professionals,
familiar with the proper execution of the item. The
advantage of these on-line evaluations is that they
enable corrective action to be taken on defective items
before those items reach the patient. Of course, such
on-line evaluations do not subtitute for patient evaluations, since numerous ward-related factors will contribute
to food acceptability before it reaches the patient.

Another consideration for testing concerns the patrons
eating in the hospital dining room/cafeteria. Clearly,
ambulatory patients who eat there deserve equal consideration with ward patients. Moreover, the ratings assigned
to the food served in the hospital dining room/cafeteria
may serve as a form of control against changes occurring
in the sensory quality of the food due to transportation
and distribution on the ward. Unacceptable ratings
obtained on the wards for food items that are found to be
acceptable in the cafeteria may indicate a failure in the
delivery function. In addition, the opinions of the
hospital staff members who eat in the cafeteria are
important to the food service manager, as they constitute
a stable set of patrons whose likes and dislikes must
also be considered.

Conducting Food Acceptance and Preference Tests

Once the nature of the desired information has been
established (preference versus acceptance), the specific
food items of interest have been chosen, the perceptual
attributes of interest have been selected, and a scale
has been chosen, one is then ready to conduct the test.
However, as in any field test, an attempt must be made to
maintain stringent controls over sampling and testing,

while accommodating the special requirements of the hospital setting. To assist in this endeavor, the following
is a simplified set of procedural guidelines for collecting acceptance data via a typical rating card format,
such as the one shown in Figure 4. These procedures are
representative of those that should be used in collecting
any type of sensory data from hospitalized patients,
keeping in mind both the necessary experimental controls
and the specialized nature of the respondents. Also, as
stated above, because it is frequently necessary or
desirable to assess the opinions of ambulatory patients
or staff eating in the hospital dining room/cafeteria,
guidelines for collecting data in this type of environment are also presented. Although certain aspects of the
procedures for collecting acceptance data do not apply to
preference testing (because actual food items are not
evaluated), many of the guidelines that are related to
sampling, distribution of forms, and patient-surveyor
interactions should also be adhered to during preference
testing.

Testing on the Wards

A. Time of Testing
   1. Acceptance tests, by definition, must be carried
out when the food is available for the patient to taste.
This means at meal times. Collecting acceptance data
after a patient has already eaten, or between meals, will
produce data that are neither valid nor useful.
   2. Patients should be asked to fill out the response
cards as soon as they receive their trays. This means
that either the person(s) conducting the test must be
present when the tray is taken to the patient's room or
else the response cards must be available on each
patient's tray prior to meal delivery. The former
procedure is preferable, because only by having someone
present in the patient's room can proper control be
maintained over the conditions of testing.

B. Sampling Patients
   1. A random sample of patients should be chosen.
This requires sampling patients from all wards at each
meal. Do not collect data on a particular food item from
patients on only one or two wards. This may bias the
results, especially if the cart for that particular ward
goes up late, if the trays on that ward are delayed in
being distributed, or if other unexpected events occur on

the ward. Also, within any ward the choice of patients should be random.

2. While random selection of patient respondents is the goal, one should not leave response cards if a patient is not in his room when the tray is brought in. Also, response cards should not be left with a patient who is likely to be occupied for some time (talking with his doctors), is ill at the time (may have an upset stomach and will not eat right away), or is otherwise not likely to be eating immediately (may be sleeping). Patients on special diets must not be inadvertently included in tests of regular diet items.

3. Anonymity of responses must be guaranteed to all respondents in order to ensure valid judgments and candid comments.

C. Choice and Number of Items to Test at a Meal

1. Although the menu items to test are chosen prior to the actual test period, care should be taken when choosing the particular items to be tested at any given meal and by any given patient. Specifically, if a food item is usually served at the dinner meal, then it should be evaluated only at the dinner meal, in spite of any difficulties that may arise due to nonavailability of personnel at this time. Acceptance data collected on a dinner item served at breakfast or lunch will surely show lower acceptability than they would if that item were served at its proper meal.

2. If an item is usually served at more than one meal, it should be tested at all the meals at which it is normally served. For example, coffee may be selected by many patients at breakfast, but may only be selected by coffee lovers at lunch or dinner. Collecting data on coffee only at lunch or supper may produce biased results, representing only the opinions of a subgroup of the patient population.

3. The number of items tested at any one meal or by any one patient can vary considerably, depending on the number of independent responses desired for each item. That is, if the patient is only requested to rate the overall acceptability of the item, several items may be tested at a meal (Sather and Calvin, 1960). However, if several different types of responses are needed for each item (temperature, flavor, etc.), then fewer items should be tested. Creating fatigue or boredom among patients because of too-frequent testing will have a negative effect on their responses.

4. Special diet items should always be evaluated separately from regular diet items.

D. Distributing Response Cards

1. If response cards are distributed by placing them on patient trays at a central site, then explicit instructions about completing the card must be available to the patient. Also, details on how to return the card must be made explicit. As stated previously, however, this method of conducting a test is less desirable than having personnel go to each patient's room. Patients will regard more seriously a survey/response card that is handed to them by a person, than one that simply appears on the tray with their meal. Also, without a test person in the room it is impossible to determine whether the patient made the rating immediately upon receiving the food or after he got back from the clinic, x-ray, etc., when the food was cold and, therefore, not representative. Explaining intructions is also impossible in this testing format, and it should only be used if there is no other feasible method for collecting the data.

2. When distributing the response cards, personnel must be careful not to bias the patient. A typical request for participation might be stated: "Excuse me. We're conducting a survey today on (food item name). Would you mind taking the time to fill out a card to give us your opinion of the item?" If the answer is "yes," the patient should be given the response cards and a pencil and told that someone will collect them later. If the answer is "no," one should simply thank the patient and leave. Do not pressure the patient if he/she declines to participate. Data collected from such patients are likely to be biased negatively.

If a patient seems too ill to participate, simply say, "I'll come back on another day when you're feeling better."

3. There are certain things that personnel should not say when approaching a prospective respondent. Do not say such things as "Would you please fill out this card? We want to see how good the carrots taste" or "We want to get some information on the carrots, now that we have this new system of cooking." Comments such as these will bias the person either positively or negatively and must be avoided. In general, the less the patient knows about the reason for the test, the more valid will be the response.

Testing in the Dining Hall/Cafeteria

Most of the above guidelines apply when tests are conducted in the hospital dining room/cafeteria. However, the following additional points should be kept in mind:

1. Patients or staff in the dining hall should be asked to fill out a card as soon as they sit down with their trays, so that the food is still at the appropriate temperature when they make their ratings. A less desirable method is to distribute cards from the end of the serving line. This method is only acceptable if it does not interfere with the smooth progress of the line.
2. Survey persons should circulate among the tables, watch for someone who has taken the test item, and then approach that person a manner similar to that described above for ward patients.
3. Survey persons should be sure to hand out cards throughout the meal, not just at the beginning of the meal or just at the end. A food item that may be hot and flavorful at the start of the meal may get cold and lose its flavor after being in a steam table for some time.

Automated Data Collection

While the procedural requirements for proper collection of food acceptance data can be time-consuming, several automated approaches are available that will reduce the time necessary for the analyzing the data. Two relatively inexpensive methods for automating data collection involve the use of optical scanning and punch-card response formats. The survey form shown in Figure 2 is an example of an optical scanning format for collecting perference data; Appendix B shows the same format applied to a questionnaire on food service systems. Similar response formats are commonly used in nationwide standardized test programs. Using such a printed response format, patients merely darken the appropriate box or boxes. Once the forms have been collected, they can be "read" into a computer file, using one of a variety of available automated optical scanning devices. Subsequent data analysis can be carried out using available computer programs. Alternatively, a punch-card format like that shown in Figure 6 can be used. Here, a printed computer card can be placed in a holder specially designed for it. Patients, using a stylus, punch a hole in the card

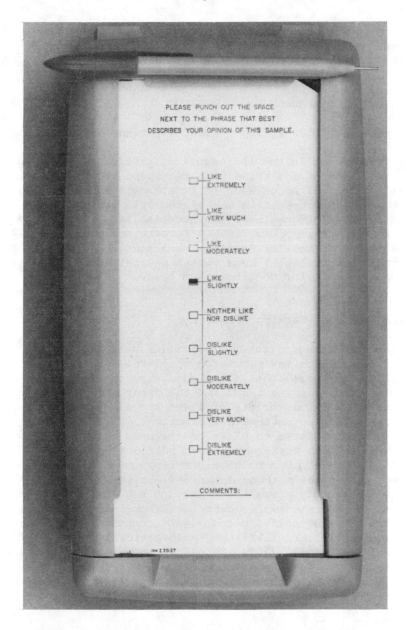

FIGURE 6 Punch card format applied to food
acceptance testing. The printed computer response
card is placed in a specially designed holder and,
using the stylus at the top, the patient punches a
hole in the card corresponding to his response
choice.

corresponding to their response choice. Once punched, these cards are ready for batch processing on the computer.

HOSPITAL FOOD SERVICE: ASSESSING PATIENT SATISFACTION

Systems Factors of Importance to Patient Satisfaction

As pointed out in the introduction, problems in hospital patient feeding can arise from two sources: the food and the system. Although each is independent of the other, the problems inherent in the system will ultimately be reflected in judgments of the acceptability of the food. Many of these important system factors are common to all hospital food service systems; others may be specific to certain hospitals. I have chosen several of the more common factors for consideration below.

Menu Items and Serving Frequency

Although the ingredients, preparation, and delivery of food to patients may result in menu items of excellent quality, the particular items placed on the menu, the frequency of serving them, and the opportunity of patients to select among a variety of items are all important variables affecting patient satisfaction. The first problem, choosing items to place on the menu, requires knowledge of patient preferences for individual food items. This information can be obtained via long-term preference tests, using the methods described earlier. However, as noted previously, repeatedly serving high-preference items is not the sole answer. Even highly preferred foods, if served too frequently, become less acceptable, as demonstrated by Zellmer (1970) and mathematically delineated by Balintfy et al. (1974, 1975) and Rogozenski and Moskowitz (1975). To obtain information on these desired levels of serving frequencies, the frequency preference scales described previously should be employed.

Menu Selection

The opportunity to choose from a variety of menu items is an important factor affecting patient satisfaction. Glew

(1970, 1973) has demonstrated increases in the acceptability of hospital food by varying the choice of entrees.
Opportunity to choose portion sizes for menu items is
also a frequent request of patients; those with large
appetites frequently complain of the lack of adequate
portions, while patients with small appetites frequently
complain about the waste in the system. In general,
providing patients with the chance to choose among alternatives will always increase satisfaction, regardless of
the aspect of service being left to their selection.

Description of Menu Items

Variety and choice in a menu will only increase satisfaction if the entries for the menu items are unambiguous
and descriptive. Items having exotic or ambiguous names
have been shown to be less well liked and are less often
chosen than items with simpler, more descriptive names
(Schutz et al., 1972; Rucker et al., 1973; Kincaid, 1975).
This problem is even more pronounced in pediatric wards,
where it has been shown that an item such as "Molded
Waldorf Salad" may be interpreted as "moldy" food, "Egg
Souffle" could be translated into "egg pie," and "Consomme
Julienne" may only remind a child of "a movie star"
(Bachrach, 1970). Clearly, the use of nondescriptive
adjectives in food item names should be avoided, and con-
sideration should be given to providing short descriptions
of the actual ingredients and preparation methods for
items that may be ambiguous.

Menu Combinations

In addition to the above menu factors, the combination of
items in a meal is also important. Although frankfurters
and sauerkraut might make an acceptable meal for most
people, frankfurters and cauliflower may not. Eindhoven
and Peryam (1959a,b) have presented data for a wide
variety of pairs of menu items, showing that the preference rating for the pair is not simply the mean of the
preference ratings for the individual items. In more
recent work, Moskowitz and Klarman (1977) have published
compatability indices (based on magnitude estimates of
perceived compatability) for pairs and triplets of foods.
Table 4 is taken from their data and shows geometric mean

TABLE 4 Geometric Mean Compatability Value for Entree-
Vegetable Pairs

| Vegetable | Entree | | | | |
	Liver	Corned Beef	Frank-furters	Chicken	Ham
Peas	53.8	83.5	52.2	140.4	135.4
Corn	48.3	70.4	49.2	114.9	100.8
Cauliflower	80.3	56.2	60.3	116.0	111.6
Sauerkraut	14.6	105.2	201.9	21.3	45.0
Tomatoes	79.0	68.0	107.3	68.7	90.6

SOURCE: Adapted from Moskowitz and Klarman, 1970.

compatability values for various pairs of entrees and
vegetables/starches. Here we can see that frankfurter
and sauerkraut is more than three times as acceptable as
frankfurter and cauliflower.

In related research, Rogozenski and Moskowitz (1975)
have analyzed the relative importance of items within a
meal and their contribution to the acceptability of the
whole meal.

They used an additive equation of the form:

Menu Hedonic Rating = k_1
(Hedonic Rating of Entree)   + k_2
(Hedonic Rating of Starch)   + k_3
(Hedonic Rating of Vegetable)   + k_4
(Hedonic Rating of Salad)   + k_5
(Hedonic Rating of Dessert)   + k_6.

They arrived at the following set of weights, in which
the greater the weighting value the more important is the
food to the overall rating of the meal:

k_1 = ENTREE   = 2.07
k_2 = STARCH   = 0.53
k_3 = VEGETABLE = 0.42
k_4 = SALAD   = 0.25
k_5 = DESSERT   = 0.57
k_6 = CONSTANT = 5.68

Clearly, the entree is the primary determinant of the
acceptability of the meal, and the salad is the least
important of its components.

Portion Size

As mentioned previously, portion size is an important
factor in patient's satisfaction with hospital food
service. No less so is it an important economic consideration for hospital food service directors. However,
portion size may be more likely to be perceived as a
problem in the hospital cafeteria. In a recent multihospital study (Maller et al., 1980) ward patients judged
the portion sizes of menu items as significantly larger
than did either ambulatory patients or staff eating in
the hospital cafeteria. Since ward patients also had
lower mean appetites (self-judged), it would appear that
their inactivity produces less discontent with portion
size than does the greater activity level of ambulatory
patients and staff. Contributing to the greater dissatisfaction with portion size in the cafeteria is that staff
members paid for their meals, creating greater expectations of portion size.

Tray Delivery Time and Demeanor of Servers

Arrival time of meals is a complaint frequently heard
from hospitalized patients. This is to be expected,
given the wide range of normal daily meal patterns among
individuals. However, consistency in time of meal
arrival will allow the patient to adjust to any new time
schedule. The demeanor of people serving trays is also
important. Cheerful personnel, whether food service
employees or nursing staff, can improve the patient's
general attitude at meal time, and this will affect
perceived satisfaction with the meal.

Food Tray Appearance and Cleanliness

The appearance of the food tray and the cleanliness of
dishes and silverware can have a significant impact on
patient perceptions of meal acceptability. A clear case
of this effect occurred in some data collected by our

laboratory (Maller et al., 1980), which showed that ward patients were significantly more satisfied with the attractiveness and cleanliness of dishes, silverware, and trays than ambulatory patients and staff eating in the hospital cafeteria. The care and scrutiny given to patient trays during the tray assembly process contrasts sharply with typical cafeteria practices in which silverware is left in open binds, napkins and other utensils are left for self-service, etc. These differences in procedures were clear causes of the differences in ratings in that study and indicate the contribution of these factors to perceived satisfaction with the system.

Dining Environment

The dining environment in which most patients eat is their hospital room. In newer hospitals, where rooms are large, cheerfully decorated, and comfortably furnished, eating in the confines of one's room may not be aversive. However, in older hospitals, where room environments may be less than optimal, the effects of dining environment on satisfaction may be significant. Group dining versus dining alone has also been cited as a major factor affecting rate of recovery of patients from illness (Ronco, 1972). Herz et al. (1978) have developed several alternative modes of ward dining based on the use of day rooms.

Food Preparation and Delivery Methods

Several reviews of the effects of hospital food preparation and delivery systems on food quality have been published (Rinke, 1976; Matthews, 1977; Herz et al., 1978). However, information on the effects of alternative food systems on the quality of hospital food is still needed (Bunch et al., 1976). Dr. Dahl's paper (in this volume) reviews some of the more recent data on the effects of such systems. I simply wish to mention that, although food preparation methods will have a direct influence on food acceptability, other, more subtle effects may result from patient inferences about the method of food preparation. For example, in a conventional cook-serve operation, the food is hot-plated and brought to the ward in an insulated or hot-cold cart. The effect of the cart is primarily on the temperature

integrity of the food. In a recent study of hospitals
that use hot-plating, approximately 28 percent of all
patients were dissatisfied with the temperature of hot
food items and approximately 25 percent were dissatisfied
with the temperature of cold food items (Maller et al.,
1980). Cook-chill and cook-freeze systems that rethermalize food on the wards can eliminate much of this temperature moderation during transport.

However, if patients are allowed to observe the
rethermalization process on the ward, many will assume
that the food is frozen, possibly brought in from a
vendor, and thus will rate it as being less acceptable
than food items that they believe come "hot from the
kitchen." This factor has been suggested as the possible
reason for higher acceptability ratings for food items
prepared using a hot-plating system, as contrasted with
the same food items prepared using several cold-plating
systems (Cardello et al., 1981). Unraveling such cogni-
tive effects from the direct effect of these systems can
be difficult without adequate controls against patient
knowledge of the system.

Special Diets

Unlike many other types of institutional food service,
hospital food service is complicated by the requirement
for large numbers of modified food items to accomodate
special diets. Because these food items are frequently
formulated with lower-than-normal levels of seasonings
(low sodium, low sugar) or are drastically restricted in
nature (soft, fluid-only), potential problems for food
acceptance exist. Interestingly, however, in a recent
attempt to investigate the notion that restricted diets
are less acceptable than regular diets, patients on midly
restricted diets (low sodium, diabetic, no added sodium,
and soft diet) rated the acceptability of restricted menu
items no differently than did patients receiving regular
diets (Maller et al., 1980). These results do not support
the clinical lore that patients have an unfavorable reaction to modified diets, although it should be pointed out
that grossly modified diets, such as fluid-only, were not
examined in this study. Mrs. McNutt's paper, later in
this volume, describes recent efforts to improve the
quality of special diet items.

Relative Importance of Factors to Overall Acceptability

In view of the wide array of factors contributing to the perceived acceptability of hospital meals, the question of the relative importance of these factors becomes important. Tables 5 and 6 from Herz et al. (1978) provide relevant information on this point. In their study, opinion data were obtained on the various meal factors listed in Tables 5 and 6 for both patients eating on the ward and patrons eating in the hospital cafeteria. Responses to these items were then regressed (using multiple linear regression) against ratings of overall meal acceptability. The resultant beta weights provide an index of the relative importance of each item to overall meal acceptability. Table 5 shows the ranking in terms of importance (beta weights) for the ward patient data; Table 6 shows the same data for cafeteria patrons. As can be seen, the appearance and aroma of the food are

TABLE 5   Meal Factors in Rank Order of Their Importance Toward Patients, as Determined by Multiple Linear Regression

Factor	Beta Weight[a]
Appearance and aroma of food	0.41830
Temperature of cold food items	−0.12575
Attractiveness of dishes, silverware, tray	0.12997
Tenderness of meat	0.12987
Size of portions	0.07087
Variety of items to select	0.08515
Cleanliness of dishes and silverware	0.06750
Temperature of hot food items	−0.03559
Food served when you want it	0.01173
Thoroughness of cooking vegetables	−0.00377
Seasoning of food	[b]

[a]The beta weight indexes the degree of importance of the factor to overall patient acceptance of the mean (from Herz et al., 1980).
[b]Not included in regression equation because it provided no further predictive power.

TABLE 6 Meal Factors in Rank Order of Their Importance
To Cafeteria Patrons, as Determined by Multiple Linear
Regression

Factor	Beta Weight[a]
Appearance and aroma of food	0.27501
Cleanliness of dishes and silverware	0.16146
Temperature of hot food items	-0.13281
Tenderness of meat	0.12343
Variety of items to select	0.10234
Size of portions	0.08343
Seasoning of food	0.05985
Temperature of cold food items	-0.02782
Attractiveness of dishes, silverware, tray	[b]
Thoroughness of cooking vegetables	[b]
Food served when you want it	[b]

[a]The beta weight indexes the degree of importance of
the factor to overall patient acceptance of the mean
(from Herz et al., 1980).
[b]Not included in regression equation because it
provided no further predictive power.

the most important factors contributing to the meal
acceptability for both groups. For ward patients the
temperature of cold food items; the attractiveness of
dishes, silverware, and tray; and the tenderness of meat
are also important factors. For cafeteria patrons the
cleanliness of dishes and silverware, temperature of hot
food items, tenderness of meat, and variety of items are
important. The major differences between the groups seem
to be the greater importance of the cleanliness of dishes
and silverware for cafeteria patrons and the greater
importance of the temperature of hot items over cold
items in the cafeteria.

METHODS FOR ASSESSING PATIENT SATISFACTION
WITH SYSTEM FACTORS

When attempting to assess patient satisfaction with system
factors, management must develop a food service system

survey. Such a survey may either take the form of a printed opinion questionnaire, or the form of a detailed personal interview with patients. The interview format provides maximum latitude in probing the underlying reasons for patient responses. However, if the data are to be treated quantitatively, then at a minimum a <u>structured</u> interview is necessary. A structured interview simply standardizes the topics and questions to be asked in the interview, as well as the response format for each question. In that way the frequencies of responses to each item can be calculated and used to analyze the data statistically, while still allowing maximum flexibility to explore the underlying reasons for the responses. Whether system surveys are printed or are conducted by personal interview, the survey should be conducted during the patient's stay and not upon discharge, when his memory for certain aspects of the food service system may be poor.

Because the methods for developing reliable and valid surveys are too time-consuming to be discussed in any detail here, the interested food service practitioner is referred to several excellent sources for both technical and nontechnical readers recommended by the American Statistical Association (Tanur, 1972; Hauser, 1975; Williams, 1978).

System surveys in the form of printed questionnaires are by far more easily administered than interview surveys. Appendix B contains one such hospital food service system questionnaire that was used very successfully in a recent multihospital survey. The development of this instrument is described in Maller et al. (1979), and data from the survey have also been reported in Maller et al. (1980).

Patient-Dependent Factors Affecting the Perception of Hospital Food

Feeding hospitalized patients is more complicated than most other institutional food service operations because of the unique requirements and conditions. Patients differ on a wide range of demographic variables and can be affected by a variety of disease states and medications. They are also in a uniquely stressful situation and are beset by a variety of motivational and affective problems. Each of the above factors can affect their perceptions of the food and food service of the hospital.

Effects of Disease State

Numerous disease states will produce distortion or
decrements in the patient's senses of taste and smell
that will affect the perception of food. These various
deficits or symptoms are clinically categorized as
follows:

Ageusia--a total loss of taste perception.
Hypogeusia--a decreased or diminished sensitivity in
detecting and/or recognizing (identifying) the taste
qualities.
Hypergeusia--an increased or heightened sensitivity in
detecting and/or recognizing taste qualities.
Dysgeusia--an unpleasant distortion in the perception
of taste qualities, e.g., a persistent or repulsive taste.
Anosmia--a total loss of odor perception.
Hyposmia--a decreased or diminished sensitivity in
detecting and/or recognizing (identifying) odor qualities.
Hyperosmia--an increased or heightened sensitivity in
detecting and/or recognizing (identifying) odor qualities.
Dysosmia--an unpleasant distortion in the perception
of odors, e.g., a persistent, repulsive odor.

Table 7 lists disease states that have been demonstrated to affect taste or smell and the specific type of
clinical anomaly that has been identified (Maller and
Cardello, 1978). The list is long, and while systematic
relationships between these disease states and food preference or acceptance have not been clearly demonstrated,
the alert dietitian should be aware of the potential
effects of these disease states on patients' assessment
of hospital food.

Effects of Medication and Therapy

Various drugs used in the treatment of hospitalized
patients have been shown to produce alterations in taste
perception (Carson and Cormican, 1976). Table 8 lists
these drugs and their known effects.
Even therapuetic procedures may have effects on the
perception of food, as demonstrated by the loss of taste
and odor acuity in patients on maintenance hemodialysis
(Atkins-Thor et al., 1978; Schiffman et al., 1978). As
with disease states, the hospital dietitian should be
aware of the possible contribution that a patient's

TABLE 7   Summary of Disease States Causing Dysfunctions
in Taste and Smell Perception

Diseases	Dysfunctions	
	Taste	Smell
Oral Cavity and Salivary Glands		
Sjogren's syndrome	#	#
Type I familial dysautonomia	#	#
Disordered oral sensations	#	.
Endocrine, Nutritional, and Metabolic		
Addison's disease	++	.
Cystic fibrosis of pancreas	+,%,%,%,	+
Diabetes mellitus	=,#,%	.
Essential hypertension	#,%	.
Carcinomatosis	#,%	.
Hypogonadism--Turner's syndrome	#	#
Hypothyroidism	#	#
Zinc Deficiency	#	.
Digestive System		
Acute Perihepatitis	.	#
Cirrhosis	#	#
Infectious Diseases		
Leprosy	#	.
Mental Disorders		
Depression	#	.
Schizophrenia	*	.
Miscellaneous		
"Idiopathic hypogeusia and dysgeusia"	#,*	#,*
Drugs--thiol containing	#	.
Surgical trauma	*	.
Head trauma	#	#

Key: % = normal; + = hypergeusia or hyperosmia;
# = hypogeusia and hyposmia; * = dysgeuisia and sysosmia;
. = undetermined

SOURCE: Maller and Cardello, 1980.

TABLE 8 Effects of Medications on Taste Perception

Drug	Taste Dysfunction
Amphetamines	Decreased sweet sensitivity in some: differs with individuals
	Increased bitter sensitivity
Anesthetics	
Cocaine	Decreased sensitivity, especially sweet and bitter
Cocaine	Decreased bitter and sweet sensitivity
Amydricaine	Decreased bitter and sweet sensitivity
Amylocaine	With high intake, loss of salt detection, decreased bitter sensitivity
Isococaine and tropacocaine	Decreased sweet sensitivity
Benzocaine	Increased sour sensitivity
Amethocaine	Increased bitter sensitivity
Lipnocaine	Decreased salt and sweet sensitivity
Acetyl sulfosali-cylic acid	Decreased sensitivity
Clofibrate	Decreased sensitivity
Dinitrophenol	Loss of salt taste; general hypogeusia
D-Penicillamine	General decrease in sensitivity
5-Fluorouracil	Some alterations in bitter and sour sensitivity
	Increased sweet sensitivity
Griseofulvin	Decreased sensitivity
Insulin	With prolonged use, decreased sweet and salt sensitivity
Lithium carbonate	Strange, unpleasant taste
5-Mercaptopyridoxal	Altered taste
Phenindione	Decreased sensitivity
Phenytoin	Decreased sensitivity
Oxyfedrine	Decreased sensitivity
Antithyroid agents	
Methimazole	Decreased sensitivity
Methylthiouracil	Decreased sensitivity

SOURCE: Carson and Cormican, 1976.

medication may have on his perception of the food, when evaluating complaints from certain patients.

Effects of Demographic, Motivational, and Affective Variables

A host of demographic and psychological variables may also affect judgments of food acceptability by hospitalized patients. These factors include age, sex, length of stay in the hospital, mood, appetite, satisfaction with previous meals, satisfaction with health care, and feelings of anxiety over being in the hospital (Glew, 1970; Maller et al., 1980). Related factors that have been shown to be of importance in evaluations made by staff members who eat in the dining rooms include age, educational level, and satisfaction with work and salary (Maller et al., 1980). Specifically, meal acceptability has been found to be significantly higher in male patients than in female patients (Glew, 1970) and in older patients and staff than in younger patients and staff (Maller et al., 1980). Concerning the latter point, it has been suggested that older individuals are more tolerant and less critical of the quality of food because they have diminished taste and olfactory sensitivity. A similar trend among staff members, showing that those with higher education have more favorable opinions of the meals (Maller et al., 1980) may simply be due to the fact that more-educated staff members are likely to be older.

Concerning the effects of length of stay, it has been shown that ambulatory patients (who have longer average stays than ward patients) show a significant decline in their judgements of the perceived acceptability of hospital meals as length of stay increases (Maller et al., 1980).

Another significant correlation has been observed between the ratings of all past meals eaten at a hospital and the ratings of the acceptability of test meals (Maller et al., 1980). Pearson product-moment correlations between these two ratings were significant ($p < .001$) for ward patients ($r = .51$), ambulatory patients ($r = .44$), and staff members ($r = .55$), suggesting that the perceived acceptability of previously eaten meals significantly affects the acceptability of subsequent meals. If past experience with meals at a hospital has been good, it is more likely that a given meal will be rated positively than if past experience has been bad. Thus, early impressions influence subsequent evaluations of food acceptability.

For motivational and effective variables, it was shown in the study by Maller et al. (1980) that the opinion of a meal is positively correlated with the respondent's mood. Similarly, it was found that ward patients' opinions of a meal were positively correlated with their self-reports of appetite and with the expressed importance of mealtime to them on that day. Also, signifi-

cantly correlated with the patients' opinions of the food
was their satisfaction with the nurses' and doctors' care
and their comfort (ease) in the hospital setting. These
latter findings support those of Sheatsley (1965), who
showed that patients are more likely to rate hospital food
as good or excellent if other aspects of their hospitalization are satisfactory. For the staff, satisfaction
with their work and salary were positively correlated
with their opinion of the food, thus paralleling the
observations with patients.

AN APPLIED EXAMPLE: PATIENT EVALUATIONS OF FOOD DELIVERED BY FIVE DIFFERENT TRAY DELIVERY SYSTEMS

In order to demonstrate the application of the above
methods, I will now describe some preliminary results
that we have obtained in a study of five different patient
tray delivery systems at Moncrief Army Hospital, Fort
Jackson, Columbia, South Carolina. These tests were
carried out for the Operations Research and Systems
Analysis Office at Natick Laboratories. Other aspects of
work on this project will be discussed elsewhere in this
volume. In particular, Ronald Bustead provides details
on the newly designed cook-freeze system at Moncrief.

Methods

The delivery systems that were evaluated consisted of
three cold-plating systems (3-M, Sweetheart, and
Aladdin), one hot-plating system (Therma-Tray), and a
control system that was already in service at the
hospital and that was based on hot-plating and delivery
in a hot/cold cart. A brief description of these systems
follows.

   The 3-M Integral Heating System is designed to store,
reheat, and deliver up to 24 patient trays. Cold-plated
meals go from the trayline directly into the cart for
chilled storage until meal time. Trays are then heated
within the cart, usually at a location near the final
delivery site. Each cart plugs into a wall-mounted power
supply. After the food items have been heated, the mobile
cart is used to deliver and retrieve trays to and from
patients. Food is rethermalized in dish ovens that have
an inner resistive coating to convert electrical energy
into heat. Built-in sensors control the amount of heat

delivered to the food. The dish oven also serves as the patient's meal plate.

The Aladdin Rethermalization System is designed to heat menu items and to serve as the storage, delivery, and retrieval vehicle. Food is plated cold into specifically designed server base trays with insulated covers and transferred to mobile carts. The carts are then transported to selected serving areas on the ward and rolled into refrigeration units. Food is rethermalized in the patient tray within the refrigerator. Each of 24 tray shelves in each cart has three independently operating heating units to provide heat to food items. After rethermalization, carts are removed from the refrigeration units and used to deliver patient trays.

The Sweetheart Feeding System Cart also reheats food in the patient tray and serves as the delivery and retrieval vehicle. However, battery power distinguishes it from the other systems. Food can be reheated in transit to the ward; no wall outlets are required.

The Therma-Tray System differs from the above three in that it is a hot-plating system. Food is hot-plated into insulated trays and immediately delivered to the patient. High plating temperatures and uninterrupted delivery are essential for sustained temperature integrity.

The control system consisted of an older hot/cold cart system that had been in operation at the hospital prior to these tests.

Test and Control Sites and Survey Populations

Each of the four tray delivery systems was tested for one 10-day period. Moncrief Army Hospital is a 300-bed facility that was chosen as a test site for a systems analysis of its entire food service operation. During each test period, the two medical/surgical wards (both located on the same floor of the hospital) served as testing sites. The medical/surgical wards were selected because of their stable and commonly high patient census as compared to other wards. During test periods one ward was designated as the test ward (9-West) and the other the control ward (9-East). During all tests the control ward continued to use the hot-plating delivery system in use throughout the hospital. The near-perfect symmetry of the floor plan (each wing [ward] had an identical pattern of rooms, nursing station, nourishment center, etc.), combined with their sole occupation of the ninth floor, ensured adequate control over extraneous variables that might confound differences between the ratings obtained from the test and control patients.

While no adjustments were made to normal hospital admissions policy for assignment of patients to the two wards, no major demographic differences between test and control patient populations were observed during the duration of testing. While the nursing staffs were different on the test and control wards, the staff on each ward was the same during all four test periods. Moreover, while the cooks and food service personnel who handled the loading and delivery of the trays were different for the test and control wards, the same personnel served their respective wards during all four test periods.

Survey Instruments

The survey instrument used with the patient populations was the Consumer Opinion Card shown in Figure 4. It consisted of five rating scales to be completed by the patient, as well as space for open-ended comments.

The reliability and validity of this card had been previously evaluated (Waterman et al., 1975) and had been shown to be superior to other forms with similar formats.

Survey Procedures

During each of the four 10-day test periods, 30 meals were evaluated--three meals per day. For each period, the master menu was adjusted so that the same 30 meals would be served during each test period. During this time, 67 individual food and beverage items were designated for evaluation. Of these, 48 were hot entrees, starches, vegetables, and beverages, while 19 were cold entrees, desserts, and beverages. Although all 67 regular menu items were served on the wards during this time period, the number of patients actually eating these items varied considerably. The two factors responsible for this were the number of special diets sent to the ward at any given meal and the individual food preferences of the patients, many of whom would not eat or sample a particular item because of personal preferences.

Survey personnel were present on the wards when meal trays were distributed; they accompanied the tray server (usually one of the nursing staff) to the patient's room. Only patients who were present in their rooms, physically well enough to fill out the rating cards, and ready to eat their meals were requested to participate. This ensured that qualitative judgments of the food items were valid; i.e., items were not cold or dried out when eaten. If a patient was ready to eat, he was requested to complete one or more of the food rating cards after being informed of the reasons for the survey and consenting to participate. Each patient was asked to evaluate a maximum of three food items, with one rating card being left for each item to be evaluated. Completed cards were collected approximately 30 minutes later, after patients had finished eating. Over the four test periods, approximately 4,000 food acceptability cards were collected.

Results

The data were analyzed by separating the hot food items from the cold food items and then calculating the mean ratings assigned to each food item for each test system and for the control data collected during each of the four test periods. Since each of the test systems was tested during a different 10-day period and during different parts of the spring and summer, any obtained differences in ratings of food acceptability among the test systems could be due to certain factors existing at the test site during the time of testing. These might include such factors as personnel vacations, which could have resulted in different food service workers, temporary failure of kitchen equipment, differences in season of year that may have affected patient preferences for certain hot and cold foods, etc. In order to control for these possible effects, the ratings for food items obtained on each of the four test systems were analyzed by comparing them to the ratings for those same items obtained on the control system during the period in which the test system was evaluated.

Table 9 shows the results of these comparisons for hot food items on the judged attributes of temperature and overall acceptability. The numbers to the right of each test system name show the proportion of hot food items that had higher ratings under that system than under its corresponding control. Differences among proportions

TABLE 9 Comparison of the Four Test Delivery Systems for Patient Ratings of Temperature and Overall Acceptability of Hot Food Items[a]

Temperature	
Sweetheart	0.667*
3-M	0.444*
Therma-Tray	0.313†
Aladdin	0.261†
Overall acceptability	
Therma-Tray	0.406*
3-M	0.343*†
Sweetheart	0.263†
Aladdin	0.053†

[a]The numbers in the right column are the proportions of food items for which the particular test system had better mean scores than the control system. Proportions with the same superscript are not significantly different (p < .05) from one another.

were tested for significance using a Z-test, and proportions having the same superscript did not reach significance at the .05 probability level.

Overall the Sweetheart system had the highest proportion of hot food items that were rated hotter than the control. However, this proportion was not significantly different from those for the 3-M or Therma-Tray systems. On "overall acceptability," the Therma-Tray and 3-M systems had the highest proportions, although neither Sweetheart nor Aladdin was significantly different from 3-M.

Table 10 shows the same analysis, but for the cold foods. Because certain cold items were not selected during the Sweetheart test period, the data set was considered too small to include in the analysis. Thus, only three test systems are listed in Table 10. Although the proportions shown in Table 10 differ, none was statistically different from another.

The above results for perceived temperature can be compared to the results for objective temperatures on these systems, as are reported by Ronald Bustead later in this volume. Anticipating his viewgraph on mean tempera-

TABLE 10 Proportions of Cold Food Items for Which the
Test Systems had Better Mean Scores Than the Control
System[a]

Temperature
   3-M   0.583
   Aladdin   0.571
   Therma-Tray   0.300

Overall acceptability
   3-M   0.417
   Therma-Tray   0.273
   Aladdin   0.143

---

[a]The Sweetheart system is not included because of
insufficient data.

tures for the various systems, we can show the Sweetheart
system as having the highest temperatures for hot food
items. This result corresponds well with the data in
Table 9. However, his viewgraph also shows the Sweetheart
system to have the highest temperatures for cold food
items. Unfortunately, the number of cold food items
evaluated here was too small to analyze separately in our
data. Of interest, however, in both Tables 9 and 10, is
that on "overall acceptability" the proportions for all
systems are less than .500. This means that for each
system, a greater proportion of items was rated more
acceptable under the control system than under the test
systems.

In order to get a more complete picture of the performance of the control system, the data for the control
system were collapsed across all four test periods. The
mean ratings across 11 items (hot and cold) was then
compared for all five systems (four test systems and the
control). Table 11 shows the mean ratings for "temperature" and "overall acceptability," along with the results
of Neuman-Kuels contrast tests ($p < .05$) on the differences among means.

A different picture now emerges from the data. On temperature, the Sweetheart system performs least well, with
the control system having the next lowest ratings. As was
suggested by the proportions in Tables 9 and 10, the
"overall acceptability" ratings are highest for the
control system.

TABLE 11 Comparison of the Mean Ratings Across All Food
Items for Each Test System and the Control[a]

Temperature
  3-M   3.73*
  Therma-Tray   3.57†
  Aladdin   3.54†
  Control   3.38††
  Sweetheart   2.85§

Overall acceptability
  Control   5.72*
  Therma-Tray   5.71*
  3-M   5.47†
  Sweetheart   5.00††
  Aladdin   4.65§

---

[a]Mean ratings with different superscripts are
significantly different ($p < .05$).

That the Sweetheart system should change from first to
last on temperature ratings (Tables 9 and 11) is curious.
Clearly, this system performed well when compared to its
control, but poorly when compared with all other systems
independently. The possible reason for this resides in
the data of Table 12. Here we see the mean ratings for
temperature and overall acceptability that were obtained
by the control system during the four test periods. A
sharp decline can be seen in the temperature ratings for
the control system during the Sweetheart test. Since the
factor responsible for this decline in ratings was not
evident at the time of testing, it is not known whether
this effect operated only on the control sytem or had
commensurate effects on the Sweetheart system. Consequently, to conclude simply that the Sweetheart system
did not perform well on temperature ratings compared to
other systems (Table 6) is not warranted, as this poor
performance may have been due to confounding variables,
which, when period of test is controlled (Table 9),
reveal the Sweetheart system to be the best for hot
foods. The moral of this is that while collecting data
on patients' perceptions of hospital food may be easy,
interpreting their causal effects can be much more
difficult.

TABLE 12   Mean Ratings Across All Foods for the Control
System During Each of the Four 10-Day Test Periods

Test Period	Temperature	Overall Acceptability
3-M	3.64	5.81
Sweetheart	2.44	5.66
Therma-Tray	3.64	5.69
Aladdin	3.70	5.68

Last, in Tables 9-11 relative differences among the
systems can be seen when one compares their ratings on
temperature with their ratings on overall acceptability.
Table 13 shows Pearson product-moment correlation coefficients among all pairs of the five judged attributes.
High positive correlations can be observed among the
attributes of "overall acceptability," "appearance,"
"flavor," and "texture." However, the attributes of
"temperature" are relatively independent of all others.
This independence of "temperature" ratings from all other
attribute ratings explains the differences found in comparing temperature with overall acceptability in Tables
9-11 and also points to the important association of the
flavor, texture, and appearance of food with its judged
acceptability.

SUMMARY

I have attempted to review some basic concepts, methods,
and data related to the assessment of patient perceptions
of hospital food and food services. What must be kept in
mind, however, is that each hospital is unique and has
its own requirements and problems. It is for this very
reason that hospital food service managers and dietitians
should be familiar with the basic techniques for collecting reliable and valid data on patients' acceptance and
preferences for food and on their satisfaction with food
service system factors.
    As a final point of perspective, the following is the
official dietary (menu) of London Hospital in 1875 (Pavy,
1975):

TABLE 13 Correlations Among Judged Attributes

	Appearance	Temper-ature	Flavor	Texture
Overall acceptability	.589	.258	.708	.773
Appearance		.359	.667	.568
Temperature			.406	.160
Flavor				.636

FULL DIET FOR MEN AND WOMEN

Daily--12 oz of bread. 8 oz of potatoes. 1 pint of porter.
Breakfast--Gruel.
Dinner--Sunday and Thursday--6 oz of boiled mutton.
        Monday, Wednesday, and Saturday--6 oz of roast
        mutton.
        Tuesday and Friday--6 oz of roast beef.
Supper--1 pint of broth.

   As the above diet obviously demonstrates, we have come
a long way in improving hospital food during the past
century; and as the remainder of this symposium will no
doubt indicate, we are well on the road to another century
of challenge and progress in this important area of
health care.

REFERENCES

Atkins-Thor, E., B. Goddard, J. O'Nion, R. L. Stephen,
    and W. J. Kolff. 1978. Evaluation of the relationship
    between taste acuity and zinc tissue levels in
    patients on maintenance hemodialysis. Communication
    reported in S. S. Schiffman, M. L. Nash, and C.
    Dackis, Reduced olfactory discrimination in patients
    on chronic hemodialysis. Physiol. Behav. 21:239.
Bachrach, B. 1970. Pediatric menu terminology. Hospitals
    44: 84.
Balintfy, J. L., W. J. Duffy, and P. Sinha. 1974.
    Modeling food preferences over time. Operations Res.
    22:711.

Balintfy, J. L., P. Sinha, H. R. Moskowitz, and J. G. Rogozenski. 1975. The time dependence of food preferences. Food Prod. Devel. (9):32.

Beard, J. 1977. Hospital food is chronically sick. Boston Globe, Aug. 31.

Branch, L. G. 1973. An Evaluation of Common Predictors of Consumer Acceptance. Technical Report No. 73-42-PR, U.S. Army Natick Laboratories, Natick, Mass.

Bunch, W. L., M. E. Matthews, and E. H. Marth. 1976. Hospital chill food service systems: acceptability and microbiological characteristics of beef-soy loaves when processed according to system procedures. J. Food Sci. 41:1273.

Burk, M. C., and E. M. Pao. 1976. Methodology for Large-Scale Surveys of Household and Individual Diets. Home Economics Research Report No. 40, Agricultural Research Service, United States Department of Agriculture. U.S. Government Printing Office, Washington, D.C.

Cardello, A. V., O. Maller, R. Kluter, and L. Digman. 1981. Patient and Staff Evaluation of Five Patient Food Stray Delivery Systems. Unpublished technical report. Science and Advanced Technology Laboratory. U.S. Army Natick Research and Development Laboratories, Natick, Mass.

Carson, J. S., and A. Cormican. 1976. Disease-medication relationships in altered taste sensitivity. J. Am. Diet. Assoc. 68:550.

Comstock, E. M., L. E. Symington, H. E. Chmielinski, and J. S. McGuire. 1979. Plate Waste in School Feeding Programs: Individual and Aggregate Measures. Technical Report No. TR-81/011, Food Sciences Laboratory. U.S. Army Natick Research and Development Command, Natick, Mass.

Croughan, N. K., B. J. Mullen, E. M. Comstock, C. A. Holden, H. G. Schutz, L. E. Grivetti, and H. L. Meiselman. 1981. An Annotated, Indexed Bibliography on Methods of Measuring Individual Food Intake. Unpublished technical report. U.S. Army Natick Research and Development Laboratory, Natick, Mass.

Eindhoven, J., and D. R. Peryam. 1959a. Measurement of preferences for food combinations. Food Tech. 13:379.

Eindhoven, J., and D. R. Peryam. 1959b. Compatability of Menu Items. Report No. 35-39. Quartermaster Food and Container Institute, Chicago, Ill.

Ellis, B. H. 1964. Flavor evaluation as a means of product evaluation. Page 187 in Proc. 11th Annu. Meet. Soc. Soft Drink Technologists.

Ellis, B. H. 1968. Preference testing methodology. Part 1. Food Technol. 22(583):49.

Feldman, J. J. 1962. Patients' opinions of hospital food. J. Am. Diet. Assoc. 40:325.

Freidson, E., and J. Feldman. 1958. The public looks at hospitals. Health Info. Found. Res. Ser. No. 4.

Glew, G. 1970. Food preferences of hospital patients. Proc. Nutr. Soc. 29:339.

Glew, G., ed. 1973. Cook/Freeze Catering, An Introduction to its Technology. Faber and Faber, London.

Gridgeman, N. T. 1961. A comparison of some taste-test methods. J. Food Sci. 26:171.

Hauser, P. 1975. Social Statistics in Use. Russell Sage Foundation, New York.

Herz, M., A. Freeman, G. Eccleston, G. Hertweck, S. Baritz, P. Short, W. O. Veneklasen, and J. Souder. 1978. Systems Analysis of Alternative Food Service Concepts for New Army Hospitals. Technical Report No. TR-78-031. Operations Research/Systems Analysis Office, U.S. Army Natick Research and Development Command, Natick, Mass.

Jones, L. V., D. R. Peryam, and L. L. Thurstone. 1955. Development of a scale for measuring soldiers' food preferences. Food Res. 20:512.

Kamen, J. M. 1962. Reasons for non-consumption of food in the army. J. Am. Diet. Assoc. 41:437-442.

Kamenetzky, J., and F. J. Pilgrim. 1958. Interpretation of Preference Ratings. Report No. 16-58. Quartermaster Food and Container Institute, Chicago, Ill.

Kamenetzky, J., F. J. Pilgrim, and H. G. Schutz. 1957. Relationship of Consumption to Preference Under Different Field Conditions. Technical Report No. 37-57. Quartermaster Food and Container Institute, Chicago, Ill.

Kincaid, J. W. 1975. Patients evaluate cycle menu entrees. Hospitals 49:71.

LaChance, P. A. 1976. Simple research techniques for school food service. Part 1: Acceptance testing. School Food Service J., 30(8):54.

Maller, O., and A. V. Cardello. 1978. The sick senses: functions of taste and smell. Prof. Nutr. 10(1):1.

Maller, O., C. N. Dubose, and A. V. Cardello. 1979. Patient and Staff Opinions of Army Hospital Food Service. Technical report, Food Sciences Laboratory. U.S. Army Natick Research and Development Command, Natick, Mass.

Maller, O., C. N. Dubose, and A. V. Cardello. 1980. Consumer opinions of hospital food and food service. J. Am. Diet. Assoc. 76(3):236.

Matthews, M. E. 1977. Quality of foods in cook/chill food service systems: a review. School Food Service Res. Rev. 1(1):15.

McCune, E. 1962. Patients' and dietitians' ideas about "quality" food. J. Am. Diet. Assoc. 40:321.

McDaniel, M. R., and F. M. Sawyer. 1981. Preference testing of whiskey sour formulations: magnitude estimation versus the 9-point hedonic. J. Food Sci. 46:182.

Meiselman, H. L., and D. Waterman. 1978. Food preferences of enlisted personnel in the Armed Forces. J. Am. Diet. Assoc. 73:621.

Meiselman, H. L., D. Waterman, and L. E. Symington. 1974. Army Forces Food Preferences. Technical Report No. 75-63-FLS. U.S. Army Natick Development Center, Natick, Mass.

Moskowitz, H. R. 1970. Ratio scales of sugar sweetness. Percept. Psychophys. 7:315.

Moskowitz, H. R. 1977. Magnitude estimation: notes on what, how, when and why to use it. J. Food Qual. 1:195.

Moskowitz, H. R. 1980. Comparing magnitude estimation and category scaling as acceptance measures: statistical approaches. Paper presented at ASTM Symposium, Philadelphia, Pa., Oct. 1980.

Moskowitz, H. R., and L. Klarman. 1977. Food comparabilities and menu planning. J. Inst. Can. Sci. Technol. Alim. 10(4):257.

Moskowitz, H. R., and J. L. Sidel. 1971. Magnitude and hedonic scales of food acceptability. J. Food Sci., 36:677.

Moskowitz, H. R., A. V. Cardello, O. Maller, R. A. Segars, and J. G. Kapsalis. 1979. Product optimization: maximizing consumer acceptance and increasing profit margins. Baker's Dig. 53:8.

Murphy, C., A. V. Cardello, and J. G. Brand. 1981. Taste of fifteen halide salts following water and NaCl: anion and cation effects. Physiol. Behav. 26:1083.

Opinion Research Corp. 1955. New Jersey Residents Talk About Their Hospitals. Opinion Research Corp., Princeton, N.J.

Pavy, F. W. 1875. A Treatise on Food and Dietetics. Churchill, London.

Peryam, D. R., and N. F. Girardot 1952. Advanced taste test method. Food Eng. 24(7):58.

Peryam, D. R., and F. J. Pilgrim. 1957. Hedonic scale
method of measuring food preferences. Food Tech. 11:9.

Peryam, D. R., B. W. Polemis, J. M. Kamen, J. Endhoven,
and F. J. Pilgrim. 1960. Food Preferences of Men in
the Armed Forces. Quartermaster Food and Container
Institute, Chicago, Ill.

Pilgrim, F. J. 1961. What foods do people accept or
reject? J. Am. Diet. Assoc. 39:439.

Rinke, W. J. 1976. Three major systems reviewed and
evaluated. Hospitals 50(4):73.

Rogozenski, J. E., Jr., and H. R. Moskowitz. 1975. A
System for the Preference Evaluation of Cyclic Menus.
Technical Report No. 75-46, OR/SA. U.S. Army Natick
Laboratories, Natick, Mass.

Ronco, P. G. 1972. Human factors applied to hospital
patient care. Human Factors 14:461.

Roper, Elmo, and Associates. 1958. The Public's Attitudes
Toward Hospitals in New York City and Their Financing
in May 1958. Elmo Roper and Associates, New York.

Rucker, M., L. Armstrong, I. Clemo, and A. Wu. 1973.
Descriptive menus enhance food acceptance. Hospitals
47:67.

Sather, L. A., and L. D. Calvin. 1960. The effect of
number of judgments in a test on flavor evaluations
for preference. Food Tech. 14(12):613.

Schiffman, S. S., M. L. Nash, and C. Dackis, 1978.
Reduced olfactory discrimination in patients on
chronic hemodialysis. Physiol. Behav. 21:239.

Schmalz, P. E. 1963. The use of sensory evaluation in the
meat industry. Page 6 in Food News and Views Bull. No.
189. Swift and Co., Chicago, Ill.

Schuh, D. D., A. N. Moore, and B. H. Tuthill. 1967.
Measuring food acceptability by frequency ratings. J.
Am. Diet. Assoc. 57:340.

Schutz, H. G. 1957. Performance ratings as predictors of
food consumption. Am. Psychol. 12:380.

Schutz, H. G. 1965. A food action rating scale for
measuring food accepance. J. Food Sci. 30:365.

Schutz, H. G., M. H. Rucker, and J. D. Hunt. 1972.
Hospital patients' and employees' reactions to
food-use combinations. J. Am. Diet. Assoc. 60:207.

Sheatsley, P. B. 1965. How total hospital experience
shapes patient's opinion of food. Hospitals 39:105.

Sidel, J. L., H. Stone, A. Woolsey, and J. M. Mecredy.
1972. Correlation between hedonic ratings and
consumption of beer. J. Food Sci. 37:335.

Smutz, E. R., H. L. Jacobs, D. Waterman, and M. Caldwell. 1974. Small Sample Studies of Food Habits: I. The Relationship Between Food Preference and Food Choice in Naval Enlisted Personnel at the Naval Construction Battalion Center, Davisville, Rhode Island. Technical Report No. 75-52-FSL. U.S. Army Natick Laboratories, Natick, Mass.

Stevens, J. C. 1957. A comparison of ratio scales for the loudness of white noise and the brightness of white light. Ph.D. dissertation, Harvard University.

Stevens, S. S. 1971. Issues in psychophysical measurement. Psychol. Rev. 78:426.

Stevens, S. S. 1975. Psychophysics. Wiley, New York.

Stevens, S. S., and E. H. Galanter. 1957. Ratio scales and category scales for a dozen perceptual continua. J. Exp. Psychol. 54:377.

Sullins, W. R., Jr., W. Symington, J. R. Siebold, and J. G. Rogers. 1977. Food Preference, Acceptance and Consumption in a Simulated, Isolated-Duty Station. Technical Report No. TR-78-027. U.S. Army Natick Research and Development Laboratory, Natick, Mass.

Tanur, J. 1972. Statistics: A Guide to the Unknown. Holden-Day, San Francisco.

Twedt, D. W. 1966. New developments in measurement and attitude scales. Paper presented at the American Marketing Association, Chicago Chapter, February 1966.

Waterman, D., H. L. Meiselman, L. Branch, and M. Taylor. 1974. The 1972 Westover Air Force Base Food Preference Survey and Reliability Study. Technical Report No. 75-25-25-FSL. U.S. Army Natick Laboratories, Natick, Mass.

Wells, W. D. 1965. Communicating with children. J. Res. 52:2.

Williams, W. H. 1978. A Sampler on Sampling. Wiley, New York.

Wyant, K. W., H. L. Meiselman, and D. Waterman. 1979. Air Force Food Habits Study. Part I. Method and Overview. Technical Report No. TR-79-041. Food Sciences Laboratory. U.S. Army Natick Research and Development Command, Natick, Mass.

Zellmer, G. 1970. Food acceptance vs. serving frequency. Hospitals, 44:75.

FOOD PREFERENCE SURVEY

U.S. ARMY NATICK RESEARCH AND DEVELOPMENT COMMAND

JANUARY 1977

86

Instructions for all questions: Read each question and mark the correct answer by filling in the appropriate oval, like this ①②●④ or by marking the oval opposite the correct answer. Several of the questions need more than one answer. Please read the special instructions carefully.

1. Indicate your AGE at your last birthday.

1st Digit	2nd Digit
⓪①②③④⑤⑥⑦	⓪①②③④⑤⑥⑦⑧⑨

EXAMPLE:
If you are 21 years old: Darken oval ② in the left column and darken oval ① in the right column.

2. Indicate your HEIGHT in feet and inches.

FEET	INCHES
④⑤⑥⑦	⓪①②③④⑤⑥⑦⑧⑨⑩⑪

3. Indicate your present WEIGHT in pounds.

1st Digit	2nd Digit	3rd Digit
⓪①②③	⓪①②③④⑤⑥⑦⑧⑨	⓪①②③④⑤⑥⑦⑧⑨

EX. 137 pounds Darken → ① ③ ⑦

4. Indicate your RACE/ETHNIC BACKGROUND.
- ○ Caucasian/White
- ○ Negro/Black
- ○ Oriental
- ○ Mexican American
- ○ Other (specify) _____

5. Indicate your SEX.
- ○ Male
- ○ Female

6. Indicate your MARITAL STATUS.
- ○ Married, Living Together
- ○ Single, Divorced, or Separated

7. Indicate your PRESENT GRADE.
- ○ E-1
- ○ E-2
- ○ E-3
- ○ E-4
- ○ E-5
- ○ E-6
- ○ E-7
- ○ E-8
- ○ E-9
- ○ Officer/CWO

8. Do you receive a SEPARATE RATIONS ALLOWANCE (money instead of free meals?) Indicate the correct answer.
- ○ Yes
- ○ No

9. Indicate your HIGHEST LEVEL OF EDUCATION.
- ○ Finished Grade School
- ○ High School Graduate (including GED)
- ○ Skilled Job Training After High School (Trade School)
- ○ Some College
- ○ College Graduate (include graduate work)

DC 36-025   OPTICAL SCANNING FORMS™ NEWTOWN, PA. 18940

10. How long have you been IN MILITARY SERVICE? Indicate the number of years.

YEARS

Less than one year

(1) (2) (3) (4) (5) (6) (7) (8) (9) (10) (11) (12) (13) (14) (15) (16) (17) (18) (19) (20) PLUS

11. What did you WEIGH when you ENTERED THE SERVICE? Indicate weight in pounds.

1st Digit	2nd Digit	3rd Digit
(0)	(0)	(0)
(1)	(1)	(1)
(2)	(2)	(2)
(3)	(3)	(3)
	(4)	(4)
	(5)	(5)
	(6)	(6)
	(7)	(7)
	(8)	(8)
	(9)	(9)

12. In what REGION OF THE COUNTRY did you LIVE THE LONGEST before you joined the Service? (choose one.)

○ New England (Me, NH, Vt, Mass, RI, Conn)
○ Middle Atlantic (NY, NJ, Penn)
○ East North Central (Oh, Ind, Ill, Mich, Wisc)
○ West North Central (Minn, Ia, Mo, ND, SD, Neb, Kan)
○ South Atlantic (Del, Md, DC, Va, WVa, NC, SC, Ga, Fla)
○ East South Central (Ky, Tenn, Ala, Miss)
○ West South Central (Ark, La, Okla, Tex)
○ Mountain (Mont, Ida, Wyo, Colo, NM, Ariz, Ut, Nev)
○ Pacific (Wash, Ore, Cal, Alaska, Hawaii)
○ Other Territories, Possessions or Countries

13. Indicate WHERE YOU LIVE (choose one.)

○ On post bachelor quarters (barracks)
○ On post family quarters
○ Off post bachelor quarters (alone)
○ Off post quarters with other airmen or friends
○ Off post with parents or close relatives
○ Off post family quarters

14. For MEALS PREPARED AT HOME or in the BARRACKS, do you. . .

○ prepare all of them yourself?
○ prepare 75% of them yourself?
○ share preparation 50/50 with others?
○ prepare 25% or less?
○ prepare none; Someone else does all the cooking?

15. What TYPE OF COOKING or SPECIALTY FOODS do you like best? Indicate your TOP THREE CHOICES.

○ Chinese ○ Greek ○ Natural Foods ○ Seafood
○ French ○ Italian ○ Polish & Eastern European ○ Vegetarian
○ Fast Foods (hamburgers, etc.) ○ Japanese ○ Soul ○ Other (specify) _____
○ German ○ Jewish ○ Southern
○ General American Style ○ Mexican (Not Mexican) ○ Spanish

DC 36-023 OPTICAL SCANNING FORM by NEWTOWN, PA. 18948

16. How many PEOPLE usually EAT MEALS WITH YOU?
Indicate one answer for Each Meal.

BREAKFAST
○ I don't usually eat this meal
○ None, I eat alone
○ 1 to 3 other people
○ 4 to 6 other people
○ 7 to 10 other people
○ More than 10 people

LUNCH
○ I don't usually eat this meal
○ None, I eat alone
○ 1 to 3 other people
○ 4 to 6 other people
○ 7 to 10 other people
○ More than 10 people

DINNER
○ I don't usually eat this meal
○ None, I eat alone
○ 1 to 3 other people
○ 4 to 6 other people
○ 7 to 10 other people
○ More than 10 people

17. How much has your WEIGHT CHANGED over the PAST YEAR?

My Low Weight Was:

My High Weight Was:

18. Are you CONCERNED about your PRESENT WEIGHT?
○ Yes
○ No

If your answer to this question was NO, you may turn to the NEXT PAGE.
If your answer was YES, please CONTINUE.

19. Which of the following describe your DIETING METHODS?
Mark all answers that apply.

○ I eat more to GAIN weight.   ○ I no longer eat certain foods.

○ I skip meals to LOSE weight.   ○ I cut out between-meal snacks.

○ I cut down on the amount I eat at meals.

20. Are you taking any MEDICATION regularly for weight loss/gain?
○ Yes (please specify) _____
○ No

21. How could the DINING FACILITY alter their MENU to aid in your weight program? Mark one answer for each food type.

Food Type	They Should Serve:		
MEATS	○ more ○ fewer	or	○ different or ○ OK as is
VEGETABLE	○ more ○ fewer	or	○ different or ○ OK as is
POTATOES	○ more ○ fewer	or	○ different or ○ OK as is
BREADS	○ more ○ fewer	or	○ different or ○ OK as is
SALADS	○ more ○ fewer	or	○ different or ○ OK as is
DESSERTS	○ more ○ fewer	or	○ different or ○ OK as is
DRINKS	○ more ○ fewer	or	○ different or ○ OK as is

DC 36-024   OPTICAL SCANNING FORMS™ NEWTOWN, PA. 18940

Food Preference Survey

Instructions

Your answers to the following questions will help the Armed Forces Menu Planners put foods which you want on the menu. This is not a test. We are interested in your opinion so please do not check your answers with your friends.

On the following pages, please indicate HOW MUCH YOU LIKE OR DISLIKE each food and HOW OFTEN YOU WANT TO EAT the food. If you have never tried the food item or have never heard of it, fill in the oval in the first column labelled NEVER TRIED and leave the rest of the line blank.

If you are familiar with a food on the list and would like to eat it, you should fill in an oval in the column 'Like or Dislike'. In order to say how much you like or dislike a food, look at the following scale.

1	2	3	4	5	6	7	8	9
dislike extremely	dislike very much	dislike moderately	dislike slightly	neither like nor dislike	like slightly	like moderately	like very much	like extremely

Notice that the rating of 5 is neutral, meaning that you neither like nor dislike the food. Ratings below 5 indicate dislike, while ratings above 5 indicate like. Fill in the oval of the number which best describes your feelings for the particular food item. Remember to mark every food item except the ones which you have never tried.

Example:

If you like Danish Pastry very much, you would fill in:

    ① ② ③ ④ ⑤ ⑥ ⑦ ● ⑨

If you dislike it slightly, you would fill in:

    ① ② ③ ● ⑤ ⑥ ⑦ ⑧ ⑨

DC 36-026 OPTICAL SCANNING FORMS™ NEWTOWN, PA. 18940

After rating HOW MUCH YOU LIKE OR DISLIKE THE FOOD, continue across the same line to the last two columns labelled 'How Often You Want To Eat The Food'. Decide how many days per month you would like to eat the food. If you want a food 3 meals or more on the same day, it should still be counted as one day. For any number of days from 01 to 30, fill in two ovals, one in each column. If you never want the food, fill in the two zeros, one in each column.

Please note the following examples:

Example 1

If you would like to eat a food 18 days per month, you would mark,

⊖●⊗⊛ | ⊖⊖⊖⊖⊖⊖⊖⊗●⊛

As you can see, the number you chose (18) has been filled in, one digit per column. You should fill in only one oval per column, but both columns must have one oval filled.

Example 2

If you would like a food only once a month, fill in 01.

●⊖⊗⊛ | ⊖●⊗⊛⊛⊛⊛⊛⊛⊛

In this example, the number you chose (1) has only one digit. In case this, you fill in the 0 in the left column and fill in the 1 in the right column.

If you do not want the food at all, you should mark the zero in each column.

This is not a survey of how much you like foods served in the Armed Forces. We are interested in how much you like these foods in general. Think of the food in a general way, rather than any particular time you have eaten it.

Remember, if you are not familiar with the food item, mark the first column labelled NEVER TRIED and leave the other columns blank. If you are familiar with the item, then first rate HOW MUCH YOU LIKE OR DISLIKE THE FOOD and then indicate HOW OFTEN YOU WANT TO EAT THE FOOD.

DC 36-027 OPTICAL SCANNING FORMS™ NEWTOWN, PA. 18940

6 8 8 5 2 5 8

1	2	3	4	5	6	7	8	9
dislike extremely	dislike very much	dislike moderately	dislike slightly	neither like nor dislike	like slightly	like moderately	like very much	like extremely

	NEVER TRIED	HOW MUCH you like or dislike the food (1-9)		HOW OFTEN you want to eat the food in days per month (01-30)
001 Tea	○	① ② ③ ④ ⑤ ⑥ ⑦ ⑧ ⑨	⓪ ① ② ③	⓪ ① ② ③ ④ ⑤ ⑥ ⑦ ⑧ ⑨
002 Roast Turkey	○	① ② ③ ④ ⑤ ⑥ ⑦ ⑧ ⑨	⓪ ① ② ③	⓪ ① ② ③ ④ ⑤ ⑥ ⑦ ⑧ ⑨
003 Strawberry Shortcake	○	① ② ③ ④ ⑤ ⑥ ⑦ ⑧ ⑨	⓪ ① ② ③	⓪ ① ② ③ ④ ⑤ ⑥ ⑦ ⑧ ⑨
004 Celery & Carrot Sticks	○	① ② ③ ④ ⑤ ⑥ ⑦ ⑧ ⑨	⓪ ① ② ③	⓪ ① ② ③ ④ ⑤ ⑥ ⑦ ⑧ ⑨
005 Boiled Pigs' Feet	○	① ② ③ ④ ⑤ ⑥ ⑦ ⑧ ⑨	⓪ ① ② ③	⓪ ① ② ③ ④ ⑤ ⑥ ⑦ ⑧ ⑨
006 Hot Turkey Sandwich with Gravy	○	① ② ③ ④ ⑤ ⑥ ⑦ ⑧ ⑨	⓪ ① ② ③	⓪ ① ② ③ ④ ⑤ ⑥ ⑦ ⑧ ⑨
007 Sliced Tomato Salad	○	① ② ③ ④ ⑤ ⑥ ⑦ ⑧ ⑨	⓪ ① ② ③	⓪ ① ② ③ ④ ⑤ ⑥ ⑦ ⑧ ⑨
008 Braised Liver with Onions	○	① ② ③ ④ ⑤ ⑥ ⑦ ⑧ ⑨	⓪ ① ② ③	⓪ ① ② ③ ④ ⑤ ⑥ ⑦ ⑧ ⑨
009 Tomato Juice	○	① ② ③ ④ ⑤ ⑥ ⑦ ⑧ ⑨	⓪ ① ② ③	⓪ ① ② ③ ④ ⑤ ⑥ ⑦ ⑧ ⑨
010 Peas	○	① ② ③ ④ ⑤ ⑥ ⑦ ⑧ ⑨	⓪ ① ② ③	⓪ ① ② ③ ④ ⑤ ⑥ ⑦ ⑧ ⑨
011 Cooked Turnips	○	① ② ③ ④ ⑤ ⑥ ⑦ ⑧ ⑨	⓪ ① ② ③	⓪ ① ② ③ ④ ⑤ ⑥ ⑦ ⑧ ⑨
012 Fried Rice	○	① ② ③ ④ ⑤ ⑥ ⑦ ⑧ ⑨	⓪ ① ② ③	⓪ ① ② ③ ④ ⑤ ⑥ ⑦ ⑧ ⑨
013 Corned Beef	○	① ② ③ ④ ⑤ ⑥ ⑦ ⑧ ⑨	⓪ ① ② ③	⓪ ① ② ③ ④ ⑤ ⑥ ⑦ ⑧ ⑨
014 Jellied Fruit Salad	○	① ② ③ ④ ⑤ ⑥ ⑦ ⑧ ⑨	⓪ ① ② ③	⓪ ① ② ③ ④ ⑤ ⑥ ⑦ ⑧ ⑨
015 Apricot Pie	○	① ② ③ ④ ⑤ ⑥ ⑦ ⑧ ⑨	⓪ ① ② ③	⓪ ① ② ③ ④ ⑤ ⑥ ⑦ ⑧ ⑨
016 Cheeseburger	○	① ② ③ ④ ⑤ ⑥ ⑦ ⑧ ⑨	⓪ ① ② ③	⓪ ① ② ③ ④ ⑤ ⑥ ⑦ ⑧ ⑨
017 Sausage Links	○	① ② ③ ④ ⑤ ⑥ ⑦ ⑧ ⑨	⓪ ① ② ③	⓪ ① ② ③ ④ ⑤ ⑥ ⑦ ⑧ ⑨
018 Banana Cake	○	① ② ③ ④ ⑤ ⑥ ⑦ ⑧ ⑨	⓪ ① ② ③	⓪ ① ② ③ ④ ⑤ ⑥ ⑦ ⑧ ⑨
019 Lima Beans	○	① ② ③ ④ ⑤ ⑥ ⑦ ⑧ ⑨	⓪ ① ② ③	⓪ ① ② ③ ④ ⑤ ⑥ ⑦ ⑧ ⑨
020 Skimmed Milk	○	① ② ③ ④ ⑤ ⑥ ⑦ ⑧ ⑨	⓪ ① ② ③	⓪ ① ② ③ ④ ⑤ ⑥ ⑦ ⑧ ⑨
021 Pizza	○	① ② ③ ④ ⑤ ⑥ ⑦ ⑧ ⑨	⓪ ① ② ③	⓪ ① ② ③ ④ ⑤ ⑥ ⑦ ⑧ ⑨
022 Split Pea Soup	○	① ② ③ ④ ⑤ ⑥ ⑦ ⑧ ⑨	⓪ ① ② ③	⓪ ① ② ③ ④ ⑤ ⑥ ⑦ ⑧ ⑨
023 Ice Cream	○	① ② ③ ④ ⑤ ⑥ ⑦ ⑧ ⑨	⓪ ① ② ③	⓪ ① ② ③ ④ ⑤ ⑥ ⑦ ⑧ ⑨
024 Simmered Sauerkraut	○	① ② ③ ④ ⑤ ⑥ ⑦ ⑧ ⑨	⓪ ① ② ③	⓪ ① ② ③ ④ ⑤ ⑥ ⑦ ⑧ ⑨
025 Steamed Rice	○	① ② ③ ④ ⑤ ⑥ ⑦ ⑧ ⑨	⓪ ① ② ③	⓪ ① ② ③ ④ ⑤ ⑥ ⑦ ⑧ ⑨
026 Buttered Noodles	○	① ② ③ ④ ⑤ ⑥ ⑦ ⑧ ⑨	⓪ ① ② ③	⓪ ① ② ③ ④ ⑤ ⑥ ⑦ ⑧ ⑨
027 Swiss Steak	○	① ② ③ ④ ⑤ ⑥ ⑦ ⑧ ⑨	⓪ ① ② ③	⓪ ① ② ③ ④ ⑤ ⑥ ⑦ ⑧ ⑨
028 Hot Fudge Sundae	○	① ② ③ ④ ⑤ ⑥ ⑦ ⑧ ⑨	⓪ ① ② ③	⓪ ① ② ③ ④ ⑤ ⑥ ⑦ ⑧ ⑨
029 Green Beans	○	① ② ③ ④ ⑤ ⑥ ⑦ ⑧ ⑨	⓪ ① ② ③	⓪ ① ② ③ ④ ⑤ ⑥ ⑦ ⑧ ⑨
030 Chitterlings	○	① ② ③ ④ ⑤ ⑥ ⑦ ⑧ ⑨	⓪ ① ② ③	⓪ ① ② ③ ④ ⑤ ⑥ ⑦ ⑧ ⑨
031 Pork Chop Suey	○	① ② ③ ④ ⑤ ⑥ ⑦ ⑧ ⑨	⓪ ① ② ③	⓪ ① ② ③ ④ ⑤ ⑥ ⑦ ⑧ ⑨
032 Lasagna	○	① ② ③ ④ ⑤ ⑥ ⑦ ⑧ ⑨	⓪ ① ② ③	⓪ ① ② ③ ④ ⑤ ⑥ ⑦ ⑧ ⑨
033 Hamburger	○	① ② ③ ④ ⑤ ⑥ ⑦ ⑧ ⑨	⓪ ① ② ③	⓪ ① ② ③ ④ ⑤ ⑥ ⑦ ⑧ ⑨
034 Fish Chowder	○	① ② ③ ④ ⑤ ⑥ ⑦ ⑧ ⑨	⓪ ① ② ③	⓪ ① ② ③ ④ ⑤ ⑥ ⑦ ⑧ ⑨
035 Corned Beef Hash	○	① ② ③ ④ ⑤ ⑥ ⑦ ⑧ ⑨	⓪ ① ② ③	⓪ ① ② ③ ④ ⑤ ⑥ ⑦ ⑧ ⑨
036 Hot Pastrami Sandwich	○	① ② ③ ④ ⑤ ⑥ ⑦ ⑧ ⑨	⓪ ① ② ③	⓪ ① ② ③ ④ ⑤ ⑥ ⑦ ⑧ ⑨
037 Rice Pudding	○	① ② ③ ④ ⑤ ⑥ ⑦ ⑧ ⑨	⓪ ① ② ③	⓪ ① ② ③ ④ ⑤ ⑥ ⑦ ⑧ ⑨
038 Apple Crisp	○	① ② ③ ④ ⑤ ⑥ ⑦ ⑧ ⑨	⓪ ① ② ③	⓪ ① ② ③ ④ ⑤ ⑥ ⑦ ⑧ ⑨
039 Tossed Green Salad	○	① ② ③ ④ ⑤ ⑥ ⑦ ⑧ ⑨	⓪ ① ② ③	⓪ ① ② ③ ④ ⑤ ⑥ ⑦ ⑧ ⑨
040 Baked Tuna & Noodles	○	① ② ③ ④ ⑤ ⑥ ⑦ ⑧ ⑨	⓪ ① ② ③	⓪ ① ② ③ ④ ⑤ ⑥ ⑦ ⑧ ⑨

DC 36-028 OPTICAL SCANNING FORMS by NEWTON, PA. 18940

1	2	3	4	5	6	7	8	9
dislike extremely	dislike very much	dislike moderately	dislike slightly	neither like nor dislike	like slightly	like moderately	like very much	like extremely

	NEVER TRIED	HOW MUCH you like or dislike the food (1-9)		HOW OFTEN you want to eat the food in days per month (01-30)
041 Baked Yellow Squash	○	① ② ③ ④ ⑤ ⑥ ⑦ ⑧ ⑨		⓪ ① ② ③　⓪ ① ② ③ ④ ⑤ ⑥ ⑦ ⑧ ⑨
042 Deviled Eggs	○	① ② ③ ④ ⑤ ⑥ ⑦ ⑧ ⑨		⓪ ① ② ③　⓪ ① ② ③ ④ ⑤ ⑥ ⑦ ⑧ ⑨
043 Veal Parmesan	○	① ② ③ ④ ⑤ ⑥ ⑦ ⑧ ⑨		⓪ ① ② ③　⓪ ① ② ③ ④ ⑤ ⑥ ⑦ ⑧ ⑨
044 Stuffed Green Peppers	○	① ② ③ ④ ⑤ ⑥ ⑦ ⑧ ⑨		⓪ ① ② ③　⓪ ① ② ③ ④ ⑤ ⑥ ⑦ ⑧ ⑨
045 Fried Chicken	○	① ② ③ ④ ⑤ ⑥ ⑦ ⑧ ⑨		⓪ ① ② ③　⓪ ① ② ③ ④ ⑤ ⑥ ⑦ ⑧ ⑨
046 Fruit Cup	○	① ② ③ ④ ⑤ ⑥ ⑦ ⑧ ⑨		⓪ ① ② ③　⓪ ① ② ③ ④ ⑤ ⑥ ⑦ ⑧ ⑨
047 Lentils	○	① ② ③ ④ ⑤ ⑥ ⑦ ⑧ ⑨		⓪ ① ② ③　⓪ ① ② ③ ④ ⑤ ⑥ ⑦ ⑧ ⑨
048 Carrot, Raisin & Celery Salad	○	① ② ③ ④ ⑤ ⑥ ⑦ ⑧ ⑨		⓪ ① ② ③　⓪ ① ② ③ ④ ⑤ ⑥ ⑦ ⑧ ⑨
049 Mushrooms	○	① ② ③ ④ ⑤ ⑥ ⑦ ⑧ ⑨		⓪ ① ② ③　⓪ ① ② ③ ④ ⑤ ⑥ ⑦ ⑧ ⑨
050 Enchiladas	○	① ② ③ ④ ⑤ ⑥ ⑦ ⑧ ⑨		⓪ ① ② ③　⓪ ① ② ③ ④ ⑤ ⑥ ⑦ ⑧ ⑨
051 Vegetable Juice	○	① ② ③ ④ ⑤ ⑥ ⑦ ⑧ ⑨		⓪ ① ② ③　⓪ ① ② ③ ④ ⑤ ⑥ ⑦ ⑧ ⑨
052 Peaches (Fresh)	○	① ② ③ ④ ⑤ ⑥ ⑦ ⑧ ⑨		⓪ ① ② ③　⓪ ① ② ③ ④ ⑤ ⑥ ⑦ ⑧ ⑨
053 Beer	○	① ② ③ ④ ⑤ ⑥ ⑦ ⑧ ⑨		⓪ ① ② ③　⓪ ① ② ③ ④ ⑤ ⑥ ⑦ ⑧ ⑨
054 Hashed Brown Potatoes	○	① ② ③ ④ ⑤ ⑥ ⑦ ⑧ ⑨		⓪ ① ② ③　⓪ ① ② ③ ④ ⑤ ⑥ ⑦ ⑧ ⑨
055 Cabbage	○	① ② ③ ④ ⑤ ⑥ ⑦ ⑧ ⑨		⓪ ① ② ③　⓪ ① ② ③ ④ ⑤ ⑥ ⑦ ⑧ ⑨
056 Sweet Rolls	○	① ② ③ ④ ⑤ ⑥ ⑦ ⑧ ⑨		⓪ ① ② ③　⓪ ① ② ③ ④ ⑤ ⑥ ⑦ ⑧ ⑨
057 Spinach	○	① ② ③ ④ ⑤ ⑥ ⑦ ⑧ ⑨		⓪ ① ② ③　⓪ ① ② ③ ④ ⑤ ⑥ ⑦ ⑧ ⑨
058 Cream of Mushroom Soup	○	① ② ③ ④ ⑤ ⑥ ⑦ ⑧ ⑨		⓪ ① ② ③　⓪ ① ② ③ ④ ⑤ ⑥ ⑦ ⑧ ⑨
059 Savory Bread Stuffing	○	① ② ③ ④ ⑤ ⑥ ⑦ ⑧ ⑨		⓪ ① ② ③　⓪ ① ② ③ ④ ⑤ ⑥ ⑦ ⑧ ⑨
060 Chef's Salad (with Meat & Cheese)	○	① ② ③ ④ ⑤ ⑥ ⑦ ⑧ ⑨		⓪ ① ② ③　⓪ ① ② ③ ④ ⑤ ⑥ ⑦ ⑧ ⑨
061 Sweet Potato Pie	○	① ② ③ ④ ⑤ ⑥ ⑦ ⑧ ⑨		⓪ ① ② ③　⓪ ① ② ③ ④ ⑤ ⑥ ⑦ ⑧ ⑨
062 Buttered Carrots	○	① ② ③ ④ ⑤ ⑥ ⑦ ⑧ ⑨		⓪ ① ② ③　⓪ ① ② ③ ④ ⑤ ⑥ ⑦ ⑧ ⑨
063 Low-Calorie Soda	○	① ② ③ ④ ⑤ ⑥ ⑦ ⑧ ⑨		⓪ ① ② ③　⓪ ① ② ③ ④ ⑤ ⑥ ⑦ ⑧ ⑨
064 Buttermilk	○	① ② ③ ④ ⑤ ⑥ ⑦ ⑧ ⑨		⓪ ① ② ③　⓪ ① ② ③ ④ ⑤ ⑥ ⑦ ⑧ ⑨
065 Fried Clams	○	① ② ③ ④ ⑤ ⑥ ⑦ ⑧ ⑨		⓪ ① ② ③　⓪ ① ② ③ ④ ⑤ ⑥ ⑦ ⑧ ⑨
066 Pork and Beans	○	① ② ③ ④ ⑤ ⑥ ⑦ ⑧ ⑨		⓪ ① ② ③　⓪ ① ② ③ ④ ⑤ ⑥ ⑦ ⑧ ⑨
067 Strawberry Chiffon Pie	○	① ② ③ ④ ⑤ ⑥ ⑦ ⑧ ⑨		⓪ ① ② ③　⓪ ① ② ③ ④ ⑤ ⑥ ⑦ ⑧ ⑨
068 Ham	○	① ② ③ ④ ⑤ ⑥ ⑦ ⑧ ⑨		⓪ ① ② ③　⓪ ① ② ③ ④ ⑤ ⑥ ⑦ ⑧ ⑨
069 Refried Beans	○	① ② ③ ④ ⑤ ⑥ ⑦ ⑧ ⑨		⓪ ① ② ③　⓪ ① ② ③ ④ ⑤ ⑥ ⑦ ⑧ ⑨
070 Braised Trake	○	① ② ③ ④ ⑤ ⑥ ⑦ ⑧ ⑨		⓪ ① ② ③　⓪ ① ② ③ ④ ⑤ ⑥ ⑦ ⑧ ⑨
071 Bananas	○	① ② ③ ④ ⑤ ⑥ ⑦ ⑧ ⑨		⓪ ① ② ③　⓪ ① ② ③ ④ ⑤ ⑥ ⑦ ⑧ ⑨
072 Cola	○	① ② ③ ④ ⑤ ⑥ ⑦ ⑧ ⑨		⓪ ① ② ③　⓪ ① ② ③ ④ ⑤ ⑥ ⑦ ⑧ ⑨
073 Avocado Salad	○	① ② ③ ④ ⑤ ⑥ ⑦ ⑧ ⑨		⓪ ① ② ③　⓪ ① ② ③ ④ ⑤ ⑥ ⑦ ⑧ ⑨
074 Frijole Salad	○	① ② ③ ④ ⑤ ⑥ ⑦ ⑧ ⑨		⓪ ① ② ③　⓪ ① ② ③ ④ ⑤ ⑥ ⑦ ⑧ ⑨
075 Burritos	○	① ② ③ ④ ⑤ ⑥ ⑦ ⑧ ⑨		⓪ ① ② ③　⓪ ① ② ③ ④ ⑤ ⑥ ⑦ ⑧ ⑨
076 Fresh Coffee	○	① ② ③ ④ ⑤ ⑥ ⑦ ⑧ ⑨		⓪ ① ② ③　⓪ ① ② ③ ④ ⑤ ⑥ ⑦ ⑧ ⑨
077 Buttered Mixed Vegetables	○	① ② ③ ④ ⑤ ⑥ ⑦ ⑧ ⑨		⓪ ① ② ③　⓪ ① ② ③ ④ ⑤ ⑥ ⑦ ⑧ ⑨
078 Beef Stew	○	① ② ③ ④ ⑤ ⑥ ⑦ ⑧ ⑨		⓪ ① ② ③　⓪ ① ② ③ ④ ⑤ ⑥ ⑦ ⑧ ⑨
079 Guacamole Dip	○	① ② ③ ④ ⑤ ⑥ ⑦ ⑧ ⑨		⓪ ① ② ③　⓪ ① ② ③ ④ ⑤ ⑥ ⑦ ⑧ ⑨
080 Roast Pork	○	① ② ③ ④ ⑤ ⑥ ⑦ ⑧ ⑨		⓪ ① ② ③　⓪ ① ② ③ ④ ⑤ ⑥ ⑦ ⑧ ⑨

DC 36-029 OPTICAL SCANNING FORM by NCR TRON, FL 10000

1	2	3	4	5	6	7	8	9
dislike extremely	dislike very much	dislike moderately	dislike slightly	neither like nor dislike	like slightly	like moderately	like very much	like extremely

	NEVER TRIED	HOW MUCH you like or dislike the food (1-9)		HOW OFTEN you want to eat the food in days per month (01-30)
081 Devil's Food Cake	○			
082 Chili Con Carne	○			
083 Grapefruit Half (Fresh)	○			
084 Fried Shrimp	○			
085 Vegetable Soup	○			
086 Fruit Flavored Yogurt	○			
087 Tacos	○			
088 Grilled Lamb Chops	○			
089 White Cake	○			
090 Eggs to Order	○			
091 Peaches (canned)	○			
092 Submarine Sandwich	○			
093 Stewed Tomatoes	○			
094 Fruit Flavored Gelatin	○			
095 Wheat Germ	○			
096 Lemonade	○			
097 Beef Stroganoff	○			
098 Fried Okra	○			
099 Grilled Ham & Cheese Sandwich	○			
100 Corn Fritters	○			
101 Pound Cake	○			
102 Lemon Meringue Pie	○			
103 Boston Cream Pie	○			
104 Chocolate Milk	○			
105 Roast Beef	○			
106 French Fried Onion Rings	○			
107 Chocolate Chip Cookies	○			
108 Brussels Sprouts	○			
109 Waldorf Salad (Apples, Celery & Raisin)	○			
110 Milk Shake	○			
111 Hot Chocolate	○			
112 Potato Salad	○			
113 Sloppy Joe	○			
114 Cheesecake	○			
115 Oranges	○			
116 Meat Loaf	○			
117 Ham	○			
118 Pears (Fresh)	○			
119 Cracker Sandwiches	○			
120 Creamed Onions	○			

DC 36-030 OPTICAL SCANNING FORMS, INC. NEWTON, PA. 18940

⊐ ⊞ ⊞ 旦 ⊐ 旦 ⊞

1	2	3	4	5	6	7	8	9
dislike extremely	dislike very much	dislike moderately	dislike slightly	neither like nor dislike	like slightly	like moderately	like very much	like extremely

	NEVER TRIED	HOW MUCH you like or dislike the food (1-9)		HOW OFTEN you want to eat the food in days per month (01-30)
121 Coconut Raisin Cookies	○	①②③④⑤⑥⑦⑧⑨	⓪①②③	⓪①②③④⑤⑥⑦⑧⑨
122 Chocolate Pudding	○	①②③④⑤⑥⑦⑧⑨	⓪①②③	⓪①②③④⑤⑥⑦⑧⑨
123 Cantaloupe	○	①②③④⑤⑥⑦⑧⑨	⓪①②③	⓪①②③④⑤⑥⑦⑧⑨
124 Omelet	○	①②③④⑤⑥⑦⑧⑨	⓪①②③	⓪①②③④⑤⑥⑦⑧⑨
125 Creamed Ground Beef	○	①②③④⑤⑥⑦⑧⑨	⓪①②③	⓪①②③④⑤⑥⑦⑧⑨
126 Milk	○	①②③④⑤⑥⑦⑧⑨	⓪①②③	⓪①②③④⑤⑥⑦⑧⑨
127 Asparagus	○	①②③④⑤⑥⑦⑧⑨	⓪①②③	⓪①②③④⑤⑥⑦⑧⑨
128 Potato Chips	○	①②③④⑤⑥⑦⑧⑨	⓪①②③	⓪①②③④⑤⑥⑦⑧⑨
129 Coffee Cake	○	①②③④⑤⑥⑦⑧⑨	⓪①②③	⓪①②③④⑤⑥⑦⑧⑨
130 Iced Tea	○	①②③④⑤⑥⑦⑧⑨	⓪①②③	⓪①②③④⑤⑥⑦⑧⑨
131 Onion Soup	○	①②③④⑤⑥⑦⑧⑨	⓪①②③	⓪①②③④⑤⑥⑦⑧⑨
132 Banana Split	○	①②③④⑤⑥⑦⑧⑨	⓪①②③	⓪①②③④⑤⑥⑦⑧⑨
133 Spaghetti with Meatballs	○	①②③④⑤⑥⑦⑧⑨	⓪①②③	⓪①②③④⑤⑥⑦⑧⑨
134 Chicken Noodle Soup	○	①②③④⑤⑥⑦⑧⑨	⓪①②③	⓪①②③④⑤⑥⑦⑧⑨
135 Sherbet	○	①②③④⑤⑥⑦⑧⑨	⓪①②③	⓪①②③④⑤⑥⑦⑧⑨
136 Applesauce	○	①②③④⑤⑥⑦⑧⑨	⓪①②③	⓪①②③④⑤⑥⑦⑧⑨
137 Barbecued Spareribs	○	①②③④⑤⑥⑦⑧⑨	⓪①②③	⓪①②③④⑤⑥⑦⑧⑨
138 Buttered Ermal	○	①②③④⑤⑥⑦⑧⑨	⓪①②③	⓪①②③④⑤⑥⑦⑧⑨
139 Fried Eggplant	○	①②③④⑤⑥⑦⑧⑨	⓪①②③	⓪①②③④⑤⑥⑦⑧⑨
140 Tomato Soup	○	①②③④⑤⑥⑦⑧⑨	⓪①②③	⓪①②③④⑤⑥⑦⑧⑨
141 Buttered Peas & Carrots	○	①②③④⑤⑥⑦⑧⑨	⓪①②③	⓪①②③④⑤⑥⑦⑧⑨
142 Pork Hocks	○	①②③④⑤⑥⑦⑧⑨	⓪①②③	⓪①②③④⑤⑥⑦⑧⑨
143 French Fried Potatoes	○	①②③④⑤⑥⑦⑧⑨	⓪①②③	⓪①②③④⑤⑥⑦⑧⑨
144 Collard Greens	○	①②③④⑤⑥⑦⑧⑨	⓪①②③	⓪①②③④⑤⑥⑦⑧⑨
145 Granola	○	①②③④⑤⑥⑦⑧⑨	⓪①②③	⓪①②③④⑤⑥⑦⑧⑨
146 Mixed Nuts	○	①②③④⑤⑥⑦⑧⑨	⓪①②③	⓪①②③④⑤⑥⑦⑧⑨
147 Tuna Salad Sandwich	○	①②③④⑤⑥⑦⑧⑨	⓪①②③	⓪①②③④⑤⑥⑦⑧⑨
148 Raisins	○	①②③④⑤⑥⑦⑧⑨	⓪①②③	⓪①②③④⑤⑥⑦⑧⑨
149 Pork Chops	○	①②③④⑤⑥⑦⑧⑨	⓪①②③	⓪①②③④⑤⑥⑦⑧⑨
150 Cherry Pie	○	①②③④⑤⑥⑦⑧⑨	⓪①②③	⓪①②③④⑤⑥⑦⑧⑨
151 Hot Tamales	○	①②③④⑤⑥⑦⑧⑨	⓪①②③	⓪①②③④⑤⑥⑦⑧⑨
152 Baked Potatoes	○	①②③④⑤⑥⑦⑧⑨	⓪①②③	⓪①②③④⑤⑥⑦⑧⑨
153 Nut Cookies	○	①②③④⑤⑥⑦⑧⑨	⓪①②③	⓪①②③④⑤⑥⑦⑧⑨
154 Cornbread	○	①②③④⑤⑥⑦⑧⑨	⓪①②③	⓪①②③④⑤⑥⑦⑧⑨
155 Fishwich	○	①②③④⑤⑥⑦⑧⑨	⓪①②③	⓪①②③④⑤⑥⑦⑧⑨
156 Bacon	○	①②③④⑤⑥⑦⑧⑨	⓪①②③	⓪①②③④⑤⑥⑦⑧⑨
157 Plain Yogurt	○	①②③④⑤⑥⑦⑧⑨	⓪①②③	⓪①②③④⑤⑥⑦⑧⑨
158 Cole Slaw	○	①②③④⑤⑥⑦⑧⑨	⓪①②③	⓪①②③④⑤⑥⑦⑧⑨
159 Frankfurters	○	①②③④⑤⑥⑦⑧⑨	⓪①②③	⓪①②③④⑤⑥⑦⑧⑨
160 Cottage Cheese & Fruit Salad	○	①②③④⑤⑥⑦⑧⑨	⓪①②③	⓪①②③④⑤⑥⑦⑧⑨

DC 36-031 OPTICAL SCANNING FORMS™ NEWTOWN, PA. 18940

⊞ ⊞ ⊞ ⅗ ⊽ ⅘ ⊞

1	2	3	4	5	6	7	8	9
dislike extremely	dislike very much	dislike moderately	dislike slightly	neither like nor dislike	like slightly	like moderately	like very much	like extremely

	NEVER TRIED	HOW MUCH you like or dislike the food (1-9)		HOW OFTEN you want to eat the food in days per month (01-30)
161 Buttered Whole Kernel Corn	○	①②③④⑤⑥⑦⑧⑨	⓪①②③	⓪①②③④⑤⑥⑦⑧⑨
162 Western Sandwich	○	①②③④⑤⑥⑦⑧⑨	⓪①②③	⓪①②③④⑤⑥⑦⑧⑨
163 Broccoli	○	①②③④⑤⑥⑦⑧⑨	⓪①②③	⓪①②③④⑤⑥⑦⑧⑨
164 Pineapple Juice	○	①②③④⑤⑥⑦⑧⑨	⓪①②③	⓪①②③④⑤⑥⑦⑧⑨
165 Fried Fish	○	①②③④⑤⑥⑦⑧⑨	⓪①②③	⓪①②③④⑤⑥⑦⑧⑨
166 Cold Cereal	○	①②③④⑤⑥⑦⑧⑨	⓪①②③	⓪①②③④⑤⑥⑦⑧⑨
167 Stewed Prunes (canned)	○	①②③④⑤⑥⑦⑧⑨	⓪①②③	⓪①②③④⑤⑥⑦⑧⑨
168 Cranberry Juice	○	①②③④⑤⑥⑦⑧⑨	⓪①②③	⓪①②③④⑤⑥⑦⑧⑨
169 Baked Chicken	○	①②③④⑤⑥⑦⑧⑨	⓪①②③	⓪①②③④⑤⑥⑦⑧⑨
170 Cottage Cheese	○	①②③④⑤⑥⑦⑧⑨	⓪①②③	⓪①②③④⑤⑥⑦⑧⑨
171 Baked Tuna & Noodles	○	①②③④⑤⑥⑦⑧⑨	⓪①②③	⓪①②③④⑤⑥⑦⑧⑨
172 Raisin Pie	○	①②③④⑤⑥⑦⑧⑨	⓪①②③	⓪①②③④⑤⑥⑦⑧⑨
173 Peanut Butter & Jelly Sandwich	○	①②③④⑤⑥⑦⑧⑨	⓪①②③	⓪①②③④⑤⑥⑦⑧⑨
174 Mashed Potatoes	○	①②③④⑤⑥⑦⑧⑨	⓪①②③	⓪①②③④⑤⑥⑦⑧⑨
175 Soft Serve Ice Cream	○	①②③④⑤⑥⑦⑧⑨	⓪①②③	⓪①②③④⑤⑥⑦⑧⑨
176 Brown Rice	○	①②③④⑤⑥⑦⑧⑨	⓪①②③	⓪①②③④⑤⑥⑦⑧⑨
177 Funistrada	○	①②③④⑤⑥⑦⑧⑨	⓪①②③	⓪①②③④⑤⑥⑦⑧⑨
178 Tomato Juice	○	①②③④⑤⑥⑦⑧⑨	⓪①②③	⓪①②③④⑤⑥⑦⑧⑨
179 Buttered Zucchini Squash	○	①②③④⑤⑥⑦⑧⑨	⓪①②③	⓪①②③④⑤⑥⑦⑧⑨
180 Beef Stroganoff	○	①②③④⑤⑥⑦⑧⑨	⓪①②③	⓪①②③④⑤⑥⑦⑧⑨
181 Watermelon	○	①②③④⑤⑥⑦⑧⑨	⓪①②③	⓪①②③④⑤⑥⑦⑧⑨
182 Grilled Steak	○	①②③④⑤⑥⑦⑧⑨	⓪①②③	⓪①②③④⑤⑥⑦⑧⑨
183 Baked Macaroni & Cheese	○	①②③④⑤⑥⑦⑧⑨	⓪①②③	⓪①②③④⑤⑥⑦⑧⑨
184 Banana Salad	○	①②③④⑤⑥⑦⑧⑨	⓪①②③	⓪①②③④⑤⑥⑦⑧⑨
185 Fruit Cocktail (canned)	○	①②③④⑤⑥⑦⑧⑨	⓪①②③	⓪①②③④⑤⑥⑦⑧⑨
186 Hot Cereal	○	①②③④⑤⑥⑦⑧⑨	⓪①②③	⓪①②③④⑤⑥⑦⑧⑨
187 Buttered Cauliflower	○	①②③④⑤⑥⑦⑧⑨	⓪①②③	⓪①②③④⑤⑥⑦⑧⑨
188 Clam Chowder	○	①②③④⑤⑥⑦⑧⑨	⓪①②③	⓪①②③④⑤⑥⑦⑧⑨
189 Harvard Beets	○	①②③④⑤⑥⑦⑧⑨	⓪①②③	⓪①②③④⑤⑥⑦⑧⑨
190 Bacon, Lettuce & Tomato Sandwich	○	①②③④⑤⑥⑦⑧⑨	⓪①②③	⓪①②③④⑤⑥⑦⑧⑨
191 Lasagna	○	①②③④⑤⑥⑦⑧⑨	⓪①②③	⓪①②③④⑤⑥⑦⑧⑨
192 Prune Juice	○	①②③④⑤⑥⑦⑧⑨	⓪①②③	⓪①②③④⑤⑥⑦⑧⑨
193 Doughnuts	○	①②③④⑤⑥⑦⑧⑨	⓪①②③	⓪①②③④⑤⑥⑦⑧⑨
194 Brownies	○	①②③④⑤⑥⑦⑧⑨	⓪①②③	⓪①②③④⑤⑥⑦⑧⑨
195 Apple Pie	○	①②③④⑤⑥⑦⑧⑨	⓪①②③	⓪①②③④⑤⑥⑦⑧⑨
196 Grits	○	①②③④⑤⑥⑦⑧⑨	⓪①②③	⓪①②③④⑤⑥⑦⑧⑨
197 Peanut Butter Cookies	○	①②③④⑤⑥⑦⑧⑨	⓪①②③	⓪①②③④⑤⑥⑦⑧⑨
198 Orange Juice	○	①②③④⑤⑥⑦⑧⑨	⓪①②③	⓪①②③④⑤⑥⑦⑧⑨
199 Pancakes	○	①②③④⑤⑥⑦⑧⑨	⓪①②③	⓪①②③④⑤⑥⑦⑧⑨
200 Instant Coffee	○	①②③④⑤⑥⑦⑧⑨	⓪①②③	⓪①②③④⑤⑥⑦⑧⑨

DC 36-032 OPTICAL SCANNING FORM by NCS Trwin, Pa. 15068

OPINIONS OF FOOD SERVICE AT MILITARY HOSPITALS

BEHAVIORAL SCIENCES DIVISION
FOOD SCIENCES LABORATORY
U.S. ARMY NATICK R&D COMMAND
NATICK, MASSACHUSETTS

Name _____

We are from the U.S. Army Research & Development Command at Natick, Mass. The Army has asked us to evaluate the quality of the food service they provide. Thus, we would like you to fill out this questionnaire. We also would like to find out whether your reason for being in the hospital influences your opinion of the food service and whether the medication affects your appetite. Therefore, please write your name on the top of this page, so that we can obtain your diagnosis and medication schedule. We will record this information on your questionnaire, assign to it an arbitrary number, and then remove and destroy this first page. In this manner all your responses will be kept confidential and there will be no way to identify your response. Your participation is voluntary and will be of value in improving the food service. If you have any questions about how to fill out this form, the person who distributed the questionnaire will be glad to answer them.

Please do not discuss your responses to the questionnaire with your fellow patients until all of you have returned the questionnaire.

SAMPLE: If your age is 24, mark box "2"

Under 18	18 – 25	26 – 50	51 – 65	Over 65
1	2	3	4	5

1 2 3 4 5

DC 36-114 OPTICAL SCANNING FORMS™

1. What is your current status?
   1) Military person
   2) Dependent of military person
   3) Retired military person
   4) Dependent of retired military person
   5) Other

   | 1 | 2 | 3 | 4 | 5 |

2. Age?

Under 18	18-25	26-50	51-65	Over 65
1	2	3	4	5

   | 1 | 2 | 3 | 4 | 5 |

3. Sex?

Male	Female
1	2

   | 1 | 2 |

4. Height?

Under 5'	5'-5'6"	5'7"-6'	6'1"-7'	Over 7'
1	2	3	4	5

   | 1 | 2 | 3 | 4 | 5 |

5. Weight?

Under 100 lb.	100 - 140	141 -180	181 - 220	Over 220
1	2	3	4	5

   | 1 | 2 | 3 | 4 | 5 |

6. Education?
   1) Finished grade school
   2) High school graduate (includes GED)
   3) Skilled job training after high school
   4) Some college
   5) College graduate
   6) Post graduate training

   | 1 | 2 | 3 | 4 | 5 | 6 |

7. Race?
   1) White/Caucasian-American
   2) Black/Negro/African-American
   3) Asian American/Japanese/Chinese/Korean/Filipino/Samoan/Guamanian
   4) Hispanic-American/Chicano/Spanish-surnamed
   5) Native-American/American Indian/Hawaiian/Eskimo/Aleut
   6) Other

   | 1 | 2 | 3 | 4 | 5 | 6 |

8. How long have you been at this hospital?

1-2 days	3-7 days	8-14 days	15-30 days	Over 30 days
1	2	3	4	5

   | 1 | 2 | 3 | 4 | 5 |

9. How many meals have you eaten at this hospital?

1-3 meals	4-6 meals	7-12 meals	13-25 meals	Over 25 meals
1	2	3	4	5

   | 1 | 2 | 3 | 4 | 5 |

DC 36-115 OPTICAL SCANNING FORMS™

10. What is your current diet?

Regular	Special or Modified
1	2

1 2

11. When you are not in the hospital, how many days do you eat your breakfast away from home during a typical week?

Never	1-2 days	3-4 days	5 days	6-7 days
1	2	3	4	5

1 2 3 4 5

12. When you are not in the hospital, how many days do you eat your mid-day meal away from home during a typical week?

Never	1-2 days	3-4 days	5 days	6-7 days
1	2	3	4	5

1 2 3 4 5

13. When you are not in the hospital, how many days do you eat your evening meal away from home during a typical week?

Never	1-2 days	3-4 days	5 days	6-7 days
1	2	3	4	5

1 2 3 4 5

14. Which meal did you just finish eating?

Breakfast	Mid-day meal	Evening meal
1	2	3

1 2 3

15. Where did you eat this meal?

Dining hall	Private room	Semi-private room	Ward
1	2	3	4

1 2 3 4

16. How long has it been since you have eaten this meal?

Less than 1 minute	1-10 minutes	11-30 minutes	31 minutes-1 hour	Over an hour
1	2	3	4	5

1 2 3 4 5

17. When you are not in the hospital do you normally eat this meal?

Yes	No
1	2

1 2

18. How much of your meal did you eat?

None	Some	Most	All
1	2	3	4

1 2 3 4

19. How do you feel about hospitals in general?

Very Upset	Moderately Upset	Neither Upset nor Relaxed	Moderately Relaxed	Very Relaxed
1	2	3	4	5

1 2 3 4 5

DC 36-116 OPTICAL SCANNING FORMS™

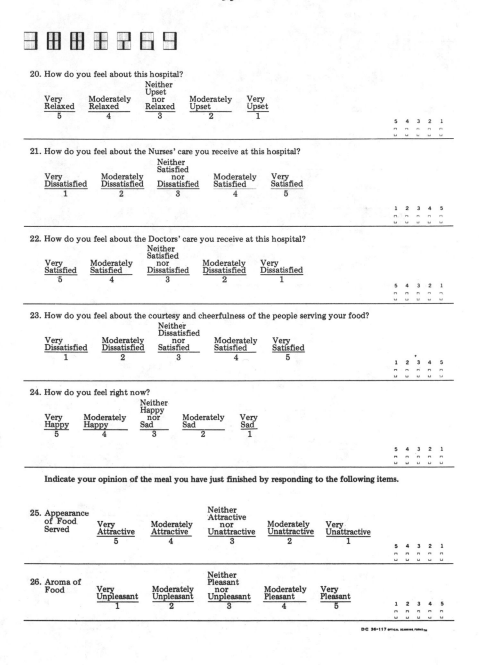

20. How do you feel about this hospital?

Very Relaxed	Moderately Relaxed	Neither Upset nor Relaxed	Moderately Upset	Very Upset
5	4	3	2	1

21. How do you feel about the Nurses' care you receive at this hospital?

Very Dissatisfied	Moderately Dissatisfied	Neither Satisfied nor Dissatisfied	Moderately Satisfied	Very Satisfied
1	2	3	4	5

22. How do you feel about the Doctors' care you receive at this hospital?

Very Satisfied	Moderately Satisfied	Neither Satisfied nor Dissatisfied	Moderately Dissatisfied	Very Dissatisfied
5	4	3	2	1

23. How do you feel about the courtesy and cheerfulness of the people serving your food?

Very Dissatisfied	Moderately Dissatisfied	Neither Dissatisfied nor Satisfied	Moderately Satisfied	Very Satisfied
1	2	3	4	5

24. How do you feel right now?

Very Happy	Moderately Happy	Neither Happy nor Sad	Moderately Sad	Very Sad
5	4	3	2	1

Indicate your opinion of the meal you have just finished by responding to the following items.

25. Appearance of Food Served

Very Attractive	Moderately Attractive	Neither Attractive nor Unattractive	Moderately Unattractive	Very Unattractive
5	4	3	2	1

26. Aroma of Food

Very Unpleasant	Moderately Unpleasant	Neither Pleasant nor Unpleasant	Moderately Pleasant	Very Pleasant
1	2	3	4	5

DC 36-117 OPTICAL SCANNING FORM™

27. Variety of Items to Select

Too Large	Moderately Large	Neither Large nor Small	Moderately Small	Too Small
5	4	3	2	1

5 4 3 2 1

28. Seasoning of Food

Too Bland	Moderately Bland	Neither Bland nor Spicy	Moderately Spicy	Too Spicy
1	2	3	4	5

1 2 3 4 5

29. Size of Food Portions

Too Large	Moderately Large	Just Right	Moderately Small	Too Small
5	4	3	2	1

5 4 3 2 1

30. Food Served When You Want It

Too Late	Moderately Late	On Time	Moderately Early	Too Early
1	2	3	4	5

1 2 3 4 5

31. Cleanliness of Dishes and Silverware

Very Clean	Moderately Clean	Clean	Moderately Dirty	Very Dirty
5	4	3	2	1

5 4 3 2 1

32. Attractiveness of Dishes, Silverware and Tray

Very Unattractive	Moderately Unattractive	Neither Attractive nor Unattractive	Moderately Attractive	Very Attractive
1	2	3	4	5

1 2 3 4 5

33. Thoroughness of Cooking Vegetables

Too Overcooked	Moderately Overcooked	Neither Overcooked nor Undercooked	Moderately Undercooked	Too Undercooked
5	4	3	2	1

5 4 3 2 1

34. Tenderness of Meat

Too Tough	Moderately Tough	Neither Tough nor Tender	Moderately Tender	Too Tender
1	2	3	4	5

1 2 3 4 5

35. Were your hot food items the temperature you like them when you ate them?

Yes 1 No 2

1 2

36. Were your cold food items the temperature you like them when you ate them?

Yes 1 No 2

1 2

37. How is your appetite when you are feeling well?

Excellent 4 Good 3 Fair 2 Poor 1

4 3 2 1

DC 36-118 OPTICAL SCANNING FORMS

38. How is your appetite today?

Poor	Fair	Good	Excellent
1	2	3	4

1 2 3 4

39. How do you feel right now?

5   4   3   2   1

5 4 3 2 1

40. What is your opinion of <u>all</u> the meals you have eaten in this hospital?

Very Good	Good	Neither Good nor Bad	Bad	Very Bad
5	4	3	2	1

5 4 3 2 1

41. At this time, do you have any pain or soreness in any part of your body?

Yes	No
1	2

1 2

42. If No to the above item, go to Item 43. If Yes, how intense is your pain or soreness at this time?

Mild	Discomforting	Distressing	Horrible	Excrutiating
5	4	3	2	1

5 4 3 2 1

43. How important is mealtime to you compared to your other activities when you are not in the hospital?

Very Important	Moderately Important	Neither Important nor Unimportant	Moderately Unimportant	Very Unimportant
5	4	3	2	1

5 4 3 2 1

44. How important was mealtime to you <u>today</u>?

Very Unimportant	Moderately Unimportant	Neither Important nor Unimportant	Moderately Important	Very Important
1	2	3	4	5

1 2 3 4 5

45. Do you add to, or replace, your meals at this hospital with items of food other than those on the hospital menu?

Yes	No
1	2

1 2

DC 36-119 OPTICAL SCANNING FORM™

46. If No to the previous item, go to Item 47.

   If Yes, indicate where you obtain the food items. (You may indicate more than one.)

   Vending Machine . . . . [1]

   Relative or Friend . . . . . [2]

   Fellow Patient . . . . [3]

   Nurse . . . . [4]

   Other . . . . [5]

47. Did you have enough spoons, forks, knives, napkins, plates?

   Yes   No
   1   2

48. If Yes to the above item, go to Item 49.

   If No, what items were you missing? (You may indicate more than one.)

   Knife . . . . [1]

   Fork . . . . . . [2]

   Spoon . . . . [3]

   Napkin . . . . [4]

   Plate . . . . [5]

49. How do you feel about the future?

Very Optimistic	Moderately Optimistic	Neither Optimistic nor Pessimistic	Moderately Pessimistic	Very Pessimistic
5	4	3	2	1

50. Did you receive all the food items which you ordered?

   Yes   No
   1   2

51. If Yes to the above item, go to Item 52.

   If No, were food items

Missing	Added	Substituted
1	2	3

52. Do you feel that your answers to this questionnaire will lead to improvements in the food service at this hospital?

   Yes   No
   1   2

Please continue on next page.

In order to give you an opportunity to make some specific suggestions to improve the food service, please answer the following items. Write your suggestions directly on the questionnaire.

53. Which food item(s) from today's meal did you not finish and/or touch?

<u>Did not finish</u>   <u>Did not touch</u>

a. _____   a. _____

b. _____   b. _____

c. _____   c. _____

d. _____   d. _____

<u>Why did you not finish?</u>   <u>Why did you not touch?</u>

a. _____   a. _____

b. _____   b. _____

c. _____   c. _____

d. _____   d. _____

54. Please list any foods for which you noticed a change in taste and/or smell before being admitted to the hospital and after being admitted to the hospital. Also note after each of the foods you list what it is about it that has changed.

Food changes before hospitalization   Food changes after hospitalization

a. _____   a. _____

b. _____   b. _____

c. _____   c. _____

d. _____   d. _____

55. For what medical problems are you being evaluated and/or treated?

_____

_____

56. What changes in the food service would make your stay in the hospital a more comfortable one? Please list them below.

a. _____

b. _____

c. _____

d. _____

e. _____

Thank you for your assistance.

DC 36-121 OPTICAL SCANNING FORM™

Date:

Installation:

SUPPLEMENTAL SHEET

Diagnosis: Primary _____ Secondary _____

Medications Patient receiving at time he or she filled out this questionnaire:

1. _____ 4. _____

2. _____ 5. _____

3. _____ 6. _____

Special or Modified Diet Information

_____

_____

Which food items on the tray were not finished and/or touched?

<u>Not finished</u>   <u>Not touched</u>

1. _____ 1. _____

2. _____ 2. _____

3. _____ 3. _____

How much did Patient eat?

None	Some	Most	All
1	2	3	4

1 2 3 4

Did the Patient experience any difficulties in completing the questionnaire?

Yes	No
1	2

1 2

If Yes, explain the difficulties.

Observations and/or Remarks:

DC 36-122 OPTICAL SCANNING FORMS™

A Food Service Manager's Perceptions of Meal Quality

Barbara J. Bobeng

At Massachusetts General Hospital, we have one patient
menu--selective--and one cafeteria menu. With these, we
have to satisfy a lot of people. We have 1,080 beds and
serve about 7,500 meals daily.

Recently, I was working with a planning committee for
our graduate program, and we frequently used the term
"quality food." Finally somebody suggested that I write
an operational definition that we could use in planning.
This is the definition that we adopted and use: "Quality
food is food which has been selected, prepared, and served
in such a manner that the food is microbiologically and
chemically safe, retains or enhances sensory properties,
conserves nutrients, and is acceptable to the consumer."

In discussing meal quality I will focus on two areas.
The menu is an important component of meal acceptability.
The functional factors that we as managers consider in
menu planning obviously affect the final acceptability of
the meal by the consumer. Parameters of food quality
also affect meal acceptability.

COST

Today most of us are managing food services under
financial constraints; and it sounds as if it will get
worse. The budget or amount of money available determines the type of meal to be planned and provided. In

Barbara J. Bobeng, Ph.D., R.D., is Assistant Director,
Dietary Department, and Associate Professor, Institute of
Health Professionals, Massachusetts General Hospital,
Boston.

restaurants, one plans and prices a menu according to
"what the traffic will bear." In a sense this is also
true for hospitals. Our patient charges are based on a
predetermined level of quality or service. For me this
means that the menu and service that I can provide are
somewhat less than the Copley Plaza or Ritz Carlton
hotels. It does not mean that I cannot provide quality
or acceptable meals.

In menu planning we should look at the total cost--
food and labor--per item provided. Items with a lower
food cost frequently have a higher labor cost, and vice
versa. In addition, we should consider the cost of the
items selected. We can plan for a high-cost item if it
is offered on the same menu with a lower-cost item that
is more popular.

PLANNING CYCLE

The average length of patient stay is an important consideration in determining the length of the menu cycle.
Many hospitals have been able to implement 1 week or 2
week cycles successfully with the shorter hospital stays.
To avoid the "roast beef or chicken every Sunday" syndrome, many hospitals use an 8-day cycle. We have longer
patient stay, about 12 days, and use a 3-week cycle menu.

One still must consider the number of long-term
patients. We have an extensive substitution list of menu
items always available for patients. For example, a large
number of patients on our orthopedic service are young
and male and request a standard lunch of a cheeseburger,
french fries, and beer. This is acceptable to them, and
to me, if allowed by the physician.

THE MEAL PATTERN

There are pros and cons to be offered for the different
meal patterns that have been implemented in hospitals.
As a manager, a three-meal-a-day plan with a heavier meal
at noon is probably better. We have a greater concentration of production personnel available at noon, whereas
at the evening meal we schedule large numbers of part-
time personnel for service.

The timing of meals is also a consideration. Breakfast
service is dependent on when employees can get to work.
One must consider transportation, weather, etc. In Boston

"The T," when it runs, runs on a different schedule on Sunday and holidays, starting operation one-half hour later than on weekdays. The evening meal must be scheduled in accordance with the Joint Commission of the Accreditation of Hospitals requirement that not more than 15 hours elapse before breakfast.

As food service managers, we have to reconcile these factors with constraints from the medical and nursing services and with patient preferences. I believe we all recognize that to a hospitalized individual food is more than just eating.

POPULARITY

In planning menus we must have knowledge of the people to be served. Considerations may include race, religion, and ethnic background, as well as regional preferences. For example, all types of seafood are common menu items in Boston; this is not true in Iowa.

Psychological factors are involved in the development of our attitudes and behavior toward food. As managers we must recognize our own food likes and dislikes to minimize their effect on menu planning. For example, I will not eat a banana. I have to force myself to include bananas in menus and menu items. Obviously, patients have similar attitudes that affect menu selection and acceptability.

Preference surveys should be done by managers to determine both popularity of menu items and frequency of serving. You have already heard about some of the methods to use. Roast beef may be popular but not when served at every meal. Although this type of information frequently appears in trade journals, popularity should be determined by each hospital. This would then take account of the racial, religious, ethnic, and regional background of the typical mix of patients. I know one of the hospitals across town is represented here today; and I am sure that food service director would have more items that would appeal to the Chinese population than I would have to have on my menu, which has to emphasize the Italian population.

PRODUCTION CAPABILITY

To produce a given menu, several resources must be considered. Labor is our most valuable and costly resource.

The number of labor hours, as well as the number of personnel available at a given time, affects the menu that can be produced. Some menu items or prepreparation can be scheduled during slack periods to produce for peak periods, but the effect on quality must be considered. We should try to achieve a balanced workload in each production unit each day, avoiding overloads of either lengthy or last-minute preparation. A disgruntled or overworked labor force can affect food quality and meal acceptability.

The skills and abilities of personnel should also be considered in menu planning. Individuals should have the skills to meet production requirements. One factor easily overlooked is scheduling of employees' days off. Relief personnel may not have the skill or efficiency of regular personnel to meet production requirements. One can plan menus that are less complicated or use convenience items at these times.

Equipment utilization should be considered for production capability. The menu should balance the use of oven, steam, frying, or top-of-the-range cooking. The purpose of this is twofold--to avoid overburdening a piece of equipment or a production area. The latter case could lead to safety hazards.

SERVICE CAPABILITY

As with production, labor must be considered with service. If a menu is tedious to serve, personnel may become either careless or slow, affecting either the attractiveness or time of service. The menu should provide for a balanced workload at trayline stations for a given meal, as well as a daily balance.

Equipment for holding and serving may affect the menu. The availability of sufficient china, glassware, and flatware should be considered. Often overlooked is the possible impact of menu items and combinations on the dishroom.

STABILITY OF MENU ITEMS

Some menu items are affected by the system. For example, breakfast eggs may be a problem. Some items deteriorate in temperature, color, or texture during the time lapse between production and service. Items that present a

problem in a given type of system can be eliminated from
a menu, or a new recipe can be devised.

This has been a brief discussion of some factors considered in menu planning. The menu itself does contribute to meal acceptability. Obviously, a menu selected
by a patient and containing some familiar and liked food
items will be more acceptable.

The other component of meal acceptability is quality
food. Parameters of quality food are sensory and nutritional attributes and safety. Sensory factors are the
most evident and, therefore, generally are the basis for
consumer acceptance.

SENSORY CHARACTERISTICS

We generally plan menus to include variety in the sensory
characteristics of menu items. Frequently we see a menu
as we plan it, with certain items combining to form a
meal. A patient may not select the items that we had
intended to go together; however, the meal may still be
acceptable to that patient.

First, we visualize the meal and meal arrangement. I
see both the plate and the tray with an uncluttered,
attractive appearance. Neatness counts to preclude drips
and spills in placing items. Accuracy is important to
comply with dietary restrictions and for satisfaction.

For visual appeal, variety in color is important. An
all-white meal, such as sliced turkey, mashed potato, and
cauliflower, could be a "turn off," especially on white
china. Garnishes can be used to add color. Preserving
the natural color of food is both visually appealing and
a signal to other senses. Broccoli that is olive green
is unappealing and probably not crisp-tender. Cauliflower
that is off-color may also be overcooked and unacceptable.

Variety in shape or form of menu items can add eye
appeal. The white meal I just mentioned did have variety
in shape and form; only the color was monotonous. All
items in a sauce or all items scooped presents an
unappealing plate. Shape and form can easily be varied
using dicing and cutting machines.

Visual appeal is also affected by the size of portions.
For many patients, too much food is unappealing. The
patient may feel defeated and not even try to eat. Many
hospitals use smaller portion sizes for patients than for
cafeteria patrons. A smaller plate, 8-inch instead of
9-inch, can also be used. In this way the meal appears

normal, and the patient is more likely to try to eat.
For patients who want and can eat more food, larger
portions can be made available.

Texture, the structure and mouthfeel of the food, is
another sensory characteristic. Adjectives used to
describe texture include crisp, soft, hard, and chewy. A
variety of textures in a meal provides a more pleasing
experience. Soup with crisp crackers; roast beef, mashed
potato, and broccoli; ice cream with a brownie--all are
combinations that vary in texture. Again, we should pay
attention to conserving the intended texture of food
during preparation and service. For example, to me
vegetables should be crisp-tender. I do recognize that
my Southern friends may disagree on this. There are, of
course, diets for which texture is intentionally
modified--liquid or mechanical soft.

Consistency is the firmness, density, or viscosity of
foods. Adjectives used to describe consistency include
runny and firm. Variety again adds appeal. A plate with
meat and gravy, creamed potatoes, and Harvard beets may
be unacceptable. The runny consistency of the three
items would be visually unappealing and would mix flavors.

Flavor is an important component of sensory quality
acceptability. We all want food to taste good. This can
be a problem with patient food service, however, because
the patient's sense of taste may be affected by his
medical treatment. Some diets, especially those with
sodium restrictions, are unappealing to many individuals.
We should provide menus with a variety of flavors: sweet,
sour, mild, strong, etc. For low-sodium items, other
seasonings can be used to enhance the natural flavor of
food.

The degree of doneness of food may affect acceptability through a variety of sensory characteristics. If
too well cooked, vegetables may have an undesirable color
and texture. Meat may change in flavor as well as in
color and texture.

A final factor in sensory quality is the temperature
of food. Menus with a variety of temperatures--some hot
and some cold items--are appealing, but only if served at
the intended temperature. A cold, crisp salad should not
be room temperature; milk should not be lukewarm nor
should ice cream be melting; and, of course, hot food
should be hot.

NUTRITIONAL REQUIREMENTS

The nutritional requirements of individuals should be considered. This is especially important for us, because we are providing all meals and because patients frequently have different nutritional needs to restore them to health. More careful attention to nutritional adequacy is needed when food choices are limited by availability, preferences, or acceptability, or by abnormal digestion or metabolism.

A house or general diet is planned to meet the nutritional needs of patients who do not require dietary modifications. Patients may have a selective menu or be served a nonselective menu. Dietitians or technicians should review the patient's selective menu for nutritional accuracy. For patients with either a selective or nonselective menu, food consumed should be reviewed for nutritional adequacy. Patients whose selection or consumption is inadequate should be counselled, the physician should be informed, and recommendations made when appropriate.

Some modification of the general diet is usually required for a patient recovering from an acute illness or trauma. Frequently, the diet must be modified in texture or amount. The objective of dietary treatment is to provide fluids, energy, and other essential nutrients in a form that can be utilized and to return the patient to a general diet as soon as possible. Some organic, functional, and metabolic disorders require an increase or decrease of the energy value of the diet. This affects nutritional adequacy and necessitates meal acceptability. Modifications in fat, protein, or mineral share a similar impact. No matter how carefully a modified diet is calculated, the key is eating. We must provide a meal that the patient finds tempting and acceptable.

One factor that cannot be overlooked is nutrient retention. If we plan a menu to provide nutritional adequacy for the patient, production and service processes should be controlled to conserve the nutrient contribution of the particular food to the total diet.

SAFETY

We are responsible for providing the patient with safe food, both chemically and microbiologically.

Poisonous or toxic materials allowed in a food service area are those necessary for maintaining the establishment, cleaning or sanitizing equipment and facilities, and controlling insects and rodents. These materials must be clearly labeled, used correctly, and stored separately from each other and from food. In hospitals, care must also be taken that food on a patient unit is clearly labeled and stored separately from medications or other materials.

Microbiological safety of food can be controlled by attention to four major critical control points: ingredient control and storage, equipment sanitation, personnel sanitation, and time-temperature. The relationship of time and temperature at all process stages for potentially hazardous foods is based on the zone of growth for microorganisms in food. Microbiological control should preclude a foodborne disease outbreak that could be harmful or fatal to individuals who are already in a debilitated condition.

I have presented some of the factors that I consider part of meal quality and acceptability. As a food service manager, I have also included some considerations from the perspective of the patient. First, that is who I serve and who you serve. Second, I recently had my first experience as a patient. I am not recommending surgery to all of you, but it does put the patient in a different perspective when one has been one. I had major surgery and was hospitalized for six days. This experience was beneficial from many standpoints, but one is that now I can appreciate the patient's point of view. I was a patient at Massachusetts General Hospital, and I would recommend it and the food to anyone.

Alternatives for Menu Item Flow in Hospital Patient Feeding Systems

Barbara J. Bobeng

For a variety of reasons, hospitals have implemented
alternative food service systems. Hospitals may operate
different systems for patient and nonpatient feeding
and/or operate a mixed system depending on the menu
item. When we talk about the system and menu item flow,
we are generally referring to hot menu items, such as
soups, entrees, vegetables, and starches.

The three alternative food service systems that will
be discussed are the conventional, cook-chill, and cook-
freeze systems. An assembly-serve or convenience system
will become one of the three systems, depending on the
temperature state of the menu item. For example, if a
frozen entree is thawed and plated cold, it becomes part
of a cook-chill system.

I will briefly present the systems and the major
process stages through which menu items flow to the
patient. Other papers of the symposium emphasize specific
process stages, describing the state of the art in equipment and the effects of the processes on quality.

Figure 1 shows the process stages in the conventional,
cook-chill, and cook-freeze systems. Through procurement,
preparation, and heating the systems use similar processes. It is the food preservation or storage treatment
use after heating that differentiates the systems. In
the conventional system, menu items are stored hot; in
the cook-chill system, in a chilled state; and in the
cook-freeze system, in a frozen state. After items are

Barbara J. Bobeng, Ph.D., R.D., is Assistant Director,
Dietary Department, and Associate Professor, Institute of
Health Professionals, Massachusetts General Hospital,
Boston.

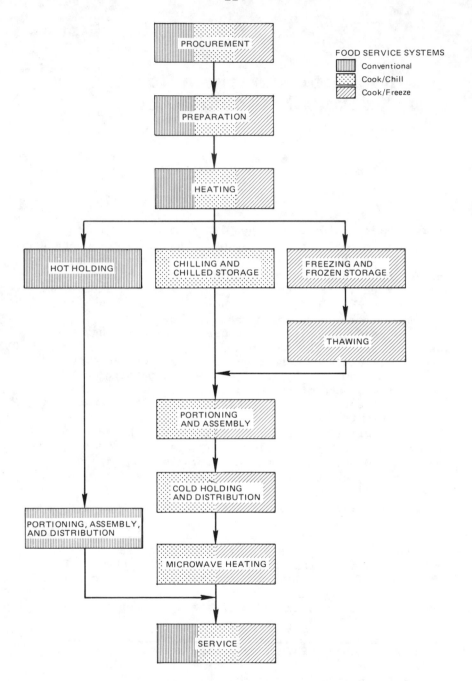

FIGURE 1 Comparison of hospital food service systems.

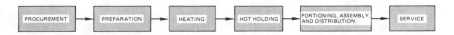

FIGURE 2 Hospital conventional food service systems.

thawed from the frozen state, processes in the cook-freeze
system are similar to those in the cook-chill system.

Briefly, the conventional system (Figure 2) consists of
traditional quantity food production. After the cooking
or heating process, menu items are stored by hot-holding
between production and service. Hot holding is any heated
storage treatment, such as holding in steam tables or
warming cabinets. Portioning, assembly, and distribution
includes any activities in a centralized area to prepare
for distribution of trays to the patients. In a decentralized system, distribution of menu items to patient
units in bulk, using heated trucks, would occur before
portioning and assembly of the tray. Service includes
any activities related to delivery of the meal tray to
the patient.

In the cook-chill system (Figure 3) menu items are
cooled to below 45°F and stored at refrigerated
temperatures for about one day--chilling and chilled
storage. Portioning and assembly is similar to the
conventional system, except that hot menu items are
cold. Cold holding and distribution may include storage
of the patient meal tray in a refrigerated truck for
distribution to the patient unit, or on a rack for
distribution and then storage in a refrigerator located
in the patient unit. Microwave heating is a terminal
heat treatment given to menu items prior to hot service.
These stages may vary somewhat depending on the equipment
used. Service is similar to the conventional system,
including those activities related to delivery of the
meal tray to the patient.

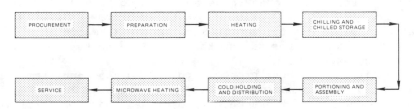

FIGURE 3 Hospital cook-chill food service systems.

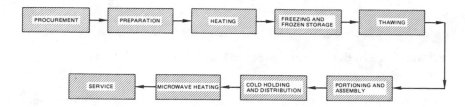

FIGURE 4 Hospital cook-freeze food service systems.

     In the cook-freeze system (Figure 4) after heating,
menu items are frozen and stored at 0°F or below for
weeks or months--freezing and frozen storage. Thawing is
a refrigerated storage process designed to increase the
temperature of the entree to above freezing. After
thawing, process stages for menu items in the cook-freeze
system are identical to those of the cook-chill system.
Again, processes may differ somewhat among cook-freeze
systems, depending on equipment used and whether menu
items are frozen in individual portions, as plated meals,
or in bulk.
     Later in the symposium the effects of meal assembly,
meal distribution, and meal service on the quality of
food are addressed. Procurement, preparation, and
heating can also affect quality of the menu items.
Quality must be controlled throughout menu item flow to
ensure that a quality meal is presented to the patient.
     Procurement includes establishing specifications, pur-
chasing, receiving, inspecting, and storing ingredients
for menu item production. The goal of in-process control
is to conserve the inherent quality of these ingredients.
     Preparation includes all food handling activities
prior to heating, such as peeling, grinding, mixing, and
shaping. Control mechanisms for personnel and equipment
sanitation and time-temperature should be designed to
provide for the microbiological quality of the menu
items. Recipes may need to be adjusted to provide for
sensory quality. For example, in the cook-freeze system,
recipes for sauces frequently require a waxy maize
starch. Some recipes adjust the quantity and type of
seasoning used.
     Heating is any heat process applied to the menu item,
such as baking, steaming, frying, or roasting. Depending
on the menu item, it has been recommended that potentially
hazardous foods be heated to 165°F-170°F to destroy the
vegetative cells of common pathogens. Some menu items

are commonly given heat treatments to less than 165°F in a conventional system to preserve sensory quality. Temperatures must be controlled in subsequent process stages to minimize bacterial contamination and/or growth. Time and temperature of hot holding must be controlled to preserve the nutritional quality of the menu items. In the cook-chill and cook-freeze systems, the endpoint temperature for heating menu items should be established, recognizing that there will be a second heat treatment before meal service. A milder heat treatment during the initial heating should contribute to conserving both the nutritional and sensory quality of the menu item. Times and temperatures must be controlled throughout the menu item flow to minimize bacterial contamination and growth. in the final heat treatment, the menu item should reach a temperature of 165°F-170°F to assure microbiological control.

This brief overview of the three food service systems—conventional, cook-chill, and cook-freeze—through the production and heating phase, is followed by detailed discussion of the meal assembly, meal distribution, and meal service phases. Food production techniques may vary among systems; and the next presentations suggest some alternatives for producing menu items, especially modified diet meals.

Food Production Alternatives for Modified Diet Meals

Justin M. Tuomy

The U.S. Army Natick Research and Development Laboratories
are dedicated to the personal support of the military
man--clothing, shoes, body armor, tentage, air drops,
food, etc. Although it is an Army installation, it has
responsibility for food research and development and
engineering for all of the armed forces. Thus, it has
responsibility for an operation estimated to cost $10
billion a year. To accomplish this there are three
separate organizations at Natick Labs. They are the
Operations Research System Analysis Office (ORSA), the
Science and Advanced Technology Laboratory (SATL), and
the Food Engineering Laboratory (FEL). In FEL there are
two operating divisions. One is the Food Service Equipment Division, and the other is the Food Technology
Division (FTD), of which I am Chief.

In the Food Technology Division there are four
branches--Animal Products, Plant Products, Food
Packaging, and Experimental Kitchens--a total of almost
90 people with a wide range of skills in various food
disciplines. They include dietitians, home economists,
food technologists, food packaging specialists, military
food service people, and chemical and mechanical
engineers. Our responsibilities are in the so-called
hardware area--individual food items and rations,
existing feeding systems, food specifications, production
engineering, technical support to procurement and to the
individual services. We deal with dining halls serving
2,000 customers, dining halls serving 80 customers,

Justin M. Tuomy is Chief, Food Technology Division, Food
Engineering Laboratory, U.S. Army Natick Research and
Development Laboratories, Natick, Massachusetts.

submarines feeding over 100 sailors for 90 days with no
resupply, small groups manning missile sites 100 miles
from nowhere, patrols in the jungles, patrols in the
Arctic, patrols in the desert, astronauts, war-reserve
food stored for up to 8 years, feeding for medical
service in combat, and so on. While a lot of our work is
just plain institutional feeding, some of it is on the
frontiers of food science. For example, how do you feed
people under stress conditions? We do not brag enough
about it, but we are the foremost laboratory in the world
on feeding under stress conditions.

What I am leading up to is that our work involves food
and food service under just about any condition you can
imagine. From this I have developed a series of truisms
that I would like to share with you, because I hope they
will provide you with the ideas and the enthusiasm to
implement those ideas that can make real differences or
provide new perceptions in your own jobs.

TRUISM NO. 1: EVERYONE WHO EATS AT LEAST ONE MEAL A DAY IS A FOOD EXPERT

Food professionals run into this attitude all of the
time. Who is to say the individual is not right? At
least, he should be as far as his own likes and dislikes
are concerned. Where we have a greater problem is with
management. Common is the idea that we are a bunch of
loafers because "Where's the problem with food? You can
buy all you want at the supermarket down the street."
This becomes a never-ending educational problem. Those
of us who have captive consumers have the worst time,
because the consumers cannot vote with their feet and
their dollars on the quality of our operations. Or,
imagine a situation like ours, in which the R&D operation
is a world away from our customers and there is no
real-dollar bottom line that entitles us to a pat on the
back or a kick somewhat lower.

TRUISM NO. 2: EVERY FOOD PROFESSIONAL IS AN EXPERT IN EVERY ASPECT OF FOOD SCIENCE, TECHNOLOGY, AND ENGINEERING

This is more insidious and potentially more dangerous
than the preceding truism, since it can result in all
kinds of problems, ranging from little glitches to great

catastrophes. We have found problems many times with equipment that has apparently been designed without any input from food professionals familiar with the intended use. Worse yet, we have found problems rampant in food service operations. Sometimes, the truism comes from ignorance or nonawareness that experts in food-related disciplines have a lot to offer. At other times, it seems to be a jealous guarding of one's private preserves. One of the things we are very conscious of is that food doesn't care who eats it. At one time the various armed services were, and still are in many instances, very parochial; and if one service had a new food service thing, the other services immediately had to have one bigger and better. This attitude has changed a great deal. We have recently designed a new compact food packet for use in assault, nonresupply situations at the request of the Marine Corps. Now that they have seen how good it is, the Navy wants it for battle station feeding, and the Army wants if for special forces and rangers. In the past the Navy and the Army would have insisted that they have separate packets.

When we worked with the Walter Reed Army Medical Center cook-freeze system, we found that food preparation and handling in genral were little different than at an Air Force facility at Warren Air Force Base in Wyoming, which was also using a cook-freeze system. The only differences were in special uses such as hospital special diets. We further proved that many of the techniques used in industry could be applied effectively at Walter Reed. So, don't look down your nose at fellow food professionals just because they work in different sectors. They might have a lot to offer in making your job easier and better.

TRUISM NO. 3: MOST FOOD SERVICE OPERATIONS THAT DO NOT HAVE A PROFIT AND LOSS STATEMENT ATTACHED TO THEIR DAILY OPERATIONS ARE RUN FOR THE CONVENIENCE OF THE OPERATOR, WITH CUSTOMER SATISFACTION COMING IN FOR LIP SERVICE ONLY

This type of thing is frequently found in the armed services, where the dining hall operator has little incentive to increase his own workload by attracting more customers. It may sound odd to mention "attracting more customers" to those who have not experienced the armed forces and so visualize GIs being lock-stepped into the dining halls. Not so, except in such cases as basic training. Tests have shown that of all those entitled to a free meal and with the freedom of choice, only 40 percent or less take advantage of that free meal. In some cases I have seen it as low as 20 percent. When a number of customer-oriented changes are made, this can be raised to 70 or more percent. It can never reach 100 percent for various reasons, including the fact that a number of people do not eat three meals a day. Is this true only of the armed services? My observations lead me to say that it is not. Many nonprofit facilities are faced with the same problem. Attendance at meals can be increased by a knowing, caring, forceful management.

It bothers me more than anything else when operators are not running their operation for their own convenience, nor are they running it for their customers. Instead, they seem to be running it for every other reason in the book, from having a nice computer printout to being able to have long conferences on company time. Even worse is that they do not know or admit that this the case. You must know of facilities that are run this way. But have you ever stood off and looked at yourself and your operation? Are you so caught up in daily trials and tribulations that you are placing your customer last on your list of priorities? Is your customer a figurehead at the top of the priority list only to drop out of sight when push comes to shove?

We at Natick Labs make every effort to think of our work only in terms of what it will do to improve the lot of our customer, the GI, wherever he or she may be, whether it is floating around the Indian Ocean, stationed in Germany, or out in the jungle some place. As a result, I have a habit of asking some "stupid" questions, such as: "Why can't that patient have a better tasting special diet?" The answers I get are usually revealing, ranging from a blank stare to "He is too sick to care." I am amazed how many times I have heard that last one. Basically, the answers are negative and slanted toward not rocking the boat. It is a delight to meet the individual who says: "How can we do it?" That is the attitude I am hoping all of you have; and I am hoping that you will carry away from this symposium germs of ideas by which you can really make your customer's days more happy.

TRUISM NO. 4: THE DIFFERENCE BETWEEN MEDIOCRE
FOOD AND MARVELOUS FOOD IS ONLY A HAIRSBREADTH,
EASILY BRIDGED BY CLOSE ATTENTION TO MINOR DETAILS

In other words a little tender, loving care. If you want
to prove this sometime, just give two separate kitchens
that have never worked together the same recipe and the
same raw materials, let them go to it, and then compare
the end products. The odds are you will find differences,
probably major ones. We find it all the time in the armed
services and not just because we have over 2,000 dining
facilities worldwide. The first thing you will say is
that it demonstrates a lack of training. Basically, you
are right. But I lay most of the blame on supervision
and management.

One of the first things I do when involved in evaluating a dining facility is to have my people run a series
of complete and very thorough yield tests and work studies
on a number of food items. Invariably, these will show
major problems--probably that the recipe is not being
followed even though everyone in the place swears on a
couple of stacks of Bibles that it was followed to the
last tenth of a gram and the last second of timing. It
is amazing what yield tests on a process from start to
finish will reveal.

I did this once with liver sausage production when I
was head of quality control for Oscar Mayer & Company and
learned a lesson. All kinds of complaints of product
variation and poor quality were being received, but
production supervision took the adamant stand that every
batch was made exactly the same way. They were dead
wrong. There wasn't a single variance from specification
that was of any size that would be noted by a casual
observer--just a lot of small things. When they were
corrected and the quality was back, not even sophisticated taste panels could detect differences from batch
to batch or day to day. That, by the way, made fervent
supporters of quality control from supervisors who had
been skeptical. The key here and the most important
thing to remember is that big problems usually stand out
like sore thumbs and can be attacked directly. It is the
combination of a lot of little variations that is the
insidious villain.

Of course, a lot of factors enter into the customer's
perception of food quality; but do not ever forget that
it is his and only his perception that counts. Our
studies have shown that food presentation, decor, and a

lot of other things also make a big difference. But food
is one of the most important things.

Why does this happen to us professionals? We are
lazy. We do not have a viable quality control program.
We assume our cook personnel are well trained. We assume
they have remembered their good training of 30 years ago
and have not picked up any bad habits. We never look at
the garbage pail. We never run a yield test on any
portion of our operation. We just never think of the
person eating our output as a person and a customer.

TRUISM NO. 5: THE INITIAL REACTION OF WE NORMAL
PEOPLE TO THE SUGGESTION OF A CHANGE IS:
"NO WAY! IT WON'T WORK!"

The biggest challenges in my work have come when someone
told me it wouldn't work. When I first got into research
and development, I had a boss whose standard answer to
practically every one of my proposals was "It won't work!"
I received eight patents under that boss and I do not know
how many scientific publications because I was egged on
by that challenge. But I have not found it easy since I
became a boss to reverse the process and accept new and
different ideas myself. It just does not seem a standard
part of human nature to accept change when it is proposed
by someone else. However, I found that by going over in
the corner every once in a while and talking severely to
myself I can not only accept new ideas but encourage and
reward them. Let me tell you, it is rewarding to me.

But, whatever you do, don't automatically respond to
any new idea with: "Nice, but it won't work in my
facility." Instead, say to yourself: "What could I do
to make it work?" Be positive instead of negative about
new ideas.

Food Production Alternatives for Modified Diet Meals

Carol P. Shaw

Many of the varied projects that we are conducting at
U.S. Army Natick Research and Development Laboratories
are concerned with hospital feeding programs, and it
seems that our efforts in this area are increasing. We
in the Food Engineering Laboratory have done such things
as producing guides for the cook-freeze system at the
Walter Reed Army Medical Center (Young et al., 1977;
Darsch et al., 1978; Darsch et al., 1979a; McNutt et al.,
1979; Shaw et al. 1979a,b,c); evaluating patient tray
delivery systems (Darsch et al., 1979b; Shaw et al.,
1979d), surveying restaurant menus; evaluating
cook-freeze systems (Shaw et al., in press); and, most
recently, surveying quality assurance practices in 22
nonmilitary hospitals.

I would like to acquaint you with some of the work we
have done with modified diet items; give you ideas of how
you can improve the flavor of some of your modified diet
products, and briefly review the results we found in our
survey of quality assurance practices currently used in
nonmilitary hospitals. Above all, I would like to
emphasize the consumer as the end product user of the
modified diets.

EXPANDING DEMAND FOR MODIFIED DIETS

Although we are reaching a stage in which our patient
population is getting more elderly, we have to realize

Carol P. Shaw, B.S., is a food technologist, Food
Engineering Laboratory, U.S. Army Natick Research and
Development Laboratories, Natick, Massachusetts.

that today's patients on modified diets are not just the very elderly, the very infirm, or the very ill. Indeed, they are apt to be young, as well as apt to be less ill, and to have hearty appetites.

When we read in the newspapers daily articles such as those by Craig Clairborne on how to prepare low-sodium foods, when diet cookbooks reach the top of the best-seller list, when traditional French cooking is being replaced with the nouvelle cuisine, and when the jogger next door as well as several of one's relatives need specially prepared meals, we must realize the growing demand for modified diets from both hospital patients and the general public.

In 22 nonmilitary hospitals surveyed almost 50 percent of the patients were on modified diets (Table 1).

MEETING THE NEEDS

What are hospitals doing today to satisfy the needs of the modified diet patient? If patients on modified diets comprise 50 percent of the hospital census, is 50 percent of the attention being given to producing quality foods to serve them? Or is the special diet preparation still being hidden away in a small corner of the kitchen with few, if any, checks on quality? In our survey, we have seen some progress. The day of the doctor's requesting and receiving tailor-made menus for each special diet patient has largely disappeared. Instead of 60 to 80 types of modified diets, most hospitals are using 8 to 12. Sodium levels are being monitored by patients and dietitians together. The improved nutritional education of young doctors and the increased reliance on the dietitian seem finally to be having an effect. Commercial production of many types of modified diet items is increasing. Although one hears complaints about the cost and quality of some of the items, the development of a good commercial base will give dietitians a wider range of options. Much work still must be done to improve these commercial foods, and judgments must be made to use only those of high quality. The number of jars of baby food and other special dietary products of questionable quality still in most hospital storerooms somewhat attests to the quality of the food the patients are being fed.

Other outdated approaches are still being used. Often modified diet items, if they are not hidden away in a little corner, are simply taken from the regular items.

TABLE 1 Hospitals Visited in Quality Assurance Survey

Hospital Name	Hospital Location	Hospital Type	Type of Ownership	Food Service Operation	No. of Beds	Type of Food Service Operation	Modified Diets (%)
Bethany Medical Center	Kansas City, Kans.	Medical Surgical	Private	In-House	425	Conventional	40
Brattleboro Retreat	Brattleboro Vt.	Psychiatric Nursing	Private	ARA	180	Convenience Conventional	50
Central Wisconsin Center	Madison, Wis.	Disabled Children	State	In-House	793	Conventional	50
Exeter Hospital	Exeter, N.H.	Medical Surgical	Private	SAGA	200	Conventional	50
Glover Memorial Hospital	Needham, Mass.	Medical Surgical	Community	ARA	102	Conventional	50
Hospital of the University of Pennsylvania	Philadelphia, Pa.	Medical Surgical	Private	Custom Mgmt. Corp.	700	Cook-Chill	55
Lahey Clinic	Burlington, Mass.	Medical Surgical	Private	Seiler's Corp.	200	Conventional	60
Madison General Hospital	Madison, Wis.	Medical Surgical	Community	In-House	500	Conventional	33
Massachusetts General Hospital	Boston, Mass.	Medical Surgical	Private	In-House	1092	Conventional	46
McLean Hospital	Belmont, Mass.	Psychiatric	Private	In-House	328	Conventional	25
Medical Center of South Carolina	Charleston, S.C.	Medical Surgical	State	ARA	550	Conventional	50-55

Hospital	Location	Type	Ownership	Foodservice	Beds	Method	%
Memorial Hospital	Pawtucket, R.I.	Medical Surgical	Private	ARA	312	Conventional	55
Mercy Hospital	Des Moines, Iowa	Medical Surgical	Private	In-House	500	Cook-Chill	30
Middleton Memorial Hospital	Middleton, Conn.	Medical Surgical	Private	ARA	380	Conventional	55-60
Norwood Hospital	Norwood, Mass.	Medical Surgical	Community	In-House	267	Conventional	40
Portsmouth Hospital	Portsmouth, N.H.	Medical Surgical Maternity	Private	SAGA	145	Conventional	50
University of Kansas Medical Center	Kansas City, Kans.	Medical Surgical	State	In-House	780	Cook-Freeze	40
University of Wisconsin Medical Center	Madison, Wis.	Medical Surgical	State	In-House	555	Cook-Chill	45
Women's and Infants Hospital	Providence, R.I.	Maternity Surgical	Private	SAGA	163	Conventional	10
Veterans Administration Hospital, Boston	Boston, Mass.	Medical Surgical Psychiatric	Federal	VA	801	Conventional	50
Veterans Administration Hospital, Brockton	Brockton, Mass.	Medical/ Surgical Psychiatric	Federal	VA	916	Conventional	60
West Jersey Hospital	Voorhees, N.J.	Medical	Community	In-House	236	Cook-Freeze	65

Thus, to prepare beef stew, one removes a portion of it for bland diets before the onions and spices are added and a portion for low-sodium diets before the salt is added. For patients needing pureed items, the product is simply pureed and served without alteration. For liquid diets, water is added to the pureed product. The results are as one might expect. The bland items certainly taste bland; the low-sodium items are noticeably lacking in salt; the pureed items look and taste unappetizing; and the liquid items not only taste like watery beef stew, but the particles usually settle to the bottom of the glass. Another alternative is even easier--serve patients pureed baby foods or nutritional supplements and ready-prepared foods, even if the quality may be somewhat substandard.

It is possible for a hospital to feed every patient food equivalent to that found at home or on the commercial market. When we were asked by the Walter Reed Army Medical Center to develop production guides for their cook-freeze system, we did it with the goal of providing each patient with quality food. When we developed more than 300 production guides for modified diet patients, we had the same goal as for regular diet patients--the production of highly acceptable modified diet items for patients with special dietary restrictions. There is no reason for special diet patients to be expected to eat unappetizing foods.

THE DEVELOPMENT PROCEDURE

Special care and attention went into producing the modified diet items for the Walter Reed Medical Center. To be sure, it takes just a little more effort to prepare a beef stroganoff for a patient who is on a modified diet; but that extra effort is especially important if these patients are going to continue to adhere to their diet restrictions and be satisfied customers of the hospital. We started developing the recipes by first consolidating the number of diets. Walter Reed had 88 different types of special diets; there is no way a hospital can give proper attention to each of this number of diets and produce consistently high-quality items. We consolidated the major restrictions into:

(1) a combination of calorie-restricted, low-saturated-fat, low-cholesterol, diabetic, and bland diets

(2) a combination of sodium-restricted, saturated-fat-restricted, cholesterol-restricted, diabetic, and bland diets

(3) a pureed diet

(4) a dental liquid or thinned, strained diet

(5) a renal diet

This gave a manageable number of diets to begin our work. We found it relatively easy to combine several restrictions into one diet. The items were first prepared according to the original, unmodified diet recipe; then they were modified until we considered the item to be of good flavor and quality. The products were next evaluated by a technological panel for color, appearance, odor, flavor, and texture. Each approved item was placed at -10°C for storage at 1, 2, 3, 6, and 12 months. Some items requested were not suitable for a cook-freeze system or for the Walter Reed tray delivery system and were not approved. But there are sufficient, well-liked items suitable for each system, so that there is no reason to serve substandard meals. Nutritional analyses were made of each item, and the production guides and storage results were published in technical reports.

SPECIAL NEEDS

Among the modified diet items developed for the Walter Reed Medical Center, the "dental liquids" or thinned, strained entrees serve as an illustration of the undocumented needs of special diet patients.

Because the military has a relatively high percentage of young, exuberant soliders who get into at least their share of accidents, a high number break their jaws and must have them wired shut for 6 to 8 weeks. During this time they need a liquid diet. Natick Laboratories developed a group of freeze-thaw-stable items tasting like components of a normal meal. Items were produced that would be smooth and flavorful and would not settle to the bottom of the glass. Products such as thinned, strained green beans, mashed potatoes, chicken cacciatore, and caramel custard were all acceptable in a liquid form and provided variety to the usual liquid nutritional supplements. Because fresh meat has a very gritty or sandy texture when reduced to a fine particle size, and because commercially available pureed meats have an undesirable flavor, freeze-dehydrated meat that pulverizes

easily to a fine power was used as a base for entrees.
The procedures for making these products were sent to
Walter Reed and published as a technical report (Shaw et
al., 1979c).

AN EXAMPLE

During this development period, a young man broke his jaw
in a softball game at Natick Labs. We used him as a test
subject and gave him some dental liquid samples and a survey questionnaire. The local newspapers reported the incident, complete with a clever cartoon. The Boston press
then reported the incident, and a Boston television station conducted an interview. A fact sheet was developed to respond to inquiries and soon the dental liquid
products were being reported in such diverse media as the
Chicago Tribune, the Wall Street Journal, the American
Dental Association news releases, the Canadian Broad-
casting Company, the Journal of Oral Surgery, and the
Journal of the American Dietetic Association.
    Within a few months Natick Labs was inundated with hun-
dreds of requests for information and for samples of these
liquid products from professional people and private individuals. Many of these people were in desperate need of
flavorful liquid diet items. They included not just those
with broken jaws and recent oral surgery, but many with
throat cancer, laryngectomies, hiatal hernias, and other
conditions often requiring liquid foods for the rest
of their lives.
    The original products, made with freeze-dehydrated
meat, were not easily adaptable for use in small hospitals or by out-patients. We are now developing completely
freeze-dehydrated powders that can be packaged in individual portions and reconstituted easily with hot water.
Thus, a hospital or out-patient will be able to open a
package of powdered, freeze-dried chicken with wine, or
beef with spaghetti sauce, add a cup of hot water, blend
for a few seconds in a blender, and have a flavorful,
nutritious liquid entree, sippable through a straw. This
relatively obscure feeding problem well illustrates the
needs for modified diet products in today's market.

PRODUCING QUALITY PRODUCTS

But how does one actually produce quality food? In the
literature, many references discuss the quality of

hospital food, defining this quality and describing how
to measure it. Thus, we gain some knowledge of procedures for quality assurance, taking dietary audits, and
measuring acceptability. Under quality assessments there
is usually a check-off for flavor; it is "satisfactory"
or "unsatisfactory." How to obtain that satisfactory
flavor is usually not addressed. Other factors such as
serving temperatures are much more easily measured and
receive much more documentation and discussion.

During developmental work on modified diet items, the
question is often asked: "How can one produce a bland
item that does not taste bland, or a low-sodium item in
which the lack of salt is not readily noticeable?" It
was clear that some practical suggestions for use in
formulating flavors would be of interest.

Almost 30 years ago a paper (which is now considered a
classic) was published by L. B. Sjöstrom and S. E.
Cairncross (1953) of Arthur D. Little, Inc., entitled
"What Makes Flavor Leadership?" In this study, eight
different brands of food items that were outstanding
sales leaders in their fields were examined to discover
any common flavor characteristics that separated them
from lower-selling brands. These were all nationally
sold products, so there were no large concessions to
regional preferences. Such diverse items as catsup,
prepared mustard, salad dressing, canned luncheon meats,
cola drinks, chocolate bars, peanut butter, and gelatin
desserts were examined. This work has now been updated
at Arthur D. Little and, although not yet published, the
results are again very similar. The old ground rules of
flavor still hold true. There are certain qualities
essential to successful food products, no matter what
their market. It is the application of many of these
qualities that are sought in developing modified diet
items.

THE QUALITIES

The first quality is blended flavor. Thus, when one
wants sweet and sour pork, for example, the sweet, sour,
pork, and spicy flavors should be perceived at almost the
identical moment. Time intensity studies have been
published in which the actual time intervals between
recognizable flavor characteristics are measured (Neilson,
1977). Blended flavors do not mean bland flavors. One
needs recognizable, identifying characteristics to provide

interest. Therefore, in a teriyaki steak the beef, garlic, ginger, and soy flavors provide interest, but they must be blended so that the total impression is teriyaki, not its individual components. Many especially well blended and complex flavors are found in nature as well as in well-blended food products. Over 300 volatile compounds have been identified in heated beef (Van Steaten, 1977), but flavor chemists have not yet been able to produce a totally satisfactory meat flavor. Blended products are hard to describe and reproduce; consider, for example, the uniqueness of the flavor of Coca-Cola, Hershey's chocolate, and Campbell's soups.

Cooks have long known that long cooking, simmering, or marinating aids in blending flavors. Salt, in addition to being an interest note, aids the flavor blend. Thus, when reducing the sodium content, one especially needs a good blend of other interest notes to make the lack of salt not readily apparent. Interest notes from allowable herbs may make any bland items seems to taste spicy.

THE FLAVOR SEQUENCE

The order of the appearance of flavor notes is important. An initial impact of pleasant flavor is as important as initial impressions elsewhere. Everyone is familiar with items that leave a bland initial impression, as if one were chewing on cotton or sawdust, only to have the flavor bloom later. This is apt to occur in pureed meats, especially chicken. Introducing allowable seasonings along with broth and altering the fat content will create a faster initial flavor impact. Many products have unpleasant characteristics, but if the initial impression is pleasant, unpleasant flavors may be hidden in the overall blend and may actually add interest to the product.

Just as the initial impression is important, so also is the lasting impression. The bitterness of artificial sweeteners detracts particularly because it tends to linger in the mouth after other flavors have disappeared. Blending this bitter taste in with other flavors makes it less a detriment. Coffee, for example, is inherently bitter, and one expects bitterness as part of the flavor blend. The quick disappearance of flavors encourages one to eat more of a product. If the flavor lasts in one's mouth for a long period, there is little incentive to take another bit or swallow.

BLENDING OF FLAVORS

Another term used in descriptive sensory analysis is "body of flavor." Even if one thinks of a product as a series of recognizable flavor characteristics appearing in a certain order, there is still something lacking in the overall flavor picture. Most products have unrecognizable or unidentifiable flavor notes that add to the fullness of the product. In fruits, for example, there are complex esters adding to the fullness of the natural product that are not found in items such as Kool-Aid-type fruit drinks. Methylanthranalate alone, for example, will not give a full grape flavor, nor will amyl acetrate give a complete banana flavor. In American and continental cooking we have relied heavily on such items as butter, eggs, milk, and cream to give a full rich body of flavor to sauces, casseroles, and desserts. Restricting such items in low-calorie, low-fat, and low-cholesterol diets becomes a challenge if one is to still retain a fullness of flavor. Careful blending of flavors, often at subthreshold levels, accompanied by the use of low-fat beef, chicken, or fish stock, allowable cheeses or cheese flavorings, and natural fruit flavors, will increase the complexity of the flavor blend and add a full-bodied impression to the final product.

In formulating and testing products for modified diets, I would urge dietitians cooks to think about the flavor sensations produced in food: Is there a well-blended flavor giving an impression of fullness and richness? Is there a good, quick initial impact of flavors? Is the aftertaste low and pleasant, and are there enough interesting flavors to cause patients really to want to eat the food? There can be no doubt that the patient is the final arbiter of food quality, that likes and dislikes are omnipresent, and that serving temperatures are as important as are aesthetic features such as color and garnishes. However, I wonder if some lack of literature on how to produce quality flavored products is because we know so little about flavor itself and because of the almost unbelievable complexity of flavor chemistry.

TIME REQUIREMENTS

To develop modified diet items in a manner to produce superior quality requires additional time and labor. The University of Kansas Medical Center, for example, reported that it takes 3 months to develop properly a recipe from its inception through consumer acceptance. However, very few hospitals spend even close to this amount of time in recipe development. To offset these requirements, I would suggest that the following recommendations be considered:

1. The consolidation of as many diet modifications as possible. Although much progress has been made, most hospitals are still attempting to tailor too many diets to relatively obscure requirements. It is not that optimum nutritional management is not needed for a variety of diets, but rather that these diets be combined to the greatest extent possible. It is far more likely that better quality items can be prepared by careful attention to larger batches of combination diets than by preparing small amounts of each individual diet modification.

2. Freeze as many modified diet items as possible. Although much is written and discussed about the relative merits of the cook-freeze, cook-chill, and conventional systems, no one system is ever used to the exclusion of others. In a cook-freeze system, some items will always be prepared conventionally; conversely, in a conventional system, there are always items that have been frozen sometime in their history. To prepare larger batches of labor-intensive, low-volume modified diet items to freeze for later use can be very cost-effective.

3. If erratic quality is a problem in a given facility, consider the use of the restaurant-type menu, in which the same items are offered just as they would be in a restaurant. In our hospital surveys it was obvious that the daily repetition of items led to much more consistent quality. There are several ways of adding variety to a restaurant menu; and if the use of this menu means substituting a large variety of poor-quality items with fewer items of high quality, then it should certainly be considered. A restaurant menu can be used effectively with modified diet patients. Consolidating the number of diets offered, coupled with producing the same high-quality items each day, can give more appetizing selections from which a patient can choose. It is better to select one entree from a choice of five good ones each day than to have a seemingly endless variety of poor-quality food. Some hospitals have worked their low-sodium and other diet restrictions into one general restaurant menu. In this way the patient learns to select food in the same manner as he must when he leaves the hospital.

In giving these recommendations, our main purpose has
been to show ways to make management more aware of the
production of modified diet items. But is there an
awareness of the quality of food being given to each
modified diet patient? While there may be only a few
patients on each diet modification, these few together
will probably comprise about 50 percent of the patient
population. Are they getting 50 percent of the attention?

THE QUALITY ASSESSMENT SURVEY

I have made several references to the survey just completed on the quality assessments in hospitals. I would
like briefly to summarize some of the findings of this
survey as an informational base for discussions at this
symposium.

Food service contracting has become a reality in
military hospitals. Thus, it is becoming critical to
have methods of measuring and monitoring quality to
ensure that contract-operated hospitals are delivering to
their patients quality food equivalent to that from
in-house facilities. As a first step in developing
monitoring procedures, we undertook a survey of 22
nonmilitary hospitals to determine what quality assurance
practices are currently being used. By patterning
military procedures after those in general use, we hope
to avoid the overregulation and excessive paperwork too
often prevalent in government operations.

The 22 hospitals surveyed (Table 1) included small,
medium, and large facilities; private, community, state,
and Veterans Administration hospitals; conventional,
cook-chill, and cook-freeze operations; and in-house and
contract-operated facilities. A more even geographical
distribution would have been preferred, but economic
factors led us to focus mainly on hospitals along the
Eastern seaboard and in the Midwest.

Although a wealth of information was obtained from
this survey, I will highlight only a few of the most
important findings.

1. Ingredient Specifications Most hospitals have
their own ingredient specifications. Those operated by
food service contractors used contractor-approved vendors.
The leverage of being able to discontinue immediately the
association with a vendor delivering substandard goods
gives private hospitals an advantage not always possible

with the federal government and some state government
procurement systems.

2. <u>Ingredient Control</u> About 50 percent of the
hospitals surveyed controlled the ingredients delivered
to the cooks. Those on restaurant-type menus found
ingredient control and many other control procedures
easier than those hospitals on cycle menus.

3. <u>Time-Temperature Controls</u> Production schedules
usually determined the time before serving that items
were prepared. However, this approach was quite loosely
structured in many hospitals. Methods of controlling
time-temperature standards from production to patient
varied considerably, and many hospitals reported an
inability to serve food to patients at temperatures
required by public health regulations. One hospital on a
cook-freeze system has temperatures of each item recorded
after rethermalization in microwave ovens. Generally,
and with good reason, cook-chill and cook-freeze systems
were more careful about time-temperature controls than
conventional systems.

4. <u>Adherence to Recipes</u> The methods used to adhere
to recipes varied greatly. One hospital, a long-term
psychiatric facility, does not use any recipes but
encourages innovation and creativity by their cooks. The
University of Kansas Medical Center, in many ways a
pioneer in hospital quality assurance, emphasized end
item product description in monitoring standardization of
cooking, thus trying to eliminate preference judgments.

5. <u>Nutritional Data</u> All hospitals had the nutritional
values of each recipe calculated. However, all agreed
that this was meaningless without careful monitoring of
patient selections and plate waste.

6. <u>Microbiological Tests</u> No hospitals were currently
doing any routine food microbiological testing. Hospitals
generally did test the cook-chill, cook-freeze systems at
the beginning of their operations, but they discontinued
testing because of the high cost and lack of positive
results. Some hospital laboratories did occasional
surface or equipment testing, and one hospital dietary
department used simple commercial kits for testing
surfaces and equipment. These kits are easy to use and
often are useful in training personnel in sanitation.

7. <u>Sanitation</u> The most detailed and structured
assessments were in the area of sanitation. The various
checklists and audit forms were usually quite detailed
and specific, especially in hospitals operated by food
service contractors. However, no clear correlation was

found between the number of checklists and the visible
sanitary conditions. Management's enforcement of good
sanitary practices seems to be the prime factor in good
sanitation.

8. Test-Tray Assessments Many hospitals relied
heavily on test or dummy assessments for checking tray
accuracy, attractiveness, cleanliness, food temperatures,
and food quality. When conscientiously carried out,
recorded, reported, and followed up, these test-tray
assessments seemed effective. Some hopitals included a
nondietary employee on test-tray assessments.

9. Sensory Evaluations

Informal Most hospitals had one person, usually
the tray line supervisor, responsible for checking
temperatures and taste of all items before plating.
This was less apt to be done in hospitals using a
restaurant menu. A few hospitals had test-tray
evaluations by all cooks before serving. This peer
evaluation seemed important in encouraging each cook
to produce the best-quality product possible.

Formal The cook-chill and cook-freeze operations
were more apt to have formal sensory panel sessions
the day after the products were prepared. Eight- to
ten-member panels were common and included a wide
range of dietary employees. Other hospitals often
conducted formal sensory evaluations to compare
products from different vendors, test new recipies, or
evaluate problem items. As diversified a panel as
possible was recommended.

10. Patient Acceptability Ratings All hospitals
conducted patient acceptability surveys, usually monthly
or quarterly. The results were often transmitted to the
hospital management, and high patient acceptability
ratings were considered extremely important. However,
many hospitals felt interviews gave more informative
results. Dismissal questionnaires were regarded as less
important, generally because of a low rate of return.

11. Cafeteria Acceptability Ratings Generally,
relatively little was done in surveying cafeteria
patrons. many felt that sales were the most reliable
indicator of acceptability. Several hospitals left
comment cards for suggestions periodically, and one food
service contractor did tray assessments with customers
similar to those done on the patient floors.

Although this survey of hospitals provided much background information on current quality assurance practices,

our impression is that formal quality assurance audits
alone were no guarantee of high-quality food. This
impression, of course, parallels industrial experiences.
Many small hospitals were quite unaware of the quality
checks they had built into their systems.

If I had to summarize the most important ingredient in
promoting hospital food service quality today, I would do
it in two words: good management. The hospitals operating under good management teams are well aware who they
have to please--not just the Joint Commission of the
Accreditation of Hospitals nor the hospital management,
not just the district or regional manager or the public
health inspector, but the patient in Room 111 with a
broken leg, the coronary patient in Room 204, and all
those hard-working employees looking forward to lunch in
the cafeteria. Although the adage "you can't please all
of the people all of the time" is undoubtedly true, I do
hope your goal will be to "please all of the people most
of the time."

REFERENCES

Darsch, G., C. Shaw, and J. Tuomy. 1978. Storage Study of
Frozen Entree Items Developed for Walter Reed Army
Medical Center. NATICK/TR-78/006 (AD A091 769).

Darsch, G., C. Shaw, and J. Tuomy. 1979a. Examination of
Patient Tray Food Service Equipment: An Evaluation of
the Sweetheart Food Service Cart. NATICK/TR-79/026 (AD
A071 571).

Darsch, G., R. Young, C. Shaw, and J. Tuomy. 1979b.
Entree Production Guides for Modified Diets. Part IV.
Modified Meat Substitute Entrees. NATICK/TR-79/013 (AD
A079 958).

McNutt, J., M. Branagan, J. McPhee, L. Albertini, and M.
Klicka. 1979. Entree Production Guides for Modified
Diets. Part V. Renal Diet Items. NATICK/TR-79/014 (AD
A083 141).

Neilson, A. J. 1977. Time intensity studies. Drug
Cosmetic Ind. 80:452-534.

Shaw, C., G. Darsch, G. Legris, Y. Masuoka, and J. Tuomy.
1979. Entree Production Guides for Modified Diets.
Part I. Consolidated Modified Meat Entrees.
NATICK/TR-79/010 (AD A079 949).

Shaw, C., G. Darsch, and J. Tuomy. 1979. Examination of
Patient Tray Food Service Equipment: An Evaluation of
the Alpha Cart. NATICK/TR-79/036 (AD A083 161).

Shaw, C., G. Darsch, and J. Tuomy. In press. Survey of Hospitals Using a Hotel-Menu Approach in Patient Tray Feeding.

Shaw, C., V. Loveridge, G. Darsch, and J. Tuomy. 1979. Entree Production Guides for Modified Diets. Part II. Pureed Bland Entrees. NATICK/TR-79/011 (AD A073 718).

Shaw, C., V. Loveridge, G. Darsch, and J. Tuomy. 1979. Entree Production Guides for Modified Diets. Part III. Pureed Bland Entrees. NATICK/TR-79/012 (AD A069 183).

Sjöstrom, L. B., and S. E. Cairncross. 1953. What makes flavor leadership? Food Technol. 7(2):56-58.

Van Steaten, Ed. 1977. Volatile Compounds in Food. Fourth edition. Central Institute of Nutrition and Food Research, TNO.

Young, R., C. Shaw, G. Darsch, J. Tuomy, and G. Walker. 1977. Meat and Fish Entree Production Guides Prepared for Walter Reed Army Medical Center. NATICK/TR-77/005 (FEL 77-004) (AD A004 476).

Food Production Alternatives for Modified Diet Meals

Jessie W. McNutt

There is little information on modified diet meals in the
literature on food production. Recipes for these modified
diets generally involve small quantities of ingredients
for meals to be prepared as needed. Each hospital has
its own recipe file, to which dietitians and cooks have
contributed over the years, and such modified diet menus
may show little variety. For example, plain sliced beef
or sliced chicken may be served four or five times per
week to the patient on a modified diet.

In the past, Army hospitals have had a very large
collection of recipes and special diet recipes. Each
hospital had its own favorites; and when recipes were
combined with those from all the hospitals, the task of
computerizing them became monumental, since there were
more than 4,000.

As a step toward standardizing these recipes, Colonel
Particia Accountious, who was then in the Office of the
Surgeon General and Chief Dietitian for the Army, decided
that all Army hospitals should use the Armed Forces Recipe
Service file and that modified diet recipes should be
developed based on this file. This Army project, called
"Modification of the Armed Forces Recipe File for Medical
Facility Use," was funded in October 1980 and is to be
completed by October 1, 1982. Besides using the same
recipes as the rest of the military, the Army hospitals
will also be using the same basic ingredients in their
preparation.

Jessie W. NcNutt, R.D., is Research Home Economist,
Experimental Kitchens, Food Engineering Labroratory, U.S.
Army Natick Research and Development Laboratories,
Natick, Massachusetts.

BACKGROUND

I should like first to give a little historical background
on this recipe file and the feeding of the military. I
joined the Army in World War II as a hospital dietitian,
and before one month had passed I was assigned to a hospital going overseas. One of the first things I learned
as we set up our hospital in England was that we had no
recipes and no diet manual. The cooks had had some training and seemed to have some recipes in their heads, and
I, too, had some recipes in my head. Modified diets overseas consisted of soft diets, liquid diets, and any type
of diet that doctors requested that could be implemented
with foods available. Actually, there were manuals that
had been written for the cooks, bakers, managers, and
inspectors, but they were not available in either of the
hospitals where I was assigned.

Following World War II, each of the services developed
its own recipe manual. Then in June 1967, a directive
from the Assistant Secretary of the Army established a
Department of Defense Recipe Service. A Department of
Defense task group had determined that a standard recipe
service was feasible and desirable. It would increase
efficiency and economies in food planning, preparation,
and service and would eliminate duplication of effort in
recipe development, testing, and publication.

The Department of the Navy became the editors, with
responsibility for the development, publication, and
distribution of standard recipes. Dietitians from the
four services (Army, Navy, Air Force, and Marines)
divided up the food categories and arbitrarily selected
"the" recipe for the first publication. Each year, one
or more categories of foods was chosen for possible
improvement. From time to time there were also changes
in ingredients and packaging, and there was always the
addition of new food items to be used by the military.

ASSIGNMENT TO NATICK LABORATORIES

Natick Army Research and Development Laboratories was
given the responsibility for testing and standardizing
recipes and for coordinating the field testing of new
recipes.

After Natick had tested and standardized a recipe or a
group of recipes, they were forwarded to the editors, who
sent them out in increments to the other members of the

Recipe Committee for comments. Each of the four services was represented on this committee and returned individual comments not only to the editor but also to each committee member. The Natick representative would then resolve any comments and discuss them on the phone with the editors. A final recipe represented the thinking and interests of all the users. The members saw each recipe before and after final editing.

The consolidated Armed Forces Recipe Service file was printed and distributed in 1969. It is mandatory for all military services to use these recipes. They are written for 100 servings, and the procurement of food by the military is based on the ingredients in the recipes.

By 1975 there had been four changes to the basic file. So many of the recipes had been changed in some way that the committee decided a total revision was in order.

This was accomplished last year, and the present file contains a total of 1,509 recipes and variations, plus 88 guideline cards and 61 colored photographs.

This recipe file is referred to as TM10-412 by the Army. It has been given other names by the Navy, Air Force, and Marine Corps. The recipe file, which is the basis of the menu for the military, will also be the basis of the menu for Army hospitals. It is available from the Superintendent of Documents, U.S. Government Printing Office, for $36.00 for the recipes and $3.50 for the index.

ARMY HOSPITAL DIET MANUAL DEVELOPMENT

At the same time that a completely new Armed Forces Recipe Service file was being published, a new Army hospital diet manual was also being written. It will be known as TM8-500, Nutrition Support Handbook, and will probably be published in 1982. It was developed and edited by Major Donna Ranger, R.D., Special Projects Officer of the Academy of Health Science, San Antonio, Texas. Major Ranger sent all the food lists for the special diets to us in the Experimental Kitchens of Natick, and we were able to begin this project in January 1981. Major Ranger is our consultant when problems arise. Incidentally, the first Army Hospital Diet Manual, which we did not have in World War II, was published in 1957 and was used by both the Army and Air Force.

Initial guidance for this project--the Modification of

Armed Forces Recipes for Hospital Facilities--came from
Colonel Jessie Brewer, Office of the Surgeon General.
The following are some of our guidelines: (1) Recipes
will be written for 10 portions, as there are many small
hospitals in the Army. (2) Directions are also to be
given for freezing modified diet items, as this will make
it possible to have an inventory of these items. (3) The
Office of the Surgeon General will encourage the use of
blast freezers if any of the hospitals wish to purchase
them. (4) This project will be completed by October 1982.
(5) Recipes will be published, but will be completely
separate from the Armed Forces Recipe File. (6) Dental
liquid diets, or, as we call them, thinned, strained
diets, may not be necessary as part of these recipes if
these diets can be purchased from industry. (7) Soy-
extended ground beef, which is a part of military feeding,
will not be used by the hospitals. (8) Entree recipes
will be the first developed. (9) Those production guides
already developed for Walter Reed Army Hospital will be
included among these recipes. There are some that have
no AFRS recipe counterpart.

Food lists and tables from the new Army Hospital Diet
Manual are very clear and easily understood. The bland
diet includes any food prepared without black pepper,
chili powder, or red pepper. So, all of the modified
diets can easily be made bland, as can most of the
regular foods served in the hospital. The American
Diabetes Association and American Dietetic Association
food exchanges are referred to in the food lists as
Calorie Exchanges.

DIETARY EXCHANGES

For those who are not familiar with the American Dietetic
Association dietary exchanges, there are six major exchange lists--milk, vegetable, fruit, bread, meat, and
fat. Exchanges are foods in specific measures that can
be substituted (or exchanged) for other foods in the same
list. As an example, to substitute for a slice of bread
in the diet, any one of the following could be used:
one-half cup of cooked spaghetti, noodles, or macaroni;
one-half cup of cooked cereal; one-half cup of mashed
potato; one-fourth cup of sweet potato; and many others.
One vegetable exchange is one-half cup of any 1 of about
30 different vegetables, each containing about 5 grams of

carbohydrates and 2 grams of protein (25 calories). A
fruit exchange has very specific measures for different
fruits, as there is a wide variation in the amount of
carbohydrate per weight of different fruits. For example,
one small orange can be exchanged for only two dates, and
one-half cup of grapefruit juice is the equivalent of
one-quarter cup of grape juice or one-third cup of apple
juice. Each of these fruit exchanges would contain 10
grams of carbohydrate, or 40 calories.

The Diet Manual also has sodium calorie exchanges and
renal exchanges. While the recipes are written for 10
portions, we have specified that each meat portion is
three exchanges, or can be 15 portions of two meat
exchanges.

SELECTION OF RECIPES FOR MODIFICATION

To begin the project, entrees in the AFRS file were surveyed to determine suitability for modification. There
were approximately 75 entrees that could be modified for
different diets. Approximately 16 of these could be
written without testing, using the Walter Reed production
guides.

It is our aim to make the modified diet recipes as
similar to the AFRS recipes as possible; but our main
goal is that they must taste good, be attractive, and be
highly acceptable. When feasible, five different modified
diet recipes are developed for each regular recipe. They
are: (1) sodium-restricted, calorie-restricted, bland;
(2) calorie restricted, bland; (3) ground meat; (4)
thinned strained; and (5) renal diet. There are special
recipes for each of these five diets, and each recipe is
especially formulated to give a product that is appetizing, freezes and reheats well, is seasoned to give a
full blending of flavors, and makes the patient who eats
it feel he is having the same food as the other patients
in the same room. For example, the ground meat pineapple
chicken and the thinned strained pineapple chicken are
not merely the regular recipe put through a food chopper
or liquefied in a blender. We have served the low-
calorie pineapple chicken with the regular pineapple
chicken in a luncheon in the Experimental Kitchens, and
our guests rated the calorie-restricted version equal to
the regular. Both received high ratings.

When a vegetable, as with stuffed peppers, stuffed

cabbage, or Syrian beef stew, is an important part of the
entree, the modified diet recipe has been developed for
two or three meat exchanges and one vegetable exchange.
If the vegetable is a minor part of the recipe, or considerably less than one vegetable exchange, we have
chosen to ignore it. For example, our modified diet
pizza recipe contains two tablespoons canned tomato per
serving, which would be only 1 gram of carbohydrate--
hardly worth considering as a vegetable exchange. Before
we publish the recipes, we will have determined the
nutrient contribution of all of the modified diet recipes.
Table 1 shows the armed forces recipe for Syrian beef
stew for 100 patients; Tables 2-6 show its modifications.

EQUIPMENT NEEDS

Thus far in our testing, very little equipment has been
needed for recipe development. We have used an electric
skillet; a griddle; a 4-quart saucepan for top-of-the-
stove cooking; and a 13- by 9-inch roasting pan for oven
cooking. A blender is needed for the thinned strained
diet items, and a food grinder makes more attractive
ground meat than a food processor. No doubt other equipment will be needed as we continue, but we wish to keep
the preparation procedures as simple as possible. Though
developed for 10 portions, the recipes can be scaled up
for use with larger equipment.

In formulating the recipes that contain a sauce or a
gravy, a modified edible starch is used. This type of
starch is essential for the stability of sauces that are
to be frozen. These sauces contain no fat and minute
amounts of carbohydrates, so they can be considered "free"
foods. They add to the attractiveness of the portion,
keep the food moist, protect the item from oxidation
during freezer storage, and in addition add to the flavor.

So far, in the write-up of the recipe we have given no
suggestions on packaging the item to be frozen. For the
small hospital, it is probably best to package in individual portions, which is what we have done in our own
testing. It also makes portioning easier on the serving
line because items will be ready for the trays. However,
if the hospital has many modified diets, it may be
preferable to freeze in bulk, with the exception of the
renal diet items, which should always be carefully
weighed in individual portions.

TABLE 1 Armed Forces Recipe Service Recipe (Regular Diet Recipe)--Syrian Beef Stew

Yield 100 Portions (2 Pans)   Each Portion: 1 Cup Stew plus 3/4 Cup Rice
Pan Size: 18- by 24-Inch Roasting Pan   Temperature: 400°F Oven; 350°F Oven

Ingredients	Weights	Measures	Method
Shortening, melted or salad oil	4 oz	1/2 cup	1. Grease bottom of each roasting pan with 1/4 cup shortening or salad oil; place an equal quantity of meat in each pan.
Beef, diced, thawed	30 lb		
Salt	8 oz	3/4 cup	2. Combine salt, pepper, garlic, cinnamon, allspice, and brown sugar; sprinkle an equal quantity over meat in each pan.
Pepper, black		2 tbsp	
Garlic, dehydrated		1 tsp	
Cinnamon, ground		1/4 cup	
Allspice, ground		1/4 cup	
Sugar, brown	6 oz	1 cup	3. Cook in 400°F oven, about 1 hour.
Water, hot		2 gal	4. Add 1 gal water to each pan. Cover; simmer 1 1/2 hours in 350° F oven.
Beans, green, frozen	8 lb	4-2 lb pg	5. Add an equal quantity of beans, onions, and tomatoes to meat in
Onions, dry, cut into 8 wedges	3 lb	3 qt	

Tomatoes, canned cut into pieces	12 lb 12 oz	1/2 gal (2-No. 10 cn)
Starch, corn	10 oz	2 cups
Water, cold		1 qt
Rice, steamed		4 3/4 gal

each pan. Stir to combine. Cover; simmer 1 to 1 1/2 hours or until beans are tender.

6. Blend cornstarch and water to make a smooth paste. Slowly add half of cornstarch mixture to ingredients in each pan. Blend thoroughly. Cook 5 minutes or until thickened.

7. Prepare 1 recipe for steamed rice (Recipe No. E-5).

8. Serve stew over 3/4 cup rice.

NOTE:
1. In Step 1, 30 lb beef pot roast diced in 1 to 1 1/2-inch pieces may be used. Trim beef to remove excess fat and gristle.

2. In Step 5, 3 lb 5 oz dry onions A.P. will yield 3 lb onions cut into wedges.

3. In Step 5, 1 lb (1 No. 10 cn) canned dehydrated uncooked green beans or 1 lb 10 oz (1 No. 2 1/2 cn) canned dehydrated compressed green beans or 12 lb 10 oz (2 No. 10 cn) canned green beans may be used. Prepare dehydrated green beans according to instruction on container. Drain dehydrated or canned beans before adding to meat mixture; reduce cooking time to 45 minutes.

4. In Steps 2 through 6, a steam-jacketed kettle or roasting pans (18 by 24 inches) on top of range can be used to brown and cook meat and vegetable mixture.

5. Other sizes and types of pans may be used. See Recipe No. A-25.

TABLE 2 Recipe for Modified Diets (Calorie-Restricted, Bland)--Syrian Beef Stew

Yield 10 Portions
Pan Size: 4-Quart Saucepan

Each Portion: 3 Oz Cooked Beef and
1/2 cup Vegetable

Percent	Ingredients	Weights	Measures	Grams	Method
54.57	Beef, diced, thawed	4 lb		1,814	1. Trim all visible fat from beef.
					2. Brown beef in saucepan.
0.42	Salt		2 tsp	14	3. Combine salt, garlic, cinnamon, and allspice; sprinkle over meat.
0.12	Garlic, dehydrated		1 tsp	4	
0.06	Cinnamon, ground		1 tsp	2	
0.06	Allspice, ground		1 tsp	2	
6.83	Water		1 cup	227	Add water, cover, and simmer gently 1 hour or until tender.
17.06	Tomatoes, canned crushed	1 lb, 4 oz	2 1/2 cups	567	4. Remove meat. Save 1/2 cup liquid for use in Step 6. Cool.

| 3.40 | Onions, dry, chopped | 4 oz | 3/4 cup | 113 |
| 17.06 | Beans, green, frozen | 1 lb, 4 oz | | 567 |

5. Add tomatoes, onions, and green beans to remaining liquid. Cover and simmer 1/2 hour or until vegetables are tender.

| 0.42 | Starch, edible, modified | 1/2 oz | 4 1/2 tsp | 14 |

6. Using cooled liquid, add starch to form a slurry. Add to vegetable mixture while stirring. Heat to simmering.

7. Portion 3 oz meat with 1/2 cup vegetable.

NOTE: 1. In Step 1, 4 lb beef, diced, thawed (beef for stewing, frozen, diced, USDA IMPS) will yield 2 lb cooked diced beef after trimming.

2. In Step 2, a nonstick vegetable spray may be used to prevent sticking.

VARIATION: 1. For 2 meat exchanges and 1 vegetable exchange, use 2 lb, 12 oz beef in Step 1, to yield 10 2-oz portions beef and 10 1/2-cup portions vegetables.

TABLE 3 Recipe for Modified Diets (Sodium-Restricted, Calorie-Restricted, Bland)--Syrian Beef Stew

Yield 10 Portions
Pan Size: 4-Quart Saucepan

Each Portion: 3 Oz Cooked Beef and 1/2 cup Vegetable

Percent	Ingredients	Weights	Measures	Grams	Method
54.81	Beef, diced, thawed	4 lb		1,814	1. Trim all visible fat from beef.
					2. Brown beef in saucepan.
0.12	Garlic, dehydrated		1 tsp	4	3. Combine garlic, cinnamon and allspice; sprinkle over meat.
0.06	Cinnamon, ground		1 tsp	2	
0.06	Allspice, ground		1 tsp	2	
6.83	Water		1 cup	227	Add water, cover, and simmer gently 1 hour or until tender.
17.13	Tomatoes, canned crushed	1 lb, 4 oz	2 1/2 cups	567	4. Remove meat. Save 1/2 cup liquid for use in Step 6. Cool.

3.41	Onions, dry, chopped	4 oz	3/4 cup	113
17.13	Beans, green, frozen	1 lb, 4 oz		567
0.42	Starch, edible, modified	1/2 oz	4 1/2 tsp	14

5. Add tomatoes, onions and green beans to remaining liquid. Cover and simmer 1/2 hour or until vegetables are tender.

6. Using cooled liquid, add starch to form a slurry. Add to vegetable mixture while stirring. Heat to simmering.

7. Portion 3 oz meat with 1/2 cup vegetable.

NOTE: 1. In Step 1, 4 lb beef, diced, thawed (beef for stewing, frozen, diced, USDA IMPS) will yield 2 lb cooked diced beef after trimming.
2. In Step 2, a nonstick vegetable spray may be used to prevent sticking.

VARIATION: 1. For 2 meat exchanges and 1 vegetable exchange, use 2 lb, 12 oz beef in Step 1, to yield 10 2-oz portions beef and 10 1/2-cup portions vegetables.

TABLE 4 Recipe for Modified Diets (Meat, Ground, Bland)--Syrian Beef Stew

Yield 10 Portions
Pan Size: 4-Quart Saucepan

Each Portion: 6 Oz

Percent	Ingredients	Weights	Measures	Grams	Method
53.20	Beef, ground, thawed	2 lb, 8 oz		1,134	1. Cook beef in its own fat until it loses its pink color, stirring to break apart. Drain or skim off excess fat.
18.95	Tomatoes, canned	14 oz	1 3/4 cups	404	2. Add tomatoes, green beans, brown sugar, salt, cinnamon, and allspice. Heat to simmering; simmer 2 minutes.
6.67	Beans, green, frozen	5 oz	1 cup		
1.08	Sugar, brown		2 tbsp	23	
0.56	Salt		2 tsp	12	
0.03	Cinnamon, ground		1/4 tsp	0.7	
0.03	Allspice, ground		1/4 tsp	0.7	3. Make slurry with starch and water. Add to meat mixture while stirring. Bring to simmer.
0.52	Starch, edible, modified		3 1/2 tsp	11	
18.96	Water, cold	14 oz	1 3/4 cup	404	4. Place in blender and puree 10 seconds.
					5. Portion in 6-oz servings. Garnish with chopped pimientos if desired.

TABLE 5 Recipe for Modified Diets (Thinned Strained)--Syrian Beef Stew

Yield 10 Portions
Pan Size: 4-Quart Saucepan

Each Portion: 8 Oz (1 Cup)

Percent	Ingredients	Weights	Measures	Grams	Method
24.85	Beef, ground thawed	1 lb, 9 oz		714	1. Combine beef, water, tomatoes, beans, brown sugar, soup and gravy base, salt, cinnamon, allspice, and pepper. Simmer 5 minutes.
32.23	Water	2 lb	1 quart	926	
14.97	Tomatoes, canned	15 oz	2 cups	430	
5.01	Beans, green frozen	5 oz	1 cup	144	
2.02	Sugar, brown	2 oz	1/3 cup	57	
0.97	Soup and gravy base beef flavored	1 oz	3 tbsp	28	2. Place in blender and blend on high speed 2 minutes or until smooth.
0.70	Salt		1 tbsp	20	
0.07	Cinnamon, ground		1 tsp	2	
0.03	Allspice, ground		1/3 tsp	0.8	
0.01	Pepper, black ground		1/8 tsp	0.2	
2.57	Margarine	2 1/2 oz	1/3 cup	74	3. Make a roux with margarine and flour.
0.28	Flour, what, general purpose		1 tbsp	8	4. Add blended ingredients to roux and heat to simmer while stirring.
0.49	Starch, edible modified	1/2 oz	1 2/3 tbsp	14	5. Make a starch slurry with starch and water.
15.80	Water, cold	1 lb	2 cups	454	6. Add to blended mixture while stirring. Heat to simmer.

TABLE 6 Recipe for Modified Diets (Renal Diet)--Syrian Beef Stew

Yield 10 Portions
Pan Size: 4-Quart Saucepan

Each Portion: 30 Grams Cooked Beef
50 Grams Cooked Green Beans
30 Grams Sauce

Percent	Ingredients	Weights	Measures	Grams	Method
26.84	Beef, diced, thawed	1 lb, 4 oz		567	1. Cut dices in half (approximately 10-gram pieces). Do not trim fat.
1.33	Salad oil	1 oz	2 tbsp	28	2. Brown beef in salad oil.
0.47	Onions, dry, minced		1 tbsp	10	3. Add onion, garlic, cinnamon, and allspice and saute 1 minute.
0.19	Garlic, dehydrated		1 tsp	4	
0.08	Cinnamon, ground		3/4 tsp	1.7	
0.08	Allspice, ground		3/4 tsp	1.7	
16.09	Water	12 oz	1 1/2 cups	340	4. Add water, cover, and simmer 1 hour or until tender. Remove meat and save for Step 9.

155

	Ingredient				Procedure
34.88	Beans, green, frozen	1 lb, 10 oz		737	5. Simmer green beans in seasoned liquid from meat, 10 minutes or until beans are tender. 6. Remove green beans and save liquid for sauce in Step 8.
2.04	Lemon juice	1 1/2 oz	3 tbsp	43	7. Combine lemon juice, sugar and starch. Blend well.
1.33	Sugar, granulated	1 oz	2 tbsp	28	
0.57	Starch, edible, modified		1 1/3 tbsp	12	8. Add starch mixture to reserved liquid while stirring, and heat to simmer.
16.09	Liquid from meat and green beans plus water if needed	12 oz	1 1/2 cups	340	9. Assemble each portion as follows: 30 grams cooked beef, 50 grams green beans, and cover with 30 grams sauce.

NOTE: 1. One portion contains approximately 8.5 grams protein, 40 milligrams sodium, and 6.16 milliequivalents potassium.

2. In Step 1, beef, diced, thawed (beef for stewing, frozen, diced, USDA IMPS) was used.

THE TESTING PROCEDURE

Each product developed in the experimental kitchens is tested by a small panel of dietitians or food technologists for overall quality. This same panel tests the product again after 0°F storage at 3 months and 6 months.

Cutter Army Hospital, Fort Devens, Massachusetts, agreed to test the modified diet recipes in the hospital cafeteria. The dietitian there reports that so far they have been very good. Some of the recipes have also been included in the modified diet menus at Moncrief Army Hospital, Fort Jackson, South Carolina, where the modified diet items are prepared and frozen in quantities of 50 to 100 servings. In August when I was there, the production schedule listed 100 portions sodium-restricted, calorie-restricted, bland pizza and 100 portions calorie-restricted bland pizza. This was one of our new modified diet recipes, developed for 10 portions, and consisted of one bread exchange and one meat exchange. After conferring with the dietitians, we decided to change the recipe to two meat exchanges and increase it to 100 portions each. The cook and I started preparing 200 individual pizzas. It soon became apparent that this was going to take all day. The recipe was immediately adapted for a sheet pan to be cut after baking (20 portions to the pan), with special consideration for the pizza to fit on the special entree dish to be used.

The preparation of these many different diet items, however, can take a long time each day in the diet kitchen. Why not then make them in quantity ahead of time and freeze them? Just because a hospital is on a cook-serve system, there is no reason modified diet items could not be prepared ahead of time and be available when needed. On this small scale, one needs a blast freezer, freezer space for storage, and a system of inventory. The modified diet menu and the inventory would be the basis of producing these items.

DISCUSSION

QUESTION: Would you predict the future of retort-cooked, pouch-packed foods? Will they replace frozen foods?

TUOMY: I don't know if this question is asking about my official position or my personal position on the subject of whether the pouch foods will replace frozen foods. The official position is that they probably will

sometime in the future. My personal position is that
they won't. So you can take your pick. The pouch foods
are really a very good quality canned food, but they are
still a canned food. They are processed to sterility.
They are excellent for our operational rations, and I
think they are good for special purposes at home, for
camping, and that sort of thing. But in this country at
least, where we have abundant refrigeration, I cannot see
them at this time or at any time in the near future
replacing frozen foods, unless the cost of energy gets so
high that we cannot afford to have refrigerators.

QUESTION: Will we be given a list of the recipes
mentioned, where they can be purchased, what is the order
name and number? Also the list of exchanges?

TUOMY: I assume that you are talking about the dental
liquid mixtures and where they can be purchased. Of
course, we don't know that at the moment. We know that
some firms are interested in making them; and I assume
that once they do, they will advertise them. However, we
have technical reports on all of these special diets that
we made for Walter Reed Hospital, and we are perfectly
willing to send them to whoever asks for them. The
requests for the dental liquid have been the highest
response of any we have ever had in technical reports.
For the other various modified diets, we also have
technical reports. If you would like to have them, leave
your name with Carol Shaw, Jessie McNutt, or me. If you
provide your name and address, we will be happy to send
them to you. They are public publications, and as long
as we have any in stock we will send them out.

QUESTION: Are the Natick modified diet and dental
liquid recipes available to the general public?

TUOMY: The answer is: Certainly. They are paid for
by the general population's tax money, and the general
population is welcome to them. The fact is we are happy
when people come in and ask for results of our work. It
makes us feel good that we are doing something.

QUESTION: Have there been any recent studies on the
energy costs of the three different systems--conventional,
cook-chill, and cook-freeze?

TUOMY: There have been some energy studies. They are
in the literature. I have not read them for some time,
so I can't remember them enough to quote from them. But
if you go into the literature, you will find them. In
those energy studies there are a lot of "ifs." It all
depends upon how long you are going to store your frozen
foods and so on. It is very difficult to quantify the
various systems because of the variations in them.

QUESTION: Do you have any ideas why hospitals using restaurant-style menus have had fewer quality control problems?

TUOMY: As an old production man who worked 10 years in industry, I can tell you one thing. If you have fewer items and are making larger volumes, you can exercise tighter control. As a former quality control man, I was always happy to get into that situation. It is when you are making small amounts of any one item and changing items every day that you get into quality problems. My guess as a quality control man is that as soon as you start using a restaurant menu you are cutting down the number of your products and you are making much more of any given product. So therefore, you will control it tighter.

SHAW: I think that is true basically. But I think the other thing is that you are using the same recipes day after day even in a conventional system. So, if your ingredients are prepared by an ingredient preparation area, and brought to the cooks, it is immediately noticeable if they are different from day to day. The end product should be the same from day to day. There is just that constant repetition along with larger volume of items that makes the whole process easier to manage and control.

QUESTION: With energy costs being what they are, it has been suggested that all ingredients be added simultaneously to reduce the amount of cooking time. If this is the trend, what effect will this procedure have on modified diet flavoring?

SHAW: I think in any recipe you have, there are certain reasons for adding ingredients at different times. Obviously, when you are making a cake, you know that it makes a difference whether you add things all at once or one at a time. I think, generally, to add as many ingredients together as you can at one time is certainly a good idea both from energy-cost and labor-cost viewpoints. In some ways, such as adding your spices and herbs early, you will increase the blending effect that you will get from the cooking together of these items. So, I think the answer is yes; to a point, it is good to add as many things together as you can. But there are some cases where you have to add things in increments.

State-of-the-Art Review of Health Care Patient Feeding System Equipment

Paul Hysen and Jeanne Harrison

Major advances in technology, engineering, and design
concepts have been responsible for the development of new
health care oriented food service systems in recent years.
New and existing equipment items have been designed or
modified to support cook-chill, cook-freeze, convenience,
or the more traditional conventional systems. The selection of equipment to support a food service program has
become more critical due to the increasingly complex requirements of hospitals and medical centers. The availability of more equipment options and the escalation of
construction, labor, and equipment costs have also added
to the significance of the system/equipment decision.
Equipment must be appropriately selected to support not
only the preparation process, but also the tray assembly
process, the meal distribution process, and the meal
service process.

Before cook-freeze, cook-chill, and convenience food
service systems came into existence, the major equipment
selection dilemma faced by the manager of a conventional
food service system was what source to purchase the equipment from and which brand or manufacturer to buy. While
these details of equipment purchase are still important,
several other questions must be answered first. These
questions or key decision points are assembled in Figure
1 as a schematic representation of options and their
interrelationships. State-of-the-art equipment is available for conventional, cook-chill, cook-freeze, or convenience food service systems. Qualitatively satisfactory

Paul Hysen is President and Jeanne Harrison, R.D., is
Senior Associate of Hysen & Associates, Inc., Food
Systems and Facilities Planners, Novi, Michigan.

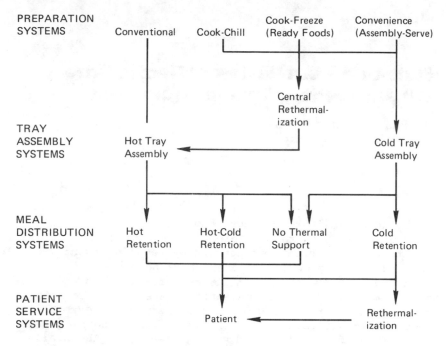

FIGURE 1 Hospital patient food service system matrix.

food service programs exist throughout the United States
using each of these major preparation systems. While the
criteria used for the selection of any system is individual, selection of one system or another can enhance some
options and preclude others at the tray assembly, meal
distribution, and meal service points. A detailed discussion of food preparation systems and selection criteria
for these systems is presented in other sections of these
symposium proceedings.

This paper presents basic information regarding the
selection of state-of-the-art equipment that will support
quality hospital patient care feeding programs. While it
must be recognized that a food service system is an
integrated process, or a continuum from food receipt to
patient consumption, for purposes of presentation clarity
information will be presented in three sections: meal
assembly system, meal distribution system, and meal
service system.

MEAL ASSEMBLY SYSTEM

Meal assembly includes all activities that relate to patient tray preparation (see Table 1). These assembly activities can occur in one location within the hospital food service kitchen (centralized tray assemby) or in numerous locations closer to patient bed areas throughout the hospital or medical center (decentralized tray assembly).

Figure 2 is a schematic representation of the variations of the meal assembly process that are presently in use in health care settings throughout the United States. Equipment required for the different assembly systems has been designed to support a variety of requirements, including the need to maintain sufficiently hot or cold food temperatures to minimize bacterial growth as defined by various regulatory authorities, the need to maintain high-quality appearance and taste for maximum patient acceptance, and the need to promote efficiency of labor utilization.

While a complete patient meal tray ready for service consists of hot, cold, and ambient components, the definitions adopted can be that hot tray assembly refers to assembly systems supported with soup, meat, vegetables, and starches that are hot (140°F or above) at time of tray assembly; whereas cold tray assembly refers to assembly systems supported with these components in either chilled, frozen, or ambient states. Typically, cold tray assembly implies a downstream rethermalization process.

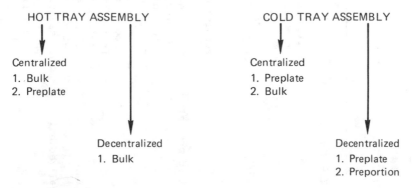

FIGURE 2 Major tray assembly systems.

TABLE 1 Meal Assembly System

Major Tray Assembly System	Benefits	Constraints
Hot tray assembly		
Centralized bulk	Quality control is easier to achieve when assembly occurs in one location. Food is produced, assembled, distributed, served, and eaten within a narrow time period, thus reducing potential food handling errors resulting from increased processing sophistication.	Immediate delivery of the tray from the point of assembly to the patient bedside is required to ensure satisfactory quality. Coordination between the nursing department, materials management department, and the dietary department must be excellent to ensure immediate delivery of patient trays.
Centralized preplate	Menu variety is enhanced. A large inventory of food items can be maintained, including a variety of special diet items. Economies of scale due to large batch production, including special diet items, can be achieved. A wider array of menu items can be offered at each meal to enhance patient meal selection oportunities.	The equipment is sophisticated and requires extensive employee retraining and education to ensure that proper procedures are followed. The system is equipment-dependent. Equipment performance may, in some cases, be difficult to ensure.
Decentralized bulk	The assembly point is close to patient areas, making both normal tray delivery and late tray delivery easier to accommodate.	A multiplicity of assembly points requires more supervision labor. Large capital equipment cost required for increased number of assembly areas.

Cold tray assembly

Centralized preplate	Menu variety is enhanced. A large inventory of food items can be maintained. The assembly process can be scheduled by the food service manager to optimize labor utilization; it does not have to occur just prior to mealtime.	Equipment is sophisticated and requires extensive employee retraining and education. Some food items cannot be accommodated in the system. Acceptance in some community settings has been low due to the system's highly structured and uniform appearance.
Centralized bulk	Menu variety is enhanced. A large inventory of food items can be maintained. The assembly process can be scheduled by the food service manager to optimize labor utilization; it does not have to occur just prior to mealtime.	Some food items cannot be accommodated in the system.
Decentralized preplate or preportion	Menu variety is enhanced. A large inventory of food items can be maintained. Response time to patient food selections and diet changes is minimized. Appropriate temperatures of food items can be regularly achieved.	A large capital outlay for decentralized unit equipment is required.

Hot Tray Assembly

Three hot tray assembly systems are commonly found: hot centralized bulk, hot centralized preplate, and hot decentralized bulk. Examples of each of these systems in use today and the type of equipment they are using are given below.

Hot Centralized Bulk

With this system, entree items are held hot after production and served as quickly as possible to the patient. This is accomplished by placing prepared foods into steam table pans and covering and placing the pans into hot food-warming cabinets, where they remain until placed in steam table compartments for use during tray assembly. (Note that steam tables should have a heat-generating source above the food item as well as below when on the tray assembly line.) The period of time between production, assembly, distribution, and service is minimal in a hot centralized bulk system. Therefore, a major consideration is the physical proximity of the production and assembly areas. These two areas must be close to each other in order for the system to function to its maximum capability.

Hot Centralized Preplate

After the food is produced, it is portioned into individual or combination containers. Each container is then quickly frozen and typically encapsulated in some form of protective film and placed in cassettes (food storage racks). When food items are ready to be used, they are tempered (allowed to thaw in a controlled environment), then centrally reheated in a conveyor microwave oven prior to placement on a tray during the assembly process. Food is ordered electronically in this system, allowing it to remain in a chilled environment until it is needed for a specific tray. When it is needed, the food is retrieved, heated, and assembled. The production and assembly areas can be some distance apart because food is sent to the assembly area chilled. The assembly equipment is operated independently of the production equipment, with the chilled and frozen storage acting as the connecting link.

A recent variant to the system described above is a hot centralized preplate system that depends on chilled rather than frozen storage, and bulk rather than individual portion pack containerization. Food items (meat, vegetable, and starch) are plated in a chilled state during the actual assembly process and brought up to serving temperature by a conveyorized combination microwave/convection oven.

Hot Decentralized Bulk

Like the hot centralized bulk system, the hot decentralized bulk system depends on a narrow time period between production, assembly, distribution, and service. The major difference is that instead of the patient tray being assembled in one location, the food products are produced in one location (usually a form of central kitchen) and transported in heated and/or chilled trucks to various locations throughout the hospital for assembly at a site near the patients. Equipment to maintain temperature must be provided at each location. This equipment can include food warmers, steam tables, roll-in refrigeration, rack carts, and a conveyor belt. Since some food items do not transport or hold well (e.g., fried or grilled foods), cooking equipment (more appropriately called "finish cooking" equipment) is usually provided to enhance the quality of the final product.

Cold Tray Assembly

Cold, chilled, or frozen food can be assembled using a decentralized preplate system, a decentralized preportion system, or a centralized preplate or bulk system.

Centralized Preplate

This system differs from the hot food systems in that all food is rapidly chilled immediately after production. After it is chilled, it is preplated either for freezing or for storage in a chilled state. Equipment required to complete this process can include a precooler, a blast freezer, an L-bar sealer, a shrink tunnel, front-loading mobile rack shelving, rack carts, roll-in refrigeration, and a conveyor for the assembly process.

Centralized Bulk

Food items are produced in large quantity, chilled in
large quantity, stored in bulk containers, and assembled
from a chilled state on individual patient trays for
distribution, typically to decentralized pantries where
the meal is rethermalized prior to service. Equipment
unique to this system would be pump/fill stations;
tumbler chillers; large walk-in coolers for long-term
storage; and high-velocity, quick recovery roll-in
chillers. An assembly conveyor with refrigerated support
and storage equipment would also be required, as it would
be for the centralized preplate system previous described.

Decentralized Preplate or Preportion

A decentralized preplate or preportion system refers to
the place of assembly of preplated or preportioned chilled
or frozen entree items. In this example, food is assembled for the patient tray in a location remote from the
central production area and close to the patient. This
system has found acceptance in an acute care setting
where high priority is given to those patients who require
demand feeding due to the critical nature of their illness. To support this system, roll-in refrigeration,
rack carts, and an assembly area or conveyor belt are
needed, as well as a major form of rethermalization
equipment.

Conveyor Systems

Whether decentralized or centralized, each assembly area
requires support equipment to assemble the trays. The
size of the area, the number of trays to assemble, and
the type of production system and its sophistication will
determine the type of conveyor system required to provide
support.

Figure 3 indicates options for tray assembly equipment.
The options include manual conveyors, such as the flat
belt conveyor or tray slide; simple mechanical conveyors,
such as the skatewheel or roller types; and motorized
conveyors, such as the semiautomated computer-controlled
conveyors, straight line conveyors, and a circular
"merry-go-round" conveyor.

MANUAL

↓

Tray Slide

SIMPLE MECHANICAL

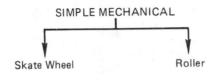

Skate Wheel   Roller

MOTORIZED

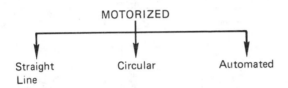

Straight   Circular   Automated
Line

FIGURE 3   Meal assembly process--
conveyors.

MEAL DISTRIBUTION SYSTEM

The process of meal distribution includes all activities
relating to the systematic movement of assembled tray
units from the point of assembly to the patient area.
This discussion will focus on thermal retention/support
systems involved in the meal distribution process (see
Table 2).
   Figure 4 shows the major categories for thermal
retention/support systems. They include: hot thermal
retention/support, hot and cold thermal retention/
support, no thermal support, and cold temperature support.

Hot Thermal Retention Systems

Three types of equipment are typically used to keep food
hot during distribution. The first of these is the pellet
system. With pellets, temperature is retained through
the use of a heated enclosure system. The bottom half of
the enclosure is metal, usually stainless steel, with an

TABLE 2   Meal Distribution System

Major Meal Distribution System	Benefits	Constraints
Hot thermal retention systems		
Pellet system	Support equipment and system operation are conventional and uncomplicated. There is no requirement for a special plate; any standard-sized china. No special insulated delivery cart is required.	Provisions for maintenance of cold items such as milk, salads, jello, ice cream, etc., are not made. Hot food cannot be held for a long period of time (more than 45 minutes). Additional serviceware pieces need to be inventoried, stored, transported, and washed.
Insulated components	Only the dinner plate and food are heated; there are no pellet bases to heat. It is simple in operation, requiring no special pellet dispensers to purchase. There is no burn hazard to the attendant or patient because there is no hot pellet base or pellet disk. No special insulated delivery cart is required.	Additional serviceware pieces need to be inventoried, stored, transported, and washed. Attractive insulated components are often taken home by patients as useful momento of their hospital experience.
Heat support cart	Thermal energy can be controlled to plate and/or bowl as required. The cart allows for food to remain heating until tray is removed for service to the patient.	Special sophisticated motorized carts and special trays with heaters are required. The potential for maintenance/repair problems is high. The cart and the trays are dependent

Each cart has an insulated drawer for ice cream and other frozen desserts.
Heat energy continues to be supplied to food during the transportation process.

on the use of disposable dishes.
Disposable dishes could be uneconomical from an operational cost standpoint and could be considered unacceptable from an aesthetic perspective.
No provisions are made for maintenance of cold food items at proper temperatures except ice cream.

Hot and cold thermal retention systems

Pellet and sublimation refrigeration

A synergistic heat maintenance effect is achieved.
Simplicity of cart construction and ease of sanitation.
The cart is lightweight, which provides for ease of mobility.

The operational cost and complexity of the required carbon dioxide cooling system is a consideration.
Patient trays are not completely assembled at a central assembly point. Final assembly occurs in patient areas.

Split tray

Centralized supervision and control of the total assembly process.
No reassembly of tray components is required in the patient areas.
Good temperature retention of both hot and cold items.
The system accommodates late trays within a reasonable period.

The cart is heavy and bulky. A motorized version may be required if any ramps are to be negotiated.
The carts are difficult to sanitize.
The initial cost of the cart is high and maintenance costs can be high.
Due to the relatively heavy weight and limited maneuverability, carts and wall surfaces are subject to damage.

Match-a-tray

Same as described for split tray except that consolidation is required on the patient level.

Same as described for split tray. Additional labor must be applied at the patient area to reassemble the complete patient meal.

TABLE 2 Continued

Major Meal Assembly System	Benefits	Constraints
Insulated trays	Maintains hot and cold zones well without external heat or refrigerant sources. Simplicity of transport is achieved. It does not require a heavy, enclosed delivery cart. Stacked trays protect and insulate food. There is less load on the dishwashing facility due to disposables. There are no complex components to repair, replace, or maintain.	The purchase of special disposable dishes results in higher operational costs. Food holding time is limited to 45 minutes. The long-range cost could be substantially higher than other systems due to disposable and lease costs. Hot foods may take on a "steamed" appearance in the hot compartment due to its relatively small volume and lack of venting. Possible adverse patient reaction to eating from a compartmentalized tray. Trays can be difficult to sanitize completely due to deep cavity construction. The top and bottom tray compartments do not nest; more storage area required. Rigid presentation and placement of dishes is a limitation of the system.
Insulated components	Only the dinner plate and food are heated. There are no pellet bases to heat. It is simple in operation, requiring no special pellet dispensers to purchase.	Additional serviceware pieces need to be inventoried, stored, transported, and washed. Attractive insulated components are often taken home by patients as

171

	There is no burn hazard to the attendant or patient because there is no hot pellet base or pellet disk. No special insulated delivery cart is required.	useful momentos of their hospital experience. Hot food holding time is limited to 30 minutes; cold food items can be held longer.

No thermal support

| Covered tray | The tray is a simple standard unit. The equipment cost of the system is low. | Requires an immediate and responsive transportation system.
High labor component is required for transportation process.
No thermal support is available for entree and other food items. |

Cold temperature support system

| Umbilical refrigerated cart | Lightweight cart.
Carts are simply constructed and easily sanitized.
Low maintenance of refrigeration machinery due to its permanent location. | No thermal support is provided during the actual transportation process; it depends on the residual cold effect achieved by precooling the cart. |
| Roll-in refrigerator cart combination | Standard manufactured equipment is utilized, e.g., roll-in refrigerator and upright enclosed tray cart.
Cart is lightweight, simply constructed, and easily sanitized. | No thermal support is provided during the actual transportation process. |

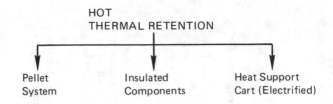

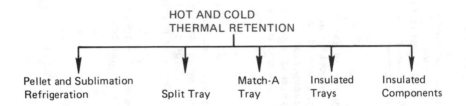

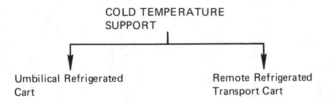

FIGURE 4 Meal distribution system.

integral heat energy storage reservoir. An insulated
container is sometimes used for thermal support to the
hot beverage and the soup. Several new types of pellet
systems have been introduced that are much improved compared with the original pellet design. The most original
of these uses the retained heat of melted wax (stearic
acid) as its heat energy source.

Benefits of the pellet system can be described as
follows: There is no requirement for a special plate of
a specific size or material; any standard-size china dish
with heat-retaining capability may be used. There is no

requirement for a special insulated delivery cart when pellets are used; carts can therefore be lightweight for easy maneuverability. The system is designed to support the temperature and moisture content of the food as it is placed on the dish originally. This offers management the assurance that the food will arrive in a condition similar to what it is when it leaves the assembly area, if delivery is accomplished within the system's time limits.

Constraints of the system can also be described. This system only maintains hot food items; there is no provision for maintenance of cold items. There is a limit to the amount of time the system can safely support appropriate hot temperatures. Hot foods cannot be held longer than 45 minutes. The system also requires additional serviceware pieces, including pellet bases and special pellet heating dispensers that have to be inventoried, stored, handled, and sanitized.

Insulated components are an alternative method to the pellet system used for temperature retention. Here, the main entree dish is encapsulated with an insulated dome cover and insulated bottom liner. Insulated components are used for soup and hot beverages and may also be used for cold food items. Numerous manufacturing companies now offer this system on a lease or purchase basis.

Benefits to using this system include the following: There is no burn hazard to the food service worker or patient because no component is heated to a high temperature; only the dinner plate and food are heated. It is a simple operation, requiring no special heating equipment to be purchased. There is no requirement for the use of special insulated delivery carts; therefore, the light-weight, easy-to-maneuver carts are acceptable. This system depends on appropriate temperatures at the time the food is put into or on the insulated component.

Constraints of the system include the following. The hot food holding time is limited to no longer than 30 minutes. There is no capability for raising temperatures, so if temperatures are inappropriate at the time of tray assembly, then holding time is further reduced. This system requires many additional serviceware pieces to be inventoried, stored, handled, and sanitized three times daily. In addition, hospitals that have used this system have found that because the insulated components are attractive and appealing to the patient, they are often taken home as a useful memento of the hospital stay.

A third alternative used to keep food hot during

distribution is the motorized, self-powered heat support cart with heating units and disposable dishes. The cart provides for individual heat control of each tray via a self-contained battery power source in the cart and individual heaters under the plate and bowl positions on the tray.

The benefits of this system include the fact that the heat can be controlled to the plate and/or bowl as needed. The cart allows for heat energy to be supplied to the food during the transportation process and to continue heating until the tray is removed to be served to the patient. Each cart has an insulated drawer for ice cream and other frozen desserts to be stored until they are ready to be placed on the patient tray prior to service.

The constraints include the following: It is a complex system that requires sophisticated motorized carts and special trays with heaters. It has the potential to produce maintenance/repair problems that some hospital maintenance departments may not be familiar with. At the present time it is dependent on the use of disposable dishes. In addition, the unit makes no provision for the maintenance of cold food temperatures except ice cream and frozen desserts.

Hot and Cold Thermal Retention Systems

Four approaches are commonly used to maintain food temperatures. The first is the pellet and sublimation refrigeration system. This is a relatively lightweight cart that separates hot and cold food in different compartments. The hot food temperature is maintained using pellets and a synergistic heat maintenance effect resulting from containing the pellets and the hot food in one compartment separate from the cold items.

This system depends on the food being plated at appropriate temperatures, because the equipment is planned to maintain, not boost, temperatures. The benefits of the system include cold food temperature maintenance in addition to the hot food maintenance. The cart is simply constructed, resulting in ease of sanitizing.

The operational cost and complexity of the carbon dioxide system that supports the cold temperature compartment is a constraint to the system. In addition, patient trays are not completely assembled at a central point. Final assembly still must occur in the patient area, without direct supervision.

With the split tray approach, patient trays are assembled with hot and cold food items on the same tray. They are then placed into a mobile cart that has hot and cold chambers. The tray straddles a center divider, with hot temperature maintenance support on one side and a cold compartment on the other.

The split tray system provides for good temperature retention for both hot and cold food items and can accommodate holding late trays for a reasonable period of time without significant deterioration. An additional benefit is that there is no reassembly of tray components in the patient area--both hot and cold items are on one tray.

The constraints of the split tray system are as follows. The cart is heavy and bulky; a motorized version may be required if the hospital or medical center has any significant ramps that must be negotiated during distribution. The weight and limited maneuverability of these carts can result in wall surface damage within the hospital. In addition, the cart is difficult to sanitize, maintenance is usually high, and its initial cost represents a significant investment.

The match-a-tray was a predecessor of the split tray. With this approach, one tray is used for the patient's hot food components and one tray for the accompanying cold food. Both are transported in one cart with hot and cold compartments. The hot and cold components are consolidated onto one tray immediately prior to service.

The benefits and constraints of this system are similar to those of the split tray system (see above). Another constraint results from the additional labor at the patient area to reassemble the complete meal. This process is usually accomplished without direct supervision, allowing for the possibility errors in reassembly of patient meals.

The original version of the insulated tray system used stackable trays with permanent or disposable dishes and reusable beverage containers. Separate temperature zones within the stackable tray created columns of temperature support. The trays and lids were lightweight and could be easily stacked on a lightweight cart for transportation to patient areas. More recent versions consist of total enclosure trays that in effect encapsulate each food component or each temperature group of components for thermal support. Units are available for use with disposableware, permanentware, or a combination of serviceware types.

The benefits of the system are as follows. There are no complex components to repair, replace, or maintain.

Dishwashing is reduced when disposable dishes are used. The trays maintain hot and cold zones without external heat or refrigeration sources. Thus, the system is easy to use and dependable.

The constraints of the system can be described as follows: The system is primarily made available on a lease basis. The long-range cost of this arrangement should be explored as well as such short-range advantages as little or no capital investment. It may be substantially higher in cost than other distribution systems in the long range. The holding time is limited to 45 minutes. During this time, some hot foods take on a steamed appearance. In addition, the rigid presentation and placement of the dishes can be a menu planning constraint. Some patients have an adverse reaction to eating from the rigidly compartmentalized tray. The top and bottom tray compartments do not nest, so storage space must be planned accordingly.

No Thermal Support

This system, if in fact it can be described as a system, uses no thermal support or retention equipment to maintain food tempratures and can best be exemplified by the covered tray. It is most commonly employed when a tray must be transported only a short distance, or in some cases for late trays when they are called for, prepared, and immediately delivered.

The cost of the covered tray is low initially, and the maintenance costs are low. The construction of the tray is simple, making it easy to sanitize.

The constraints of the system are as follows: It requires an immediate responsive transportation system. There is no thermal support available for the entree and other hot food items that lose temperature rapidly and become qualitatively less desirable.

Cold Temperature Support

A transportation cart that is designed to maintain chilled food temperatures yet does not require mechanical refrigeration equipment to be part of the basic transportation unit is an umbilical refrigerated cart. Cold trays are assembled, loaded into an enclosed insulated cart, and transported to remote pantry areas where they are con-

nected to a wall-mounted or floor-borne refrigeration
unit. As needed, the trays can be removed from the refrigerated cart and rethermalized for each patient. In
some installations the carts are attached to the refrigeration unit and cooled before they are loaded with
patient trays for distribution.

The carts are lightweight and simply constructed;
therefore they are easy to transfer and sanitize. The
refrigeration machinery is also a low-maintenance item,
making this a low-maintenance system.

The constraints include the fact that there is a requirement for refrigeration equipment in the main kitchen
and on the patient floors. This additional refrigeration
makes the system more expensive to install. The system
also requires equipment to rethermalize meals prior to
service to patients.

The most commonly employed form of cold environmental
support to patient food trays awaiting subsequent rethermalization and service is through the use of a roll-in
refrigerator/cart combination. A standard roll-in refrigerator, either a single- or multiple-door configuration,
is provided in each decentralized pantry unit. An upright, usually enclosed tray cart containing the patient
food trays is placed within the refrigerator. If the
cart is of the enclosed type, doors provided on the cart
are opened prior to placement in the refrigerator, thus
effecting proper chilled air circulation to the food.

Since this system uses standard manufactured components, initial capital costs are generally reasonable;
and maintenance cost is favorably affected. However,
since standard components imply standard sizes or dimensions, design flexibility is reduced, and trays and other
components must be selected to fit units available.

MEAL SERVICE SYSTEM

The final stage in patient tray handling systems is the
meal service system (see Table 3). This includes all
activities that relate to the delivery of the assembled
meal tray to the patient room or eating area. This
discussion will focus on cold delivery systems that
require rethermalization before service to the patient.

TABLE 3 Meal Service System

Major Meal Service System	Benefits	Constraints
Microwave ovens	The food is cooked very rapidly. "On-demand" patient feeding can be achieved.	Food is easily overcooked, and some foods tend to rethermalize unevenly, leaving hot and cold spots. Food does not brown, causing some foods to have an unnatural appearance. A trained operator is required to rethermalize all food products. Employee training is essential to the success of the program. Maintenance of microwave ovens can be a significant cost factor.
Convection ovens	Oven cavities can accommodate 12 to 30 meals at a time; thus higher efficiency can be achieved in the rethermalization and reassembly process as compared to a microwave system.	The speed is increased as compared to a conventional still air oven; however, the process is not as fast as a microwave oven. Some food products experience excessive cooking losses; in others, there is a thickened surface layer on the food from the rethermalization process. Some food products do not rethermalize to a uniform temperature.
Infrared ovens	Food is rethermalized at a faster speed than conventional still air ovens. Oven cavities can accommodate 16 to 24 meals at a time; thus higher efficiency can be achieved in the rethermalization and reassembly	Energy consumption for rethermalization is comparatively high. Soups are not accommodated by the infrared equipment and must be separately handled. Dishes and covers become very hot in the rethermalization process.

Integral heat ovens and carts

process as compared to a microwave system.
Minimum intervention by employees is required to rethermalize food.
Efficiency and speed of service is enhanced due to multiplicity of meals rethermalized at the same time.
Integrally heated dish acts as "pellet" system to continue to provide thermal support to hot food after service to patient

Food products may burn to or stick to the heated dish.
Certain food items, such as soup or hot breakfast cereals, are difficult to rethermalize.
Dishes must be sprayed with a release agent to prevent sticking when using certain food items.
Warewashing time is increased, particularly for the breakfast service, because of the food that sticks to dishes.
Ongoing operation costs are comparatively high due to replacement and lease costs.
An inflexible presentation of the tray and rigid placement of items when employing the cart-borne system.

Contact plate heater carts

Reduced pantry labor due to rethermalizing and refrigerating patient trays in the delivery cart.
Allows pantry to be reduced in size and lowers equipment cost by eliminating need for reheating ovens.
Minimum intervention by employees after assembled tray has been dispatched from main tray assembly location.

Cart maintenance may be a problem due to complex electrical components.
Special trays and dishes are required--usually disposable dishes--which can increase operating costs.
Rethermalization can only be done from the chilled state, not from the frozen state.
The cart is presently being field-tested; its performance has not been proven.
Operating cost appears to be high, based on preliminary data available.
An inflexible presentation of the tray and rigid placement of items are aesthetic limitations of the system.

Rethermalization of Patient Meal Components

Five major types of equipment are used in the rethermalization of patient meals: microwave ovens, convection
ovens, infrared ovens, integral heat ovens and carts, and
contact plate heater carts.

The first of these, the microwave oven, is an oven
cavity in which short waves of electromagnetic energy
travel at near the speed of light. This energy is
absorbed by the food, which then generates heat through
increased molecular action. The cavity of the oven is
not heated except for the steam that is formed as the
food heats. With this system, individual plates of cold
food are reheated just prior to meal service to the
patient. One meal at a time is reheated and, for this
reason, most systems depend on more than one microwave
oven per pantry.

The benefits of this system can be described as
follows. The system delivers hot meals to the patient
very rapidly. Each microwave oven can rethermalize one
meal every minute, which is particularly advantageous for
late trays or for demand feeding food service programs.

The constraints of this system can also be described.
Certain foods such as fried chicken cannot successfully
be reheated, requiring some menu adjustment. Food can
easily be overcooked and in some cases unevenly cooked,
requiring special attention to plating procedures in the
assembly process. If original cooking is to be done,
certain foods such as meats and desserts do not brown,
causing them to have an unnatural appearance. The success
of this system is dependent upon the individuals responsible for the rethermalization. Employee training and
monitoring programs are essential.

Convection ovens use a heated oven cavity and a fan
during the cooking process. The fan is used to disturb
and strip away the relatively cooler layer of air that
would lie next to the food product in a still-air oven,
thus bringing hot air in contact with the food to speed
the rethermalization process. Convection ovens can accommodate many plated meals at one time.

This system does provide hot meals because they are
heated in close proximity to patients. There are no
special trays, plates, or covers to purchase, inventory,
and wash.

The constraints of the system include the fact that
mass reheating of various types of entrees does not offer
any thermal selectivity for individual entree heating

requirements. This could result in some products being
overheated and some products being undercooked; therefore,
for best results, this system discourages individual variations in size or composition of entrees. In addition,
some food products demonstrate excessive cooking losses,
while others demonstrate a thickened surface layer on the
food from the rethermalization process.

The third type of rethermalization equipment, though
less frequently used, is the _infrared_ _oven_. Infrared
ovens use electrically generated radiant heat energy
applied to the top and bottom of dishes positioned in the
oven cavity. With this system, food is cooked at a speed
generally matching that of a convection oven or of the
integral heat oven described later.

The constraints of the system include the following:
The equipment configuration does not currently provide
for rethermalization of soup or hot breakfast cereals.
Also, the food must be approximately the same thickness;
otherwise, food items will heat unevenly, resulting in
some plates not achieving appropriate temperatures.

A fourth system for the rethermalization of cold food
is the _integral_ _heat_ _oven_ _and_ _cart_. This system uses an
integrally heated dish that is actually a small electronic
impulse-resistance oven. Here, plates with contactors and
wiring imbedded in the plate bottom receive and distribute
heat evenly throughout the dish. The impulse action of
the timing mechanism of the oven helps eliminate scorching
during the rethermalization process.

The benefits of this system can be described as follows: The speed of the meal service is enhanced because
24 meals can be rethermalized at the same time. The
system requires a minimum amount of intervention from
food service workers to accomplish rethermalization. The
construction of the dish with the contactors and wiring
in the bottom has the potential to reduce the overheating
that can be a problem when food is rethermalized. In
addition, the heated dish acts as a pellet system, continuing to provide thermal support to the food after it
is served to the patient.

The constraints can be described also: The dishes
must be sprayed with a release agent to prevent sticking
when using certain food items. Because the dishes have
wires and contactors in the bottom and are usually leased
from the manufacturer, they increase the on-going operational cost of the system. The system, when employed in
its newest car-borne configuration, requires a rigid
placement of items on the tray, resulting in an inflexible

presentation. Warewashing time is increased, particularly for the breakfast service, because of food that sticks to the dishes from that meal. In addition, it takes the same amount of time to heat 1 meal as it does to heat 24 meals. The system does not have the capability to respond rapidly to individual meal service, resulting from late trays or demand feeding food service programs.

The contact plate heater provides the fifth system to rethermalize in-patient hospital food. With a contact plate heater cart, food is portioned into dishes that exactly fit holes or cutouts in a tray. The position of the dish determines whether or not a food item will subsequently be rethermalized when a cart containing multiple trays is placed in a rethermalization cabinet (modified roll-in refrigerator). Physical contact between the plate heater in the rethermalization cabinet and the bottom food container (dish) accomplishes heat transfer. This is an example of a heat conduction system.

The benefits of the system include the following: The system requires minimal intervention by employees after the assembled tray has been dispatched from the main assembly area to the patient service area. Trays are efficiently refrigerated and rethermalized in the same delivery cart, which minimizes the amount of handling required in the patient pantry area. This allows the pantry to be reduce in size and lowers the equipment cost of the pantry by eliminating the need for rethermalization ovens. At the present time the system can be purchased or leased.

The constraints of the system are as follows: The cart is presently being field-tested. Its performance has not been proven. Preliminary data available at this time seem to indicate that the system costs will be high. The system requires special trays and dishes that must be purchased or leased. The tray presentation and placement of individual items are inflexible. Because the cart is sophisticated in its construction, it can be assumed that there will be increased maintenance requirements. In addition, the system can only reheat from the chilled state; it cannot reheat from the frozen state.

SUMMARY

The health care food service industry has long sought the attention of high-technology designers and manufacturers. Food service managers have longed for the ability to tell success stories of the application of advanced state-of-the-art technology rather than being relegated to describing their systems as conventional and traditional food service systems. In fact, many equate "conventional" and "traditional" with old fashioned and antiquated.

As we enter the high-tech era, we should learn from those who have preceded us. An appropriate example would be the computer or data-processing industry. Certainly, no industry is advancing faster technologically; computer capability is increasing as rapidly as computer costs are falling. What 5 years ago filled a good-sized room and cost $500,000, now sits on a desk and costs one-hundredth of that amount. Yet the industry leaders of the computer age uniformly agree that it is not the hardware (equipment) that counts, it is the software (management systems) that determines the success or failure of a specific application.

And so it is also with the health care food service industry. If we are distracted by exciting technology and we allow ourselves to focus on equipment selections first, we are bound to fail. Modern technology can provide us with an infinite variety of equipment combinations and system configurations--so many that we will completely lose sight of our goal. And what was our goal? Patient feeding--providing a nutritious, attractive, appetizing meal, pleasantly served at the appropriate time. That is a very human goal, not a cold technological, equipment-driven goal.

To achieve our patient-oriented goal, we should begin our development process by being results-oriented rather than equipment-oriented. Establish the program goals, the human goals, the qualitative goals, and the economic goals, and then apply state-of-the-art technology to support and enhance the process for the benefit of the patient.

SELECTED BIBLIOGRAPHY

Avery, A. 1980. A Modern Guide to Foodservice Equipment. CBI Publishing, Boston, Mass.
Ball, E. W., and K. Durfee. 1978. Hospital airline galley. In Abstracts of Health Care Management Studies. Wesley Medical Center, Chicago, Ill.
Beaton, M. 1976. Tray system cuts labor, improves food. Dimensions in Health 53(6):30-31.

Berkman, J. 1976. Cooking in the new age. Food Manage. Mag. November:40-44, 72.

Berkman, J. Personal communication. Cedars-Sinai Hospital, Los Angeles, Calif.

Brown, B., and P. R. Doyon. 1974. An automatic electronic food system. Hospitals 47(63).

Deignan, P. 1978. Food services merge to contain costs and enhance menu. Hospitals 52 (19):157-162.

Deignan, P. Personal communication. United Hospitals, St. Paul, Minn.

Donovan, A. C., and O. B. Ives. 1966. Hospital Dietary Services, A Planning Guide. Public Health Service Publication No. 930-C-11. U.S. Government Printing Office, Washington, D.C.

Doyon, P. 1981. A Hospital Assesses the Results of a Seven Year Experiment in its Food Service and Dietetics Department Using Cook-Chill, Cook-Freeze Preparation Methods and Electronic, Food Component Retrieval, with Automatic Tunnel Microwave Rethermalizing. Unpublished report. West Jersey Hospital, Voorhees, N.J.

Doyon, P. Personal communication. West Jersey Hospital. Camden, N.J.

Ellis, C. 1976. Old, new meld in ready foods system. Mod. Healthcare 6(1):41-43.

Fee, T., and E. Wilson. 1977. Ready foods provide opportunity to improve service flexibility. Hosp. Admin. Can. 19(4):16, 18-20, 22-24, 26, 27, 30.

Henning, J., and D. Tanis. 1974. Are ready foods ready now? Mod. Healthcare 1(2):65-66, 68.

Herz, M., et al. 1977. Analysis of Alternative Patient Tray Delivery Concepts. Army Natick Research and Development Command, Natick, Mass.

Herz, M., et al. 1978. A Systems Analysis of Alternative Food Service Concepts for New Army Hospitals. Army Natick Research and Development Command, Natick, Mass.

Herz, M. L., and J. J. Souder. 1979. Preparation systems have significant effect on costs. Hospitals 53(1):89-92.

Hysen, P. 1980. Food Production and Patient Service System Evaluations. Unpublished report. Hysen & Associates, Novi, Mich.

Kazarian, E. A. 1969. Work Analysis and Design for Hotels, Restaurants and Institutions. AVI, Westport, Conn.

Kazarian, E. A. 1977. Food Service Facilities Planning. AVI, Westport, Conn.

Keefe, R. T., and S. A. Goldblith. 1973. Hospital feeding via microwave kitchenettes: a cost analysis. Abstr. Hosp. Manage. Stud. 27(8):16, 18-19, 22-23.

Koncel, J. 1976. Planning pervades conversion to cook/chill system. Hospitals, 50(22):87-92.

Koogler, G. H., and S. Nicholanco. 1977. Analysis of a decision framework for prepared food systems. Hospitals 51 (February).

Kotschevar, L. H., and M. E. Terrell. 1977. Food Service Planning: Layout and Equipment. John Wiley & Sons, New York.

Kotschevar, L. H., and M. E. Terrell. 1977. Food Service Planning: Layout and Equipment. 2nd ed. John Wiley & Sons, New York.

LeBourdais, E. 1977. Improve service with the cook-freeze process. Dimensions in Health Service 54(6):25-26.

Livingston, G.E., and G. M. Chang. 1979. Food Service Systems, Analysis, Design & Implementation. Academic Press, New York.

Mental health facility reduces labor costs with new food service system. 1977. Mod. Healthcare 7(1):62-63.

Millcross, J., M. A. Hill, and G. Glew. 1974. Consequences of a switch to cook-freeze. Hospitals 48(17):118, 124-126.

National Sanitation Foundation Standards. 1973. National Sanitation Foundation, Ann Arbor, Mich.

Patrick, A. 1977. Robots in the kitchen. Dimensions in Health Service 54(6):22, 24.

Peddersen, R., et al. 1973. Increasing productivity in foodservice. Inst./Vol. Feed Mag.

Reference Guide, Sanitation Aspects of Food Service Facility Plan Preparation and Review. 1978. National Sanitation Foundation, Ann Arbor, Mich.

Rinke, W. 1976. Three major systems reviewed and evaluated. Hospitals 50(4):73-77.

Shea, L. A. 1974. Heat-retaining capabilities of selected delivery systems. J. Am. Dietet. Assoc. 65(4):430-436.

Sneider, R. M., and R. P. LeMay. 1979. An evaluation of meal tray systems. Abstr. Health Care Manage. Stud. 15.

Stockdale, L., M. E. Matthews, and B. Mateicka. 1972. Streamlining central tray assembly. Hospitals 46.

Unklesbay, N. F., et al. 1977. Foodservice Systems: Product Flow and Microbial Quality and Safety of Foods. Research Bulletin 1018. University of Missouri--Columbia College of Agriculture, Agriculture Experiment Station.

186

Unklesbay, N. 1977. Monitoring for quality control in
alternate foodservice systems. J. Am. Dietet. Assoc.
71(4):423-428.
Wilson, R. L. 1977. Major food service systems as applied
to St. Elizabeth medical center: review, evaluation,
and recommendations. Abstr. Health Care Manage. Stud.

DISCUSSION

QUESTION: Of the tray assembly systems addressed,
which offers the least potential for error, incorrect-
food-on-tray type of error. In other words, which system
is the most simple?

HYSEN: I don't know if I really have an answer. I
can only say that we started out many years ago--putting
this in a historical perspective--with decentralized tray
assembly operations, with the hot cart going up to the
floors. That's the only way that we were assured of
getting at least lukewarm food to the patient. But that
exposed us to very high risk in terms of having a lot of
semitrained people dealing with foods under minimal or no
supervision. So, with the advent of temperature retention
systems and temperature suppport systems (we were able to
centralize that process), thanks to good old Henry [Ford]
we were able to put a conveyor belt in and streamline
that process and also reduce staffing. We also think
that we reduced errors because we could apply direct
supervision under centralized controlled conditions.

We are now going back to some extent to decentralizing
operations for qualitative reasons. I think you're going
to lose control, and I think management can handle that
if they can bring a level of control to them. For years
Detroit was the automotive capital of the world and all
of the major automotive companies produced all of their
products in Detroit. Now, for various and sundry reasons,
manufacturers are building plants in California, in
Florida, in the Sun Belt states, and in many other
locations, accepting the fact that it might be more
cost-effective to produce all cars, all widgets, or all
television sets in one location, but for other reasons to
be diversified, perhaps to better serve the market. Our
market is the patient; so again we have to look at what
is the best system in terms of patient service.

QUESTION: Where do you store the food in the cold tray
assembly preplate process while you build inventory for
the one-hour liquid nitrogen? Doesn't quality
deteriorate?

HYSEN: Yes, obviously. Somebody wanted to get into liquid nitrogen because that was the state of the art at the time. That's where the bells and whistles could be found, and everybody wanted to be there. That's not a good application--food should be produced, heated, cooled as rapidly as possible, and wrapped and then frozen. You don't want that product to be stored for a week or so until you get around to freezing it, to build up enough to turn on the liquid nitrogen tunnel. But liquid nitrogen is 270°F below zero; it is very difficult to keep, so you have to keep it in a vacuum-insulated dryer flask, and it cannot be kept under pressure. It has to be allowed to escape through the atmosphere. In one hospital with about 200 beds, a very small liquid nitrogen tunnel was used. Even under that application more of the liquid nitrogen evaporated than was used in the freezing tunnel, because the distributor would only bring in 300 gallon vials. By the time the vial was needed, most of the liquid nitrogen had evaporated.

QUESTION: With the more technical advanced components of patient feeding systems, where do we find the employees?

HYSEN: I don't know.

QUESTION: How much training is envisioned and how does it affect employee retention and turnover?

HYSEN: An excellent question. When you're dealing with the state of the art, you're dealing with infor- mation that has not been totally disseminated. Let me put this in an analytic context. When we automated our consulting office a couple of years ago, we brought in word processing units rather than typewriters. These have screens and are very neat--they type as fast as 200 words per minute. They never make a mistake or misspell anything, but it takes about a month to train somebody how to operate them, and, consequently, with normal employee turnover it's difficult to deal with in an office environment with advanced equipment. When you hire someone, she or he may be familiar with an IBM executive or selectric typewriter, which is generally available, but they perhaps have not seen a CPTA 1000 word processor--and there's going to be training involved. One has to recognize that, and you're not going to find employees who are familiar with microwave ovens and con- vection ovens and decentralized operations. And, in a health care employment network, people come in, they're trained, they work out, and then they end up in materials management or some other area. You are dealing with a more sophisticated system. Your opportunities for hiring are diminished, and your training has to be stronger.

QUESTION: Which of the three motorized tray assembly conveyors is most labor-efficient? How many trays per minute is the average of each?

HYSEN: I have seen, personally, a motorized tray assembly process from two trays per minute under very bad conditions to ten trays a minute. That's quite a scale. Ten trays a minute has been achieved under nonselective menu conditions in a state institution or a city hospital with no selection and very limited diets. In a standard operation very high rates can be achieved. Under normal tray assembly conditions with normal menus, five to eight trays per minute can be expected. In a chilled food program, production will increase because hold-ups will be fewer and less difficult to handle. You don't find high-tech employees--you train them. In a market where there are only two to four hospitals, the associate hospital in town is unlikely to have the same kind of system. Finding employees with the skills that you need is generally difficult.

QUESTION: You said that a two-week supply of preplated entrees only takes an hour or so to go through that liquid nitrogen tunnel--that the tunnel was used 26 hours a year. How would you justify this?

HYSEN: I am not attempting to justify it.

QUESTION: Which system has better heat retention qualities and what is the approximate time period of heat retention? Unitized base with metal cover? Unitized base with insulated cover?

HYSEN: The insulated cover with the same time period does provide some significant improvement in the heat retention quality of that system, as opposed to a metal cover. The metal covers are very durable; however, they tend to stay with us too long and they start getting banged up and dented and they look like they have been through three wars. But they still do their job, so we keep them. Less expensive plastic covers unfortunately have to be replaced more often, but they are about comparable to the metal cover in heat retention quality.

QUESTION: SECO is producing a pellet with a waxlike substance that liquefies on heating no more than 300°F. It holds a higher heat longer than metal unitized pellets.

HYSEN: Yes, there are some pellets coming out. SECO has one, but it encapsulates a wax substance in the base unit rather than employing a piece of metal as the heat sink. The waxy substance is safe material; it is bee's

wax--nothing more than steric acid. It goes through a
phase change just like water does when it changes to ice,
and the delayed heat of fusion added to the specific heat
of that product gets a little better effect off that.
Again, the manufacturer has provided us with some time-
temperature curves that we have not verified ourselves,
but the system seems to provide better heat retention
than a straight pellet system.

QUESTION: The more moving parts you have in a system,
the more chance you have for electrical failure.

QUESTION: What if a monorail loses power half-way
there? What does the patient eat?

HYSEN: The automatic car transportation systems are,
I would have to say, near the end of their life-cycle.
We saw a lot of activity in that area in the early 1970s
(everybody wanted an automatic car transportation system
until they had one). Then, they found out that they
replaced $2.00-an-hour cart pushers with $5.00-an-hour
technicians to maintain that system and yet needed to
keep the $2.00-an-hour cart pushers because the system
was unreliable. In the very first one I saw, the food
service department gave up using the system at all for
the first 6 months. For the food service workers, this
was a centralized tray assembly with decentralized microwave ovens. They finally adopted a process where they
would make up all their trays and keep the carts down in
the walk-in refrigerator, and just before mealtime the
food service workers would push the carts and rethermalize
the product. This is not a typical situation. It became
more and more typical when people realized getting the
cart to the patient was just a small part of the problem.
You needed somebody to push that cart down and put it in
a refrigerator and make sure that it was secure, that it
was under proper temperature control, and that other
things started happening in the pantry at the appointed
time like making coffee and getting things ready for meal
service. Now who is going to run the pantry--is that
going to be food service or nursing service? Well, a lot
of hospital designers thought it should be nursing service. After all, food service is part of total patient
care, and total patient care should be a responsibility
of the nursing staff. Nurses should rethermalize the
food. Nurses didn't want to rethermalize the food--
nurses are not food-oriented. So, there are a few
facilities that still operate with the nursing service
doing the rethermalizaton. When food service departments
took over that process again, food service workers had to

leave the kitchen tray assembly area and go to the patient
areas to accomplish the rethermalization process. If
they had to go up there anyhow, why not take the cart at
the same time? A lot of facilities have avoided use of
the automatic cart transportation system; they just push
the carts up.

QUESTION: How do the insulated trays compare with
either the unitized base with metal cover or unitized
base insulated cover for heat retention?

HYSEN: They are comparable. In any of those systems,
particularly the insulated tray or the insulated component systems, you need to be very careful of the food.
If you can put food in hot at the appropriate temperature,
chances of having a successful process are enhanced.
There is a significant difference between those two
systems.

QUESTION: What is the difference of heat loss between
insulated trays with disposable dishes and insulated
trays with heated dishes?

HYSEN: There is a significant difference between
disposable dishes and china dishes when used with an
insulated tray. An insulated tray does not provide any
energy; its theory is to encapsulate and maintain that
heat energy or, in the cold side, to store heat energy.
The mass of a disposable dish is not very significant in
relationship to the to the mass of the food; consequently,
it is not going to add anything.

If you can use a permanent dish that has some mass to
it and if you heat that dish, you have a better system
with longer heat retention time because you're adding
energy. The dish now becomes an energy source; it is now
a pellet. So we find that insulated tray systems work
much more successfully at breakfast, particularly with a
heated dish. Eggs, pancakes, or something of that nature
have a lot of mass to maintain temperature, so the dish
does add significantly to the overall performance of that
system.

QUESTION: Who manufactures the dry-ice cart system?

HYSEN: Is it still available? St. Mary's in Ann
Arbor, Michigan, is the only hospital I know that's using
such a cart.

QUESTION: How often is dry ice added to the cold
retention side of the cart?

HYSEN: It's not. The hospital using that dry ice
cart is not adding dry ice any longer. They used to add
the dry ice prior to every meal to chill down the center

section. They no longer chill the center section, but they are still splitting the hot components and using the hot pellet system for the soup and the coffee off to the side. They found that the dry ice only added a 5° temperature difference on the cold side. They still separate the two so that the pellet system does not radiate heat into the cavity of the cold food.

QUESTION: What about the trayveyor system for tray distribution?

HYSEN: There are a couple of new facilities using the trayveyor, a tray distribution system that takes trays from a central location directly up to patient floors located above the central assembly point. It is not very much used these days because we have an opportunity to have a kitchen directly below the patients' floors. The trayveyor system is good for only that one purpose and that is to go directly up and deposit trays on the floors above. That is a very commonly employed tray distribution system.

QUESTION: A correction that I would like to offer. The Sweetheart cart is not plugged in for heat maintenance; rather it is battery operated.

HYSEN: The Cryovac system is sometimes referred to as the Kap-Cold system, a process where you cook food to 80 percent doneness. It is primarily a kettle-based operation. Anything that you can pump out of a kettle is appropriate to this system. You cook out of a kettle at a temperature typically of 185°F-190°F. As the food goes into a pouch or bag--that is a multirated bag that has a very high oxygen barrier--it is aseptically packaged at that temperature. Then the bag is sealed and goes into a water ice bath at about 30°F for 45 minutes to 1 hour where it is tumbled and the product temperature is brought down very rapidly. You have now encapsulated the product and stopped the cooking process; you have aeseptically packaged it giving it a 30- to 45-day shelf life. There are some here in the audience, Ray Peddersen from LDS Hospital in Salt Lake City and someone here from United Hospitals in St. Paul, who have been operating Kap-Cold systems for some time. United Hospitals has been operating for 3 years now; Ray started earlier this year. In Michigan, Elias Big Boy, the largest restaurant chain the state, installed the Cryovac Kap-Cold system about 3 years ago and was having trouble with some of the cream soups. They distribute products out of a central commissary to about 160 locations throughout Michigan, and they were having trouble with Canadian cheese soup and clam chowder. They were operating strictly a cook-chill operation with open kettles, and it only involved cooling down and pumping the food into pure pack containers for shipment to their units. The Kap-Cold was much less expensive than to go into a full freezing process. It is a system that has demonstrated itself and is going to respond with very high quality in some very specific applications.

Effect of Meal Assembly, Meal Distribution, and Meal Service on Sensory Quality of Food

Carol Anne Dahl

Glew (1973) comments that sensory qualities are at their best at the moment of purchase for cold foods or immediately after cooking for hot entrees. Newer hospital food service systems, such as cook-chill and cook-freeze, involve three additional processing steps after cooking: meal assembly, meal distribution, and meal service. Without strict managerial control, additional time and handling during these process steps will decrease the sensory qualities of food at service. Although meal assembly, distribution, and service functions have been an integral part of the newer hospital food service systems since 1960, published information related to management and control of these functions has not become common knowledge. Thus, the first purpose of this paper is to consider aspects of sensory quality of food that are related to meal assembly, meal distribution, and meal service.

Sensory quality of food is a complex concept in food service systems. Ward (1979) suggested that sensory quality of food may have greater meaning in food service than in food manufacture because of the complex sensory and psychological interactions: between components and courses, between the courses themselves, between food and the beverages consumed with the meal, and between the food eaten and the entire ambience of the meal, including the standard of service, the room, the decorations, the noise level, and presence of the other patients.

Carol Anne Dahl, Ph.D., R.D., is Assistant Professor of Food Service Systems Management at Michigan State University, East Lansing.

Sensory quality of food in a food service system is also a complex concept because it must be considered from a systems perspective; all processing steps in a food service system have a cumulative effect on the quality of food at the point of service. Sensory quality of food begins with menu engineering and systems design and is closely related to detailed purchase specifications, standardized food formulations, and closely monitored storage techniques. Meal assembly, meal distribution, and meal service procedures will also cumulatively affect the ultimate sensory quality.

Eating food, one of life's basic necessities, can also be one of life's greatest pleasures. Eating hospital food is frequently considered a necessity rather than a pleasure. Hospital patients are without a choice of eating facility, and they are confined to their "environment" (bed) more closely than are other clients of institutional food services--in schools or industrial cafeterias, for instance.

MEAL ASSEMBLY

As Dr. Bobeng suggests elsewhere in these proceedings, meal assembly "includes activities in a centralized area to prepare the patient meal for distribution of trays to the patient." Meal assembly is frequently the most important step in determining the visual appeal of meals. How the meal looks is usually the first and most important message of sensory quality received by the patient.

Plating Procedures

Placing food on the correct type of plate according to predetermined patterns or criteria is called plating. Plating involves the dish or other food container as well as the food intended for service.

Plating procedures are significant in a food service setting for two reasons:

1. For visual appeal: Pleasing arrangements of food on a dish heighten the visual appeal of the meal. Orderly and neat presentation of food on the plate suggests to the patient that the food is clean and has been carefully handled.

2. To facilitate reheating: Different plating
procedures facilitate various types of reheating.

Plating for Visual Appeal

People tend to eat with their eyes. Give them food and,
if they like the looks of it, they will like the taste of
it. Restaurants practice showmanship on the plate for
profit; health care institutions can adopt similar
practices.

Attractive food is a matter of taste and attention and
is not dependent on food cost, labor, or the type of food
service system. Attractive food can be served in any
operation. Axler (1974) identifies five elements that
contribute to the visual appeal of a plated meal.

1. Composition of the dish. The food items on the
plate have unity and wholeness.
2. Good use of color. A single appealing color, or
complementary or contrasting colors may be used.
3. Good contrast in texture and shape: Shapes, forms,
and textures contrast with other shapes, forms, and textures. The banana split and the hamburger are excellent
examples.
4. Pleasing relationship of food to dish: The food
fills the plate or other service container in an aesthet-
ically pleasing manner.
5. Identification of food: The patient can easily
and correctly identify all food items.

An example of poor planning for sensory quality at
meal assembly would be an all-brown dinner served on a
single, thick, heavy 9-inch institutional china plate--
brown meat with brown gravy, brown potatoes with brown
gravy, and brown vegetable au gratin. Or, consider a
white dinner consisting of off-white pork chops accompanied by off-white sauerkraut, off-white potatoes, and
off-white-to-yellow applesauce. Some institutions have
mastered the art of uniform presentation; everything is
portioned with an ice cream scoop.

Like the restaurant consumer, the hospital patient
demands more than satiety and balanced nutrition. He
responds to the total eating experience, the taste and
smell of food and the pleasant anticipation of the food
stimulated by its visual appeal. The food service operation's solution, of course, is to look at the total eating

experience as the customer sees it. Which is more appealing, the dry breakfast cereal in the box in an institutional bowl, or the dry breakfast cereal out of the box in a sparkling glass bowl topped by a piece of fresh fruit? Which is more appealing, a plate awash in chicken a la king, or the chicken a la king in a pastry shell? Which is more appealing, a closed ham and cheese sandwich seemingly cut in two with a hatchet, or the same sandwich, open faced, with overlapping rolls of ham and cheese on one side of the bread and tomato slices on a lettuce leaf on the other side?

To see meal presentation more effectively, the food service director can examine color photographs of the food trays. In so doing, he might ask himself the following questions:

1. What is it? Vegetable soup or Manhattan clam chowder? If it looks like vegetable soup, how can the patient be made to see that it is clam chowder?

2. Does anyone want to eat the food on this tray the way it looks?

3. Is the meal's appearance consistent with the care and quality of production?

4. What would it take to make this item more attractive? More fit to be served in a fine restaurant? It might be 2¢ worth of cheese or 3¢ worth of anchovies. A garnish should compliment the flavor of the food and its color.

5. Why use that particular dish? Is it too large? Is it too small? Is it the same thick, heavy institutional dish that the patient sees every day? How can the plate, platter, or tray be used as a frame for the food?

6. Is the meal neat as assembled?

Both attractive and ordinary foods become more appealing when they are well arranged on the service container. The food service director may only occasionally have control over plate size, shape, and color, but always has control over food arrangements on the plate, as well as the arrangement of plates on the tray.

The Plate The plate should be clean and unmarked. Chipped or cracked plates must be discarded for microbiological reasons. Portioning should be neat. Plates of food splattered with food or gravy drippings by tray line personnel working too fast detract considerably from the food design on the inside of the dish and, of course, from the overall appearance of the tray.

Arrangement of Food on the Plate   To arrange food on plates attractively, the food director must consider the patient's perspective. The patient is seated before the plate. Rather than seeing a circle, he sees a near side and a far side. Height of food on the plate is also noticed. Axler (1974) presented the following guidelines for arrangement of food on a plate.

   1.   Establish a back and front to the plate; build from the back to the front. Left-right symmetry is not necessary; left-right balance is necessary.
   2.   Make sure that one point on the plate is the focus, but not necessarily the physical center.
   3.   Vary the height of the food items so that the plate has three definite dimensions. Mounds are better than blobs, rolls better than slices, shingled layers better than piles, and so on.
   4.   Vary the form and texture of the items. Avoid three mounds, three circles, all squares, all cubes, and so on.
   5.   Place items with contrasting colors next to each other; separate similarly colored items.
   6.   Use the rim of the plate or an even border of the plate as a frame, and keep the food in the well. When something extends beyond the border, make the effect a dramatic accent.
   7.   Make the arrangement simple, using as few elements as possible to make a pleasing composition that will cover the plate.
   8.   Arrange the food so that the eye travels into the plate, not away from it, following lines made by the food. The bones of chops, for example, can point in and up rather than down and out.
   9.   Place larger, heavier-appearing items on the inside of the composition and lighter pieces on the outside.
   10.   Use an odd number whenever possible--three, five, or seven pieces of vegetable rather than four, six, or eight.
   11.   The importance of garnishing cannot be over-emphasized.

Portion Size   Portion size is controlled by the food service system. Overly large portions can result in food

waste and expense to the food service system or in over-
eating, and discomfort to the patient. Patients of different weight, sex, and age may prefer different portion
sizes. Portion size should be a selective item on a
hospital patient's menu whenever feasible. Quantity of
food served can also be controlled by the patient when
menu item categories not previously checked on the menu
are not served.

Packaging During meal assembly and distribution, all
foods are to remain covered (USDHEW, 1976). This regulation results in sandwiches and salads wrapped in
plastic, and individual packets for salt, sugar, and
cream; domed or covered items make up the rest of the
tray. Such wrappings are not in congruence with meals
served at home or in restaurants. These wrappings may
give an institutional appearance to the tray. Unwrapping
the food just prior to bedside delivery may remove some
of that institutional aura.

Plating to Facilitate Reheating

Various reheat subsystems are used by hospitals. Franzese
(1981) surveyed short-term care hospitals in New York City
and determined that 15 percent use a food service system
in which food is reheated by microwave energy, while 4
percent have implemented a subsystem in which food is
reheated by conduction. Each reheat subsystem has plating
procedures specific to the subsystem to facilitate adequate and even reheating. Reheat subsystems using
microwave radiation involve intricate plating techniques;
recommendations for plating in microwave reheat subsystems
follow.
    The shape of plates used for food in a microwave reheat
subsystem is important. The ideal container to microwave-
heat food evenly is the donut shape because no center
exists for underheating, and food will receive about the
same amount of heat overall. However, in food service
operations, food is usually heated on a dinner plate
(round, oblong, or square), and the dinner plate usually
contains more than one food item, such as meat, vegetable,
and starch. Thus, there are three types of food, each
with its own heating characteristics, and no donut-shaped
plates. For such a meal, the vegetable requires the least
heat. The required plate would then have a lot of center

space (square plate, airline style), because the center area, heating more slowly, would protect the vegetable and all foods would arrive at the same temperature in the same heating period. Plating procedure manuals have been developed by most hospitals using microwave ovens. The manuals usually include directions for plating and a picture of the completed entree dish.

For microwave reheating the generalization may be made that foods at the outside edge of the plate will heat quickly. Thus, hard-to-heat foods should be placed at the outside of the plate. Hard-to-heat foods include thick meat, mashed potatoes, compact foods like lasagna, thick ends of chops, fish fillets or chicken pieces, and meats covered with thick sauce. Conversely, food on the inside of a plate will heat slowly. Easy-to-heat foods should be placed on the inside of the plate for microwave-heating. Easy-to-heat foods include uniform small pieces (peas), thin sliced meat, seafood $\leq 1/2$ inch thick, breads and other bakery items, casseroles, foods in sauce, narrow ends of chops, fish fillets, and chicken pieces.

Occasionally, easy-to-heat foods may be placed on the rim of the plate or hard-to-heat foods may be placed in the center of the plate. The alternative is to modify the heating characteristics of the food. Heating characteristics or times may be modified using the following techniques:

1. Containerize. Place small vegetables like peas in a small dish. Containerization makes foods harder to heat.
2. Change the shape of the food. For instance, cut potatoes in different forms. Large shapes make foods harder to heat. Conversely, smaller pieces make foods easier to heat.
3. Add sauce or gravy to make food harder to heat.

To summarize, follow these rules for plating in a microwave subsystem:

1. Know easy- and hard-to-heat foods.
2. Develop and follow plating diagrams.
3. Place hard-to-heat foods on the outside of the plate.
4. Place easy-to-heat foods on the center of the plate.
5. Consistently use correct portion size.
6. Use plate covers to prevent dehydration in heating,

to reduce splatter, and to decrease cleanup time. Plating recommendations for other types of reheat subsystems are readily available from equipment manufacturers and experienced users.

Plating Procedures: Specifications

Plating procedures can be formalized through development, distribution, and use of specifications. The goal, of course, is to achieve a constant quality in meals at point of service to patients. Consistency in visual appeal and predictable reheating results add to long-term patient and personnel satisfaction.

Plating specifications may be in written or in picture form. Since it is generally accepted that a picture is worth a thousand words, photographs, possibly Polaroid, available to tray line personnel could aid in standardizing plating arrangements. In the future, mechanical methods for portioning may be more readily available and would eliminate human error as a factor in plating.

Quality of Menu Items on the Tray Line

Selective menus coupled with special diets requires having numerous items available for possible placement on patients' trays. Beef, for example, may be regular, low-fat, or low-salt; with gravy or without; in 1-, 2-, or 3-ounce portions; rare, medium, or well done; roasted or boiled; cold or hot. To decrease the requirement for numerous items on a tray line, the preferred strategy has been to combine diets so that the patient on a low-fat diet also gets low-salt and/or low-calorie servings. Combining special diets may result in an unnecessary decrease in calories or in the sensory quality of food for some patients. When special diets must be combined because of limited space during meal assembly, special consideration should be given to the types of diets combined, and potentially complicated food items should be reevaluated for exclusion from the menu.

Centralized Meal Assembly

A centralized tray assembly process results in better control of meal appearance, plating procedures, and neatness, since all activities are usually under the control of one supervisor, Such control is a major factor in providing consistency in quality of the meal.

Temperature of Meal Assembly Environment

Air-conditioned or refrigerated environments used for meal assembly may reduce the temperature of hot foods during meal assembly. Temperatures of hot foods should be monitored throughout the meal assembly process.

Pellet Systems

Care must be taken to ensure that unitized bases are heated early enough to be hot when meal assembly begins. Much of the sensory appeal of a meal is related to temperature at service.

Training Meal Assembly Personnel

Tray line personnel training should stress the importance of neatness for food on plates, as well as of plating arrangements. The importance of the visual appeal of food to patients has been discussed.

Time of Complete Meal Assembly

Meal assembly in hospital food service systems is generally completed on a belted tray line. Two or more food service personnel usually work beside the belted tray line, adding individual menu items to patients' trays according to selections previously marked on a menu. The personnel may average from two to six trays per minute. Partial or completely mechanized tray line assembly units may soon achieve state-of-the-art status and decrease assembly time.

Total time for a meal assembly depends on the size of the insitution. A 500-bed hospital averaging four trays/ minute would require approximately 2 hours for meal assembly. Such time periods, even with food at room temperature, are viewed as microbiologically safe (USDHEW, 1976). Taking such time could also cause undesirable changes in food temperature when food is not properly refrigerated

or held hot. Temperatures of milk or jello could rise
from 7°C/45°F to 13°C/55°F in less than 1 hour. If
refrigerated carts were to be used to transport the milk
or jello to patient areas within 45 minutes, temperatures
would probably be too high for optimal sensory satisfaction.

Temperature of Food Items at Meal Assembly

Conventional hospital food service systems generally cook
food on the day of service, place it into steam tables
for hot holding, and then put it onto plates for service.
The temperature of foods plated hot should be $\geq 60°C$
(USDHEW, 1976). Newer food service systems precook food
items from one to several days in advance of service,
chill or freeze the food items until the day of service,
and then place them (temperatures $\leq 7°C$) onto plates.
Food that is plated chilled will be reheated before
service to patients.
   Cardello et al. (1981) compared the effect on sensory
quality in food of five food delivery systems—two hot-
plating delivery systems (Control and Therma Tray) and
three cold-plating delivery systems (Sweetheart, Aladdin,
and 3-M). Each system was tested for 10 days; 68 individual food and beverage items—72 percent hot entrees,
28 percent cold entrees—were designated for evaluation
of appearance, temperature, flavor, texture, and overall
quality by hospital patients on a medical surgical ward.
Results indicated that the major difference among delivery
systems was between hot-plating and cold-plating systems.
Food served from hot-plating systems was preferred by
patients because reheating previously cooked and frozen
food had adverse affects on its quality at point of service. The temperature of food served from the cold-
plating system by 3-M had the most favorable rating,
while the system by Aladdin was preferred by cooks for
its compactness and its ability to keep food cold.

Meal Assembly Checklist

A meal assembly checklist could be developed by food
service directors and used by tray line supervisors to
further ensure high sensory quality in food. Such a
checklist might include the following items:

1. Tray Appearance
    a. Is the standard tray setup used as in the diagram?
    b. Are the items correctly placed on the tray?
    c. Are the portions of uniform size and shape as stated in the standard?
    d. Are the items neatly placed and portioned?
    e. Is the tray overcrowded?
    f. Are the dishes free from cracks, stains, or dents?
    g. Is the tray attractive in color and shape?
    h. Are the food items correctly placed on dishes?
    i. Are the hot food items correctly placed for heating?
    j. Are the cold food items correctly placed?
    k. Are the napkins, silverware, condiments, cups, or mugs in their respective places?
    l. Do the items on the tray correspond with the coded items listed on the menu?

2. Tray Accuracy
    a. Do the items on the tray correspond with the coded items listed on the menu?
    b. Are the utensils, condiments, cups, and saucers provided on the tray?
    c. Does the condiment kit correspond with the coded items listed in the menu?
    d. Is the food on each component of the tray the right item allowed in the diet?
    e. Are there items on the tray that are not supposed to be there?

It is well to develop a standard tray line checking technique to help the supervisor increase accuracy and speed. This technique will not be difficult if the menu format supplies a good eye transfer and movement from the product on the tray to the menu. The most modern technique to improve tray line accuracy is the optical scanner together with universal product coding. Research may lead to a computerized system, in which accuracy is checked by the computer through signals from the menu items themselves.

MEAL DISTRIBUTION

Meal distribution may involve heated, ambient-temperature, or chilled food transported in heated, ambient-tempera-

ture, or chilled environments. Time-temperature histories
of food during meal distribution are critical factors
that have sensory as well as microbiological implications
for food quality.

Hot-Holding

Of possible food-environmental temperature combinations
during meal distribution, holding hot food hot has caused
the greatest concern. Glew (1973) concluded that the use
of heated transport or hot cupboards in any food service
system must result in palatability losses.

Hot-holding food--warm-holding is the similar term used
in Europe--is a technique used during meal distribution in
hospitals that incorporates a stationary steam table or
movable cart. Hot-holding was studied in several inves-
tigations at the Swedish Food Institute, Göteborg, Sweden,
and proves to be a most effective means of destroying the
sensory quality of food previously achieved by careful
choice of raw materials and of processing and storage
conditions (Bengtsson and Dagersbog, 1978). Quality loss
in hot-holding can be reduced by proper control of the
environment and temperature, but the most effective
countermeasure is to minimize the time between preparation or reheating and serving (Bengtsson and Dagersbog,
1978).

Karlstrom and Jonsson (1977) concluded that the
greatest quality losses from hot-holding are due to sensory attributes. According to these authors, potatoes
are most affected, followed by fish and meat. Similarly,
Hill et al. (1977) reported that creamed potatoes prepared from fresh potatoes deteriorated in flavor even
after only 15 minutes of hot storage. Dehydrated potatoes
do not exhibit such change even after 60 minutes of hot
storage. Hansson et al. (1972) also determined that hot-
holding had the most deleterious effect on flavor. They
found that potatoes were the most sensitive, followed by
peas, fish cakes, and hamburgers.

Bengtsson and Dagersbog (1978) determined that hot-
holding two or more hours strongly reduced the sensory
quality of beef slices and patties. Precooking differences of the beef products in this cook-freeze system
were not noticeable following two hours of hot-holding.

Requirements for microbiological quality in food,
however, may conflict with requirements for maximizing
sensory quality. Grater (1979) states that the drive for

higher standards of cleanliness and prevention of cross-contamination has affected food quality. Of highly serious concern to the caterer is legislation on storage temperature requirements for cooked food awaiting service. Retaining food at temperatures of 74°C and above can have disastrous effects on quality.

What are the possible corrective measures? Hill et al. (1977) concluded that since hot-holding is so destructive to vegetables, vegetable products should be consumed directly following reheating and not be subjected to further hot-holding. If necessary hot-holding should be $\leq$30 minutes. Jonsson et al. (1977) concluded that the most suitable hot-holding temperature varies among foods. Corrective measures recommended by Karlstrom and Jonsson (1977) include regulation of time, temperature, and air humidity, and choice of proper cooking method.

Paulus et al. (1978) evaluated sensory quality of meat entrees after hot-holding. The entrees evaluated were sauerbraten, chicken fricasseee, meat loaf, beef goulash, and fried sausage. Conclusions were that meat entrees could be held hot at least 3 hours without major decreases in food quality. Generally, the study indicated a steady decline in other food products held 0 to 5 hours.

Rambeck (1979) states that from a technical point of view the physical transportation and in-transit storage of foods held hot as completed during meal distribution should not create any quality problems. When problems do occur, they are, with very few exceptions, due to the human factor. More information, education, and discipline are the remedies for such situations.

Hot-holding equipment is to be used to keep hot foods hot ($>$60°C/140°F), not to heat cold foods (USDHEW, 1976). Foods placed in hot-holding equipment should be $>$77°C/170°F in order to retain temperatures of 60°C/140°F for less than 1.5 hours.

Cold-Holding

The Food Service Sanitation Manual (1976) recommends holding chilled food at <7°C/45°F. Length of storage is not specified. Foter (1963) stored food at 7°C/44°F for 4 days without growth of salmonella or staphlococci. Longree (1972) recommends storing chilled food at 4°C/40°F and using it within 1 day. Since recommendations for cold-holding during meal distribution are almost always only a matter of minutes, the effects on sensory quality are assumed to be minimal.

Cold-holding equipment is generally designed to hold cold food cold rather than to chill warm food. Food service operators should consider putting only foods already chilled to 7°C/45°F into cold-holding equipment.

Time of Meal Distribution

The hospital food service system should be designed to minimize time of meal distribution. This can be accomplished by (a) scheduling meal assembly as close to meal service as possible, (b) locating the meal assembly area as close as possible to the meal service area(s), (c) training meal distribution personnel to complete their tasks effectively and efficiently, and (d) keeping meal distribution equipment in excellent repair.

Effect of Delays During Meal Distribution

Ten hospital food service directors informally surveyed by telephone in 1981 by Dahl considered delays to be the most serious problem in meal distribution systems. With pellet systems, the longer the time from assembly to service, the greater the transfer of heat from the pellet to cold food on the trays. Similar observations were made regarding the Sweetheart serving system. Delays of hot carts caused the food not only to lose temperature, but also to become dehydrated.

Meal Distribution Checklist

A meal distribution checklist developed by management could be used by supervisors to ensure additional control and feedback on sensory quality of food. Items that might be considered on a checklist for meal distribution include the following:

1. Time of distribution
   a. Record time cart (food items) leaves meal area assembly.
   b. Record time cart (food items) arrives at meal service area recorded.
   c. Record reason for any delays.
   d. Compare actual distribution time to standard distribution time.

Delays could be caused by human error or by mechanical failure. A computer-routed food cart could get lost on a monorail system.

    2. Temperature rise/fall during distribution
        a. Record the temperature of a hot food and of a cold food on a dummy tray when cart leaves meal assembly area and again when cart arrives at meal service area.
        b. Compare temperature changes to a standard.
    3. Damage to plated food items
        a. Were any food items dislodged during distribution?
        b. Any liquid food items spilled?
        c. Are patient identification tags in place?

MEAL SERVICE

In newer hospital food service systems, meal service to patients frequently involves a second heat treatment for food. Reheating food enhances sensory quality by achieving proper temperature for consumption. The length of the meal delivery process will affect the temperature of the food, as well as patient expectations. The attitudes of personnel delivering and retrieving patient trays will also affect patients' perceptions of present and future meals.

Throughout this paper the importance of quality in food has been stressed. To communicate quality, management must make standards for quality available to fellow workers in written or pictorial form. To determine if the standards are being met, management must have a method to measure and evaluate the quality under consideration. This philosophy should be applied equally to sensory quality of food at service, as well as to the temperature of food after cooking or to nutritional content.

Service standards should be evaluated by service supervisors and service personnel. Standards may be developed for the following areas: temperature after reheating and at service measured by thermometer; appearance and shape evaluated using a colored photograph; size and weight measured on a scale; and taste, odor, and texture evaluated using a dummy tray.

A product should meet standards within a prescribed tolerance limit. One that does not meet standards is not reliable and creates distrust.

Quality and standards become meaningless without constancy. Constancy or reliability of product is defined
by Nightingale (1979) as: evidence that a product or
service is consistent in both its availability and quality
characteristics over the life of the product or service.
Variables that affect the achievement of constancy
include: environment, materials, technology, "the human
variable," control, structure, and administration.

Maller et al. (1980) reported that for 1,597 individuals the perceived acceptability of previously eaten
meals significantly affected the perceived acceptability
of subsequent meals. If past experience with meals at a
hospital had been positive, it was more likely that a
meal would be rated more highly than if past experience
with hospital food had been negative. Initial or early
impressions did influence subsequent evaluations of food
acceptability.

Thus, constancy may be one of the most important
qualities a hospital food service director has to offer
patients. As excellence builds up trust in patients, the
entire eating experience could become the highlight of
the day.

Reheat Subsystems

Reheating decreases the sensory quality of food; this
disadvantage must be overcome by minimizing the effects
of reheating. Any food service system that reheats food
is serving food requiring different sensory quality parameters than food served in traditional cook-serve systems.
Systems with reheat subsystems are less desirable than
conventional food service systems. (Zallen et al., 1975;
Matthews, 1977). Zallen et al. (1975) reported that sensory scores of beef loaves served without prior storage
and reheating were significantly ($p \geq 0.01$) higher than
for similar products stored and reheated. Bobeng and
David (1978) reported similar results. Sensory scores
for color of meat and uniformity of color were significantly different for conventionally prepared beef loaf
and beef loaf prepared in cook-chill or cook-freeze
systems. They attributed the difference to the second
heat process in cook-chill and cook-freeze systems and
indicated that the beef loaf was darker, more streaked,
and more nonuniform than beef loaves prepared in the
conventional system. On the other hand, Glew (1968)
concluded that precooked frozen food reheated was as

acceptable to patients as traditional catering methods involving hot-holding.

In view of the previous cautions, the following goals are presented to minimize the undesirable effect of reheating.

Minimal processing should be one goal of a reheat sub-system. In addition to raising temperature, reheating precooked foods results in moisture loss and a possible decrease in nutrient content as great as 10 percent (Dahl and Matthews, 1978, 1979b, 1980a,b; Dahl et al., 1981). According to Bengtsson (1979), all of these further changes during reheating of precooked foods are detrimental to food quality. Thus, it may be concluded that to optimize reheating is to minimize reheating. Stated another way, optimal reheating would include the lowest acceptable temperature for microbial safety (74°C or 165°F) the highest yield, and little or no change in color, texture, flavor, or nutritional value.

Constancy in quality should be a second goal of reheating. Ideally, during reheating the whole load of food items in the equipment cavity should be heated at the same rate, to the temperature and moisture distribution representing optimal sensory quality, nutritional value, and retention of juices (Bengtsson, 1979). Unfortunately, current equipment technology does not permit this goal to be realized (Dahl and Naidu, 1981).

Complications that result from inadequate design of reheat equipment have been summarized by Bengtsson (1979).

1. Food may be overheated. Results are excessive surface drying, moisture loss, decreased yield, and color and texture changes that produce significant losses in sensory quality.

2. Food may be underheated. Results are temperatures less than optimal at service, which may lower sensory acceptability.

3. Uneven heating will give a combination of sensory losses similar to over- and underheating.

4. Foods heated in plastic or paperboard packaging may become overheated, causing deformation, melting, or even charring or burning of the packaging material. The accompanying release of volatiles may partially or completely ruin sensory qualities of the food.

5. Accumulations of food debris, fats, and juices on heating surfaces will become oxidized and/or pyrolyzed, and volatiles from these material will give off-flavors to the food being reheated. Another associated problem

is equipment cleaning, as well as the concern for the possibility of microbial growth when temperatures are 60°C/140°F.

Reheat Methods

Reheat may be completed in food service settings using any of serveral types of equipment.

Forced-Air Convection Oven A common application of the forced-air convection oven is that of reheating precooked foods in bulk or in single-portion trays. Reheating time in the convection oven will depend on how well heating power is balanced to the rate of heat uptake of the food load (Bengtsson, 1979). Load controls on such ovens are advantageous. Reheating at too slow a rate can cause product dehydration; reheating at too fast a rate may result in high surface temperatures.

Forced-air convection ovens, as well as other large food service equipment, demonstrate temperature variability. Bengtsson (1979) showed temperature ranges of 20°-40°C (68°-104°F) in a forced-air convection oven operating at 250°C/482°F unloaded, and a temperature variation of 35°C/95°F in and between samples of food heated in a forced-air convection oven. Dahl and Matthews (1979a) reported similar figures for beef loaf cooked in a forced-air convection oven.

Effects of uneven temperature distribution on sensory quality of foods include reduction of consistent product quality within and among batches. Areas of the food may be overdone or overheated at the edges, while interiors may not have been reheated to appropriate temperatures for optimal sensory satisfaction.

Steam injection into forced-air convention ovens raises the relative humidity of the air and reduces surface evaporation from products. Bengtsson (1979) cites decreased cooking time as an additional advantage of steam injection. Controlled steam injection should be considered as an element of equipment redesign.

Rapid circulation of air over food in a forced-air convection oven and the high temperatures used encourage the deposition and charring of food and fat spills on walls, heating elements, and fans. When such spills burn they may cause off odors in the food. Catalytic or pyrolytic cleaning are features that have been introduced to help alleviate these problems.

Microwave Radiation As a reheat instrument, a microwave oven will: increase the temperature in food, cause approximately 10 percent loss of moisture and nutrient content, and lower the microbiological population. Results depend on the type, size, shape, and arrangement of food; on the power input and output of the oven; on the type of container (covered or uncovered) in which food has been placed; on the time of heating; and on the food's location in the cavity of the oven. For constant results in sensory quality, the food service manager must closely monitor and control all of the above for every portion of food. Dahl (1981b) has prepared a study kit for the American Dietetic Association that more fully describes the controls required for use of a microwave reheat subsystem.

As a reheat instrument, the microwave oven will not: brown foods, crisp foods, or act as a critical control point for food safety. When the microwave process is strictly viewed as one in which temperature is to be raised, and when the process is closely controlled by taking the temperature of each portion reheated, results can be superior to other reheat methods because the food can be heated on demand. Since meals are individually heated in a microwave oven, it must also be recognized that microwave ovens are individually fast--heating one meal--but collectively slow--heating 100 meals--when compared to conventional methods of heating.

Steam and Water Bath Steam and water baths are less frequently used as reheat methods than microwave and convection reheating. Examples of products that might be reheated by steam include food masses in bulk, such as stews and vegetables, as opposed to those already por- tioned. Examples of food items that might be reheated by a hot or boiling water bath include bulk items such as pasta and plastic-packaged items in single-serving or bulk size.

Poor heat insulation of equipment may contribute to sensory quality loss of foods reheated by steam because of prolonged reheating time and excessive condensation in the chamber. Bengtsson (1979) states that automated, efficient venting of air and draining of condensation, pressure-temperature control, and high steam-generating capacity are very important to good product quality and reproducibility in steam heating. Overpressure is also an important consideration in relation to size of food

being heated. Using high pressures and temperatures
results in overheating large products, such as potatoes,
while reducing heat time and quality loss for foods of
smaller dimensions such as peas and diced meat.

Steam-Jacketed Kettle Food reheated in a steam-jacketed
kettle (SJK) usually includes those foods that could have
been initially cooked in an SJK--stews, soups, gravies,
spaghetti sauce, etc. One major problem, especially in
SJKs over 5 gallons, is stirring. Stirring is used to
improve temperature distribution; without it deposition
and burning of food on the heating surfaces may occur,
resulting in a burnt flavor for the entire food load.
Another problem in using a large SJK that could also
result in a burnt flavor is uneven temperature distribution on the walls because of improper venting of air and
condensate inside of the steam-heated mantle.

Cart Perhaps the most advanced design to date for a
reheat subsystem is the Alpha cart. The Alpha cart, a
component of Anchor Hockings, "Chill-Therm System,"
transports food and beverages, keeps chilled food cold,
and reheats precooked frozen food. The Alpha Cart was
designed for use at Walter Reed Army Medical Center in
Washington, D.C., and began operation in 1978. Each cart
holds 20 patient trays. Each hot food item is individually reheated according to 1 of 15 reheating codes. A
reheat cycle takes 32 minutes (Shaw et al., 1979).
   Shaw et al. (1979) describes the Alpha Cart's problems
as erratic heating and not heating all foods to the
desired temperature. A partial solution was to eliminate
from the menu such hard-to-heat items as bone-in chicken,
spareribs, and pork chops, while also reducing portion
sizes. Three years following implementation, however,
Riggs (1981) reported that Walter Reed has planned to
switch from reheating in carts to reheating in microwaves.
   Other car systems designed for distribution and reheating or hot-holding are described by Cardello (1981). Cart
systems designed for reheating (3-M, Sweetheart, Aladdin)
require that food be chill-plated. The cart sytem by
Therma Tray accommodates food that is plated hot. When
Army hospital patients rated temperatures of food served
from the four cart systems, foods served from the 3-M
system received the highest ratings.

Menu Design and Reheating

Menus designed with reheat subsystems in mind contribute
to total sensory quality of food at service. Information
regarding these menu limitations is frequently available
from equipment manufacturers and from food service operators famocular with a particular subsystem. Menus should
be modified to include those foods that fit well into the
chosen system. For example, serving crisp, fried eggs
with liquid yokes for breakfast in a cook-chill food
service system with a microwave reheat subsystem is wish-
ful thinking. Reheating bone-in chicken pieces in conduction heat subsystems (3-M Integral Heat or Alpha Cart)
is usually considered too difficult because of uneven
temperature distribution. Menu limitations of water and
steam reheat subsystems require using only those foods
that can be reheated directly in water or in sealed
plastic pouches placed in boiling water.

Temperature of Food After Reheating

The Food Service Sanitation Manual (USDHEW, 1976) states
that:

> Potentially hazardous food (any food that consists
> in whole or in part of milk or milk products, eggs,
> meat, poultry, fish, shellfish, edible crustacea,
> or other ingredients, including synthetic ingredi-
> ents, in a form capable of supporting rapid and
> progressive growth of infectious or toxigenic micro-
> organisms) that has been cooked and then refriger-
> ated shall be reheated rapidly to 74°C/165°F or
> higher throughout before being served or before
> being placed in a hot food storage facility.

Temperatures recommended for microbiological safety of
foods have been cited as detrimental to sensory quality.
Paulus et al. (1978) recommends that reheating to a center
temperature 70°C/158°F should be avoided if optimal sensory and nutritional quality of vegetable-based dishes is
to be retained. The sensory values of vegetable-based
meals most subject to change were color and texture.
When potentially hazardous foods are considered, reheat
temperatures must be $\geq$165°F/74°C, based on microbiological quality. When vegetable formulations that do not
contain potentially hazardous food are considered, tem-

peratures below 74°C/165°F may be tolerated to conserve sensory quality.

Goals for temperatures of food after reheating can also be based on the temperature desired for food at service plus a distribution factor. According to the Food Service Sanitation Manual (USDHEW, 1976), temperatures of hot food at service must be 60°C/140°F or greater. Certain foods may be more acceptable at higher temperatures--for example, coffee and other hot liquids 88°C/190°F).

To calculate the distribution factor in degrees:

1. Determine the average time in minutes from reheat to service.
2. Determine heat loss per minute using the distribution containers (plate, dome, tray, etc.) of the facility.
3. Multiply minutes of distribution by heat loss per minute to obtain distribution factor:

   Distribution Time in Minutes X °C/°F Heat Loss per Minute-Distribution Factor

4. Add distribution factor to service temperature to obtain reheat temperature:

   Distribution Factor in °C/°F + Service Temperature in °C/°F = Reheat Temperature in °C/°F

For example, if soup should be served at 88°C/190°F, and distribution time is 5 minutes and heat loss is 0.55°C/1°F per minute, then

5 minutes X 0.55°C/1°F = 2.75°C/5°F distribution factor.

Reheat temperature would be

   88°C/190°F + 2.75°C/5°F = 90.75°C/195°F.

End point temperature (EPT) of food after reheating may exhibit a broad range if all portions are monitored. Dahl and Naidu (1981) prepared beef loaf, potatoes, and peas in a simulated hospital cook/chill system to compare EPT of foods after being reheated in conduction, convection, and microwave subsystems according to manufacturer's directions. Equipment used for the study is listed in Table 1. Mean EPT and standard deviations appear in

TABLE 1   Equipment Used to Compare End Point Temperature
of Foods After Reheating

Reheat Method	Hospital Subsystem Manufacturer
Conduction	3-M
Convection	Crimsco
Microwave Radiation	Hobart

SOURCE: Dahl and Naider, 1981.

Table 2. According to the Food Service Sanitation Manual
(USDHEW, 1976) all EPTs of beef loaf and potatoes should
have been >74°C/165°F. Percentages of occurrences in
which EPT did not reach >74°C/165°F are shown in Table
3. Table 3 indicates that when beef loaf, potatoes, and
peas were reheated as a meal, the percentage of time EPTs
<74°C/165°F increased. When food items were reheated
as a meal, the conduction reheat subsystem had the
largest mean percent time (80 percent) when EPT did not
reach 74°C/165°F. Further, the conduction reheat subsystem was the only one in which time-temperature were
completely preset by the manufacturer. Results of this
study should indicate to management the importance of
continual temperature monitoring and the necessity to
examine and improve upon manufacturer's directions for
such subsystem operations as plating, menu design, and
time-temperature of heating.

Plate Selection and Reheating

In most food service reheat subsystems, the reheat container is also the serving dish. Some subsystems, such
as Alpha Cart and 3-M Integral Heating Modules, require a
specific type of container; others, such as microwave and
convection reheat subsystems, permit moderate versatility
in choice of plates. Reheat containers used as serviceware will strongly influence appearance of the meal as
well as temperature retention during meal distribution.
Such factors and their relation to the sensory quality of
meals should be strongly considered at purchase.

Types of plates available for use in reheat subsystems
range from disposable paper plates used in microwave
ovens, to thick chinaware used in convection ovens, to
heavy insulated dishes used in the 3-M or Aladdin systems.
Use of disposable plastic or paperware may "cheapen" the
meal for some patients or make it less homelike for
others. Use of heavy china or insulated ware may function
as a continual reminder of the institutional setting in
which the patient finds himself. Research is needed to
improve the weight, appearance, and hot-holding capacity
of institutional tableware.

Dome Selection and Reheating

Most reheat subsystems use a dome or tray cover during
distribution and reheating. The food service director
should be aware of the detrimental effects such plate
coverings have on food quality. Condensate from hot
foods collects on the top of the dome, and when removed,
5 to 20 ml of water (2 to 4 teaspoons) may drip onto the
food. Work is needed to redesign domes either to vent

TABLE 2 Cook-Chill Food Service System: End Point
Temperature After Conduction, Convection, and Microwave
Reheat

Product	N	End Point Temperature	
		Mean	Standard Deviation
I. Conduction reheat	15-17		
Beef loaf		74.5	4
Potatoes		80.1	5
Peas		86.5	2
II. Convection reheat	14-18		
Beef loaf		74.7	12
Potatoes		62.5	12
Peas		76.9	7
III. Microwave reheat	12-23		
Beef loaf		77.6	1
Potatoes		75.9	1
Peas		78.0	2

TABLE 3 Cook-Chill Food Service Systems: Percent Time
End Point Temperature of Foods Was Less Than 74°C After
Reheating

Product	Reheat Subsystem		
	Conduction	Convection	Microwave Radiation
I. Single-item reheating[a]			
Beef loaf	31	53	04
Potatoes	31	50	10
Peas	0	15	0
Mean	21	39	5
II. Reheated as a meal[b]			
Beef loaf	75	75	22
Potatoes	83	75	0
Peas	83	13	0
Mean	80	54	7

[a]N = 3 to 12.
[b]N = 2 to 8.

the condensation better or to include water-absorbent
material in the dome construction.

A second sensory distraction of domes covering plates
containing more than one food is that the odors are combined. Patients who otherwise might enjoy the pleasing
aroma of chicken, mashed potatoes, and brussel sprouts
now detect only brussel sprouts. Plating procedures
should eliminate strong-smelling foods in the presence of
other foods under the same plate cover.

Appearance and immediate identification of food is
critical to good sensory quality. Opque plate covers do
not permit this to occur. Clear plate covers also do not
permit this to occur, since usually only the condensation
is clearly visable, and the food items are blurred. Clear
plate covers designed with water-absorbent materials would
be ideal for allowing instant identification of food items
by patients.

Aluminum foil may be used in place of domes to cover
meals in some reheat subsystems. Such subsystems include
the one manufactured by Crimsco, Inc., as well as others
that incorporate reheating with convection ovens. The

foil should be vented with small holes at the top to keep the food from becoming soggy.

Heating Capacity of Reheat Equipment

Heating capacity of reheat equipment influences the heating rate of food. Heating capacity may be thought of as the amount of heat available to the food load. Low heat capacity results in longer times for reheating, which could have detrimental effects on food quality. Higher heat capacity results in shorter times for reheating, which would theoretically have beneficial effects on sensory quality of foods. This concept, however, does not always apply to microwave reheating. With microwave ovens more power is not necessarily better power. Too great a power output in microwave ovens could potentially result in overheating some areas or some foods before others are even warm.

The Satellite Effect

Constancy of results when reheating is important to sensory quality of food. Large, complex food service systems utilizing a central commissary for preparation and satellites for reheating and service may require additional managerial effort to maintain a constant sensory quality of food at service. Cremer and Chipley (1979) studied temperature and sensory quality of beef loaf in a commissary food service system that transported food hot. Data indicated that temperature and, therefore, sensory quality varied widely among satellites. Tighter control of standards and additional traning of personnel might be used to manage these more complex situations.

Batch Technique for Reheating

The ability to batch process food during initial cooking has long been recognized as an effective technique to maximize nutritional and sensory quality. (West et al., 1977). Batch processing during reheating can be applied for similar reasons. Individual batch reheating is a feature of subsystems with microwave ovens. Such reheat subsystems eliminate the need to hold food in a heated state, which usually results in nutritional as well as sensory losses.

Comparison of the Sensory Quality of Foods in Three Reheat Subsystems

Beef loaf, reconstituted mashed potatoes, and peas were prepared in a simulated hospital cook-chill food service system by Dahl (1981a). The purpose of the study was to evaluate the effects of reheat systems on the sensory quality food at point of service. Four trials using conduction, convection, and microwave radiation subsystems were used for each product (Table 1). Panelists' scores showed a clear preference for beef loaf reheated by conduction and for peas reheated by microwave radiation (see Table 4). Similar results were reported by Bedero et al. (1980) for beef samples cooked, not reheated, by microwave-radiation and by conventional roasting. Ferguson (1981) identified specific flavor deficiencies of microwave cooked products, such as uncooked starch, low intensity in basic salt taste, and pronounced tastes of any fats and oils present. Similar work has not been reported for microwave-reheated products. In the study by Dahl (1981a), microwave reheating resulted in the highest overall satisfaction rating for two of the three foods reheated.

Practical Suggestions for Improving Reheat to Optimize Sensory Quality of Foods

1. Use minicomputers to automate and regulate the reheat process in order to improve managerial control and reduce operation variability.

2. Develop facility standards for reheated food at service, such as:

    a. Temperature measured by a prescribed method that includes type of thermometer, location of measurement in the food, time after reheating, number of samples, and method of recording--all in relation to predetermined temperature goals for specific foods.

    b. Color measured in relation to a color photograph.

    c. Weight of servings measured by a scale.

    d. Size and shape of servings measured by a drawn-to-scale diagram.

    e. Plating and tray arrangement assessed in relation to a color photograph.

TABLE 4 Results of Sensory Analysis of Products Reheated in a Cook-Chill System by Conduction, Convection, or Microwave Radiation

Sensory Quality	Beef Loaf Statistical Differences Among Reheat Methods[a]	Beef Loaf Reheat Method Preferred by Panelists	Potatoes Statistical Differences Among Reheat Methods[a]	Potatoes Reheat Method Preferred by Panelists	Peas Statistical Differences Among Reheat Methods[a]	Peas Reheat Method Preferred by Panelists
Surface	NA[b]		No		Yes	Microwave
Color	Yes	Conduction	NA		NA	
Crust	Yes		NA	Convection	Yes	Microwave
Product	Yes	Conduction	Yes	Microwave	NA	
Uniformity	Yes	Conduction	NA	Convection	NA	
Moisture	Yes	Conduction	Yes		Yes	Microwave
Odor	No		No	Microwave	Yes	Microwave
Texture	No		NA		NA	
Juiciness	No				NA	
Flavor	Yes	Conduction	Yes	Microwave	Yes	Microwave
General	Yes	Conduction	Yes	Microwave	Yes	Microwave
Overall satisfaction	NO		Yes	Microwave	Yes	Microwave

[a] $p \leq 0.05$.
[b] NA = not applicable.

SOURCE: Dahl, 1981a.

3. Improve design of reheat equipment to prevent excessive temperature variation resulting from poor heat distribution and air circulation. Continuous processing equipment may be a partial solution, since steady-state conditions are maintained at any given position along the line. However, such equipment is limited to very large operations. In the interim, Byron and Kilpatrick (1971) recommend reducing product size reduction whenever possible to reduce temperature variability.

4. Standardize instructions for reheating. These must be developed as part of the food formulation or standardized recipe.

5. Improve research. Bengtsson (1979) demonstrated the complex interrelationship among oil temperature, surface browning, center temperature of the food mass, weight loss, and sensory quality of deep fried beef patties during initial cooking. Appropriate intensity of each factor must be achieved to obtain optimum product quality after cooking. Similar study is need to optimize reheat procedures for various foods. For example, variables for microwave reheating could include: frequency, power, output level(s) of pulsed power, time, microwave field distribution (and types of compensating equipment, such as mode stirrers, rotating support tables, and shielding devices on moving wave guides), humidity, shape, mass, and container. Such studies would appear still to be a matter of empirical testing.

Postheat Hold

European food service systems often reheat and hold food warm until service. American reheat subsystems, such as the 3-M Integral Heating Module and the Crimsco Ducted Forced-Air Convection Oven, also demonstrate such capabilities. The 3-M reheat system has a hold cycle of 12 minutes in which food temperature is to be held at >60°C/140°F. Paulus et al. (1978) recommends that such hot-holding periods after reheat be limited to 30 minutes to retain optimal sensory qualities in the food.

Service of Food

Meal service is the final and the most important step relating to sensory quality of food. All other processing

steps have been initiated in support of this focal point
of a food service system.

Temperature of Food at Point of Service

To serve hot foods hot ($\geq 60°C/140°F$) and cold foods
cold ($\leq 7°C/45°F$) is both a goal and a challenge to
hospital food service operators, for microbiological as
well as sensory reasons. Temperature is well recognized
as a major factor in the sensory acceptance of food.
Appropriate serving temperatures may vary among types of
hot or cold foods.

Ten hospital food service directors were informally
interviewed by telephone in 1981. Respondents answered
questions relating to in-house goals for temperature of
food at service. Some respondents worked for food management companies and followed strict guidelines for temperatures as indicators of microbiological and sensory
quality, while others were merely estimating approximate
temperature goals based on microbiological guidelines.
In Table 5 recommendations of respondents are compared to
published temperature recommendations for food at point
of service.

Jonsson et al. (1977) reviewed temperature preferences
of subjects. Some examples were: potatoes, 63°-75°C/
145°-167°F; meatballs, 60°-75°C/140°-167°F; and pea soup,
59°-69°C/138°-156°F. The report concluded that such judgments were not consistent and must be regarded as purely
subjective. Blaker et al (1961) reported temperature
preferences of hospital cafeteria customers ranging from
46°-79°C/115°-175°F for potatoes, 49°-79°C/120°-175°F for
vegetables, and 38°-71°C/100°-160°F for meat.

Delays in Meal Service

Patient's days are highlighted by mealtimes. When meals
are served on time, the patient is most likely to be ready
to eat the food while it is still hot or cold. When meals
are late, patients become impatient and may not receive
full enjoyment from the meal.

Delays of any type in meal service after reheating
will cause additional temperature loss i food at the
rate of about 0.55°C/1°F per minute, depending on the
container. Two major causes of delay in patient tray
service were cited by 10 Michigan hospital food service

TABLE 5 Hospital Food Service Systems: Temperature
Recommendations for Food at Point of Service

Food Category	°C/°F	Literature Source	Survey of Hospital Food Service Directors 1981
Meat	38°-77°C 100°-170°F	Blaker et al. 1961	66°-71°C/150°-160°F
	66°-71°C/ 150°-160°F	Thompson and Johnson, 1963	
Soups			71°-82°C/160°-180°F
Soups with milk[a]			≤60°C/140°F
Sauce/gravy[a]			71°-82°C/160°-180°F
Vegetables and potatoes	52°-74°C/ 125°-165°F	Blaker et al., 1961	71°C/160°F
	71°-77°C/ 160°-170°F	Thompson and Johnson, 1963	
"Dip entree" (stew)			66°C/150°F
Coffee			180°-190°F
Salads			7°C/45°F
Chilled foods			≤4°-16°C/40°-60°F
Milk; other chilled beverages			≤ 4°C/40°F
Frozen items			0°C/32°F

[a]All potentially hazardous goods are to be reheated to
74°C/165°F (USDHEW, 1976).

directors in a telephone survey in 1981. One reason was
that meals were delivered to patients by nursing rather
than by food service personnel. Food service directors
had little control over availability and speed of work
among nursing personnel, especially part-time employees,
who did not always understand the importance of prompt
meal service. When nurses deliver patient trays, excellent communication and mutual training sessions are
required between the nursing and food service departments.

The second reason for delays was special handling of
patient trays. Patients who are in isolation wards or who
require assistance with eating may receive their trays
late, and certain sensory qualities may have deteriorated.
Such situations usually required special coordination
between food service and nursing personnel.

Service Personnel

Personnel delivering and picking up patient trays influence patients' evaluations of the sensory quality of a
meal. Service personnel dress, attitude (cheerful toward
patient and toward food), and amount of interaction time
with patients can serve to improve or to lower a patient's
reaction to meals. Maller et al. (1980) reported significant connections between patients' ratings of hospital
food and their satisfaction with nurses' and doctors'
care. These findings agree with the report of Sheatsley
(1965). Maller et al. also demonstrated that, for hospital staff, satisfaction with work and salary were
directly connected with opinions of the food.

How do service personnel respond to patients' praises
or complaints of meals? Do service personnel have the
background to explain limitations and benefits of the
hospital food service system to patients? Do nursing or
food service personnel deliver patient trays? Do service
personnel assist patients with the selective menu? Are
service personnel trained on a regular basis to become
aware of these factors?

Conversely, a late tray delivered in a hurry by a
harried worker who does not bother to greet the patient
can easily reinforce a negative image of hospital food.

Sensorial Responses of Patients to Food

To completely understand the meaning of sensory quality
of food in a food service setting, the food service

director must be aware of factors in addition to the food
service system that influence that sensory quality.
Among those factors are the sensorial and psychological
responses of patients to food, as well as attributes of
the meal service environment. The food service director's
understanding of the complexity of the sensory quality of
food should be thoroughly communicated to assembly, distribution, and service personnel during regular training
sessions. Such training should assist the director in
maintaining high standards.

Appearance

Appearance of a food includes the combined impact of all
visual aspects of a food--color, shape, quantity, freshness, etc. Appearance and aroma were ranked as the most
important meal factors in overall consumer acceptability
by ward patients in army hospitals. During evaluation of
an army hospital cook-freeze food service system, Bustead
(1980) showed that patients ranked perceived food service
problems in descending order of importance. Defects in
appearance and aroma, those meal factors first noticed,
were the biggest problems. Bustead attributed long
periods of hot holding as the source of these problems.

Color

Color is an important indicator of food quality. Color
may be considered separately or as a component of appearance of food. Questions that could be raised about food
color include: Is it characteristic of the food? Is the
color appealing in relation to other foods present?
   Color may indicate freshness. Ryley et al. (1977)
evaluated fresh sprouts and frozen peas after four reheat
methods. Results indicated that panelists preferred
products highest in chlorophyl and thus closer to the
natural fresh state of the product.

Form

Form or shape of a food can be considered separately or
as one aspect of appearance. Concepts related to form
include: Is the form of the food attractive? Is it
appropriate to the particular food?

Freshness

The degree of freshness perceived by patients may influence acceptance of food. Freshness may be perceived by one or more of the senses. For example, eyes may perceive an intense green color in cooked broccoli, a more satisfying color than dull green or brown. Other indicators of freshness may include the aroma of meat and the texture of vegetables.

Gloss

Kramer and Twigg (1970) suggest that gloss be considered an important aspect of appearance. Gloss is defined in Webster's as brightness or luster. Gloss on an apple may indicate a special cleaning effort; on vegetables it may indicate application of a glaze during formulation. Is the gloss appropriate to the food? Is gloss characteristic of a particular food formulation?

Flavor

Flavor is generally considered to include odor, taste, and mouthfeel (Charley, 1970). Once a food has been seen as acceptable, the patient obtains additional information about its quality using the nose and mouth. Von Sydow (1975) suggests that optimizing flavor of food products is to a large extent a matter of preserving the flavor of the ingredient raw materials or of a freshly cooked item following the principle: larger resemblance, better flavor.

Aroma

Odor is considered one of three components of flavor. The other two are taste and mouthfeel. Odor was rated along with appearance of food as the most important organoleptic component of sensory quality (Herz et al., 1978; Bustead, 1979). Odor may serve as a valuable index to the quality of a food and even to its wholesomeness and edibility. To produce an odor, a substance must be volatile; molecules of the food substance must make contact with the cilia in the nose.

Questions that might be raised about aroma of a food include: Is the aroma pleasing? Is it stimulating to the appetite? Is it characteristic of the product? What is the interaction of aromas on the same plate or tray?

Taste

Taste is sensed by taste buds on the tongue. Sensations that taste buds register are sweet (tip of tongue), salt (tip of tongue), sour (side of tongue), and bitter (back of tongue). Human senses, such as taste acuity, are sharpest around the ages of 20-25 years and after this slowly decline.

Factors to consider regarding taste include: Is the taste characteristic of the product? Is it palatable in strength? Is the product suitably seasoned?

Mouthfeel

Mouthfeel is considered one of three aspects of flavor (Charley, 1970). Components of mouthfeel include pain (as from pepper), temperature, the tactile sensations of texture (graininess, brittleness, chewiness), astringency (as from cider), and consistency.

Texture

Textural characteristics of a food may be picked up by the sense of touch in hands and mouth as well as by the sense of hearing as food is chewed. On a word association test, Sherman (1975) reported that participants indicated that over 100 characteristics may be involved in texture. Some characteristics of texture were: crisp, dry, juicy, soft, stringy, fluffy, and greasy. Texture can add greatly to sensory acceptance of foods in special diets in hospitals. When foods have relatively less taste and odor, as in bland diets, the potential importance of texture increases. Such is frequently the case for patients with gastrointestinal disturbances or those recovering from surgery. When bland diets also specify soft foods with low fiber content, other sensory factors such as color, form, and freshness must be considered.

Tenderness of meat can be considered a textural property. Purchase specifications, as well as the method of cooking and degree of doneness, influence tenderness, which was rated fourth out of ten meal factors in acceptability by ward patients in army hospitals (Herz et al., 1978).

Consistency

Consistency or viscosity can make an important contribution to mouthfeel. Ice cream can be too hard or too soft and gravies too thick or too thin. Temperature of food affects consistency. Cold syrup is thick; hot syrup is thinner. Cheese is an elastic solid at room temperature but when heated becomes a liquid.

Consistency may affect the patient's ability to handle food. Cold butter is hard to spread. Cold, hard ice cream may be difficult for elderly patients to eat.

Consistency may be also an indicator of misformulation. Curdled custard, pasty reconstituted mashed potatoes, and rubbery gelatin are examples.

Personal Factors of Patients That May Affect Sensory Quality of Food

Diets are more than a combination of nutrients; they also have psychological value. Food has no nutritional value unless it is eaten, so it must first be acceptable and palatable. Factors that make a meal acceptable can seldom be quantified because they are subjective and affected by so many circumstances. Some of these are not qualities of the meal itself.

The same patient can exhibit many mood changes in the course of a brief hospital stay. What affects the patient? How does internal conditioning affect his perception of the food served? How predictable is his reaction to a given food item from hour to hour, day to day?

Food Preference

Personal likes and dislikes of patients influence sensory acceptability of foods. Patients in the southern United States who prefer soft cooked vegetables might have a difficult time with Chinese stir fried cuisine. A patient who could not tolerate spinach as a child would

probably prefer not to be served fresh spinach as an
adult.

Based on their past experiences, consumers may not
always detect sensory qualities of foods as they are
served. Grater (1979) tells the story of the day he
decided to expand the choice of vegetables in his operation by including braised onions. A customer took one
portion of braised onions on self-service and poured
custard over it. Not only that, but he ate it! Later
when asked if he had enjoyed the food item, the customer
replied that he had not really enjoyed it, but then he
never had like baked apples very much and he would not be
having then again. Thus the question arises: What differences are there in sensory quality perceptions between
the customers and food service personnel?

Ferguson (1981) generalized about customer food preferences from results of market studies, concluding that
one-third of the population is discriminating about what
they eat, one-third is less selective, and the other third
really does not care what they put in their mouths. Information is not available to determine whether such conclusions apply to hospital patient populations.

Expectation and Choice

What does a patient expect hospital food to be like? If
recent public media presentations can affect public
opinion, expectations must be very low even before the
first meal is served. Hospital food is not infrequently
the topic of jokes and sarcasms in the medical area.

What would patients prefer hospital food to be like?
Ten hospital food service directors in a 1981 informal
telephone survey (Appendix B) believed patients most preferred a homelike quality to the food they were served.
When a person is ill, he would most often prefer to be
comfortable in his own bed in his own home. Patients
were also thought to prefer meals served to be somewhat
like restaurant meals (complete meal to include soup,
salad, entree, roll, dessert, and beverage), since
hospital room charges that include meals are viewed as
expensive.

Perceived Ease of Eating

Difficulty with self-feeding or chewing may decrease the
pleasure of food for various patients. Especially

affected are patients with newly acquired arm/hand/facial injuries, as well as elderly patients who were formerly more independent.

Ability to Taste Food

One factor that affects palatability of food is the ability to taste it. Certain medications and disease conditions have long been known to affect taste. Hollingsworth and Paffenberger (1917) reported that elevated blood glucose decreases sensitivity to sweetness. Enhanced sensitivity to taste has been reported in patients suffering from adrenal insufficiency (Henken et al., 1963) and in cystic fibrosis patients (Henkin and Powell, 1962). The latter is controversial, however, since Wotman et al. (1964) and Desor and Maller (1975) reported no differences. In contrast, Cohen et al. (1973) reported hypogenusia among thermal burn patients. Depressed taste thresholds also occur in lung cancer patients (Williams and Cohen, 1978).

Assessed Microbiological and Chemical Condition of Food

Cleanliness of dishes and silverware is used by patients and other consumers to assess cleanliness and safety of food served in hospitals (Herz et al., 1978). How many patients would knowingly eat, let alone enjoy, food that was considered unclean or unsafe?

Assessed Nutritive Value of Food

Nutritional value of foods is a popular concern. Because of their altered physical states, hospital patients are likely to be even more concerned about nutrition in food. Serving foods such as salads, chicken, and fish of recognized nutritional value could increase sensory acceptability when compared to pop, potato chips, and other fabricated foods. On the other hand, patients may assume all food served in a hospital is of high nutritional value because it is served in a hospital.

Age, Sex, and Physical Condition

Age and sex of hospital patients have been shown to influence perceived satisfaction with food served. Glew (1970) determined that for patients in hospitals in England satisfaction with food increased with age, and that males are more satisfied with food than are females. Maller et al. (1980) surveyed 1,597 patients and staff at five army medical facilities and concluded that age was the major demographic factor influencing meal acceptability. The more critical attitude of younger individuals was attributed to their possible preference for fast foods; older individuals were viewed as less discriminating, probably due to deterioration in sensory perception. In addition, physical conditions of patients, such as pain and lack of mobility, could also affect food perceptions.

Length of Hospital Stay and Hospital Schedules

Duration of hospitalization may effect a patient's ability to enjoy meals. Maller et al. (1980) reported a slight negative effect on ratings of food by patients confined for long stays. The longer the hospital stay, the more particular about, or possibly the more disinterested in, food the hospital patient may become.

Hospital schedules for patient testing frequently disrupt meal service. Meals may be interrupted or postponed. Obviously, such situations affect patient meal satisfaction as well as food quality.

Special Diets

Special diets may have a negative impact on sensory quality of meals. Diet prescriptions that exclude salt, fat, or sugar or that include large amounts of one substance at the expense of others will usually deviate from the patient's perception of what he would like to eat. Explanation of the rationale and importance of the diet, extra friendliness, and nonfood treats on the tray (flowers, decorations, etc.) can be used to alleviate frustrations caused by special diets. However, Maller et al. (1980) failed to observe an effect of special diets on ratings of meal acceptability when 1,597 individuals were surveyed.

Environmental Attributes That May Contribute
to Sensory Quality of Food

Just as the five senses of sight, sound, smell, touch,
and taste interact with the food, they also interact with
the eating environment. The whole pleasure of eating may
be spoiled if the setting is unpleasant (Rambeck, 1979).
Consumers, especially patients, appreciate having their
meals in pleasant surroundings and in good company.

Environmental factors that may add to the pleasure of
the meal include: the presence of other people, cheerful
room colors, a comfortable eating position, alternate
eating areas (areas other than the patient's bed), and
music. Environmental factors that may distract from the
pleasure of the meal include unusual and loud noises,
solitude, obtrusive odors (common in hospitals), or
presence of other patients under stress. Although hospital food service directors have little actual control
over these factors, their awarness of the conditions in
patient eating areas could be a significant contribution
to improving them. Table 6 is a summary of environmental
factors that may add to or detract from sensory quality
of a meal.

Sensory impairment of food quality due to purchase and
production is under a greater degree of control by hospital food service directors than is environmental quality
of service areas. However, the food service director may
be influential over conditions of service areas in the
following ways:

TABLE 6 Environmental Factors That Influence Sensory
Quality of a Meal Served to Hospital Patient

Positive Factors	Negative Factors
Holiday specials	Clutter at bedside
Music in background	Eating alone
Unrushed	Unusual odors
Presence of friends, others	Loud noises
Cheerful room colors	Dim light
Comfortable position	Other patients under stress
Choice of eating area	

1. Suggest alternate service areas.
2. Arrange meal service times to avoid unpleasant
stimuli.
3. Make other hospital support services aware of the
importance of environmental sensory stimuli on patient
perceptions of the sensory quality of food.

Some System Factors That May Affect Sensory Quality of Food at Meal Service

Special Events

Use of special events meals such as turkey for Thanksgiv-
ing, duck for Christmas, or hot dogs for Stadium Day, plus
decorations, can provide a much needed bright spot in a
patient's long, bed-ridden hospital stay.

Service: Evaluation

The Joint Commission on Hospital Accreditation requires
that hospitals survey patients about food quality and
that they keep these surveys on file for review. Such
surveys may be as brief as one question asked of the
hospital patient population four times per year with no
follow-up or as extensive as a survey instrument with
personal follow-up for each questionnaire completed.
Patients who have been asked to rate the food service and
have received follow-up from the food service professional will probably feel more satisfied in the long term.
People eating at home have a choice among foods, and
patients in hospitals may attain greater satisfaction
from meals when food choices are available. Patients are
frequently requested to make food choices from a printed
menu during meal service. Hospital menus may be selective, semiselective, or may offer no choice among foods
planned for service. Provision of a choice in some or
all menu item categories sets the frame of mind for the
patient's sense of satisfaction and independence. Glew
(1973) compared three hospital food service systems:
conventional with no selective menu, conventional with
selective menu, and cook-freeze with selective menu.
Food for the three systems was supplied by the same chefs
working in the same kitchens. The provision of a choice
of food increased its acceptability in all cases.

When is the best time for a patient to make meal choices? Frequently, hospitals request patients to choose meal items 24 to 48 hours ahead of service. Is this as effective as walking into a restaurant and choosing what you would like or eat 10 to 20 minutes ahead of service? The closer choice of meal items is to service, the better it reflects the patient's actual food preference for that meal.

Patient food selections from a printed menu can be enhanced by providing a stimulating variety of foods. Menus can be written to emphasize variety among menu item categories in the same meal, among selections of food in the same categories, among meals served on the same day, and among meals served at the same time each day. Variety may be emphasized by variations in color, texture, temperature, presence of meat or fish, etc. Variety can be a menu tool that assists in satisfying the wide range of patient preference and expectations for food with good sensory quality.

Degree of Doneness at Production

Degree of doneness due to initial cooking may affect such food qualities as color of roast beef and texture of vegetables even after reheating. Such effects are important at point of service, since processing has a cumulative effect on food at point of service. Preference for degree of doneness in foods may vary among geographic locations, individuals, ethnic groups, and age-groups. A patient's expectations for degree of doneness of food products should be determined by food service directors and written into standardized recipe procedures.

Meal Service Checklist

Develop a checklist for use by meal service personnel. Such questions might include:

1. Food Appearance
    a. Does the food item being checked have satisfactory color?
    b. Is there pleasant eye appeal in the variety of color and texture?
    c. Is the portion of uniform size and shape?
    d. Are garnishes properly used?

e. Is there a right texture for a particular food
item?
2. Food Taste
a. Are there any strong or undesirable flavors?
b. Is the taste desirable as to what is expected
of the product?
c. Is there any ingredient that produces an
undesirable flavor or aftertaste?
d. Is the seasoning adequate?
e. Does the product have a pleasing aroma?
3. Food Texture
a. Is the product over- or undercooked?
b. Does the moisture content make the texture
suitable to the particular food product?
c. Is the proper texture identifiable in the
product?
d. Is the product too tough and/or stringy?
e. Is the product too soft and/or mushy?

CONCLUSION

A popular definition in Sweden for food service is "an
organized form of food destruction" (Bengtsson, 1979).
Food destruction in a food service system is related to
the potential for systematic decrease in quality of food
throughout processing. The popular American image of
hospital food service has not been far afield from this
definition. The hospital food service industry must
accept the challenge to remake this image.

Sensory quality of food in a food service setting is a
challenging and complex concept. Managerial efforts to
increase sensory acceptability of food as outlined in
this paper will benefit patients, employees, and the
hospital. Patients will be more consistently satisfied.
Food service personnel will have a clearer understanding
of what output was expected of them and will be more
content; quality of work life and, possibly, productivity
will improve. Long-term profitability to the hospital
will likely ensue when patients and personnel show
improved satisfaction.

REFERENCES

American Hospital Association. 1972. Food Service Manual
for Health Care Institutions. 3rd ed. American
Hospital Association, Chicago, Ill. 312 pp.

Ang, C. Y. W., C. M. Chang, A. E. Frey, and G. E. Livingston. 1975. Effects of heating methods on vitamin retention in six fresh or frozen prepared food products. J. Food Sci. 40:997.

Axler, B. H. 1974. Focus on . . . Adding Eye Appeal to Foods. Bobbs-Merrill, Indianapolis, Ind. 110 pp.

Bengtsson, N. 1979. Catering equipment design and food quality. Pages 121-133 in G. Glew, ed., Advances in Catering Technology. Applied Science Publishers, London.

Bengtsson, N., and H. Dagersbog. 1978. Fried meat and meat patties--the influence of preparation and processing on quality and yield. Pages 147-161 in K. Paulus, ed., How Ready are Ready-to-Serve Foods? S. Karger, New York.

Blaker, G. G., J. L. Newcomer, and E. Romsey. 1961. Holding temperatures needed to serve hot foods hot. J. Am. Dietet. Assoc. 38:450-454.

Bobeng, B. J., and B. D. David. 1978. HACCP models for quality control of entree production in hospital foodservice systems. II. Quality assessment of beef loaves utilizing HACCP models. J. Am. Dietet. Assoc. 73:530-535.

Bedero, K. O., A. M. Pearson, and W. T. Magee. 1980. Optimum cooking times for flavor development and evaluation of flavor quality of beef cooked by microwaves and conventional methods. J. Food Sci. 45:613-616.

Bryon, F. L., and E. G. Kilpatrick. 1971. Clostridum perfringens related to roast beef cooking, storage and contamination in a fast food service restaurant. Am. J. Publ. Health 61:1869-1884.

Bustead, R. 1980. Meeting the challenge in hospital food service (experimental phase). In Moving into the 1980's, Proceedings of the Food Service Management Committee of the National Security Industrial Association. U.S. Army Natick Research and Development Command, Natick, Mass. March 18.

Cardello, A. V., O. Maller, R. Kluter, and L. Digmon. 1981. Patient and staff evaluation of five patient food tray delivery systems. U.S. Army Natick Research and Development Laboratories, Natick, Mass. 15 pp.

Charley, H. 1970. Food Science. Ronald Press, New York. 520 pp.

Cohen, I., P. J. Schechter, and R. I. Henkin. 1973. Hyposusia, anorexia and altered zinc metabolism following thermal burn. J. Am. Med. Assoc. 223:914-916.

237

Cremer, M. L., and J. R. Chepley. 1979. Time and temperature, microbiological and sensory quality of meatloaf in a commissary foodservice system transporting heated food. J. Food Sci. 44:317-326.

Dahl, C. A. 1981a. Cook/chill foodservice systems: sensory evaluation of beef loaf, peas and potatoes reheated by conduction, convection or microwave radiation. J. Foodserv. Syst. In press.

Dahl, C. A. 1981b. Microwave Ovens: Theory and Use in Foodservice. Study Kit. American Dietetic Association, Chicago, Ill. In press.

Dahl, C. A., and M. E. Matthews. 1978. Cook/chill foodservice systems: microwave heating precooked portions of beef loaf. J. Microwave Power 13:87-93.

Dahl, C. A., and M. E. Matthews. 1979a. Forced-air convection ovens: temperature range in oven and in beef loaf during heating. School Food Serv. Res. Rev. 3:11-15.

Dahl, C. A., and M. E. Matthews. 1979b. Hospital cook/chill foodservice systems: effects of end temperature of initial cooking on yield and moisture content of beef loaf during processing. J. Am. Dietet. Assoc. 75:34-37.

Dahl, C. A., and M. E. Matthews. 1980a. Cook/chill foodservice system with a microwave oven: thiamine content in portions of beef loaf after microwave-heating. J. Food Sci. 45:608-612.

Dahl, C. A. and M. E. Matthews. 1980b. Cook/chill foodservice systems with microwave ovens: range of temperature, yield, moisture and fat content among portions of beef loaf, potatoes, and frozen and canned green beans after microwave-heating. J. Am. Dietet. Assoc. 77:289-295.

Dahl, C. A., and Y. Naidu. 1981. Cook/chill foodservice systems with conduction, convection and microwave reheat subsystems: relative microbiological condition of beef loaf, peas, and potatoes. J. Food Sci. In press.

Dahl, C. A., J. J. Jen, and P. D. Huang. 1981. Cook/chill foodservice systems with conduction, convection and microwave reheat subsystems: nutrient retention in beef loaf, peas, and potatoes. J. Food Sci. In press.

Desor, J. A., and D. Maller. 1975. Taste correlates of disease states: Cystic fibrosis. J. Pediatr. 87:93-96.

Ferguson, V. B. 1981. Microwave and flavor: compatible? In Digest Microwave Power Symposium 1981, International Microwave Power Institute, Toronto, Ontario, Canada, June 9-12. 87 pp.

er, M. J. 1963. The time-temperature relationships in food sanitation. Cornell Hotel Rest. Admin. Q. 4:58-62.

Franzese, R. 1981. Survey examines hospitals' use of convenience foods. Hospitals 55:109.

Glew, G. 1968. Attitudes of patients to food in hospitals. Nutr. Lond. 22:195-207

Glew, G. 1970. Food preferences of hospital patients. Proc. Nutr. Soc. 29:339-343.

Glew, G., ed. 1973. Cook/Freeze Catering, An Introduction to Its Technology. Faber and Faber, London. 168 pp.

Grater, Chris. 1979. The caterer's requirement for food quality. Pages 57-63 in G. Glew, ed., Advances in Catering Technology. Applied Science Publishers, London.

Hansson, E., H. Olsson, I. Bosund, and I. Rasmussen. 1972. Changes during warm holding of food products. Naringstorskning 16:106. In Swedish, summary in English.

Harder, E. J. 1979. Blast Freezing System for Quantity Foods. CBI, Boston, Mass. 394 pp.

Henkin, R. I, and F. G. Powell. 1962. Increased sensitivity of taste and smell in cystic fibrosis. Science 138:1107-1108.

Henkin, R. I., J. R. Gil, Jr., and F. C. Bartter. 1963. Studies on taste thresholds in normal man and in patients with adrenal cortical insufficiency: the role of adrenal cortical steroids and of serum sodium concentrations. J. Clin. Invest. 42:728-735.

Herz, M., A. Freeman, G. Eccleston, G. Hertweck, S. Baritz, P. Short, W. O. Veneklason, and J. Souder. 1978. A Systems Analysis of Alternative Food Service Concepts for New Army Hospitals. Technical Report, Natick/TR-78/031. U.S. Army Natick Research and Development Command, Natick, Mass. 199 pp.

Hill, M. A., M. Baron, J. S. Kent, and G. Glew. 1977. The effect of hot storage after reheating on the flavour and ascorbic acid retention of precooked frozen vegetables. Pages 331-340. in G. Glew, ed., Catering Equipment and Systems Design. Applied Science Publishers, London.

Hollingsworth, H. L., and A. T. Paffenberger, Jr. 1917. The Sense of Taste. Moffat, Yard and Co., New York. 212 pp.

Jonsson, L., L. Ohlsson, and B. Lindholm. 1977. Comparison of the temperature-holding capacities of three different tray distribution systems. Pages 295-313 in J. Glew, ed., Catering Equipment and Systems Design. Applied Science Publishers, London.

Karlstrom, B., and J. Jonsson. 1977. Quality changes during warm-holding of foods. Pages 315-330 in G. Glew, ed., Catering Equipment and Systems Design. Applied Science Publishers, London.

Kotschevar, L. 1973. Foodservice for the Extended Care Facility. Cahners Books, Boston, Mass. 509 pp.

Kotschevar, L. 1975. Management by Menu. National Institute for the Foodservice Industry, Chicago, Ill. 381 pp.

Kramer, A., and B. A. Twigg. 1970. Quality Control in the Foodservice Industry. Vol. 1, 3rd ed. AVI, Westport, Conn. 556 pp.

Livingston, G. E., and C. M. Chang. 1979. Food Service Systems, Analysis, Design and Implementation. Academic Press, New York. 483 pp.

Longree, K. 1972. Quantity Food Sanitation. 2d ed. Wiley-Interscience, New York. 422 pp.

Maller, O., C. N. Dubose, and A. V. Cardello. 1980. Consumer opinions of hospital food and foodservice: demographic and environmental factors. J. Am. Dietet. Assoc. 76:236-242.

Matthews, M. E. 1977. Quality of food in cook/chill foodservice systems: a review. School Foodserv. Res. Rev. 1:15-19.

Nightingale, M. 1979. Questions concerning quality and reliability of the meal experience. Pages 135-141 in G. Glew, ed., Advances in Catering Technology. Applied Science Publishers, London.

Paulus, K., I. Nowak, R. Zacharios, and A. Bognav. 1978. Influence of heating and keeping warm on the quality of meals. Ann. Nutr. Alim. 32:447-458.

Paulus, K. 1979. The constraints on food quality. Pages 51-63 in G. Glew, ed., Advances in Catering Technology. Applied Science Publishers, London.

Powers, T. F. 1980. Introduction to Management in the Hospitality Industry. John Wiley & Sons, New York. 383 pp.

Rambeck, U. 1979. How can the food supplier influence quality at the catering level? Pages 72-86 in G. Glew, ed., Advances in Catering Technology. Applied Science Publishers, London.

Riggs, S. 1981. How well has Walter Reed's "revolutionary" food system worked? Rest. Inst. 88:73-75.

Ryley, J., G. C. Brookes, and M. Paul. 1977. The effect of end-cooking methods on the colour of frozen vegetables. Pages 341-346 in G. Glew, ed., Catering Equipment and Systems Design. Applied Science Publishers, London.

aw, C. P., G. A. Darsch, and J. M. Tuomy. 1979.
Examination of Patient Tray Food Service Equipment and
Evaluation of the Alpha Cart. Technical Report,
Natick/TR-79/036. U.S. Army, Natick Reserch and
Development Command, Natick, Mass. 65 pp.

Sheatsley, P. B. 1965. How total hospital experience
shapes patient's opinion of food. Hospitals 39:105.

Sherman, P. 1975. Textural properties and food
acceptability. Proc. R. Soc. Lond. B 191:131-144.

Smith, L. L. W., and L. J. Minor. 1979. Food Service.
AVI, Westport, Conn. 632 pp.

Terrell, M. E. 1979. Professional Food Preparation. 2nd
ed. John Wiley & Sons, New York. 741 pp.

Thompson, L. D., and D. Johnson. 1963. Food temperature
preferences of patients. J. Am. Dietet. Assoc.
43:209-211.

USDHEW. 1976. Food Service Sanitation Manual. DHEW Publ.
No. (FDA) 78-2081, Food and Drug Administration,
Public Health Service, U.S. Department of Health,
Education, and Welfare, Washington, D.C. 96 pp.

Von Sydow, E. 1975. Flavour--a problem for the consumer
or for the food producer? Proc. R. Soc. Lond. B
191:145-153.

Ward, A.G. 1979. Food quality, the role of the law. Pages
87-98 in G. Glew, ed., Advances in Catering
Technology, Applied Science Publishers, London.

West, B. B., L. Wood, V. Narger, and G. Shugart. 1977.
Food Service in Institutions. 5th ed. John Wiley &
Sons, New York. 839 pp.

Williams, L. R., and M. Y. Cohen. 1978. Altered taste
thresholds in lung cancer. Am. J. Clin. Nutr.
31:122-125.

Wotman, S., I. D. Mandel, S. Khotim, R. H. Thompson, A.
H. Kutscher, E. V. Zegarelli, and C. R. Denning. 1964.
Salt thresholds and cystic fibrosis. Am. J. Dis.
Child. 108:372-374.

Zaccorelli, H. E. 1972. Nursing Home Menu Planning--Food
Purchasing, Management. Cahners Books, Boston, Mass.
359 pp.

Zallen, E. M., M. J. Hitchcock, and G. E. Goertz. 1975.
Chilled food systems. Am. Dietet. 67:552.

APPENDIX A
FOOD SERVICE TEXTBOOKS

Ten food service textbooks were reviewed for content related to material covered in this paper (American Hospital Association, 1972; Zaccorelli, 1972; Kotschevar, 1973, 1975; West et al., 1977; Harder, 1979; Livingston and Chang, 1979; Smith and Minor, 1979; Terrell, 1979; and Powers, 1980). Tables of contents were reviewed to determine if topics of meal assembly, meal distribution, or meal service were addressed. Results in Table A-1 show that only 30 percent of books reviewed contained information on meal distribution and service. Only 10 percent (one book) contained information on meal assembly. Similarly, indexes of the 10 books were reviewed to determine if topics related to sensory quality of food at service were addressed. Results in Table A-1 indicate that less than 10 percent mentioned the subject. This review of textbooks shows that information on meal assembly, distribution, and service, as well as discussion of sensory quality of foods in food service systems, has received

TABLE A-1 Number of Food Service Textbooks Containing Material on Sensory Quality of Food at Meal Assembly, Distribution, and Service

Topic	Number of Books[a]
Table of Contents	
Meal assembly	1
Meal distribution	3
Meal service	3
Index	
Color of food	0
Palatability	0
Quality of food	1
Sensory quality of food	0
Taste	1
Temperature of food at service	1 (no temperature given)
Texture of food	1

[a]N = 10.

little attention. Knowledge of food service operators in these areas probably did not come from formal training if these or similar textbooks were used as the only class references.

APPENDIX B   SURVEY OF HOSPITAL FOOD SERVICE DIRECTORS

Ten food service directors were informally interviewed by telephone in June 1981. The population surveyed consisted of:

Men	60 percent
Women	40 percent
Work in Michigan	80 percent
Work outside of Michigan	20 percent

Hospitals in which the food service directors worked served 300-1,500 patient meals per day. Food service systems were conventional or cook-freeze.

Food service directors were asked the following questions.

1. What parameters would you include in a definition of the sensory quality of food?
    Patient's point of view?
    Food director's point of view?

2. What type of food service system does your facility have?
    A. Describe your meal assembly process.
    What are the effects of the meal assembly process on the sensory quality of the food at service?
    B. Please describe your meal distribution process. What do you feel are the effects of your meal distribution process on sensory qualities of the food served?
    C. Please describe your meal service process. What do you feel are the effects of your meal service process (reheat) on sensory qualities of the food served to patients?

3. Please rate 3 food qualities:

    1 = most important

Patient perspective: Food Service perspective:
___ Microbiological   ___ Microbiological
___ Nutritional   ___ Nutritional
___ Sensory   ___ Sensory

4. From the patient's perspective, why do patients eat?

Sensory satisfaction
Hunger
Nervousness
Nutrition
Other:

5. Does your facility have sensory standards for food served? Do you know of sensory standards in other facilities?

6. Do you feel that climate of service is a significant factor in a patient's appreciation of the sensory quality of food served? Which factors are positive and which negative?

DISCUSSION

QUESTION: If you are not going to be concerned about sensory quality, do I have to be concerned about microbiological quality?

DAHL: As a spokesman for sensory quality, I might look at the relative importance of sensory, microbiological, and nutritional quality. I did query 10 food service directors and try and get some impression of their overall thinking. I was surprised in that sensory quality did, in fact, come before microbiological quality. My personal viewpoint is that biological quality and chemical safety should take preeminence, even if we could achieve better sensory quality.

QUESTION: At what length of time does frozen storage begin to surpass the quality of refrigerated storage?

DAHL: Generally speaking, colder is better as far as sensory quality retention is concerned. I recently read a study that compared the quality of frozen food and the quality of refrigerated food during a 3-day storage period. The result of that study indicated that frozen storage was the preferred method of achieving better sensory quality. I would, however, caution that when

length of storage is considered, storage in a chilled
state should probably be not much more than 1 day and certainly not more than 3 days. Comparing the time in that
sense is perhaps not valid, since in a chilled system you
would think in terms of a 24-hour to 72-hour maximum
period, whereas with frozen storage you might consider
3-, 6-, or maybe even 12-month periods at a time. So,
the sensory concern is not as important as the microbiological concern.

QUESTION: In a prepared production system holding
food approximately 45 days, in your opinion is the food
quality at the point of patient service better with
frozen or with refigerated storage, assuming sanitary
packaging and quick chilling?

DAHL: I think the question refers to a comparison of
food that has been held using the Cryovac system, where
it has been cooled in a water bath and stored in an
oxygen-impermeable film for up to 45 days, and a similar
food product, that has been held in frozen storage for 45
days.

The answer to the question is "I don't know," because
I have not seen any literature reporting such a comparison. I have not tasted the same food that has been held
in a Cryovac system and in a cook-freeze holding
technique.

The second thought that I had in answering that question is that it probably depends on the type of food.
Foods such as soups may maintain excellent sensory quality
even after 45 days in a Cryovac system--probably comparable to food that has been held in a frozen state. Sensory quality of food after frozen storage is going to be
dependent on several factors: the length of time in
frozen storage as well as the barrier properties of the
wrap in which the food is stored; and some unknown factors, such as the method in which you defrost that food,
will probably affect the sensory quality. At Michigan
State, we're undertaking a study of five methods of thawing, including microwave thawing, refrigerator thawing,
and other ways in the forced air convection oven.

Meal distribution can be done without thermal support,
or it can be done hot-holding, or it can be done using
cold-holding techniques. Of these three, hot-holding is
considered by most authors as perhaps the most destructive to the sensory quality of food. Carlstrom and
Johnson in 1977 concluded that the greatest quality losses
due to hot-holding were sensory attributes. Hansen in
1972 determined that hot-holding has the most deleterious

effect on flavor, and other authors such as Grater in 1972
see a conflict between the requirement for maintaining
microbiological quality of food and requirements for maximizing sensory quality. So, some questions to think about
are: How long is the distribution time? (The time of
hot-holding can be deleterious to the effect of sensory
quality on food.) Are delays a regular occurrence in your
facility? (Delays can cause increased time for hot-
holding.)

If you're considering a system with no thermal support
during meal distribution, you, of course, have a big question about the temperature change between the time food
leaves the central area and gets to the patient service
areas. Are the hot- and cold-holding areas separated well
enough so that the hot food doesn't get cold and the cold
food doesn't get hot? And, lastly, check the temperature
of foods in all areas of the cart or hot-cold holding unit
that you may be using. How uniform are the temperatures
throughout the equipment?

One of the concerns that we have is that food service
equipment handles food in bulk or quantity. As a result
we see a large range of temperature distribution. So, we
would challenge manufacturers and operators to continually
be aware that the temperature is in an acceptable range.
Here, when we're considering meal distribution and temperatures that are held hot, those temperatures should be
140°F or higher. With reheat we have a different criteria: They should be 165°F or higher. During meal
distribution you want your hot foods to be 140°F or 60°C
at a minimum. Of course, if they go too high you have
the problem of lowering sensory quality due to the moisture loss. So, look not only at the temperatures of one
or two samples, but look at the temperature distribution
within equipment that you have.

QUESTION: Could you comment on hot-holding of canned
vegetables and canned or convenience entrees as related
to sensory quality?

DAHL: I am unaware of any research reports relating
to sensory degradation of canned vegetables; however, my
immediate response is that since they have already been
pressure-processed at 250°F or above, they have probably
gone through most of the color and texture changes and
would not experience dramatic additional changes. However, any food that you put into hot-holding will continue to deteriorate—perhaps at a slower level than
would freshly prepared vegetables. Again, we have the
effect of different market forms of food. And, by

experimentation or possibly by additional research, we may find a better answer to the question of the effect of on hot-holding different market forms of vegetables.

QUESTION: Would you comment on moisture retention under insulated covers without a hole?

DAHL: Moisture does tend to build up on the dome and drip back onto the food. I would not be worried from a sensory perspective about drying the food out; in effect, I would be worried about the opposite point: What effect is the dripping moisture gong to have on the appearance? Is it going to make it look soggy? Is it going to make the gravy look watery?

QUESTION: Don't toast or other intended dry hot foods get soggy in the system?

DAHL: Yes, they do.

QUESTION: Would it be possible to prolong the holding time of vegetables and retain their sensory quality by using frozen vegetables versus canned or by otherwise undercooking vegetables to be held more than 30 minutes?

DAHL: Yes, a very good suggestion. Undercooking is one method that is used in food service systems that have a second heat system. If you talk to chefs and cooks in various hospitals, you will find that a general practice is to initially cook foods about 75 percent of completion when you have a second heat treatment either in cook-chill or cook-freeze. A project that I undertook at the University of Wisconsin was to look at the microbiological effects of undercooking food initially and then reheating it to appropriate temperatures, which would be 165°F or higher, before service. This did turn out to be acceptable microbiological practice when beef loaf was the product.

So, the answer is that vegetables alone are generally not considered to be a potentially hazardous product. If you're anticipating a long hot-holding period, you may not even initially process the vegetables at all. You would probably want to bring them to 140°F but then not process them. This would not cook them but would more or less put them in a hot condition for the steam table or other hot holding unit. No hot-holding unit is designed to bring a food up to 140°F or any given temperature. It's only designed to maintain that temperature. The answer to the question is yes, diminish the initial cooking if you're going to plan on hot-holding.

Assuring the Microbiological Quality of Hospital Patient Feeding Systems

Gerald Silverman

INTRODUCTION

The term "microbiological quality" applied to food items
is an inclusive one that contains a number of diverse
meanings and implications. It incorporates safety and
whether or not pathogens, toxins, and other microbial
metabolites having physiological activity are present.
It also indicates the presence or absence of unacceptable
spoilage aromas and flavors. It is not always appreciated that often a further consideration, that of shelf
life, can also be involved. The relationship between
safety and spoilage, though, is not always mutually beneficial, and guaranteeing one does not necessarily guarantee the other. For example, during processing the
microflora may be drastically altered and reduced, and
normal spoilage growth patterns and their accompanying
volatiles and flavors minimized. It is then possible for
pathogens, if introduced and allowed to flourish, to
create a public health problem unaccompanied by significant spoilage indications (Ayres, 1971; Mossell, 1975).
In other instances the distinction between spoilage and
pathogens is altered by the susceptibility of the patient.
Spoilage organisms, normally benign to a healthy individual, can cause severe infections to stressed patients
(Knudsen and Bodman, 1976).

It is often difficult to state definitively that a
given food item in a hospital feeding system does not
contain any pathogen, toxin, etc., or that it has not

Gerald Silverman, Food Microbiology Group, Science and
Advanced Technology Laboratory, U.S. Army Natick Research
and Development Laboratories, Natick, Massachusetts.

been subjected to incipient spoilage. Each food item will be accompanied, unless extreme measures are taken, by a microbial flora. The resultant risk-benefit estimate for each patient can only be achieved if an effective quality assurance program (QAP) is operative. A properly designed and supervised QAP will be an important contribution in any risk-benefit calculation, not only in making an adequate safety factor achievable but also for enabling the program to be consistent.

The QAP required for hospital feeding systems should be a dynamic cost-effective program not mainly dependent on end product analysis. All elements in a facility—equipment, raw material, personnel, and procedures—have to be considered. Processing and sanitation are monitored, and the training and performance of personnel, especially supervisory personnel, are an integral part of the program. It has been noted that with proper controls acceptable products can be produced in substandard facilities, and that while one can improve the microbial quality of raw materials, unacceptable raw materials should never be used (Surkiewicz et al., 1967; Peterson and Gunderson, 1974).

Estimates are that as high as 10 percent of patients in acute-care hospitals in the United States undergo a nosocomial infection (New York Times, 1981b). Dixon (1980) noted that the second most important source for infection appears to be contaminated vehicles that carry food. The contribution of foods to this infection rate is unknown, especially for a particular hospital at which a very high nosocomial rate has been experienced.

As noted by Silverman (1976), hospitals may be considered an in-house production facility whereby a wide variety of products are produced in a technologically limited facility and delivered to a known population. While difficult to monitor with the hazard analysis-critical control point program (HACCP), the method has the advantage of being able to control all elements of its production and delivery systems. The important consideration is whether or not the system is functioning as designed and reflected in the QAP. An effective QAP should have sufficient constraints to be able to meet criteria evaluated by established tests.

FACTORS INVOLVED IN THE CONTROL OF
MICROBIAL GROWTH AND SURVIVAL

The requirements for the proliferation in food of microorganisms of public health concern are listed in Table
1. It can be seen that, either due to survival or after
the introduction of toxigenic organisms, the main factors
that will affect subsequent growth are temperature and
time, since processing reduces competing microflora, and
most foods are capable of supporting microbial growth. A
number of investigators studying a diversity of food service systems have indicated that, while they did not encounter any foods posing a public health problem, in a
great many cases either the organisms or defects in the
processing operations were present (Bryan et al., 1978)
and presented a potential hazard. Often one or more of
the requirements in Table 1 is missing, and an outbreak
occurs only upon their appearance.

Microorganisms capable of causing food infection or
intoxication appear to constitute a small number (Table
2), and they have been studied extensively so that almost
all of their growth requirements are known. Most of these
are vegetative organisms and, unlike spores, will therefore not survive normal cooking temperature. Certain of
the organisms are capable both of being infective and of
producing enterotoxins. While one agent, such as the
enterotoxins of S. aureus or the neurotoxins of C.

TABLE 1   Requirements for a Foodborne Intoxication or an
Infectious Incident

---

1. The toxigenic or infectious organism either survives
   processing or is introduced into the food item during
   processing.
2. Nontoxigenic organisms are present in low numbers or
   are incapable of inhibiting growth of pathogens.
3. Growth conditions are favorable:
   - temperature
   - nutrients, pH, Eh, oxygen concentration, moisture
     content, solutes, etc.
4. Other:
   - repair mechanisms
   - additives
   - physiological state

TABLE 2 Major Infective and Enterotoxigenic Organisms

Organism	Spore	Infective	Entero-toxi-genic	Growth Temperature (°C)
Gram-positive				
Clostridium botulinum	+	+	+	3-48
Clostridium perfringens	+	+	+	6.5-50
Staphylococcus aureus	−	+	+	10-45
Bacillus cereus	+	−	+	10-48
Gram-negative				
Salmonella sp.	−	+	+[a]	5-47
Vibrio				
parahemolyticus	−	+	+	4-42
cholera	−	+	+	15-42
Shigella	−	+	+[a]	
Escherichia coli	−	+	+	10-40
Yersenia	−	+		-2-45
Klebsiella			+[a]	

[a]Requires further verification.

botulinum, may be of more significance in food intoxication, they are also capable of being infective. In some
instances proliferation is not necessary (Bryan, 1979)
because small concentrations are sufficient for causing a
food-borne infection, although large numbers of organisms
are generally needed to cause an intoxication. As few as
10^1 organisms of Shigella and 10^3 of Vibrio cholera
are capable of infecting an adult. Others, such as Salmonella, require 10^4 to 10^5 organisms, and Clostridium
perfringens as many as 10^8 organisms.

Generation times for these organisms, which are mostly
mesophiles, depend of course on the temperature and are
usually 15-30 minutes at optimal temperatures, but Willardsen et al. (1978) observed a doubling time of 7.1
minutes at 41°C for C. perfringens. At refrigeration
temperatures, growth is either inhibited or the generation time is lengthened to hours. This is why temperatures appreciably above or below the optima are
effective for inhibiting growth.

Spoilage organisms are present on the raw material and
are often also introduced during processing and distribution. They consist of a large variety of species, many

of which are psychrophiles. The temperature range for growth of these microflora in raw food will be wide, from below 0°C to approximately 45°C. While no one organism in the microbial spectrum will grow at either end of this wide temperature range, in general, organisms that consist of psychrotrophs and mesophiles can usually compete effectively with food poisoning organisms and are responsible for protecting the consumer if temperature abuse occurs by causing spoilage. They are, however, susceptible to processing stresses, and it is their destruction that makes thermally processed foods so favorable, subsequently, as a growth medium for food poisoning organisms. Ingredients and raw foods almost always contain a significant microflora.

The importance of the quality of the raw material being used during processing should not be minimized. Processing should not salvage food that is partially spoiled. Moreover, a number of studies have demonstrated a direct relationship between the presence of hazardous microorganisms and the aerobic plate count, although some consider this relationship to be inconsistent (Silverman, 1979).

An example of the microbiological concentration of the raw materials entering the system is illustrated in Table 3, which lists the quality of the raw material from commercial sources encountered in a military feeding system (Silverman et al., 1976).

These items were not analyzed for specific pathogens or enterotoxigenic organisms. This is not unusual, since the expense and time required for the examination of specific organisms would, on a routine basis, be considerable. For this reason certain indices are employed (Table 4). Indicator organisms, or indices, are organisms for which well-defined, rapid, and economical analytical methods are available and whose presence in excessive numbers would indicate that (1) the raw material was not satisfactory, (2) the processing parameters were not correct (3) contaminants were introduced during processing, or (4) storage and delivery systems were faulty. Indices can be selected for specific products and processing situations; but they do not ensure that contamination with a specific organism that is not tested for will not occur, and they have to be employed with a great deal of judgment. Even when a particular food-poisoning organism is routinely tested for, testing can only be done in a limited manner, and the use of indices as a substitute may be thought to be inadequate. In only a few instances (Mossel, 1975) have specific food-poisoning organisms

TABLE 3 Microbiological Analysis of Ingredients Used in Frozen Foil Pack Food Items

Item	Aerobic Plate Count (CFU^a/g)	Coliform (MPN^b/g)	Fecal Coliform (MPN/g)	Staphylococcus Aureus (per gram)	Fecal Streptococci (per gram)
Raw beef	5.2×10^5	>1100	4.6	+	69
Ground raw beef	2.4×10^6	>1100	>1100	+	2
Ground raw beef	3.8×10^5	870	>1100	+	2
Raw steak	3.4×10^4	234	8.8	+	12
Raw chicken	3×10^4	110	89	−	1.5
Raw chicken	1.2×10^4	240	24	0	2
Peas and carrots	1.1×10^4	0.36	0	0	−
Green beans	4×10^2	0	0	0	0
Raw potatoes	3.8×10^5	470	0	0	5
Potato (dehydrated)	$<10^2$	0	0	0	0
Gravy mix	5×10^1	15	1.5	0	0
Seasoning mix	4.1×10^4	350	2.7	−	23
BBQ sauce mix	2.5×10^2	0	0	0	0
Rehydrated cake mix	6.7×10^2	17	0	0	0
Icing for cake	24×10^3	0	0	0	0

[a]Colony forming unit
[b]Most probable number

SOURCE: Silverman et al., 1976.

TABLE 4   Microbiological Indices

Aerobic plate count	Fecal streptococci
Anaerobic plate count	Halophilic organisms
Yeast and mold count	Osmophilic organisms
Thermophilic plate count	Spore count
Psychrophilic plate count	Direct microscopic
Coliforms	Dye reduction
Fecal coliforms	Impedence
	C-14 evolution

been related to an indice and are applicable only to a particular food. Nevertheless, the judicious use of indices, especially when combined with one or more analyses for specific organisms, can be effective after the acquisition of a data base.

The effectiveness of temperature in eliminating micro-flora is illustrated in Figure 1. Not only did the ground beef contain a significant bioburden, but other ingredients (spices, seasoning) also contributed additional organisms. Although the cooking temperatures varied widely, the bioburden was reduced to low numbers, the APC to 2,300 organisms per gram, and the indices to zero.

It can be seen that the microbial concentrations varied from 10^2 per gram for commercially processed products to over 10^6 per gram for raw ingredients such as ground beef. The latter also contained very high numbers of coliform and fecal coliform organisms. Since microorganisms are inactivated by a combination of temperature and time, it is apparent that the more contaminated raw ingredients all have to be heated for longer times to have their microbial population reduced to a reasonable concentration. Extremely contaminated foods, therefore, should not be employed. They may not only be partially spoiled, but they may also be unable to pass microbial constraints without extremely prolonged thermal processing.

The microbial flora of thermally processed foods can be stabilized by effective refrigeration (Table 5). Snyder (1981) recently noted that pasteurized (thermally processed but not sterile) foods are capable of 2 to 4 weeks of storage life. Items may behave differently—mainly those that do not cool rapidly, such as roast beef, for which an increase in microbial population was

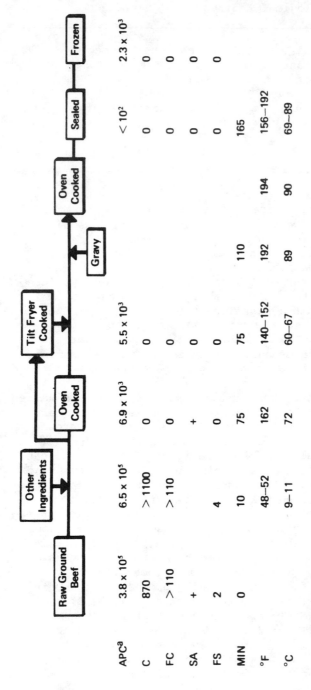

	Raw Ground Beef	Other Ingredients	Oven Cooked	Tilt Fryer Cooked	Gravy	Oven Cooked	Sealed	Frozen
APC[a]	3.8×10^5	6.5×10^5	6.9×10^3	5.5×10^3			$< 10^2$	2.3×10^3
C	870	>1100	0	0			0	0
FC	>110	>110	0	0			0	0
SA	+	+	+	0			0	0
FS	2	4	0	0			0	0
MIN	0	10	75	75	110		165	
°F		48—52	162	140—152	192	194	156—192	
°C		9—11	72	60—67	89	90	69—89	

[a]APC--aerobic plate count in colony-forming units
(CFU)/g; C--coliform is in most probable number (MPN)/g;
FC--fecal coliform in MPN/g; SA--Staphylococcus aureus/g;
FS--fecal streptococci/g; MIN--minutes to reach the
particular stage of processing; °F--degrees Fahrenheit;
°C--degrees Celsius.

FIGURE 1 The effect of processing on the microflora of beef pot pie.

TABLE 5   Microbial Analysis of Items Stored at 40°F

| Item | Microorganisms per Gram | | |
	0 Days	Mesophiles, 7-9 Days	Psychrophiles, 7-9 Days
Chicken pot pie	210	80	50
Roast beef	725	15,000	13,000
Salisbury steak	4,200	3,100	5,400
Fried chicken	4,400	80	65
Sliced ham	1,500	75	30
French fried potatoes	420	100	25
Onion rings	1,300	15	50
Onion rings (partially baked)	17,000	76,000	66,000
Oven browned potatoes	11,000	15	20
Lyonnaised potatoes	700	1,800	1,600
Lyonnaised potatoes (partially baked)	18,000	4×10^6	4×10^6
Vegetable soup	65	10	10
Cream of potato soup	200	2×10^5	2×10^5
Clam chowder	335	480	320
Cucumber salad (without vinegar)		4×10^7	3×10^7
Cucumber salad (with vinegar)		2,550	1,300
Carrot salad	4×10^5	4×10^6	3×10^6

noted. Partially baked items, such as onion rings and lyonnaise potatoes, experienced a significant increase in counts. The most obvious reason for the increase in bioburden for cream of potato soup was a failure to be rapidly cooled due to storage in a large container. The results for raw salads without dressing or vinegar are not unusual. The natural microflora, especially if there is sufficient moisture present, can proliferate during refrigerated storage unless stabilized. An effective procedure is to decrease the pH. Vinegar not only accomplishes this, but acetic acid is also bacteriostatic. Silverman et al. (1976) found that salad ingredients frequently contained a very high bioburden, having aerobic plate counts in excess of 10^7 organisms per gram and coliforms in excess of 10^3, and were positive for fecal coliform. This observation was also made by Ockerman and Stec (1980), who found that adding vegetables (shredded lettuce, tomato slices, and dressing) to sandwiches greatly increased the bioburden. Frozen foods will be completely stabilized after freezing and, in fact, some of the microflora will lose viability during storage. Growth can resume, though, after thawing.

Many items, some of which may not usually be considered to contain a large number of organisms, have in fact been found to do so. Spices can be a troublesome source of contamination (Pivnick, 1980). Those not treated with ethylene or propylene oxides contained microbial concentrations having an aerobic plate count of 10^2 to 10^7 organisms per gram, depending on the type of spice. Twenty-five percent of the samples tested had coliforms in excess of 10^3 per gram and 6 percent had E. coli present. Treatment by ethylene or propylene oxides reduced the counts from 80 to 99.999 percent, but individual spices were still capable of containing significant bioburdens.

While breakfast cereals and baked goods generally have low bactrial counts, flour and dry cereal mixes can contain bioburdens up to 10^6 organisms per gram and coliforms to 10^4, and possess E. coli (Elliot, 1980).

In addition to monitoring microbiological tests for specific organisms and indices, a QAP should include tests for monitoring the environment of the facility, the effectiveness of sanitation procedures, and processing parameters (Table 6). Most of these techniques are inexpensive and simple to employ, and some, such as an air sampler, may not have to be employed after it has been established that aerosols are not a problem.

TABLE 6   Sanitation and Processing Tests

Time	Sanitation and the environment
Temperature	- Swab test
- Thermometer	- Rodac plate
- Paper thermometer	- Contact tape
- Recorder	- Air sampler
- Temperature-time indicator	- Visual inspection

Temperature and time are the main elements in any QAP (Bobeng and David, 1977), and extreme care should be taken in the measurement of temperature. Dependence on controlling thermal processing by oven temperature is to be avoided. Instead, it is necessary to measure the internal temperature of the food item, and for items such as roasts the proper monitoring is conducted on the largest units in the oven. The cooling stage in cook-chill or cook-freeze systems also appears to be critical in that appreciable multiplication can occur if the rate is too slow (Tuomi et al., 1974; Bunch et al., 1976; Bryan and McKinley, 1979; Longree, 1980). Slow cooling rates inevitably result from storing large volumes, failing to have sufficient air circulation, covering the product while still hot, and an inadequate cooling capacity of the refrigerator unit.

The three methods--rodac plate, swab, and contact tape--used for evaluating the sanitation of food contact surfaces have different efficiencies of recovery (Silverman, 1979). This is not a critical factor if the same method is consistently used for evaluating a surface and a data base for an acceptable sanitary state is established. One should not depend completely upon visual inspection, since is it often an inadequate criterion for evaluation (Table 7). Visual inspection overestimated satisfactory surfaces and underestimated unsatisfactory surfaces. Comparable results were obtained using swabs. Similarly, the use of paper thermometers for monitoring warewashing operations will indicate whether or not the unit is operating correctly but not whether the surface of the washed item has been sanitized. Subsequent monitoring of the sanitized surface by a contact technique (rodac plate, swab, or tape) will indicate whether handling contributes any significant bioburden.

That the control of these QAP elements is extremely important is indicated by the data compiled by Bryan (1978) (Table 8). The three main factors implicated in outbreaks were a lack of adequate temperature control, followed by an inoculation from an infective source, and also a lack of sanitation. Essentially the same factors were involved in a subsequent study done on meat and poultry products, which are responsible for over 50 percent of the foodborne outbreaks (Bryan, 1980). Ham, turkey, and roast beef products were the most frequently identified sources, with sausage and chicken following.

Cremer and Shipley (1980a) obtained a time-temperature profile for scrambled eggs processed in a hospital-type food service system and found that the potential for

problems existed even though microbial counts were low.
The microflora contained a wide variety of organisms,
including S. aureus, E. coli, and a sporeformer, and they
noted that the time-temperature combinations encountered
would support microbial proliferation.

Of importance in any program, especially as a source
of contamination during or after processing, are the food
service personnel. Large numbers and a variety of organisms are associated with humans (Skinner and Carr, 1974).
All skin surfaces contain a microflora, their concentration being dependent upon personal sanitation, the use of
disposable gloves, and the degree of shedding by the individual. Heavy bioburdens have been found on the wrists,
hands, and face, indicating a requirement for the use of
disposable gloves. In an effective QAP it is essential
that gloves be worn if contact is a problem. This problem has been noted by Cremer and Shipley (1980b), who
found large number of S. epidermidis resulting from a
slicing procedure in a hospital system where gloves were

TABLE 7 Comparison of Rodac Plate Count and Visual
Evaluation

	Method of Evaluation			
	Visual	NLABS[a] A	B	Maximum Two-Plate Test[b]
Number of Tables				
Satisfactory	22	7	11	13
Unsatisfactory	5	20	16	14

[a]U.S. Army Natick Research and Development Laboratories'
standard. A: That standard used in surveys, whereby a
table is judged satisfactorily if no rodac plate count
exceeds 100 CFU/25.8 cm^2 or more than 50 percent of the
plates had counts of 50 CFU/25.8 cm^2. B: By changing
the previous constraint to 150 CFU/25.8 cm^2.
[b]Rodac plates for two locations were randomly chosen
and judged satisfactory if the maximum of the two plates
did not exceed 150 CFU 25.8 cm^2.

TABLE 8   Microbial Factors Contributing to Foodborne
Disease Outbreaks (1973-1976)

Rank	Factor
1	Inadequate refrigeration
2	Preparing food too far in advance
3	Holding food at temperatures not hot or cold enough
4	Infected personnel coming in contact with food
5	Inadequate reheating
6	Inadequate cleaning of equipment
7	Leftovers
8	Cross-contamination
9	Inadequate thermal processing
11	Contaminated raw ingredients in cooked foods
14	Obtaining foods from unsafe sources

SOURCE: F.L. Bryan, 1978.

not employed, and by Bryan and McKinley (1979), who found
S. aureus on the hands of handlers of roast beef.

Avens et al. (1978) studied whether the hazards that
can be associated with food service systems--in this case
schools--are characteristic of the type of system or the
schools themselves and found that preparation and handling
abuses were the responsibility of the schools and not the
particular system. None of the four methods studied--
conventional on-site, hot bulk-transported, cook-chill,
and cook-freeze--demonstrated any advantage in minimizing
the frequency of abuses.

METHOD OF HAZARD ANALYSIS-CRITICAL CONTROL POINT

A recent development in effectively monitoring a food
service system is the hazard analysis-critical control
point (HACCP) program (Silverman, 1979; Bryan 1981;
Snyder, 1981).

Hazard analysis identifies those processing points,
ingredients, and human elements that can affect product
safety in a significant way. Critical control points are
those processing parameters that must be accurately
controlled in order to ensure the safety of the product.

The HACCP approach identifies operations that present a constant and most hazardous potential and concentrates on monitoring these operations.

The HAACP procedure addresses itself to attaining a level of safety by combining monitoring of the processing operations with good manufacturing practices. This procedure is production oriented and lends itself most readily to a commercial production facility.

The International Commission on Microbiological Specifications for Foods (ICMSF) has developed sampling plans based upon the risk inherent for different food classifications. The risks are assigned values--Case 1, the least hazardous, to Case 15, the most hazardous. This procedure has been devised mostly for application to sampling (Table 9) of various foods and relates each food to a corresponding case, with specific indices and associated pathogens. The ICMSF method does attempt, in a general way, to match the food material, its associated microflora, and its use. This is apparent, for example, in the more stringent requirements for dried special dietary foods that are to be fed to highly susceptible consumers such as patients, infants, and the elderly.

Unfortunately, to ensure an extremely high degree of protection so as to eliminate the presence of pathogens with any degree of certainty requires a large number of samples. For example, in a lot having a 2 percent level of contamination of salmonella, with no sample allowed to contain any salmonella (c = 0), if the number of samples (n) equalled 60, two out of three lots would be rejected, and the probability of acceptance would be 30 percent, whereas, with n = 5, c = 0, one out of ten lots would be rejected.

The difficulty is that these procedures were designed in large part for the evaluation of large commercial production batches. In a hospital facility the diets are more varied and the items served may be fresh, reconstituted, cook-frozen, cook-chill, cook-serve, etc. Production lots are usually not large--in fact they can be quite small--and shelf life is generally greatly limited by refrigerated storage. Moreover, the ICMF and other schemes, although assuming hazards imposed by pathogens, were not designed to closely match the safety represented by a sampling scheme to that of patient susceptibility.

An effective QAP, in spite of frequently having severe personnel restrictions, must be capable of combining the best features of both the HACCP and the ICMSF procedures. Bobeng and David (1977) applied the HACCP model to food service systems and found that time and temperature is a

critical parameter requiring continuous surveillance.
However, they were unable (Bobeng and David, 1978) to
achieve a uniform HACCP program for food service systems
because of their diversity.

The following QAPs have been developed and tested at a
military hospital production facility for cook-freeze,
cook-chill, and fresh menu items that use a delivery system based on rethermalization (conductive) from the chill
state. Although it incorporates features of HACCP, it
depends upon a more integrated monitoring program that
utilizes microbiological data not only to monitor the
system but to establish guidelines for consumer (patient)
risk.

DESIGNING A QUALITY ASSURANCE PROGRAM FOR A HOSPITAL

The QAP should be designed to achieve the desired safety
consistently, and this should be accomplished by personnel
fully oriented as to the objectives, the rationale required to achieve them, and cost-effectiveness. Management must realize that success is measured by an absence
of problems, and that a lack of problems does not indicate that the QAP is superfluous, since the elimination
of food intoxication outbreaks and the occurrence of
extremely low incidences of food related microbial problems is a main objective of a successful and dynamic QAP.
Snyder (1981) has recently observed that an effective QAP
can be expected to reduce noncompliance to an extremely
low percentage but cannot be expected to eliminate it.

The food service equipment in a facility should be
monitored for performance characteristics and reliability.
Examples of the units in a production facility to be monitored are listed in Table 10. Management must be thoroughly familiar with the equipment and its performance.
In many instances difficulties arise in processing, not
only because of a breakdown in the performance of equipment but also from an inability to operate at required
efficiency, so that if poor cooling, lower than desired
cooking temperatures, inadequate mixing, etc. results, a
food will be inadequately processed. Equipment specifications are often misleading. For example, ovens
frequently lack temperature uniformity and are rarely
tested when loaded.

The elements in a QAP that has been designed for a
cook-freeze military facility are listed in Table 11
(elements 1 to 11) and integrate the performance of the
facility with that of management objectives. Extensive

TABLE 9 ICMSF Sampling Plans and Microbiological Limits

Product	Test	Case	Class	Plan[a] n	Plan[a] c	Limit per gram m	Limit per gram M
Breaded precooked fish	SPC[b]	2	3	5	2	10^6	10^7
	Faecal coliforms (MPN[c])	5	3	5	2	4	400
	Staphylococcus (ind)[d]	5	3	5	2	10^3	2×10^3
Frozen cooked shrimp, prawn, and lobster tails	SPC	3	3	5	1	10^6	10^7
	Faecal coliforms (MPN)	6	3	5	1	4	400
	Staphylococcus (path)[d]	9	3	5	1	10^3	2×10^3
	V. parahaemolyticus	12	2	5	0	10^2	
Fresh vegetables (to be consumed raw)	E. coli	5	3	5	2	10	10^3
	Salmonella	11	2	10	0	0	
Blanched, frozen vegetables	SPC	4	3	5	3	10^4	10^6
	Coliforms	4	3	5	3	10	10^3
Dried dietetic foods	SPC	2	3	5	2	10^4	10^6
	Coliforms or enterobacteriaceae	5	3	5	2	10	10^3
	Salmonella	11	2	10	0	0	

Product	Test	Case	Class	n	c	m	M
Dried soups, not to be cooked	SPC[b]	2	3	5	1	10^4	10^6
	Coliforms	5	3	5	2	10	10^3
	C. perfringens	8	3	5	1	10^2	10^4
	Salmonella	11	2	10	0	0	
Dried special dietary foods[e]	SPC	3	3	5	1	10^4	10^6
	E. coli	5	3	5	2	<3[f]	10
	S. aureus	9	3	10	1	10	10^2
	B. aureus	9	3	10	1	10^2	10^4
	C. perfringens	9	3	10	1	10^2	10^3
	Salmonella	15	2	60	0	0	
Frozen precooked entrees and vegetables in sauce	SPC	5	3	5	2	10^5	10^6
	Coliforms	5	3	5	2	10^2	10^4
	E. coli	5	3	5	2	<3	10^2

[a] n, number of units sampled; c, number of units that can exceed a microbiological level, m, but no sample can exceed M.

[b] Standard plate count.

[c] Most probable number.

[d] Indicator (ind) as distinguished from pathogen (path).

[e] Foods to be eaten by high risk patients; food for infants, aged, relief, etc.

[f] <3, no positive tube in a 3-tube MPN test.

end product analysis and temperature and sanitation monitoring activities are conducted to establish a data base.
Generally one tends to discover that consistency in
processing is lacking. Once the system appears to be in
control and monitoring is effective, then the frequency
of surveillance can be decreased and more selection demonstrated in the items chosen for monitoring.

The elements listed in Table 11 have also been incorporated and expanded further into a QAP for a cook-chill
and cook-freeze system for a military hospital. These
were designed to provide reliability with a minimum of
personnel and laboratory equipment. Not only are more
factors considered in the utilization of raw materials,
but also portioning and delivery systems requirements
were added (elements 12 to 14).

The system does not depend on HACCP analysis for each
product, but instead classifies products into categories
that are dependent upon their main processing parameters.
These parameters (ovens, kettles, freezers, etc.) are
monitored as "stations" with the actual temperature constraint established for each product. The monitoring of
the most critical parameters is documented by designated
personnel. In this way criticial parameters are constantly checked by a minimum of personnel.

The system depends upon the establishment of rela-

TABLE 10   Typical Processing Elements in a Hospital
Facility

Receiving and storage of ingredients and raw materials
Portioning equipment
Formulation and preparation of ingredients
Processing equipment
    - thermal (steam, microwave, fryers, ovens, kettles,
      etc.)
    - refrigerators
    - freezers
    - food preparation surfaces
    - utensils, pots, etc.
Packaging equipment
Storage of processed food
Reconstitution and portioning
Delivery
Washing and cleanup

TABLE 11   Elements in a Quality Assurance Program for a
Military Production Facility

_____

Production
   1. Known sources of raw materials
   2. Classification of foods as to risk
   3. Sanitation
   4. Time-temperature profiles
   5. Personnel training
   6. End product analysis
   7. Operational production guides
   8. Information analysis and feedback
   9. Mechanism for corrective action by management
  10. Hazard analysis--critical control point (HACCP)
  11. Production objectives
       - shelf-life
       - acceptability
       - uniform quality

Delivery
  12. Temperature-time profile for plating, storage,
       delivery, and serving
  13. Sanitation of delivery and serving surfaces
  14. Incidence of temperature abuse

_____

SOURCE: G.J. Silverman, G. J. (1982).

tively stable production procedures, and therefore standardized "operational production guides" are used for
each item. Sources of raw materials must be known, and
all ingredients that received minimal thermal processing
(hams, sausage, etc.) are analyzed prior to use. Personnel training is essential, not only for uniformity in
production and sanitation, but also to obtain their full
and effective participation. Personnel should understand
what is expected of them in material handling, processing,
temperature control, and sanitation, and the rationale
being employed. Any constructive suggestions from personnel should be evaluated and, if merited, incorporated into
the program. Serious or consistent deviations from procedures usually indicate that a portion of the QAP may not
be satisfactory and may have to be modified.
     In a hospital feeding system there are a number of
problems that should be carefully considered by the food

service staff. The menu, of course, consists of a variety of items ranging from unprocessed or minimally processed ingredients (salads, spices, juices) to more processed items (ham, salami, frankfurters), to highly in-house processed items (pork roasts, stews), to maximally processed items that are, or almost are, sterile (canned foods). Patients, in turn, will have varying rates of susceptibility and should not be fed foods posing a risk that exceeds their susceptibility. Susceptibility will vary from a risk corresponding to that of an essentially healthy person to that of immunosuppressed or burn patients. The latter might require sterile foods or carefully selected processed foods, portioned and served asceptically (Kundsen and Bodman, 1976).

A QAP for a hospital should, therefore, address the following requirements, and food service personnel may have to assess whether:

1. The contamination level of processed foods is reduced to a consistently known value. This value should be capable of being matched to the susceptibility of the consumer (patient).

2. Foods that are minimally processed or not processed should be assigned risk values and should only be fed to patients of low susceptibility.

At present it is extremely difficult to assign the degree of susceptibility of a patient except in a general sense. What can be done is to recognize that patients can be categorized as to their degree of susceptibility. Moreover, the actual risk to a patient will be the result of the susceptibility of the patient and the infectivity of the organism. As noted above, Bryan (1979) compiled the challenging dose of enteric pathogens for humans, which demonstrates the wide variation of from 10^1 to 10^8 organisms, but these values apply to healthy adults and not to more susceptible individuals.

Processing temperatures, with main emphasis on cooking and the subsequent cooling temperatures, are carefully monitored for consistency. An awareness of time constraints is necessary, and this responsibility is shared by supervisory personnel as well as the quality control representative. End product analysis is conducted on processed foods and selected ingredients and is useful mainly for the analysis of trends and for establishing the quality of raw materials. The microbiological and temperature constraints are shown in Table 12. The program is based on the principle that if the monitoring system is properly designed and conducted, the requirement for end product analysis is minimal.

It has been recommended that foods for cook-chill or cook-freeze be undercooked, since these items undergo further rethermalization prior to serving (Longree, 1980). The extent of undercooking, if undertaken, must be carefully defined and microbiologically evaluated. This technique may prove difficult to control and may result in inadequate processing. Experience with roast beef, whereby the degree of roasting could, by the use of lower temperatures for longer periods of time, result in a redder product (Federal Register, 1978), has resulted in foodborne disease outbreaks (New York Times, 1981a). Problems with roasts are further complicated by the fact that Salmonella typhimurium appears to be able to migrate within roast beef and can survive on the surface when the core temperature is 141.5°F (Blankenship, 1978). Bryan and McKinley (1979) recommend effective processing procedures for producing a safe product.

TABLE 12 Microbiological and Temperature Guidelines Used by the U.S. Army Natick Research and Development Laboratories for Cook-Chill or Cook-Freeze Foods

Microbial	Constraint
Aerobic plate count	$\leq 1 \times 10^5$ CFU/g
Coliform	$\leq 1 \times 10^2$ MPN/g
Escherichia coli	0 MPN/g
Staphylococcus aureus[a]	$\leq 1 \times 10^2$/g
Clostridium perfringens[a]	$\leq 1 \times 10^3$/g

Temperature
Cooked: 160°-165°F (71°-74°C)
Cooked-frozen: store at 0°F (-18°C)
Cooked-chill: store at 45°F (7°C)
   (cool below 50°F within 2 hours)
Reconstitute to: 140°-160°F[b]
                  45°-50°C (7°-10°C)
Roast beef: the equivalent of 145°F (63°C)

[a]Only on selected products.
[b]FDA (1976) requires 165°F.

Concurrently conducted is sanitation monitoring of food contact surfaces. After an initial survey of the facility, a schedule of testing for each piece of equipment is followed, with main emphasis on those items causing the most difficulty in either cleaning or maintenance.

Attention is also given to the sanitation and temperature profile of the delivery system. The maintenance of proper temperatures prior to delivery and the delivery of foods at safe temperatures is essential. A difficult attribute of the system is the maintenance of either elevated (>140°F) or refrigerated temperatures (<45°F) prior to patient delivery.

A study was conducted (Table 13) in a military hospital to evaluate a cook-chill, cook-freeze system. Of the initial 90 items tested, 9 were found to exceed the constraints listed in Table 12. The canned ham was a commercial product, and this problem has occurred in other military systems (Silverman, 1982). Most of the samples had excessive coliform counts, no E. coli, and three also had excessive APC counts. Notice that these products included both cook-chill and cook-freeze products and meat, vegetable, and starch items. The QAP introduced into this system has succeeded in eliminating the produc-

TABLE 13 Menu Items[a] in a Military Hospital Food Service System That Failed to Meet Monitoring Constraints[b]

Item	Constraint
Tuna salad	Coliform
Pancake	Coliform
Frankfurter	APC[c]
Roast pork	Coliform
Pancake batter	APC, coliform
Tuna salad	Coliform
Tuna casserole	APC, coliform
Canned ham	Coliform
Fried rice	Coliform

[a]First 90 production items tested.
[b]See Table 10.
[c]Aerobic plate count.

tion problems associated with these products and reducing nonconforming incidences to less than 0.1 percent.

The proper employment of a QAP, therefore, will enable a system to maximize the safety of a food service system. Without such a program the only way to measure effectiveness may be to collect data on individual food-poisoning incidents, for which there is difficulty in detection or in assigning responsibility, or by noting the occurrence of more widespread outbreaks.

REFERENCES

Avens, J. S., P. J. Poduska, F. P. Schmidt, G. R. Jansen, and J. M. Harper. 1978. Food safety hazards associated with school food service delivery systems. J. Food Sci. 43:453-456.

Ayres, J. C. 1971. Reducing Food Spoilage and Deterioration. CRC, Cleveland, Ohio.

Blankenship, L. C. 1978. Survival of a Salmonella typhimurium experimental contaminant during cooking of beef roasts. Appl. Environ. Microbiol. 35:1160-1165.

Bobeng, B. J., and B. D. David. 1977. HACCP models for quality control of entree production in food service systems. J. Food Protect. 40:632-638.

Bobeng, B. J., and B. D. David. 1978. HACCP models for quality control of entree production in hospital food service systems. I. Development of hazard analysis critical control point models. J. Am. Dietet. Assoc. 73:524-529.

Bryan, F. 1978. Impact of food-borne diseases and methods of evaluating control programs. J. Environ. Health. 40:3154-323.

Bryan, F. L. 1979. Epidemiology of food-borne diseases. In Food-Borne Infections and Intoxications. Academic Press, New York.

Bryan, F. L. 1980. Food-borne diseases in the United States associated with meat and poultry. J. Food Protect. 43:140-150.

Bryan, F. L. 1981. Hazard analysis of food service operations. Food Technol. 78-87.

Bryan, F. L., and T. W. McKinley. 1979. Hazard analysis control of roast beef preparation in food service establishments. J. Food Protect. 42:4-18.

Bryan, F. L., K. A. Seabolt, R. W. Peterson, and L. M. Roberts. 1978. Time-temperature observations of food and equipment in airline catering operations. J. Food Protect. 41:80-92.

Bunch, W. L., M. E. Mathews, and E. H. Marth. 1976. Hospital chill food service systems: acceptability and microbiological characteristics of beef-soy loaves when processed according to system procedures. J. Food Sci. 41:1273-1276.

Cremer, M. L., and J. R. Shipley. 1980a. Hospital ready-prepared type food service system: time and temperature conditions, sensory and microbiological quality of scrambled eggs. J. Food Sci. 45:1422-1424.

Cremer, M. L., and J. R. Shipley. 1980b. Time and temperature, microbiological, and sensory assessment of roast beef in a hospital food service system. J. Food Sci. 45:1472-1478.

Dixon, R. E. 1980. Control of nosocomial and other infections acquired in medical-care institutions. In E. H. Lennette, A. Balows, W. J. Hausler, and J. P. Truant, eds., Manual of Clinical Microbiology. ASM, Washington, D. C.

Elliott, R. P. 1980. Cereal and cereal products. In Microbial Ecology of Foods (ICMSF). Academic Press, New York.

FDA. 1976. Food Service Sanitation Manual. HEW Publ. No. (FDA) 78-2018. Superintendent of Documents, Washington, D.C.

Federal Register. 1978. 42(138):30791-30793.

Kundsen, R. B., and H. A. Bodman. 1976. Microbiology and hospital feeding systems. J. Milk Food Technol. 39:197-199.

Longree, K. 1980. Quantity Food Sanitation. Wiley-Interscience, New York.

Mossel, D. A. A. 1975. Critical Reviews in Environmental Control. CRC, Cleveland, Ohio.

New York Times. 1981a. Rare beef linked to illnesses. June 20.

New York Times. 1981b. One in ten patients infected in hospitals an educator finds. December 26.

Ockerman, H. W., and J. Stec. 1980. Total plate and coliform counts for fast food service sandwiches. J. Food Sci. 45:262-266.

Peterson, A. C., and R. E. Gunderson. 1974. Microbiological critical control points in frozen foods. Food Technol. 28:37-44.

Pivnick, H. 1980. Spices. In Microbial Ecology of Foods (ICMSF). Academic Press, New York.

Silverman, G. J. 1976. Microbiology of mass feeding systems: an introduction. J. Milk Food Technol. 39:196.

Silverman, G. J. 1979. Establishing and maintaining microbiological standards in food service systems. In G. E. Livingston and C. M. Chang, eds., Food Service Systems. Academic Press, New York.

Silverman, G. J. 1982. A quality assurance program for the F. E. Warren AFB. Technical report. (In press).

Silverman, G. J., D. F. Carpenter, D. T. Munsey, and D. B. Rowley. 1976. Microbiological Evaluation of Production Procedures for Frozen Foil Pack Meals at the Central Preparation Facility of the Frances E. Warren Air Force Base. Technical Report 76-37-FSL. U.S. Army Natick Research and Development Command, Natick, Mass.

Skinner, F. A., and J. G. Carr. 1974. The Normal Microflora of Man. Academic Press, New York.

Snyder, O. P. 1981. A model food service quality assurance system. Food Technol. 70-76.

Surkiewicz, B. F., R. J. Groomes, and A. P. Padron. 1967. Bacteriological survey of the frozen prepared foods industry. Appl. Microbiol. 15: 1324-1331.

Tuomi, S., M. E. Mathews, and E. H. Marth. 1974. Temperature and microbiological flora of refrigerated ground beef gravy subjected to holding and heating as might occur in a school food service operation. J. Milk Food Technol. 37:457.

Willardsen, R. R., F. F. Busta, C. E. Allen, and L. B. Smith. 1978. Growth and survival of C. perfringens during constantly rising temperatures. J. Food Sci. 43:470-476.

DISCUSSION

QUESTION: Can you comment on pretreatment of salad vegetables to extend shelf life at 40°F? Antioxidants with centrifigation are used to control oxidation. Are antimicrobial agents used to reduce microbial populations, are they successful, and to what extent?

SILVERMAN: Preservation of salads involves the chemistry and physiology of lettuce. The contamination of lettuce is such that the outer leaves are heavily contaminated with dust and dirt. The problem of improving the shelf life of lettuce is that you have to be able to control the original freshness of it. In some cases, you don't get it until it is one week to two weeks old; therefore, preservation is very difficult. A number of companies produce lettuce that has a shelf life of two weeks.

This lettuce is fairly good microbiologically, but whether you want to accept it as a top-grade product is another matter. It is collected in the field, rapidly chilled, taken directly to a processor, processed and packaged in small packages under either an inert atmosphere or CO_2, and then shipped refrigerated. The shelf life is claimed to be at least two weeks. To do this in a small facility is tricky.

Antioxidants do help, but I have found antimicrobial agents to be very tricky. First of all, you have to make sure that the lettuce is clean, without a lot of soil left. Then, you have to be very careful that you are not using bruised lettuce. Anyone who buys crates of lettuce knows that this is not an easy thing to do. Some of the lettuce is very heavily bruised when you purchase it. Antioxidants, antimicrobial agents, and centrifigation to remove water are extremely important and will work. But you have to consider the entire process and the raw material involved.

QUESTION: You talked about cooking roast beef. Would you recommend or not recommend cooking roast beef to a medium-well-done state, refrigerating, slicing, and then reheating in liquid to a minimum of 140°F.

SILVERMAN: This is what I would recommend. You have to reheat it to 140° to serve it anyway, but I would give it a minimal reheating. Now, if you want rare roast beef, you can do that. You can cook roast beef to a rare state, but you have to reheat it to 140°F for serving.

QUESTION: We have used a number of different types of thermometers. The pocket variety is most convenient and lowest in cost. But they are not always accurate and often develop "legs." Do you have any recommendations on types of thermometers?

SILVERMAN: We use the new electronic thermometers. The reason that some of the standard ones are plus or minus 3° is because that is the accuracy they guarantee. On general principle, I consider this too wide a range for our type of work. For most users, it is fairly good. The electronic type will read a tenth of a degree, and it is accurate to well within 1°. I consider that minimal for what I am doing. There is a large variety of electronic thermometers on the market, and they vary from about $180 to $200. I keep two because one is always malfunctioning.

There are problems with electronic thermometers. One is the thermometer itself, and the other is maintaining

them. Just as with delivery systems, you have problems
with the state of the art. Generally speaking, they are
reliable. We abuse ours, as we use them constantly. They
are extremely accurate. There is a bewildering variety
on the market, but I wouldn't try to recommend any one.

Effects of Current Food Service Practices on the Nutritional Quality of Foods

Thelma S. Hendricks

When one begins to search the literature for information
on the effects of current food service practices on
nutrient retention, what is found is a distressing lack
of information. No systematic, controlled research of
significance has been done on nutrient retention of food
and meals as affected by the variety of current institutional food delivery systems.

Why hasn't this research been done? With one out of
three meals consumed outside the home by the average
individual, effects of food service practices on nutrient
retention might well be significant to the nutritional
well-being of the individual. Consider, also, those
persons who exist for extended periods entirely on institutional prepared foods, such as in colleges and universities, nursing homes, hospitals, and the military. The
answer to the question "Why hasn't this research been
done?" might simply be "No money or inclination." Analytical tests for nutritional analyses are expensive.
Additionally, assay techniques for many of the nutrients
are difficult. When we take a look at the gaps of knowledge in current food composition tables, we become aware
of the complexity of the problem. However, despite the
expense, analytical problems, and time involved, the task
of evaluating the effects of current food service practices on the nutrient retention of foods is one that must
be accomplished.

Lt. Col. Thelma S. Hendricks, Ph.D., R.D., Army Medical
Specialist Corps., is Assistant Professor of Nutrition,
Department of Biochemistry, Uniformed Services University
of Health Sciences, Bethesda, Maryland.

The dearth of information on the effects of food service practices on nutrient retention was amplified by Lachance (1977), who said, "Without doubt, the most ill-defined food service nutrient information concerns the effects of holding times which can range from long-term (weeks, months) interim frozen storage to long-term (hours) cafeteria steam table holding of bulk pan foods, and to analogous periods of holding preplated trays in heated insulated mobile carts, used in catering and hospital food service."

This paper will address the effects of three food service processes on the nutrient retention of foods, namely, meal assembly, meal distribution, and meal service. I should emphasize, however, that deterioration of nutrients may occur at many levels of food-processing, storage, preparation, and service. The major culprits severely depleting nutrients during food service practices are leaching (either into cooking fluids or drippings), heat degradation, light, and oxidation. Nutrients vary considerably in their susceptibility to destruction by the culprits mentioned. Vitamins that are somewhat depleted by food service practices include A, D, E, B_6, B_{12}, riboflavin, ascorbic acid, pantothenic acid, and folacin. Thiamine and ascorbic acid have been most studied because of their instability, and the assays for these nutrients are not as difficult as for some of the others. Information on the effects of large-scale cooking on trace minerals is essentially nil.

MEAL ASSEMBLY

Since heat is detrimental to several nutrients, one would certainly expect to find differences in nutritional quality of foods held hot during meal assembly and those held refrigerated. Kahn and Livingston (1970) evaluated thiamine retention in four common dishes using a variety of food service practices. The dishes selected for study were beef stew, chicken a la king, shrimp newburg, and peas in cream sauce. Thiamine content was measured after the dishes had been freshly prepared and again after they were held for 1, 2, or 3 hours at 180°F (82.2°C) and after freezing and reheating in either microwave or infrared to 194°F (90°C) or by immersion in boiling water. The results of this study are shown in Table 1. Thiamine losses were significantly greater in the dishes that had been freshly prepared and held hot than in those that were pre-

TABLE 1   Relative Thiamine Retention in Four Common
Products   Subjected to Various Heating Treatments

Sample Treatment	Thiamine Retention (%)[a]				
	Beef Stew	Chicken a la King	Shrimp Newburg	Peas in Cream Sauce	Average of All Products
Freshly prepared	100	100	100	100	100.0
Fresh, held at 180°F 1 hr	73.5	75	76	87	78.2
Fresh, held at 180°F 2 hr	68	70	73	83	73.9
Fresh, held at 180°F 3 hr	63	63	66	76	67.4
After 10°F storage	96	96	96	96.5	96.1
Frozen, microwave heated	95	94	92.5	93	93.5
Frozen, immersion heated	85	87	86	87	86.0
Frozen, infrared heated	91	90	88	92	90.4

[a] Percent retention in relation to freshly prepared products or
frozen commercial samples.

SOURCE: Kahn and Livingston, 1970.

pared, frozen, and reheated in a microwave or infrared
oven. Reheating by immersion in boiling water also resulted in better thiamine retention than in the fresh
food held hot. Thiamine loss due to hot holding was 21.8
percent at the end of 1 hour and 32.6 percent by the end
of 3 hours. These authors calculated that the difference
in thiamine content between fresh food held hot for 3
hours and microwave-heated frozen foods was equal to 18.4
percent of the RDA for 4- to 6-year olds and 14.7 percent
of the RDA for 6- to 8-year-olds and 18- to 75-year-old
women.

Ang et al. (1975) reported the effects of hot-holding
on vitamin retention in six fresh and frozen prepared
food products. In general, the freshly prepared products
were of highest nutritive quality, and hot-holding significantly reduced thiamine and ascorbic acid content.
These studies indicate that the hot-holding of foods is
not desirable from a nutritional standpoint.

The manner in which food is handled before assembly
may also affect nutrient retention. Boyle and Funk (1972)

compared the thiamine retention in freshly prepared sliced
roast beef with beef roasts held over dry heat either
sliced or unsliced for 1 1/2 hours, and refrigerated reheated roasts. Results of this comparison are given in
Table 2. Note that the "nutrient cost" of refrigerating
the cooked roast beef, slicing, and reheating is about 14
percent. Unsliced roast beef held hot for 1 1/2 hours
had a better thiamine retention than sliced meat treated
in the same manner.

Heat Destruction

Although emphasis has been given to thiamine and/or vitamin C in these studies, one would expect other nutrients
to be similarily affected. Pantothenic acid, folacin, and
vitamin B_6 are also susceptible to destruction by heat.
Karlström and Jonsson (1977) reported the effect of hot-
holding time and temperature on the content of vitamin
B_6 in cooked cod. A dramatic loss of vitamin B_6 was
seen with increased hot-holding time and temperature, as
shown in Figure 1. As just mentioned, folacin is a nutrient at risk with heat-treated foods. In fact, one of the
earliest cases of diagnosed folacin deficiency was thought
to be a result of folacin losses during food preparation
(Zalusky and Herbert, 1961). An individual subsisting on

TABLE 2 Effects of Heat, Slicing, and Refrigeration on
the Thiamine Content of Beef Roasts

Treatment	Thiamine Retention (%)
Sliced and served immediately (internal temp., 60°C)	78.8
Held 90 minutes, unsliced (internal temp., 58°C)	79.2
Held 90 minutes, sliced (internal temp., 59°C)	76.5
Refrigerated, sliced, and reheated (internal temp., 60°C)	67.8

SOURCE: Boyle and Funk, 1972.

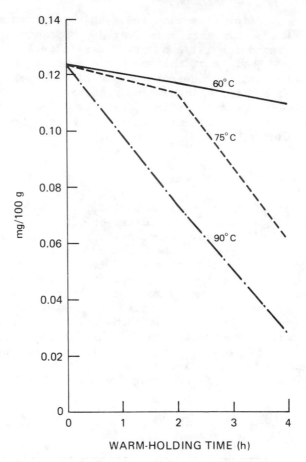

FIGURE 1 The effect of warm-holding time and temperature on the content of vitamin B_6 in cooked cod (from Karlström and Jonsson 1977).

restaurant meals of hamburgers, doughnuts, and coffee developed megaloblastic anemia due to folacin deficiency. An investigation of the restaurant practices revealed that the hamburgers were thin, had been cooked several hours ahead of time, and kept on a hot plate. The patient's physician had the beef pattie analyzed and found very little residual folate. I might add that such a diet would likely result in folate deficiency regardless of the food preparation techniques; however, the report in

TABLE 3 Percentage Retention of Ascorbic Acid Using
Institutional Preparation Methods

Vegetable	Tested Immediately (%)	Tested After Holding Over Steam 1 h (%)
Carrots	48	26
Potatoes	21	14
Spinach	21	12
Brussel sprouts	23	11
Cabbage	32	0
Cauliflower	25	20

SOURCE: Thomas, 1942.

the literature did serve to call attention to nutrient
losses during food preparation.

Usually the greatest amount of nutrient loss in vegetables occurs during the cooking process and is caused by
the leaching of water-soluble nutrients. However, additional losses do occur during hot-holding of vegetables.
Thomas (1942) reported ascorbic acid loss of institution-
cooked vegetables held hot for one hour after preparation.
The data from this study are shown in Table 3. Hot-
holding of vegtables resulted in significant losses of
vitamin C.

The method of food preparation affects nutrient retention in foods. For example, a potato that has been
boiled, diced, and pan fried (hash-browned potatoes) would
have little or no vitamin C left after holding hot for 1
hour. In contrast, a potato baked with the skin on would
have about 60 percent of the original vitamin C after hot-
hold for 1 hour (Branion et al., 1947).

In summary, hot-holding during meal assembly has pronounced effects on the nutrient content of foods. These
losses are due to heat destruction of certain nutrients,
as well as losses due to oxidation.

MEAL DISTRIBUTION

During meal distribution, one would expect to see additional loss of nutrients in foods that are held hot. Com-

parison of nutrient losses with various food distribution procedures has not been done. One study was found in which the vitamin C content of several vegetables was evaluated using two different food distribution methods (Wagner, 1971). The ascorbic acid content of food held hot in insulated containers and food held in the refrigerator for various periods and reheated in a convection oven was evaluated. The results of the study are given in Table 4. A significantly greater amount of vitamin C was lost in vegetables held for 3 hours in an insulated container than in vegetables held in the refrigerator and reheated. Note, however, that there were increased nutrient losses with increased length of refrigeration. Few studies have been done evaluating the effect of current refrigeration practices on nutrient retention. One would expect the nutrient content of vegetables to be most affected by refrigeration. In an early study, Branion et al. (1947) reported ascorbic acid content of potatoes left standing in the refrigerator for various periods of time. These values are given in Table 5. This study illustrates the loss of vitamin C with refrigeration, but again one might also expect to see this trend with other

TABLE 4 Percentage Losses of Vitamin C in Vegetables Using Two Meal Distribution Processes

Food	Held in Hot Insulated Container (3 h)	Refrigerated and Reheated[a] After 24 h	After 48 h	After 72 h
Potatoes	78.4	44.3	52.2	53.9
Brussel sprouts	88.1	23.7	29.2	40.5
Cauliflower	72.8	23.5	26.2	30.2
Red cabbage	82.1	12.2	22.1	34.6
White cabbage	89.1	39.3	49.3	61.7
Spinach	(1 h) 53.8 (2 h) 68.1 (3 h) 75.3	22.8	41.2	54.4
Green cabbage	(1 h) 61.0 (2 h) 71.9 (3 h) 80.0	17.8	35.4	53.1

[a]Heated in convention oven 320°F 15 minutes.

SOURCE: Wagner, 1971.

TABLE 5 Changes in Ascorbic Acid Content of Boiled
Potatoes Left Standing in the Refrigerator

Condition When Assayed	100 Serving Quantity Ascorbic Acid (mg/100 g)
Potatoes, raw edible portion	11.5
Potatoes, boiled	4.9
After standing in refrigerator 24 h	2.8
After standing in refrigerator 48 h	0.8
After standing in refrigerator 72 h	0.1

SOURCE: Branion et al., 1947.

nutrients. In current food service delivery systems,
cooked foods may be preplated and refrigerated for 4 to
24 hours before delivery to satellite locations and reheating. Certainly, studies should be done on nutrient
losses associated with preplated refrigerated food.

MEAL SERVICE

With cook-chill food service systems, two heat processes
are used. Very limited research has been done on the
effects of the second heat treatment on nutrient retention. Nicholanco and Matthews (1978) evaluated thiamine
retention in beef stew at four stages of handling in the
cook-chill system--raw ingredients after preparation,
after cooking, after 27 hours of chilled storage, and
after heating to 145°F in a microwave oven. The results
of this study are shown in Table 6. Note the considerable loss of thiamine following cooking, with some additional loss after refrigeration. These investigators did
not find additional thiamine loss due to microwave cooking. However, values for thiamine were not adjusted for
weight loss. In another study, Dahl and Matthews (1980)
evaluated thiamine content of beef loaf, simulating the
cook-chill system. The study design was similar to the
earlier work of Nicholanco and Matthews, i.e., thiamine

TABLE 6   Thiamine Retention in Beef Stew at Four Steps of Handing in a Chill Food Service System

Stage of Handling	Amount (mg/100 g)	Retention (%)
After preparation of raw ingredients	0.11	100.0
After cooking	0.04	36.4
After chilled storage-- 27 hours	0.03	27.3
After heating stew to 145° in microwave oven	0.03	27.3

SOURCE: Nicholanco and Matthews, 1978.

retention of beef loaf was determined after preparation of ingredients, after baking, after chilled storage, and after heating in microwave for various lengths of time. In this study, the percentage of thiamine retention was adjusted for processing losses. Data for the study are shown in Table 7. These investigators did find additional thiamine loss with microwave heating. Approximately 30

TABLE 7   Microwave-Heating Subsystem: Percent Thiamine Retention of Beef Loaf Adjusted for Processing Losses

Food Product Flow	Simulation A	B	C	Mean
Preparation	100.0	100.0	100.0	100.0
Before microwave heating	93.6	67.8	77.7	79.7
After microwave heating				
20 s	78.7	68.7	74.3	72.2
50 s	82.0	70.0	72.0	75.0
80 s	79.0	63.6	72.9	71.8
110 s	76.5	59.7	74.2	70.1

SOURCE: Dahl and Matthews, 1980.

TABLE 8   Vitamin Content of Oven Baked Potatoes Following
Chilling and Reheating in a Microwave Oven

	Oven Baked	Chilled for 24 h	Microwave Reheated	Percent Change due to Reheating
Ascorbic acid, mg	54.60	49.40	41.50	-16.0
Thiamine, mg	0.48	0.51	0.48	- 5.9
Riboflavin, mg	0.15	0.14	0.13	- 7.1
Niacin, mg	8.19	8.44	8.62	+ 2.1
Vitamin B_6, mg	1.19	1.18	1.16	- 1.7
Folic acid, µg	42.60	37.30	34.10	- 8.6

SOURCE: Augustin et al., 1980.

percent of the thiamine was lost between initial cooking
and after 110 seconds of microwave heating. About 10
percent of this loss was due to the microwave heating
process.

Augustin et al. (1980) evaluated the effects of two
heating processes on the vitamin content of potatoes.
Ascorbic acid, thiamine, riboflavin, niacin, vitamin
B_6, and folic acid content of potatoes were evaluated
after cooking, after chilling, and after reheating in a
microwave oven. Some of the data from this study are
shown in Table 8. Although not shown on the table, the
potatoes were evaluated after an initial 6 hours of
chilling, and vitamin losses were about the same as after
24 hours. Note that ascorbic acid was most affected by
microwave cooking, but there were significant losses of
other nutrients as well.

Charles and Van Duyne (1958) looked at the effect of
two heat processes on the ascorbic acid content of cooked
vegetables. Ascorbic acid content of the vegetables was
determined when raw, after boiling to doneness with half
their weight of water, after holding in a refrigerator
(39°-49°F) for 24 hours, and after refrigeration and
reheating. The results of this study are given in Table
9. Cooked broccoli, shredded cabbage, peas, and snap
beans lost significant amounts of vitamin C with refrigeration. Reheating the vegetables caused further losses;
the degree of nutrient loss due to reheating varied with

TABLE 9 Effect of Holding and Reheating on Percentage of
Ascorbic Acid Retained in Cooked Vegetables

Vegetable	Freshly Cooked	Refrigerated 1 Day	Refrigerated 1 Day, Reheated
Asparagus	86	82	66
Broccoli	88	68	60
Cabbage, shredded	73	44	33
Peas	88	52	43
Snap beans	83	41	29
Spinach	52	48	32

SOURCE: Charles and Van Duyne, 1958.

the vegetable and ranged from 8 to 25 percent. In summary, the nutritional content of vegetables that have
been refrigerated for 24 hours and reheated is definitely
not the same as the freshly cooked product.

The method of heating used during the second heating
may also affect nutrient retention. Ang et al. (1978)
evaluated thiamine and riboflavin retention in frozen
breaded, fried chicken using a variety of heating pro-

TABLE 10 Nutrient Content of Fried Chicken after
Reheating Using Various Heating Treatments

Treatment	Retention (%) Thiamine	Riboflavin
Frozen	100.0	100.0
Convection-heated, 20-25 min	89.8	90.5
Convection-heated, held 1/2 h	88.8	88.0
Infrared-heated, 14-15 min, held 1/2 h	85.5	91.5
Steam-heated, 25-33 min, held 1/2 h	89.8	86.9
Microwave-heated, 10-11 min, held 1/2 h	92.1	92.8

SOURCE: Ang et al., 1978.

TABLE 11 Relative Percentage of Thiamine Retained in Four
Products Heated by Either Microwave or Infrared

	Beef Stew	Chicken a la King	Shrimp Newburg	Peas in Cream Sauce
After freezing (-10°F)	96.0	96.0	96.0	96.5
Frozen, microwave-heated	95.0	94.0	92.5	93.0
Frozen, infrared-heated	91.0	90.0	88.0	92.0

SOURCE: Kahn and Livingston, 1970.

cedures commonly used in food service operations. The
data from this study are shown in Table 10. Microwave
heating resulted in a slightly higher retention of thiamine than infrared heating. Differences in nutrient
retention in other methods were not statistically
significant.

Recall an earlier reported study of Kahn and Livingston (1970) in which thiamine retention in four entrees
was studied using a variety of food service procedures.
These investigators evaluated differences in microwave
and infrared heating on thiamine retention in beef stew,
chicken a la king, shrimp newburg, and peas in cream
sauce. Data on the difference between microwave and
infrared heating are given in Table 11. Microwave
heating resulted in greater thiamine retention than did
infrared heating.

Ang et al. (1975) evaluated ascorbic acid, riboflavin,
and thiamine retention in 4- to 5-pound trays of mashed
potatoes subjected to various heating treatments. Data
from the study are shown in Table 12. Major losses of
vitamin C were observed with all methods of reheating;
however, both infrared and microwave were particularly
destructive to this vitamin. Microwave heating produced
better retention of thiamine and riboflavin than did
infrared heating.

In summary, the second heating process used in the
cook-chill system is detrimental to certain nutrients.
However, these nutrient losses will have to be compared
with losses in traditional food service systems in which
foods were held hot for extended periods of time. From
the literature reported, the cook-chill system, in which

TABLE 12 Vitamin Retention in Mashed Potatoes Subjected
to Various Heating Treatments

Treatment	Retention (%)		
	Ascorbic Acid	Riboflavin	Thiamine
Freshly prepared	100.0	100.0	100.0
Convenience food system handling			
Frozen thawed	93.2	98.4	91.8
Frozen reheated in convection oven, held 1/2 h	35.7	96.5	88.3
Frozen reheated in infrared oven, held 1/2 h	23.8	93.7	89.0
Frozen reheated in steamer, held 1/2 h	41.4	92.6	86.5
Frozen reheated in microwave oven, held 1/2 h	24.1	96.5	92.0

SOURCE: Ang et al., 1975.

the foods are preplated, refrigerated, and distributed
under refrigeration and reheated in a microwave oven,
seems to offer higher nutritional quality to the consumer.

SUMMARY

Much additional research is needed to document what happens to the nutritional quality of foods using current
food service practices. We have seen from the literature
reported that the research will not be easy. Nutrient
retention depends upon the type of food, the nutrient in
question, preparation techniques, length and type of storage, length of hot-holding, method of reheating, etc.
Yet, we owe it to the consumer to define the effects of
current food service practices on the nutritional quality
of the food served.

287

REFERENCES

Ang, C. Y., C. M. Chang, A. E. Frey, and G. E.
Livingston. 1975. Effects of heating methods on
vitamin retention in six fresh or frozen prepared food
products. J. Food Sci. 40:997.

Ang, C. Y., A. L. Basillo, B. A. Catu, and G. E.
Livingston. 1978. Riboflavin and thiamine retention in
frozen beef-soy patties and frozen fried chicken
heated by methods used in food service operations. J.
Food Sci. 43:1024.

Augustin, J., G. I. Marousek, L. A. Tholen, and B.
Bertelli. 1980. Vitamin retention in cooked, chilled,
and reheated potatoes. J. Food Sci. 45:814.

Boyle, M. A., and K. Funk. 1972. Thiamine in roast beef
held by three methods. J. Am. Dietet. Assoc. 60:398.

Branion, H. D., J. S. Roberts, C. R. cameron, and A. M.
McCready. 1947. The loss of ascorbic acid in the
preparation of old and freshly harvested potatoes. J.
Am. Dietet. Assoc. 23:414.

Charles, V. R., and F. O. Van Duyne. 1958. Effects of
holding and reheating on the ascorbic acid content of
cooked vegetables. J. Home Econ. 50:159.

Dahl, C. A., and M. E. Matthews. 1980. Cook/chill food
service system with a microwave oven: thiamine content
in portions of beef loaf after microwave-heating. J.
Food Sci. 45(3):608.

Kahn, L. N., and G. E. Livingston. 1970. Effect of
heating methods on thiamine retention in fresh or
frozen prepared foods. J. Food Sci. 35:349.

Karlström, B., and L. Jonsson. 1977. Quality changes
during warm-holding of foods. Pages 315-336 in G.
Glew, ed., Catering Equipment and Systems Design.
Applied Science, London.

Lachance, P. A. 1977. Effects of food preparation
procedures on nutrient retention with emphasis upon
food service practices. Page 469 in R. S. Harris and
E. Karmas, eds., Nutritional Evaluation of Food
Processing. 2nd ed. AVI, Westport, Conn.

Nicholanco, S., and M. E. Matthews. 1978. Quality of beef
stew in a hospital chill food service system. J. Am.
Dietet. Assoc. 72:31.

Thomas, M. M. 1942. Retention of ascorbic acid in
institution and home cooked vegetables. M.S. thesis,
University of Chicago.

Wagner, K. H. 1971. On the Question of Vitamin
Preservation in Food Which Has Been Treated According

to the Multimet-Multiserv Procedure as Compared to the
Preservation in Orthodox Containers. Bull. CX167.
Crown-X, Cleveland, Ohio.

Zalusky, R., and V. Herbert. 1961. Megaloblasti anemia in
scurvy with response to 50 microgm. of folic acid
daily. N. Engl. J. Med. 265:1033.

DISCUSSION

QUESTION: Is it not true that dehydrated potatoes are
usually ascorbic acid enriched and will supply all amounts
of this vitamin?

HENDRICKS: I don't use them, but some of them are.
Check the label and make sure that you're using them if
you're in a hospital food service system, realizing that
there will be some loss of the amount listed on the label.

QUESTION: Thiamin and ascorbic acid are studied in
food service systems because they are indicator
nutrients. They will be removed or destroyed in the
foods easier than other waxy fat-soluable vitamins, and
other nutrients will be present in similar or greater
quantities than either thiamin or ascorbic acid at the
point of service.

HENDRICKS: I don't think you can assume that is true.
The reason that thiamine and ascorbic acid have been
studied is because the analytical techniques for evaluations of these nutrients are better worked out. There
are many analytical problems with folic acid, Vitamin
B_6, Vitamin A, pantothenic acid, and some of the other
nutrients. When you're talking about the total diet,
thiamine and ascorbic acid are many times added to food.
I don't think you can say that if you're getting enough
thiamine and ascorbic acid, especially if you happen to
be eating a highly refined, processed, institutionalized
diet, you will be getting in enough of the other nutrients. Riboflavin and niacin seem to be more stable.
Riboflavin is very much affected by light.

Losses of ascorbic acid in vegetables in food service
systems is relatively unimportant, since vegetables are
not usually viewed as major sources of Vitamin C. However, there are some vegetables that are good sources of
Vitamin C. The tendency is to think that we get most of
our vitamins from citrus fruits and Vitamin-C enriched
drinks. It hasn't been mentioned that leaving orange
juice in the refrigerator results in some loss of Vitamin

C. It is very susceptable to oxidation, whether in the form of citrus, vegetables, or whatever.

QUESTION: Why does cauliflower have a better retention than some other vegetables?

HENDRICKS: As with the vitamin C, it is due to the oxidation (also to the water soluability). I think you were comparing it with cabbage and spinach--most of these have more exposed surface for oxidation. My guess would be that the finer the chop, the longer it is cooked, the more that you have exposed it to water, or the more surface exposed to oxidation, the greater the loss of nutrient.

QUESTION: Would you recommend that all leftover items be disposed of rather than refrigerated and reheated?

HENDRICKS: The cost would be enormous.

QUESTION: What is the overall nutritional picture? Please consider the initial vitamin content in foodstuffs in their virgin state compared to the intermediary processing of freezing and canning to meal preparation and service. Isn't there a great loss after harvest?

HENDRICKS: Yes. I alluded to that in my comments about meal assembly, distribution, and service. Certainly, from the time that the vegetables are picked, depending on whether they go directly into the refrigerator or whether they sit out, there is quite a bit of nutritional loss. We have added back certain nutrients, but definitely some of them are not there from the original product.

QUESTION: The sensory quality of meat may deteriorate due to oxidation and thus increase in rancidity. Has Dr. Dahl any information concerning this, or does Dr. Hendricks know of any nutritional measurement that is being done?

DAHL: The questions of oxidation rancidity may sometimes be thought of as a characteristic of institutional food. I mentioned oxidation rancidity as possibly occurring during initial cooking, during holding--refrigerated or frozen--and then again during the reheating process. This is the field commonly called warmed-over flavor. There are three approaches you can possibly take to head off warmed-over flavor in food at various stages in production. The three approaches that we're taking at Michigan State are first the addition of various antioxidants. There are naturally occurring antioxidants such as ascorbic acids that occur in vegetables--certain spices such as thyme and rosemary have antioxidant properties. A recent study in the <u>Journal of Food Science</u> recorded the use of protein concentrates from various items like cotton seed and peanut seed.

Second, packaging films have very significant potential for reducing warmed-over flavor. Some of the films that are used have antioxidant components, and, when this is used for vacuumed-packed foods, it is right next to the surface of the food that you are storing. These are usually applied during frozen-storage situations.

The last approach to heading off warmed-over flavor, believe it or not, is concerned with microwave ovens. This one is kind of on the ridges of "We don't really know why it works that way." I went to a meeting of the International Microwave Power Institute a few years ago. Someone came up with an interesting story. He had rendered about 40 pounds of bacon fat using the microwave oven and he didn't have a place to refrigerate this, so he put it in his garage for a year. His report was that after a year that was just as good as bacon fat that had been rendered. Is there potentially some rationale for thinking that microwave treatment may be effective because it is so fast and it doesn't result in certain chemical components that are going to trigger this oxidative process? Maybe this is a potential explanation, but anyway you want to take a better look at the effect of microwave heating both at the initial cooking and the reheating stage on the potential for development of warmed-over flavor or the potential for decreasing that development. So, warmed-over flavor is a problem in food service, and three approaches are naturally occurring: anitoxidants, packaging, and possibly microwave treatment.

The Research Project at Moncrief Army Hospital: Introduction

Jessie S. Brewer

Why is the Army conducting research in hospital food
service systems? Army hospitals have been operating
under a standardized, conventional food service system
with hot-cold food delivery carts for the past 20 years.
These carts are beginning to cost more to maintain and
need replacing. Should we replace them with hot-cold
carts and continue with a conventional system? Or should
we purchase different systems? Which is the most cost-
efficient? Which will provide better quality food for
our patients and duty personnel? The Army is building
several new hospitals to replace World War I and World
War II hospitals, and it is upgrading a series of hospitals built 20 to 30 years ago. What type of food
service should we have in these new facilities?

In April 1975, a requirement was submitted to the
Department of Defense Food RDT and Engineering Program to
examine Army hospital food service operations to determine the most cost-effective mode of serving highly acceptable, nutritionally adequate meals to patients and
authorized duty personnel in the dining room. Natick
Army Laboratories is the organization that supports this
program.

About that time the civilian hospital community was
trying new concepts in food preparation and service, such
as cook-chill and cook-freeze, and industry was introducing new tray delivery systems to support these concepts. Visiting hospitals trying new systems showed that
the directors of food services were all convinced that
their way was the way to go.

Col. Jessie S. Brewer is Chief, Dietitian Section, Army
Medical Specialist Corps, U.S. Army, Washington, D.C.

We wanted all feasible operating systems studied to determine which system was best for the Army needs. Guidance was provided to find a system that was cost-efficient and that would improve patient and duty personnel satisfaction. Energy savings became an Army priority.

As Paul Hysen has stated, "When you plan a food service system, you want to buy a tested and proven system, or recognize an untested system as a research and development effort." I might add that when you build a new facility with an untested system as a research and development effort, you run the risk of failure. This can affect the cost of capital equipment, provide unsatisfactory patient care, cause dissatisfaction of hospital staff and administration, and result in image deterioration and firing. I am seeking answers and facts on which to base the decision on what kind of food service we should have in our hospitals. This research is being conducted very methodically and one step at a time.

Many people tell me that it is good that the Army can conduct research in hospital food service, because private and local government hospitals cannot afford to do this type of research; however, even with President Reagan's support of the defense budget, obtaining money for research in hospital food service is not easy. I have not seen any headlines in the Washington Post stating: "Reagan Trying to Convince Congress to Fund Hospital Food Service Research and Development." Each year we must fight to get our project funded. It is a real challenge to convince the people wearing stars that a new system of feeding patients is necessary when a need exists to find a method of feeding troops on the modern battlefield, and especially since the Army has a reputation of serving the best food. The message is that I feel industry should develop and test new systems. Otherwise, we may never make progress.

Moncrief Army Hospital: Systems Analysis and Test Design Phase

Ronald Bustead

SYSTEMS ANALYSIS

In 1975 the Office of the Surgeon General proposed a
requirement for a systems analysis of army hospital food
service. The project was accepted into the Food Research,
Development and Engineering Program under the designation
Military Service Requirement (MSR) U.S. Army 8-4 and
started in 1976. The original statement of need was as
follows: "A requirement exists for an overall examination of hospital food service operations to determine the
most cost-effective mode of operation to serve nutritionally adequate, palatable, high-quality meals to patients
and authorized duty personnel."

The project was essentially conducted in three phases.
First, a systems analysis, documented by OR/SA Report No.
TR-78/031 dated March 1978, was conducted. Second, new
state-of-the-art patient tray systems were evaluated.
Third, an experiment to evaluate the recommended system
and document the results is now in progress.

Systems analysis is concerned with an overall system--
all the resources invested in its operation and all the
output it produces. Elements of systems analysis include
overall objectives, alternatives and related costs,
resources expended to attain the objectives, criteria
used to determine the relative effectiveness of one
alternative versus another, analysis to determine the
consequences of each alternative, evaluation of derived
results to select the preferred alternative, and conclusions that verify results by test or experimentation.

Ronald Bustead, M.S., is Operations Research Analyst,
U.S. Army Natick Research and Development Laboratories,
Natick, Massachusetts.

ARMY HEALTH CARE SYSTEM

The data collection and analysis steps of the systems
analysis yielded the following information about the Army
hospital food service system. First, the general characteristics of Army hospitals are:

- 100, 250, 550 beds
- Patient meals: 50 percent of total
- Special diets: 31 percent of patient meals (15 percent of total)
- Conventional cook-serve system
- Centralized preparation
- Hot-cold food carts
- Trays (hot + cold items) assembled on ward

Size is biased toward the 100-bed hospitals, making
mass production techniques more difficult to apply.
Special diets are fewer than would be expected. However,
this is an average. The major medical centers have a
much higher percentage of special diets, whereas base
hospitals are very low because we are dealing basically
with healthy young men and women.

The total hospital food service system was separated
into its subsystems as follows:

- Purchasing and issuing system
- Production system
- Tray assembly system
- Meal delivery system
- Management control system

Each subsystem was analyzed in an attempt to establish
independence from each other subsystem. Such independence
allows leveling the workload by decreasing the peak
activity associated with meal times. This symposium
defines an additional subsystem--meal service--which we
include under meal delivery. We did not consider that as
a separate subsystem during the original analysis, but we
do now.

The parameters necessary to define quantitatively Army
hospital food service were established as follows:

- Cost per meal
- Productivity
- Labor utilization
- Acceptability

Each parameter has a number of factors that contribute to its measurement and several ways to express the analytical result. For example, Figure 1 shows a histogram of acceptability. This histogram represents the combined patients' and cafeteria customers' opinions of food quality at five different Army hospitals, all of which use a conventional hot-cold cart. The results from the patients alone were essentially the same as this overall result.

When each of the key parameters is measured, we develop the following analytical description of Army hospital food service in 1978 dollars:

- <u>Cost per meal</u> $3.96 (65 percent labor)
- <u>Productivity</u> 2.3 meals per man-hour
- <u>Labor utilization</u> Production 31 percent, tray

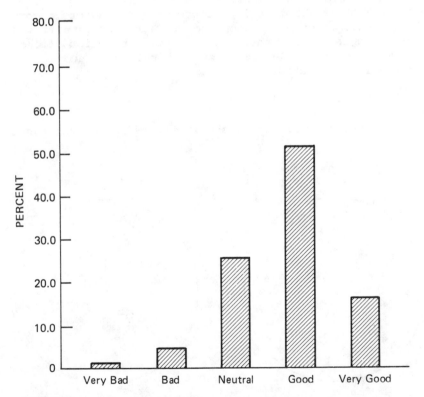

FIGURE 1 Distribution of consumer ratings for the hospital food system.

service 19 percent, management 19 percent, sanitation 16 percent, other 15 percent

• <u>Food acceptability</u> Good or better 75 percent; neutral or better 95 percent

IDENTIFYING AREAS FOR IMPROVEMENT

When we look at a budget picture and compare it to the civilian sector (Figure 2), we immediately see we are investing much more in labor. Meals per man-hour productivity for the civilian sector averages about 3.5, as compared to 2.3. The reason for this is that the Army often has to make things from scratch because its accounting system will not allow trading labor dollars for food dollars the way civilian hospitals can. However, I won't overstress labor and productivity, since food quality is the subject of this symposium.

Ranking the relative importance of meal factors according to surveys of patient opinion is a key to determining what changes the patients will accept. This list reflects patients, opinions in five Army hospitals with hot-cold cart delivery systems:

• Appearance and aroma
• Cold food items
• Attractiveness of dishes, silverware, trays

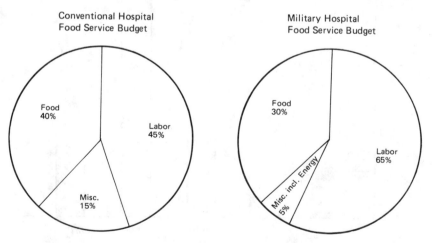

FIGURE 2 Comparison of civilian and military food service budgets.

- Tenderness of meat
- Size of portions
- Variety of items to select
- Cleanliness of dishes and silverware
- Hot food items
- Food served when you want
- Thoroughness of cooking vegetables

It is immediately apparent that patients are less satisfied with cold food temperatures than with hot food temperatures. This unexpected result exploded a generally accepted myth that hot foods were not hot enough. What temperatures were considered hot enough or cold enough? Table 1 shows the results obtained pretest at Moncrief. It can be seen that hot food temperatures vary considerably and are sometimes not very hot; yet hot food being hot enough is seventh in the patients' list of improvements needed. However, cold food temperatures are more often near room temperature. Thus, it may be the perceptive difference from room temperature that determines when a food is hot enough or cold enough.

The ultimate health care system properties, constructed from the results of the systems analysis, are as follows:

- Chilled plating of meal
- Central tray assembly
- Chilled storage of meal
- Centralized or decentralized heating
- Hot portions heated automatically

TABLE 1 Optimum Temperatures for Hot and Cold Foods

Hot Foods	°F	Cold Foods	°F
Swiss steak	112-150	Tuna salad	60-78
Deviled pork chop	114-139	Chicken salad	71-80
Turkey	128-152	Tossed salad	50-73
Beef	108-121	Apple sauce	69-78
Green beans	110-148	Chilled peaches	63-82
Rice	126-158	Lemon gelatin	57
Potato	118-158	Tomato juice	57
Coffee	154-174	Milk	51-65
Sausage	124-148		

- Multiple heating of trays
- Flexibility of serving time
- Heat maintenance of hot portion
- Cold maintenance of cold portion

The first three are self-descriptive. They allow separation of assembly from mealtimes. Number four, of course, refers to centralized heating for cafeterias and decentralized heating for patient meals. The next three ideals are realized by the new state-of-the-art, heat-in-the-delivery-cart service systems. The final two ideals also have to be met or we are back to the run-and-serve drawbacks of many previous systems.

FOOD SERVICE ALTERNATIVES

The food production subsystem has to be one of the following:

- Conventional system
- Convenience foods system (vendor supplied)
- Cook-chill system
- Frozen-ready system

When assembly, delivery, and service are added, however, the maze shown in Figure 3 develops. We chose a cook-freeze, cold plating, heat-in-the-delivery-cart system based on Figure 4, the projected annual cost graph. The bottom line, as always, is "What does it cost?" Selecting the 250-bed-size point on the horizontal axis of Figure 4 and detailing it, one achieves the results shown in Table 2.

Total cost per meal is annualized, which reflects labor savings, operating costs, and capital costs. The difference between the highest projected meal cost of $4.35 and the lowest of $2.89 is almost a dollar and a half. This looks significant, but is it? We always have to answer the question, "Are the savings enough to make changing to a new system worthwhile?" As shown below, we project a one-third labor savings with a 10-month payback period; i.e., the length of time needed to pay for new equipment and renovations is projected to be 10 months. To the military, 1 year is very good and 2 years is acceptable.

```
Present conventional
     labor costs              $904,000/yr
```

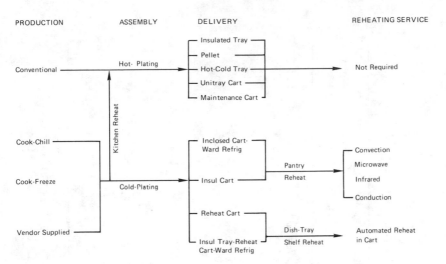

FIGURE 3   Hospital patient food service alternatives.

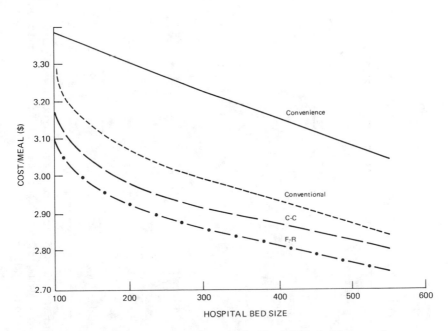

FIGURE 4   Projected annual costs in 1977 dollars of a cook-freeze production system.

TABLE 2 Cost Comparison of Alternative Configurations (thousands of dollars)

Operating Costs	Existing System	Improved Conventional	Convenience	Cook-Chill	Frozen-Ready
Labor	1,305	691	537	621	595
Food	553	534	804	534	523
Supplies	47	47	52	52	52
Energy	7	7	7	9	11
Total operating	1,912	1,288	1,400	1,216	1,181
Capital costs	1,165	1,165	1,128	1,353	1,453
Total annual cost[a]	2,056	1,430	1,541	1,388	1,366
Cost/meal	$4.35	$3.03	$3.26	$2.94	$2.80

[a]Annualized cost of labor, food, equipment, construction, energy and supplies assuming 10 year beneficial life of equipment and 25 year beneficial life of construction.

Projected cook-freeze
   labor costs $601,000
Estimated labor savings $303,000 (33%)
Total equipment cost $249,700
Estimated payback period: 10 months

The difference between the cook-chill and frozen-ready systems is only eight cents per meal, making both systems cost-effective. Further analysis was needed to pick between these systems. From the standpoint of quality the systems were judged comparable. However, the added flexibility of a frozen-ready system, able to respond to large increases in workload during an emergency, seemed more compatible with the military mission. Merely putting on more shifts would not solve the problem, since the same event that caused the emergency could cut off the supply of raw food. In addition, chilled food has to be handled much more carefully than frozen food, making the chance of mishandling error much greater with a chill system (a matter of concern to the military because of personnel turnover), which would be magnified in an emergency. These considerations far outweighed the disadvantages of increased packaging and freezer requirements and increased cost of inventory.

THE EXPERIMENT

Moncrief Army Hospital, Fort Jackson, South Carolina, was selected by the Office of the Surgeon General as the site for an experiment to determine if the projected savings can, in fact, be achieved. The sequence of the test events is as follows:

- Select and buy equipment for cook-freeze phase
- Modify facility, install equipment
- Collect pretest data
- Design menu, modify recipes, set production batch sizes
- Implement cook-freeze phase
- Evaluate new patient delivery equipment
- Repeat 1 and 2 for patient delivery phase
- Collect posttest data
- Document test results

The experiment had to be run in two phases, because the heat-in-the-delivery-cart types of equipment commercially available were in various stages of prototype development. In fact to assure reliability and performance of the equipment selected for the experiment, it was necessary to add the sixth step and evaluate the different equipment on the market. As a result, the cook-freeze phase has been operating about two years, whereas the heat-in-the-delivery-cart phase--the primary objective of the project--has been operating only about two months and has not achieved steady state. Thus, the eight and ninth steps are not yet completed.

The data collection and analysis will be thorough; Table 3 shows the areas being addressed. All contribute to measuring the effectiveness of the new system. However, the last item--costs--carries the most weight.

PRETEST ANALYTICAL RESULTS

Since the menu had to change to accommodate the new system, a computer analysis was performed to determine the effect of the changes on nutrition and cost. The new 21-day menu offered adequate nutrition, slightly exceed-

TABLE 3 Moncrief Research Project Parameters

System Objectives (Effectiveness Factors)	Specific Areas
Customer satisfaction	Patient food acceptance Patient food service surveys Patient food serving temperatures Cafeteria food acceptance Cafeteria food service surveys
Customer nutrition and safety	Menu nutrition analysis Microbiological analysis
Employee satisfaction	Kitchen worker interviews Tray delivery worker interviews Nurse interviews
System efficiency	Work sampling Meal productivity Tray assembly times Energy consumption Costs

TABLE 4   Menu Nutritional Evaluation

Nutritional Component	DDA	Before (35-day) % of RDA	New (21-day) % of RDA	New (House) % of RDA
Food energy (kcal)	3,400	123	139	161
Protein (gm)	100	159	171	199
Fat (gm)	< 40% cal	103	106	108
Calcium (mg)	800	243	278	356
Iron (mg)	14	178	185	211
Vitamin A (IU)	5,000	257	269	313
Thiamine, B_1	1.7	136	149	175
Riboflavin, B_2 (mg)	2.0	194	214	263
Niacin (mg)	22	127	138	153
Ascorbic Acid, C (mg)	60	302	317	352

ing the nutrient levels of the old menu. DDA stands for the Daily Dietary Allowances prescribed by military regulations. It must be emphasized that Table 4 represents average nutrition available from the menu and should not be confused with actual intake of any individual or group of individuals. Military issue factors were used to estimate the proportions of competing items that would be taken by the diners.

The food cost in the cook-freeze menu is comparable to the previous menu; Table 5 demonstrates that the generally more acceptable higher cost foods still appear in the new menu.

The recent increased awareness of energy consumption is illustrated in Table 6. Everything except heat and light (the kitchen is not air conditioned) has been metered out. The preliminary energy data, which does not include the new patient tray delivery system, shows an increase in energy consumption. However, energy cost is still insignificant when we recall that the total meal cost previously shown was $3.97 per meal. Even in the worst case, energy cost increased from 3 percent to 4 1/2 percent of the total meal cost. Interestingly, only about one-third of this increase is due to the freezing and the added frozen storage. Most of the rest of the increase shows up in water usage. One would suspect a

TABLE 5   Menu Costs[a]

Meal	Before (35-Day) Cost (%)	New (21-Day) Cost (%)	New (House) Cost (%)
Breakfast	0.60 (21)	0.62 (21)	0.73 (19)
Dinner	1.12 (40)	1.23 (42)	1.38 (37)
Supper	1.09 (39)	1.06 (36)	1.68 (44)
Total/Day	2.82 (100)	2.92 (100)	3.80 (100)

[a]Food prices are not current, but are based on a BDFA
of $3.29. Add $0.31 to update to today's BDFA.

leak. I'm aware that there is a general consensus developing that energy costs will defeat cook-freeze systems.
Our experience shows that it adds roughly five cents per
meal at present electric rates. Thus, electric rates must
increase by a factor of 30, while all other costs remain
constant, to approach the projected labor cost savings it
allows.

PATIENT TRAY DELIVERY AND SERVICE SYSTEMS TESTED

Figure 5 shows the delivery and service systems that were
given a 10-day evaluation. The objective was to select
the system that would best fit the concept being evaluated. It must be emphasized that selection of the Aladdin
system does not mean the other systems were unsatisfactory. All had strong points and are competitive. Aladdin
was selected because it performed satisfactorily and had
a ward refrigerator as an integral part of its system,
which eliminated the necessity for Natick Laboratories to
design and procure reheating refrigerators for one of the
other systems.

The average food temperatures for cart systems tested
are shown in Table 7. All systems tested outperformed
the control. Aladdin and Therma-Tray gave the best cold
food temperatures, but the Sweetheart system gave the
best hot food temperatures.

These data are not the best because the number of trays
in each cart was not constant and one system was not
metered (see Table 8). The 3-M figure was taken from

TABLE 6 Average Energy Costs per meal (dollars)

	Cost per Meal	Electric	Steam	Cost to Heat Water	Gas	Water Hot + Cold	Sewage	Chill Blast Thaw	Prepared Food Freezer
"Before" (6 weeks) 9/79-10/79	0.126	0.059	0.035	0.012	0.005	0.010	0.005	--	--
"Startup" (7 weeks) 10/79-12/79	0.135	0.065	0.038	0.014	0.005	0.009	0.004	--	--
Winter (9 weeks) 1/80-3/80	0.130	0.061	0.037	0.017	0.005	0.007	0.003	--	--
Spring (16 weeks) 3/80-7/80	0.156[b]	0.064[a]	0.033	0.043	0.005	0.002	0.009	0.005	0.006
Summer-Winter (28 weeks) 7/80-2/81	0.181	0.063	0.037	0.036	0.005	0.019	0.008	0.005	0.008

[a] Cost of blast freezer/rapid chiller/thaw box and prepared food freezer are included.
[b] Cost of water and heating hot water for dishwasher included after march 3, 1980; average = $0.002/meal.

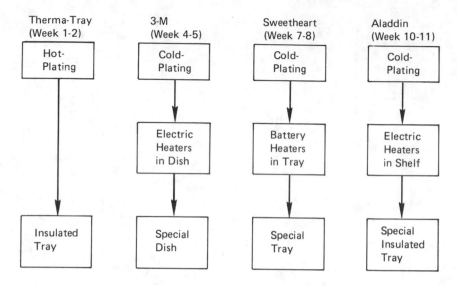

FIGURE 5 Test schedule of patient tray delivery system at Moncrief Army Hospital.

sales literature and undoubtedly presents an ideal not attainable in practice. It is included only to show that the heat-in-the-cart systems are comparable to each other and not much different from the control. Although the energy cost per meal is less than one cent, and insignificant when compared to food and labor, Therma-Tray has the

TABLE 7 Mean Temperatures for Cart Systems Tested

System	Avg. Hot	Entrees	Veg/ Starch	Breakfast	Cold[a]
Sweetheart	165	160	161	175	70
Aladdin	153	170	146	142	52
3-M	154	159	155	149	60
Therma-Tray	140	145	142	133	54
Control	130	132	130	127	62

[a]Adjusted to the same cold-starting temperature.

TABLE 8   Electricity Cost for Five Patient Tray Delivery
Systems (9-Day Average)

Cart	kWh/ Day	kWh/ Tray	Btu[a] Tray	Cost[b] Tray ($)	Cost/Cart ($) (24 Trays)
Sweetheart	7.0	0.206	703	0.0076	0.183
Aladdin	6.7	0.165	563	0.0061	0.146
3-M	Not Metered	0.07	240	0.0026	0.062
Therma-Tray	2.7 (Plate heater)	0.061	208	0.0023	0.055
Hot/Cold control	7.4	0.137	468	0.0051	0.102

[a] 3,413 Btu/kWh.
[b] $0.0371 per kWh.

lowest, requiring only a plate preheater. In fact, considering that people do not like to handle hot plates--
the factor that often defeats insulated tray systems--the
Therma-Tray energy cost could be zero if the plate preheater is not turned on, as is often the case in practice.

PRODUCTION QUALITY CONTROL

When frozen food production started, we ran a very tight
quality control function to optimize product quality and
scale to maximum batch sizes. Maximum efficiency is only
achieved with full kettles and ovens, since set-up and
clean-up time depends to a minor degree on batch size.
Each item was reheated and subjected to evaluation by a
technical panel. A 7-point scale was used, with 7 being
the best rating. Below are some of the ways the results
can be used in addition to normal quality control. First,
the ten most costly items were selected (see Table 9).
The first four items were deleted from the menu. Why
serve high-cost foods that are low in acceptability?
There are plenty of high-cost, highly acceptable foods.
   Next the ten least costly items were examined (see
Table 10). The serving frequency of the more highly
acceptable items was increased. In fact, they were

TABLE 9 Menu Items: 10 Most Costly

Overall Rating (7-Point Scale)	Item	Cost Per Serving
5.4	Creole scallops	1.141
5.6	Oriental pepper steak	1.030
5.1	Baked pork with apples	0.948
4.8	Creole shrimp	0.920
6.7	Barbecued pork spareribs	0.899
5.7	Beef stew	0.866
6.1	Beef stroganoff	0.817
6.1	Roast beef with gravy	0.790
5.5	Roast beef sandwich	0.782
5.5	Veal parmesan	0.772

substituted for the high-cost items previously deleted. This lowers cost and increases acceptability.

The same approach was used for food acceptance. First the bottom 12 were listed (see Table 11). The high-cost items were deleted, and the low cost ones were examined to see if reformulation would be expected to improve accept-

TABLE 10 Menu Items: 10 Least Costly

Overall Rating (7-Point Scale)	Item	Cost Per Serving
6.4	Creole macaroni	0.251
5.9	Chicken pot pie	0.262
6.2	Chicken a la king	0.267
5.7	Pineapple chicken	0.288
4.5	Meat pin wheels	0.293
5.6	Baked chicken with gravy	0.300
6.4	Savory baked chicken	0.313
5.8	Turkey pot pie	0.313
5.9	Baked ham, macaroni, and tomatoes	0.358
5.7	Turkey a la king	0.373

TABLE 11   Menu Items: 12 Least Acceptable

Overall Rating (7-Point Scale)	Item	Cost Per Serving
3.8	Turkey rice soup	0.031
4.5	Salisbury steak	0.407
4.5	Meat pin wheels	0.293
4.6	Chicken tetrazzini	0.463
4.8	Creole shrimp	0.920
4.9	Pork adobo	0.466
5.1	Baked pork slices with apples	0.948
5.3	Lasagna	0.425
5.3	Barbecued ground beef	0.398
5.4	Creole scallops	1.141
5.5	Chili con carne without beans	0.496

ance. In any case, every item that made this list had to be acted upon, as is always true with quality control. The data must be acted upon or the quality control effort is wasted.

Next, the top 12 food items in acceptability were examined (see Table 12). Some could be substituted for items deleted for low acceptability, whereas those that were high-cost were reformulated to lower cost. Of course, if acceptability decreased appreciably, the original formulation was retained.

In principle the cost and food acceptance quality-control system was that shown in Figure 6. The 5.5 cut-off point for food acceptability was used as action point for possible errors during food production, as were unusual yields.

In addition, a low level of microbiology monitoring was carried out. Samples would be drawn and transported back to Natick laboratories for analysis when someone was returning from Fort Jackson. Although the sampling levels were very low, gross or reccuring problems would be expected to show up. Tables 13 and 14 show the number and kinds of samples analyzed and the results. There was nothing to get alarmed about. However, we did find a meat slicer that apparently had not been cleaned well enough.

TABLE 12 Menu Items: 12 Most Acceptable

Overall Rating (7-Point Scale)	Item	Cost Per Serving
6.7	Baked tuna and noodles	0.371
6.7	Barbecued pork spareribs	0.899
6.6	Chili con carne with beans	0.340
6.4	Creole macaroni	0.251
6.4	Savory baked chicken	0.313
6.4	Chicken a la king	0.267
6.4	Chicken chow mein	0.497
6.2	Roast pork with gravy	0.537
6.1	Beef stroganoff	0.817
6.1	Swedish meat balls	0.450
6.1	Barbecued chicken	0.450
6.1	Turkey tetrazzini	0.497

RESULTS TO DATE

The only behavioral science data that has been fully analyzed are the data taken when we evaluated equipment that utilizes cold plating. All delivery equipment tested, including the hold-cold cart and Therma-Tray, delivered acceptable food. As mentioned in a previous paper, food from the hot-cold equipment rated better than the rest, but we must be careful not to take these data out of context. The menu was designed for and the food fully cooked for a hot-cold system. It was held refrigerated for service in the cold-plating equipment until the next day. The primary prupose of the evaluation was to see if the heat-in-the-delivery-cart equipment heated food with some degree of reliability and to judge compatibility with the Natick Laboratories concept.

The preliminary acceptance data from the experiment is summarized in Table 15. Clearly, food temperatures rate considerably better, whereas food acceptance remains fairly even.

Foods that reheat well rate higher when they are served hotter, whereas food that does not reheat well rates lower whether it is served hotter or not (see Table 16).

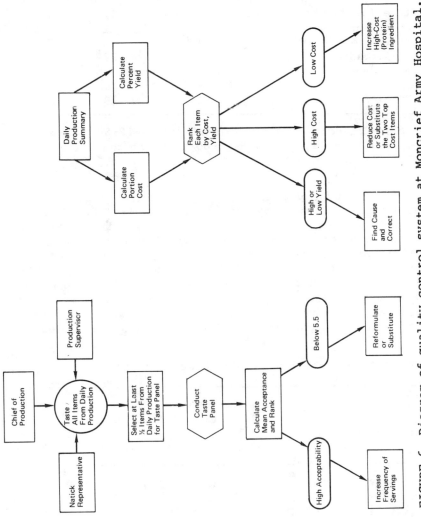

FIGURE 6   Diagram of quality control system at Moncrief Army Hospital.

TABLE 13 Microbiological Monitoring (Number and
Categories of Samples Analyzed)

Item	Frozen	Chilled
Entree (beef, chicken, etc.)	36	10
Entree (tuna, egg salads)	1	1
Vegetables, starch	1	7
Salad (tossed, cole slaw)	2	7
Gravy, sauce	4	--
Breakfast	--	4
Total	44	29

Samples Collected (No.): 4-15-80 (8), 4-22-80 (7),
5-2-80 (8), 5-13-80 (6), 5-16-80 (16), 11-26-80 (10),
2-9-81 (18).

The last area of preliminary data at this time is the
temperature/microbiology results (see Table 17). We are
now able to do more extensive microbiological evaluation
because the veterinary laboratory at Fort Gordon is analyzing about 25 samples per week in support of the equipment. There is a payoff already--three problems have been
identified. Frankfurters are fully cooked during manufacture, and the reheating cart will heat them to a satisfactory serving temperature, but they cannot be plated directly as received. They must be precooked and cooled for

TABLE 14 Microbiological Monitoring Results

Food Group (No. Samples)	Aerobic Plate Count, $<10^5$ cfu/g	Coli- forms $<100/g$	Fecal Coli- forms 0/g
Entree (46)	46	44[a]	45[b]
Tuna or egg salad (2)	2	2	
Vegetables, starch (8)	6	8	
Salad, tossed, and slaw (9)	6	5	
Gravy, sauce (4)	4	4	
Breakfast	4	4	

[a]Roast beef 250/g; meat loaf 580/g.
[b]Roast beef 10/g (E. coli)

TABLE 15 Food and Temperature Acceptance (Preliminary)

	Sample Size	No. Higher Ratings	
		Aladdin	Hot-cold cart
Temperature acceptance (hot food)	22	14	8[a]
Food acceptance (hot food)	22	12	10
Temperature acceptance (cold food)	6	5	1
Food acceptance (cold food)	6	3	3

[a]Includes three breakfast items and coffee.

TABLE 16 Comparison of Hot Cold Cart and Aladdin Systems

Food Name	Hot Cold Cart System (7/27-7/31)		Aladdin System (9/17-9/27)	
	Temperature (X)	Overall Opinion (X)	Temperature (X)	Overall Opinion (X)
Applesauce	4.3	5.7	4.0	5.8
Bacon	3.2	4.0	3.2	4.4
Baked chicken	4.1	5.3	4.0	5.0
Corn	3.6	4.7	4.0	5.8
Fruit cocktail	4.4	5.6	4.0	5.8
Hamburger	3.3	4.8	4.2	4.3
Hashed browns	3.1	4.8	3.7	4.9
Juice	4.2	5.6	4.1	5.5
Mashed potatoes	3.4	4.2	3.9	4.9
Milk	4.9	5.1	4.3	5.7
Pancakes	3.4	5.8	3.6	4.7
Pears	4.3	6.0	3.8	5.1
Peas	3.7	5.2	4.0	5.4
Roast beef	3.9	6.4	4.0	4.6
Scalloped potatoes	3.5	3.8	4.1	4.6
Squash	2.0	1.5	3.5	5.1
Swiss steak	3.2	4.9	4.1	5.2
Turkey	3.7	5.6	4.2	5.2
Turkey croquettes	3.6	4.8	4.0	6.0
Broccoli	3.8	5.1	3.5	4.8
Coffee	3.8	5.4	3.7	5.4
French toast	3.7	6.1	3.4	5.2
Mixed vegetables	3.6	5.0	3.5	5.3
Rice	3.6	5.2	3.5	3.7
Salad	4.0	5.2	3.9	5.1
Scrambled eggs	3.3	4.5	3.1	4.4
Swedish meatballs	3.7	4.8	3.6	4.9
Toast	2.8	4.2	2.5	3.3

TABLE 17 Initial New System Microbiological Results[a]

Food Group (No. Samples)	Aerobic Plate Count/g			Coliforms		
	<10⁴	<10⁵	>10⁵	<20	<50	>100
Entree (28)	22	5	1[b]	24	4	0
Potato (3)	3	0	0	3	0	0
Salad (3)	2	1	0	1	1	1[c]
Breakfast (7)	5	2	0	6	0	1[d]

[a]No significant Staphylococcus aureus detected to date.
[b]Uncooked frankfurters.
[c]Tuna salad.
[d]Pancakes.

microbiological reasons. Pancake batter was being carried over from day to day, and, when it ran low, new mix was added. Tuna and similar salads present a different problem. They are usually made a day ahead even with cook-serve systems. They are often borderline, not considered dangerous but still with counts we do not like to see. This problem was also identified in the "before" data. The recipes may include onions, celery, and peppers, which normally have significant coliform counts, whether used in raw or dehydrated form. Thus, we are inoculating a good growing medium, particularly with egg salad. We finally decided to reformulate as much as practical to avoid potential problems. After all, who wants onions in egg salad?

Some initial data on the warming-cooling performance of the Aladdin cart are shown in Table 18. The heating cycle is 36 minutes and seems adequate. If anything, there seems to be a tendency toward overheating. Few breakfast items are shown. They are difficult, and we are experimenting with different ways of plating them. On the cooling side, there is considerable variation. We do not know the cause, but suspect the fit of the insulated tray covers. Both tops and bottoms are notorious for warping, particularly after a few uses. It is obvious that if we use the minimum times shown, we have about 20 minutes if left in the refrigerator and 30 minutes if pulled out the minute the cycle is complete. Thus, someone must be there to serve from the cart as soon as the cycle ends. There is no heat maintenance cycle, a definite shortcoming.

TABLE 18   Some Aladdin Time/Temperatures

| Food | Temperature | | Time to 140°F[a] | |
	Run 1	Run 2	Min.	Max.
Broccoli	200	189	24	44
Hush puppies	147	141	4	14
Mashed potato	190	159	24	64
Pork	199	--	49	49
Fish	164	174	24	64
French toast	158	198	14	30
Carrot salad	37	37	[b]	[b]
Lettuce	37	36	[b]	[b]

[a]Inside refrigerator. Outside adds 10 minutes (about 30 percent).
[b]Reached 50°F in 14-34 minutes outside refrigerator.

Moncrief Army Hospital: Development, Implementation, and Operation of the Cook-Freeze System

William L. Goodwin, Jr.

The major emphasis of this symposium has been to examine
the effects on food quality of the meal assembly, meal
distribution, and meal service processes of conventional,
cook-chill, and cook-freeze food service systems. This
presentation is designed to describe to you the manner in
which many of the considerations described throughout the
symposium were applied in assembling a cook-freeze system
for implementation and experimentation at Moncrief Army
Hospital, Fort Jackson, South Carolina.

REVIEW OF KEY FOOD SERVICE SUBSYSTEMS

There are numerous methods of analyzing and representing
the key subsystems in a food service operation. However,
in order to maintain continuity and the proper perspective
with the first portion of the "Update on Study at Moncrief
Army Hospital, Fort Jackson, South Carolina," let's look
at food service according to the following key subsystem
breakdown:

1. Purchasing and issuing
2. Production
3. Tray assembly
4. Tray distribution
5. Tray service
6. Management control

Maj. William L. Goodwin, Jr., is Chief, Food Services
Division, Army Medical Specialist Corps, Moncrief Army
Hospital, Fort Jackson, South Carolina.

This paper will deal with the last five subsystems; no attention will be given to the purchasing and issuing subsystem.

HISTORICAL DATA--MONCRIEF ARMY HOSPITAL

Moncrief Army Hospital is a mid-size fixed Army Medical Treatment Facility located at Fort Jackson, which is near Columbia, South Carolina. It is under the command of the U.S. Army Health Services Command located at Fort Sam Houston, Texas. Moncrief Army Hospital was opened in 1972 with a constructed capacity of 410 beds. It provides a variety of general medical services to its population of active duty basic trainees, military staff, dependents, and retirees. It has a total of 12 floors, with floors 1-5 being utilized for administrative, maintenance, clinical, and medical support activities and floors 6-12 for in-patient care. Food service is located in the east end of the building, with activities on both the third and fourth floors.

In order to improve your knowledge of the detailed operation of the Food Service Division at Moncrief Army Hospital, the following statistics are provided:

Average number of meals served/day in both dining room and wards[a]	1,030
Average number of ward meals served/day[a]	459
Average patient stay[a]	5 days
Percentage of modified diets[a]	20 percent
Average monthly expenditure for subsistence[a]	$34,647.17
Average monthly value of nonprepared foods inventory[a]	$24,588.42
Personnel strength[b] (military and civilian)	55

[a] Computations based on averages during the period July 1980-July 1981.
[b] As of August 1981.

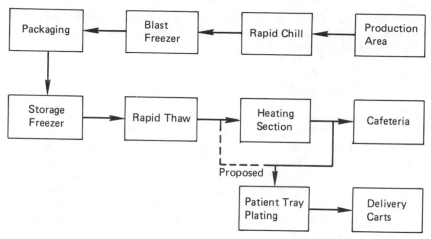

FIGURE 1 Cook-freeze system: Moncrief Hospital.

PRODUCTION SYSTEM

Cook-Freeze System Flow

Prior to entering into an explanation of the cook-freeze
system flow designed for Moncrief, the term cook-freeze
should be clarified. The use of this term does not imply
that Moncrief is totally a cook-freeze system. A total
cook-freeze system is generally a convenience food system.
The degree of cook-freeze done at Moncrief will be addressed later, but in addition to cook-freeze, cook-chill
and cook-serve items are also required to build the total
menu. Cook-freeze must be a selective process--use the
items that give the best quality with your particular
system.

Figure 1 shows the cook-freeze system flow as intended
for Moncrief Army Hospital. The initial attempt to change
from a totally conventional operation and move towards
phasing in some form of this new system from an operational standpoint occurred in 1979.

Conversion to Cook-Freeze

The conversion to cook-freeze initiated in early 1979
reached an on-line status late in the first quarter of
1980. This conversion generally followed the steps
listed below and will form the framework for my
explanation:

1. Select and buy equipment
2. Modify facility and install equipment
3. Develop production support "software"
4. Start up

Space to accommodate the conversion was the first obvious problem. An area was needed to house the refrigeration and packaging equipment necessary. To solve this problem, the existing bakeshop area underwent some equipment consolidation and relocation of certain functions into the main production area. This resulted in a bakeshop that was reduced to approximately 50 percent of its initial space. This was adequate to accommodate rapid chill, rapid blast, and packaging equipment. The storage freezer space problem was handled by constructing an additional prefab freezer adjacent to and connected to the food service loading/receiving dock. The rapid thaw equipment was able to be accommodated in the main kitchen in a location convenient to material flow. The remainder of the areas shown in Figure 1 did not pose any space problems.

Beginning at the point of production (assuming preparation is complete), the product is panned in a special half-size steam table pan and placed in a mobile open-sided wire rack for movement to the rapid chill unit. These special molded plastic pop-out pans were developed by Natick for the experiment. They are made of high-density polyethylene, withstand blast freezer temperatures of -40°F, and are sanitized and used repeatedly. The pans also have matching lids that are slotted on the corners. This permits the corners to fit through the slot and hold the lid intact during the cooling process, thereby preventing drying and freezer burn.

Food products are first processed through the rapid chill unit for loss of initial heat. The rapid chill unit installed at Moncrief is a standard Victory Rapid Chill double compartment roll-in model. This unit functions as a normal refrigerator until the timer is set. Once it is actuated, air at higher velocity and cooler temperature works to cool products down at much quicker rate than normal refrigeration. Products are loaded generally between 140°F and 150°F and cooled for approximately 3 hours to get down to 40°F or below.

Products removed from the blast freezer then have to be packaged for long-term freezer storage. Lids are removed from special molded plastic pans, and the product is popped out like a big ice cube for wrapping in clear plastic film. This is accomplished using an L-Bar Sealer

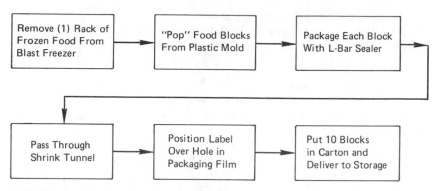

FIGURE 2   Packaging procedure.

and Weldotron Shrink Tunnel. Essentially, the product is
inserted by hand between film layers, is heat sealed
around the periphery with the L-Bar (a quick, several-
seconds-per-item process), and then automatically con-
veyed through the Weldotron Shrink Tunnel for heat
shrinking of the film to conform to the product. The
film used is Dupont Clysar polyolefin shrink film and is
available in several widths. After application of an
identification label, the frozen cubes are placed in
cardboard cartons for long-term freezer storage. Figure
2 summarizes the entire packaging procedure.

   Long-term freezer storage is accomplished in a prefab
freezer constructed as an addition to the rear loading/
receiving dock of the Food Service Division. Storage temperature is -10°F with cartons of food stored on standard
wire shelving. The freezer is approximately 12 feet by
29 feet with standard ceiling height and an anteroom to
buffer the freezer internal temperature with the outside
temperature.

   Cook-freeze items requisitioned from storage for consumption are pulled and thawed under controlled conditions. This is accomplished with a unit specifically
designed for tempering. The tempering unit installed at
Moncrief is a standard Victory Rapid Thaw three-
compartment roll-in model. This unit functions as a
normal temperature refrigerator holding cabinet until the
timer is actuated. Once it is actuated, air at high
velocity and a slightly warmer temperature facilitates
thawing. Cook-freeze cubes generally require 12 hours
for thawing. Products go from thawing cabinet to the
cafeteria for reheating and service or to tray assembly
for chilled plating.

While the selection and buying of equipment and the modification of the facility and installation of that equipment were occurring, other management decisions were made. These decisions affect final quality or, in some cases, the perception of quality as delivered to the customers. I have chosen to classify these decisions or alternatives as development of production support "software." These include such decisions as the kinds of products that should be made as cook-freeze, the menu discipline, and production guide development. Other details also fall into this category, but time constraints do not permit detailed discussion of each.

The initial experimentation with cook-freeze products required the development of production guides to accommodate cook-freeze products. A production guide is a more sophisticated version of a standardized recipe that has been tailored to the specifics of the production facility. Natick Laboratories technologists, utilizing the work that had been performed previously for the Walter Reed Army Medical Center system as a base, expanded, tested, and developed guides for the Moncrief experiment. Development was accomplished first in the lab and then in the field. Production guide development took on two distinct phases: the hard copy portion and a sensory (acceptance) portion. Production guides were brought in hard copy form from the lab, were produced and frozen, and were then rethermed and evaluated by a panel of food service and other disinterested parties (hospital staff). The results of those sensory evaluations (concentrating mainly on texture, flavor, and appearance) were then used as input to Natick technologists. Guides were revised and the process repeated with the objective being to improve the quality until all products had consistently high numerical ratings. This process continued rather intensely for approximately one year. The rating procedures and analysis techniques have been discussed earlier in the proceedings.

The approach to initial production and inventory buildup was to make as many products for cook-freeze as possible. This included soups, entrees, starch items, vegetables, and baked products. These were all regular food items--no special items for modified diets. Products being made were to supplement both the cafeteria and patient regular menu. The philosophy was to supplement the conventional menu with cook-freeze items, but not to the point of developing the "TV dinner syndrome." This was no problem for the wards, because the average patient

stay was 5 days. Concern was significant for the cafeteria menu because we have a captive audience of assigned
military personnel who must subsist in the hospital dining
room for all meals, 7 days per week. Therefore, a ratio
of approximately 50/50 cook-freeze to cook-serve menu
items was used and mainly affected the entree, starch,
and vegetable.

PATIENT TRAY ASSEMBLY, DISTRIBUTION,
AND SERVICE SUBSYSTEMS

Description-Definition of Conventional System

In order to understand the impact of conversion to a new
patient tray assembly, distribution, and service system,
one must first have an understanding of what the conventional, or previous, system was like and how it func-
tioned. Categorizing or defining the previous system is
best done by reference to Figure 3 in the paper by
Bustead. Using that figure as a guide, key in on the
conventional production system and follow the arrow
straight across. Doing this reveals a hot-plating
assembly system, a hot-cold tray delivery system (maintained by a mechanical hot-cold cart that had to be
plugged in), and a service system that requires only
passing of trays after final assembly and checking. For
purposes of this diagram, a service system in our old
system really was not required, because food was con-
tinuously maintained hot-cold.

The conventional method of patient tray assembly was a
split operation—cold foods were assembled separately
from hot and this was not a continuous process. Cold
assembly started in advance of hot-plating, with hot
items being done as close to meal time as possible in
order to optimize quality. Cold assembly was done around
a conveyor 12 feet in length utilizing three personnel.
There was a starter position (which also handled most
condiments); a position that loaded salads, desserts, and
other cold items (except milk); and a checker position
that, in addition to verifying accuracy, would load milk
and move the carts in and out of position. Cold foods
were replenished frequently from reach-in refrigerators
directly behind the conveyor line. However, mechanically
refrigerated cold units were not employed except for milk
and special cold beverages. At the time of cold assembly,
cold items were put on the tray and the tray placed in

the cart. The cart was mechanically heated-cooled and therefore had to be kept plugged in at all times. After cold assembly, the cart had to be moved back to the cart holding area and reconnected to a power source to await its turn for hot loading.

The hot food assembly area consisted of two hot food counters positioned at right angles to each other. A griddle was also adjacent for on-line preparation and direct plating of certain items (eggs for breakfast for example). One hot food counter was used for regular menu items, the other for modified diet menu items. Again, the cart had to be plugged in during the hot-loading process in order to support the mechanical heating-cooling function. Two personnel were required, one to call and load and one to plate. Hot plates were generally covered with saran wrap or foil before placing in a hot drawer.

After assembly, carts moved back to the cart-holding area, either between cold-hot assembly or after hot assembly if not going directly up to be served. The cart-holding area was approximately 15 feet wide and 22 feet long with adequate electrical reels to accommodate all carts for preheating-cooling prior to loading. Bulk loading of tea, coffee, soup, hot water, and hot cereal was also done in this area prior to dispatch to floor. Once sent to the floors, carts had to be plugged in again to maintain hot-cold temperatures, thereby decreasing flexibility. The food service attendant had to match or reassemble the hot plate with the cold tray, put on soup-cereal and beverages, and give to nursing personnel for distribution to the patient.

Preliminary Evaluation for New Patient Tray Equipment

The preliminary evaluation of new patient tray equipment was the next step in continued evaluation of the cook-freeze concept. This evaluation was accomplished May-July 1980. Figure 5 in Bustead's paper shows the systems evaluated, the test schedule, and the basic features of the system. Note that each system was tested for two weeks on one ward in the hospital. Ward 9 West was used as the test ward, and Ward 9 East was used as the control ward. The remainder of the hospital stayed on the exist-ing hot-cold cart system.

To achieve consistency with any comparative evaluation, basic rules or parameters must be established for con-

ducting the evaluation. The basic parameters of this
evaluation included the following:

1. Same menu used for all systems.
2. Same personnel involved in doing actual test and
work with each system; two military personnel from other
units were assigned strictly for the system evaluation in
order to minimize disruption to the regular operation.
3. Familiarization training was conducted with each
system by the manufacturer's representative.
4. Natick personnel collected food temperature data
on each system.
5. Natick personnel collected sensory acceptance data
among patients on both test and control systems; nurses
were also interviewed regarding their preference-
acceptance of the various systems.
6. Meal assembly for the system under evaluation was
accomplished between meal assembly periods for the
hot-cold carts.
7. Cook-freeze products were used as much as possible
on the cold-plating systems and just tempered out for
plating. Items that were best accomplished as cook-chill
were prepared one day in advance and chilled in the rapid
chill unit.

During the course of the two-week evaluation, we
focused on determining if the system performed as the
manufacturer claimed it would perform. The next logical
question after that involved its fitting our concept and
its availability on the marketplace. The concept being
pursued involved chilled plating and reheat in the cart,
preferably in a refrigerated environment. This was pre-
sumed to possess the potential for delivering the optimum
quality at a reasonable cost. Pursuit of this concept
evolved into asking the following questions about each
system:

1. Are cold foods acceptable?
2. Are hot foods hot?
3. What are limitations of the system imposed by its
design (mainly in the hot food area)? What restrictions
does it impose on the menu?

Figure 5 in Bustead's paper provides details regarding
the patient tray delivery systems tested. The Therma-
Tray system used was the traditional "Solar"-insulated
server with all components, including plate heaters.

Food was plated hot as close to serving time as possible.
The remaining systems (3-M, Sweetheart, Aladdin) all utilized cold-plating and thereby required interim refrigerated storage up to the time of reheating or rethermalization. Reheating-rethermalization occurred within the
cart. The 3-M equipment used was the cart reheat system
with some limited testing of the 3-M module. Meal reheating occurred on the patient floor at ambient temperature.
A special 3-M power supply was installed on the patient
floor to accommodate the reheating cycle. The Sweetheart
equipment utilized a cart with an energy pack that was re-
charged overnight on standard power and would reheat three
meals (without recharge) from the chilled state. The cart
was independent of any power supply during reheating; the
reheating cycle could be initiated enroute to the floors,
prior to going to the floor, or on the patient floor, but
all at ambient temperature. Cold food dishes were covered
with a special utetic lid. The Aladdin equipment evaluated was the Aladdin Rethermalization system. It consisted of an insulated tray concept with rethermalization
on the patient floor within a refrigerated cabinet. The
entire cart was placed inside the refrigerated cabinet.
A special retherm unit had to be installed on the patient
floor.

All systems included in the evaluation performed well.
They all generally did what the manufacturers claimed
they would do. My objective here has not been to go into
details regarding findings with each system, but rather
to familiarize you with the evaluation performed. Each
of you would have to evaluate all aspects of a particular
system and draw your own conclusions based on your objectives. The basic conclusion at this point is that the
cook-freeze concept and its associated method of tray assembly, distribution, and service deserved further study
and a more intense evaluation.

Conversion to New System

Based on many factors, the recommendation was made and
the decision finalized by the Office of the Surgeon
General in summer 1980 to implement the Aladdin system at
Moncrief Army Hospital during the next fiscal year for
further evaluation of the cook-freeze concept. This
evaluation should run for a period of at least one year.
The primary reason for selecting the Aladdin Retherm
system involved its availability on the market and its

fitting our projected concept, in addition to its recognized potential during the two-week evaluation phase.

For purposes of maintaining perspective, and the method used in defining the conventional or previous system, see Figure 3 in Bustead's paper. The new system can now be defined as cook-freeze and cook-chill production, cold-plating as the method of assembly, insulated tray-reheat cart-ward refrigerator as the method of delivery or distribution, and automated reheat in cart as the method of reheating-service.

Conversion to the new system involved installation of the Aladdin Retherm units on each patient floor along with other accessory equipment determined appropriate; installation of a new patient tray assembly system to facilitiate cold-plating; and installation of a walk-in refrigerator for storage-holding of assembled meals. Space was negotiated within the hospital for location of retherm units. Units are located on each floor with two back-up units located in the kitchen. Floor units are either single compartment, double compartment, or both. They are located centrally on each floor for service of both wards on each floor. Installation of these units was negotiated into the system contract fee. Installation did necessitate providing new power supplies. Accessory equipment required for the retherm areas included counterstyle freeze units and hot water dispensers. The concept was to use the freezer tops to house the hot water dispenser as well as to provide a work surface.

The walk-in refrigerator for storage-holding of assembled meals was procured as a prefab unit of approximately 15 feet by 22 feet. Installation was in the same area previously occupied by the ambient-temperature cart-storage. Compressor units were located remotely.

The patient tray assembly system equipment was purchased as off-the-shelf items and, other than minor changes in utilities, involved a simple swap-out with existing equipment plus installation of additional equipment in the same general area. All equipment is mobile. The new system is a combined operation with all items loaded in one assembly--no more split assembly. Assembly is built around a variable-speed conveyor 21 feet long. There are four mechanically refrigerated cold food counters (two deep/two shallow), a milk dispenser, mobile racks for the tray bottoms and insulated covers, and a snap-on overshelf for the conveyor that can be utilized where most advantageous. The starter unit was adapted from the previous system.

The positions on the assembly line have not changed all that much; they have just been rearranged. One position is currently being used as a starter; one is required for salad, desserts, and soups; one is required for the entree, starch, vegetable plating (does both regular and modified); and one as the checker. The checker also adds the milk and the insulated lid and moves the cart in and out of position. Salads, desserts, and soups are preportioned prior to start of assembly, but the entree, starch, and vegetable items are portioned from the bulk state with few exceptions. After the tray reaches the checker and he adds the insulated lid and milk, the tray is completely assembled except for the addition of hot or cold beverages on the patient floor. Trays are loaded onto the Aladdin cart, which holds 24 trays, does not have to be plugged-in anywhere during the assembly and distribution process, and only has to be handled once during assembly. With the exception of cups, glasses, tops and bottoms of trays, and a china side dish for eggs, the tray components are disposable. The Aladdin cart with assembled trays is stored in the walk-in refrigerated cart storage-holding area mentioned earlier until time for dispatch to the patient floors.

In advance of serving time on the ward (the amount of advance time depends on the meal, ward, and management prerogative), the carts are transported directly from the kitchen refrigerator with insulated covers. There is very little temperature change enroute. Beverages (tea, coffee, hot chocolate, etc.) are not yet on the tray. Once on the patient floor, the cart is positioned in the retherm unit and tested for electrical contact. Once this is accomplished, the unit is left until time to start retherm. The retherm unit is simply a roll-in refrigerator with connections to provide electrical energy to the cart. The insulated lid activates a microswitch that permits conduction heating to occur via a heater shelf in the cart. Cutouts in the tray bottom allow direct contact of the dish with the heater shelf. The retherm cycle takes 36 minutes; the unit is equipped with digital timers and thermometers so that the operator can constantly monitor its operating status.

Upon completion of the retherm cycle, the operator removes the cart and adds the beverages (iced tea, hot water for tea or other instant packaged beverages, and coffee). Beverages are transported to the wards (the two servers have their own beverage carts) and poured up according to tally. Individual beverages are then placed

FIGURE 3   Aladdin cart.

on the service shelf on the cart for addition to trays as
they are served. Service can occur in two modes. Either
the cart can be located in a stationary position and ambulatory patients can come to it to pick up their trays, or
the cart can be rolled room to room for delivery to bed
patients. Both methods are employed at Moncrief. The
system offers a great deal of flexibility in this regard,
because the cart is not confined to a power source during
service. With the completely assembled tray, a simple
reading of the menu and addition of the beverage speeds
up serving time considerably.

Figure 3 shows the Aladdin cart with a single retherm
unit. As was noted earlier, the retherm units are also
available in double models. The wire shelf on the front
of the cart can be popped up into position as a service
shelf when required.

While the selection and buying of equipment and the
modification of the facility and installation of that
equipment was occurring, other management decisions were
being made. These decisions involved development of patient tray "software," including the decision to preplate
or plate strictly from bulk on the line, developing the
assembly and loading schedule, how to handle modified
diets, and how to handle advance production.

As it now stands, most items are portioned from a bulk form onto the dishes during assembly. Consideration was given to preplating and freezing modified diet items in entree or entree-starch combinations in the disposable Aladdin dish, but in addition to the complications arising out of the inability to freeze all starch items, there was the problem of just not having space to physically accommodate preplates at the proper temperature during assembly. Additionally, it would have created a very labor-intensive situation in terms of packaging, freezing, and handling preplates. So modified diet items that are cook-freeze are done in 10-serving batches, with unused portions being phased into the cafeteria service. The production and service of modified diets has been simplified for cook-freeze by use of methods discussed previously in these proceedings. Modifications have been consolidated, and production guides initially developed for the Walter Reed Army Medical Center system have been adapted for use in the Moncrief Army Hospital system.

The tray assembly schedule currently being utilized calls for assembly of lunch and dinner in the morning and breakfast assembly for the next day in the afternoon. Assembly for lunch starts at 8:30 a.m. and supper at 11:00 a.m. Each meal usually requires 1 to 1-1/4 hours to complete. Breakfast assembly begins at 1:45 p.m. and generally requires slightly less time.

Food production items that are cook-freeze are no problem--they simply have to be tempered in time for use. Breakfast items are cook-chill and are done early on the day of assembly in order to allow time for quick chilling; fried and poached eggs are preplated in a china side dish; toast is made, plated, and covered but not refrigerated. All other breakfast items are panned up in bulk. Items that are cook-chill in the meat-starch-vegetable category for lunch and dinner are cooked one day in advance of use, quick-chilled, covered, and stored. Baked products are prepared in advance and portioned just prior to assembly; some products are frozen; some are conventionally prepared. Salads also are portioned right before assembly; most are made on the day of service except for the obvious ones that must be made in advance.

Conversion to the new method of tray assembly occurred with the breakfast meal on August 5, 1981, approximately a year after the decision was made to pursue further evaluation of the concept of chilled plating and reheat in the cart, preferably in a refrigerated environment.

MANAGEMENT CONTROL SUBSYSTEM

Quality Assurance Program

At the time of this writing, the total conversion to the
new system has only been in effect for several weeks.
For this reason, not all aspects of the quality assurance
program have yet been implemented, and actual results are
unavailable. However, the protocol for the quality assurance program from a managerial point of view will be
presented--it will be implemented in total during the
upcoming weeks.

Quality assurance is being approached from a broad
perspective. That is not to say that the protocol for
Moncrief is all-inclusive. There are, without a doubt,
other aspects of the total food service process that may
need to be monitored more closely once the initial protocol begins to generate feedback. The protocol for
Moncrief will consist initially of the following areas:

1. End-product analysis
2. Sanitation
   (a) Inspections
   (b) Swabs and Rodac plates
3. Time-temperature profiles
4. Food acceptance surveys

End-product analysis refers to the microbiological
analysis that will be performed on selected food samples.
Emphasis will be placed upon those items that are considered high risk, either by reason of the type of ingredients used or by the nature of the processing that they
undergo. Microbiological analysis will include aerobic
plate count, coliform count, Escherichia coli, Staphylococcus aureus (optional), Clostridium perfringens
(optional), and yeast and mold count (if necessary).
Frozen and chilled samples will be collected by personnel
at Moncrief and transported to the U.S. Army Regional
Veterinary Laboratory at Fort Gordon, Georgia, for
analysis. The number of samples collected will range
from a minimum of 16 per week to a routine of 25 per week.

Sanitation consists of two main areas, inspections and
swabs/Rodac plates. Inspections refers to routine, documented visual sanitation inspections or checklists of the
entire Food Service Division performed on at least a
weekly basis. These inspections will concentrate on areas
considered more high risk to the cook-serve process,

i.e., production equipment, temperatures on dishwasher,
pot/pan washer, etc. Supervisory personnel in production
must perform a nonwritten visual inspection on a daily
basis as part of routine, but the written inspection will
hopefully help to identify trends by improving communication and documenting corrective action taken. Swabs/Rodac
plates will be used in conjunction with the written sanitation inspection. They help to confirm the quality of
the surface sanitation being performed. Selected surfaces
will be identified and evaluated by either swabs or Rodac
plates. These surfaces include those used in food preparation and processing and contact surfaces included in
the delivery system (carts, trays, accessories). Analysis
of swabs and Rodac plates will be performed in the laboratory at Moncrief.

Time-temperature profiles refer to the in-process monitoring by trained personnel of the various production
stages and handling techniques and the manner in which
products are passed through the danger zone of microbiological activity. The objective is to ensure that products and materials, particularly high-risk items, are not
subjected to abuse as they go through the various cook-
freeze or cook-chill stages. This will be an ongoing process directed at critical processing points. The operations of food processing, filling/panning, freezing, tempering, reconstitution, plating, delivery (after heating
in ward), and warewashing will be monitored.

Food acceptance surveys are an integral part of the
feedback loop that stimulates management to direct efforts
to improve quality or service in specific areas. Surveys
will be conducted at frequent intervals in both the cafeteria and on the wards to check the quality of food and
service. The form utilized for collection of survey data
has already been discussed. Data will be compiled and
analyzed with both a look at immediate, short-range problems and the identification of long-range trends.

System Characteristics

Conversion to a new system has introduced many new
characteristics that have had a tremendous impact on
management decisions and philosophy. New meanings have
been associated with the terms production scheduling,
production control, inventory control, system training,
staffing patterns, etc. A separate symposium could be

conducted on each of them alone, and time obviously does not permit their discussion. Suffice it to be said that they are all critically important to system success.

However, there is one subject that should be noted here because it is still at the center of all action in food service--the menu or menu discipline. A brief explanation will assist greatly in understanding the project at Moncrief Army Hospital.

As was noted earlier, initial production and experimentation with cook-freeze products saw us producing soups, entrees, starch items, vegetables, and baked products. For a variety of reasons, cook-freeze items are not still being produced covering the same span of products. Reasons for change included quality of the final product, labor intensity of a given product, equipment conflicts, and storage space/logistics. For example, soups are no longer produced as cook-freeze because of low demand, inadequate packaging equipment for handling liquids, and the drain it placed on our cooling equipment. In other words, management decided that it just was not worth the effort. A full inventory is still maintained, but that inventory composition is different than when we started. For example, we still maintain quantities of approximately 110 different items. Initially, we had 85-90 different items in the freezer. We now also have to produce modified diet items that were not of interest in the original inventory buildup. The cook-freeze inventory consists largely of entree items, entree-casserole items, some starch items, sauces, gravies, modified diet items, and some baked products-- all labor-intensive items and items that do well with cook-freeze. Selectivity must be utilized in the cook-freeze decision.

The menu at Moncrief follows a 21-day cycle with a select menu for patients. Patients on modified diets are not allowed to select. The cafeteria and wards are served the same menu on the same day. Cook-freeze items are used to minimize the amount of product that must be done at the evening meals and on weekends when manpower is usually less abundant. At this time, cook-freeze entrees are used at least 50 percent of the time at lunch and dinner meals during the week on both the wards and in the dining room. The rate of use on weekends varies between 50 and 100 percent.

SUMMARY

From the viewpoint of the operator, there are no preliminary results or conclusions that can be provided at this
time beyond what has already been presented. It is still
too early. Armand Cardello and Ronald Bustead have presented data they feel is pertinent and available at this
time. Data collection is continuing in the behavioral
science/food acceptance area and the temperature/
microbiology area and will be done later in the labor
requirements area. The main point is that data collection is occurring in a very systematic manner and will be
utilized fully in formulating recommendations.

DISCUSSION

QUESTION: If any Aladdin tray has no temperature
loss, why does the cart have to be refrigerated?
GOODWIN: There is some refrigeration loss in the
Aladdin cart. Some items, such as uncovered desserts and
salads are under the little winged area, but milk is
not. That's one of the main things we have had problems
with. Over a period of time, there would be a loss
occurring; the point is to be able to take the cart up
ahead of the meal, leave it, and forget about it.
QUESTION: How do you handle hold and late trays? Is
there a microwave backup for individual trays, especially
when the food truck has been returned to the kitchen?
GOODWIN: We got into a little bit of difficulty in
the beginning with late trays because we were trying to
set aside a period of time at the end of the meal and
take all the late trays up. That became really unmanage-
able; we weren't able to get a tray to the patient until
1:30 in the afternoon. We still do that for diets that
we know are going to be late, and when patients are held
up for tests, we are retherming at a later time. We have
a backup unit in the kitchen, the Aladdin equipment, and
a double and a single unit in the kitchen as well as up
on the floor. If a patient comes in during the course of
the time that the cafeterias are open for example, we
simply have him get hot food off the line, put it on the
Aladdin tray with the insulated cover, and take it up.
We get service to the patient that way without a lot of
delay. After the cafeteria is closed, we generally have
some food left. We hold in the chilled state items that
are prepared but that we didn't use. We also have a

microwave oven in which we can heat a tray and then take it up in that manner.

QUESTION: How washable is the Aladdin cart? Can a power spray be used?

GOODWIN: We do not use a power spray--we simply sanitize by wiping down with cloth and disinfectant. That's something that we're working on with Aladdin. There is wiring inside the cart that takes care of all those microswitches and the switches in the bottom. We have been getting increasing tray counts, APC counts I guess, from doing swabs of the little tray slides in the cart indicating that there are people not cleaning very well. The point is that they are hard to clean, and we have some brushes we're going to use to try to clean those grooves out from time to time. But, I would say that they are not washable by power spraying.

QUESTION: Is there any need to change the employee's work schedule for the cook-freeze system?

GOODWIN: Basically the changes we have made to date have been that we've taken one cook and we use that individual for cook-freeze equipment Monday through Friday. He works a regular shift. He's working independent from the rest of the operation. With one person generally able to do that, we have some other folks that work the same kind of shift to handle the packaging and the movement of the food. We almost need a logistician in this kind of system to continue to move racks of food from point A to point B to point C to get it into the freezer and then to get it out and run it back through the rethaw cycle. But, that's about all that we've changed. We are now looking at tray assembly--changing and putting more folks on a straight schedule, having a core of regular people and then some early and some late. Right now we have not made those changes.

QUESTION: Have you tried putting dry toast without butter in a heat-sealed wrap before putting it on an Aladdin tray: no moisture can get to it?

GOODWIN: We tried that, but we still came out with a limp product the times that we did it, because you still have moisture and you still have heat in that cavity and it tends to make the toast limp, even though you're sealing out the moisture. We've tried buttering it and then toasting it or toasting it and buttering it afterwards; none of those things seem to work real well. If we butter it and then toast it, we can run into problems with modified diets. You can't give them butter, but the butter is in the toast. The easiest thing would be to find a simple procedure that's black and white, not gray. Then it is a lot easier on the tray line. So that is one of the reasons we decided not to do that.

QUESTION: What type of warewashing system do you use: carousel, flight-type, etc?

GOODWIN: We have a flight-type dish machine, a Hobart machine. The bottoms of the Aladdin trays fit in there without any problem between the pegs. There is a special rack to accommodate the lids. You can also have the option of changing the bed--adding a wider bed. But the problem we have is that we use chinaware in the dining room and it sits back at an improper angle. There are racks to put these trays in that hold the dishes upright. You just sit them on top of the pegs and they go through.

QUESTION: How effective are the washer tray cavities? What problems do you have in warewashing?

GOODWIN: It is difficult, with all the cavities and grooves, for all the water to drain out. If the machine is working properly it works pretty good. There is a design problem with the Aladdin tray that Aladdin thinks they can solve. Around the bottom of the tray there are some little pinholes that they use to inject foam into the cover. Those pinholes are not sealed off. Dr. Silverman knows we have been picking up some bacterial counts there because of the fact that there is water and things getting into the holes. Aladdin thinks that they can take care of that just by putting epoxy over it and sealing the holes off. Otherwise, we don't really have any problems in warewashing. Cups and glasses we wash as normal. The glasses we have for the system are a little bigger in diameter than we normally use, so they don't fit in the normal Rayburn racks. We have had to put them in a cup rack that is bigger or put them into an open rack.

QUESTION: How do you handle nourishment feedings?

GOODWIN: We have nourishment three times a day--10:00 a.m., 2:00 p.m., and 8:00 p.m. A separate person does that in tray assembly. When they take them up, it goes to a nursing station and is put in a refrigerator up there that is totally separate from where we do a retherm process.

QUESTION: How are trays handled for patients who need isolation trays?

GOODWIN: Aladdin trays are for the most part disposable anyway. All we do with an isolation tray is take along a service cart and take the tray and all those other things that go with an isolation patient--styrofoam cup, those kind of things. When we get up on the floor, we simply transfer all that to an isolation tray up there onto disposables before we take it in.

QUESTION: How many day's requirements do you keep in storage?

GOODWIN: I assume here that you are talking about the frozen inventory. It is difficult to say in terms of days, because we have a production schedule and procedure, a little model that we go through that picks amounts based on that three-week usage. Quantity is hard to determine. I don't known if we have a theoretic set pattern. We kind of base it upon usage, depending on that item as it appears on the menu. In terms of equating that inventory, the dollar value of $15,00, for example, comes out to maybe 25,000 servings of food total, including all the products that we have in the freezer. That may be a little different now. I am citing last year's figures, when we went in one day and decided to see what the inventory value was and counted how many servings we actually had.

QUESTION: Why do you repackage after blast freezing?

GOODWIN: That's a good question. We rewrap the product for a couple of reasons. This decision was made before I arrived, and I asked the same question. We did it because if we left it in a disposable aluminum pan, it is expensive. We reuse the molds, so we pop those things out and wrap them up in the foil. It packs up a little better and takes up less space that way.

QUESTION: How about sanitizing trays, carts, dishes, etc? Do you mix disposables with china?

GOODWIN: Well, I think we have already covered sanitizing. The disposables and china are mixed from the standpoint that you have a ceramic or chinaware dish for the eggs. Everything else on the Aladdin tray is disposable, is plastic of some sort. Of course, we try to use china all the way in the cafeteria.

QUESTION: Do you use a cold water chill on hot food before you place them in a blast freezer? How do you chill the product down?

GOODWIN: We make the product and let it sit out, and we've had this procedure sanctioned; we let the product sit out until it gets down to 145°-155°F, somewhere in that range. It is still out of the danger zone. We let a lot of residual heat get out that we don't want to load the refrigeration unit with. Then we put it into the cook-chill box and leave it in there 2 to 2-1/2 hours.

By that point the product is down to around 40°F. Then
we move it to the blast freezer. We don't have any kind
of cool water bath or anything that we use for chilling.

QUESTION: How do you accommodate diet order changes
and other personal transfers?

GOODWIN: Very carefully most of the time. Sometimes
we have a problem, like everybody else, with the nursing
service keeping the diet roster up to date. It's not
always our fault; it's not always their fault. We have
had occasions where a patient would come in and get lost
in the system for 3 days before we found out he was there.
It worked out that he came in on one room, checked from
that room, and they added a tray that the nursing station
didn't order through the diet roster. The patient didn't
get a tray for the next meal, so they went ahead and
called it down. This kind of thing went on for 3 days
before we discovered that this patient was legitimate and
we caught up with him. We pass out menus a couple days
ahead of time, pass them out in the morning and pick them
up in the evening. If you don't double check when your
admissions come in or if nursing service doesn't put it
down, we lose them. For diet changes we pass the rosters
out and then we get them back for a particular meal. We
send them back to nursing service just prior to meal
time. We start getting ready to take carts up around
10:30; around 10:00 we check those diet rosters. If
there are changes to be made, we make those changes
before we send the carts out. On occasion some get by
and you have to go up on the floor and catch the cart.
We try to make them before the cart leaves the kitchen.

QUESTION: Where is the site of coalition?

GOODWIN: I think we are talking about the matching of
the tray itself. We don't have to match anything upstairs
except the patient meal and the tray and add the beverage;
everything else is on that tray. The change is what you
are talking about--that occurs in the kitchen, in the
refrigerator before the cart goes out.

QUESTION: Is there a requirement for enough carts for
two or three meals at a time?

GOODWIN: Yes, there is. We have 22 regular carts
that hold 24 trays. In addition we have 5 of the mini-
carts that Aladdin has. These are really designed to be
light-load carts, "shorty" versions of the other one.
They only hold about 6 trays. We use only 8 to 9 carts
per meal.

QUESTION: Does everything have to touch the bottom of
the dish? Do you rethermalize toast? Please repeat
times of tray line.

GOODWIN: The plating is very important in this particular system. I can't overemphasize that. The cook can make a product exactly right, but if it doesn't get plated right, it doesn't come out right. Vice versa, a person can mess up the cooking and if you plate it right it may or may not come out great. Basically you have to have contact and you have to have a product that sits down. That does limit you somewhat on the menu. If you have items like a breast of chicken, then you can't get a real surface contact and you won't get good heating. Products like corn-on-the-cob won't heat very well on this system. There is a way around this. I don't know all the answers yet, but we're certainly working on it. Fried foods are difficult to do, but we found, for example, that on fried fish, if you use the old Southern method where you just use cornmeal--take a fresh fillet and use cornmeal with a small amount of flour--fry it, chill it, and put it in your system, it comes out really good. If you used a fish with an eggwash it would probably come out soggy. So there are lot of things that we need to do. We need to talk to Holly Farms chickens or someone about prefrying chicken. Maybe that is going to be an answer to some of the frying problems with chicken.

QUESTION: How do we rethermalize toast?

GODDWIN: We really don't rethermalize other than in the disposable dish sitting inside the other dish. Another way that Aladdin has recommended is to just wrap it and lay it on top of one of the cavities, so it's warm. We found that not to be what we wanted. I am not saying that it would not be acceptable to someone else.

QUESTION: Time of the tray line?

GOODWIN: We load the lunch meal in the morning starting at 8:30. For the next meal, supper, we generally start around 11:15. Our tray assembly takes an hour to put on. That is really too slow; we need to get a lot faster. The breakfast meal is done in the afternoon, starting about 1:30, and finished up before the shift gets off.

QUESTION: How do you handle hot cereals?

GOODWIN: They are cooked on the day of service. Aladdin recommends some recipes on hot cereal for this type of system. We use these and modify them a little bit. We put a little more water in and a little more ice. Basically they are cooked the day of service. We do everything for breakfast on the day we load it. Of course this is going to be served the next day. We have a cook in the morning who is preparing all the breakfast products, maybe starting at 7:00. He makes those products and puts them in the cook-chill box, so that they get chilled down by later that afternoon. Then he starts to make the products for dinner the next day, so they can be chilled. We are essentially doing things one day ahead of time. We are not totally sure that we have a hot cereal product yet that really turns out consistently. We eat more grits than oatmeal, because grits are easier to prepare.

QUESTION: For frozen entrees what rate or number of servings do you plan per package?

GOODWIN: The packages have, I would say, 10-20 servings depending on the product. If you have a bulky items like chicken, you are going to get less. If you have pork chops or that kind of thing, it's like 5 pounds to a container. And that is going to vary, depending on the product, as to how many servings you are going to get.

QUESTION: If you are on a selective menu, what do you do if the patient picks three items that do not fit the pattern of the tray?

GOODWIN: They make some strange selections: hot cakes, french toast, donut, and eggs all at one time. We try to give them that if we can, but it may mean sending two trays. We try to give them what they ask for up to a point. If a person asks for two or three things and he is only allowed one choice, we usually make the decision and give him the first item he asked for. This generally does not happen; but if there is a patient who really wants large portions, we would prefer to send him two trays.

QUESTION: Do you consider your nonselection policies for modified diets to be good idea or to be a cop-out?

GOODWIN: I think the reason that we haven't con- sidered this is that there has not been a tremendous need. We don't have that many modified diets. It is not a policy that a lot of hospitals do not have modified selects; a lot of places do. A lot of the small hospitals have modified selects; we just don't. I really don't have any other defense; it is probably something that we should have.

QUESTION: Since you do not use a restaurant-style menu, what happens to frozen items in stock that do not appear on the new menu cycle?

GOODWIN: If there is an item in stock that is not on the cycle, and we know we are not going to put that item back on the menu, we will offer it in the cafeteria as an extra until such time that we have depleted the supply.

QUESTION: Why such a long menu cycle. Is it necessary, or necessitated by a long patient or average patient stay?

GOODWIN: A lot of people think that 21 days is too short. I don't know. Some places have 8 or 9 days. We used to have that at Walter Reed and did a flip-flop version to extend it out. All the menus are on a 42-day cycle, 6 weeks. Each hospital has the option of having the menu cycle that it chooses to have. I don't know why we had 21 days. But we do have a lot of patients that are retired, or the cancer patient on occasion, that is in and out of the hospital a lot. They seem to stay longer than 5 days. Maybe that was the idea and force behind it.

BUSTEAD: I'll try to answer that. Twenty-one days is really a compromise. Originally, for people eating three meals a day, the menu was 34 days. Three meals a day in the cafeteria--you can't shorten the menu too much without boring them. We have not tried a restaurant menu because, as I mentioned, how would you like to go to the same restaurant three meals a day, 7 days a week? We did not want to run separate patient and cafeteria menus. There are two reasons for that: One is that some of the foods that are popular are difficult to serve on a cold-plating system, and Colonel Brewer made it clear that we are in business to feed the patient, so we don't want cafeteria patrons getting better food. Also, the static is simpler if everybody eats the same thing. You don't get confusion. We will have the option to change that later. We didn't want to go as short as 14 days.

QUESTION: What is the time lapse between when the trays are assembled and given to the patients and the amount of the temperature changes and the color of food items after they have been loaded in the Aladdin trays. Share some of the results; rough figures will do.

GOODWIN: We assemble trays for the lunch meal at 8:30 a.m.-9:30 a.m. and they are served around noon. So, you have several hours between. Breakfast is done the day before and served the next morning. Supper, again, is a case of a little longer time. We assemble between 11:15 and 12:15 and serve around 4:30-5:30. The temperatures on the cold food are around 38°F. When you compare that to some of the temperatures on the other systems, there seems to be an improvement, especially with milk. Milk is also cold at breakfast, because it has had a chance to sit in the cooler all night and the box cools down to about 34°F overnight. What we judge unacceptable is

below 145°F for hot and above 50°F for cold. If we get
above 55°F we are in trouble. We only have 14 minutes to
get that cart out of the refrigerator. The insulated
tray is good, but it only slows down heat transfer; it
doesn't stop it. People think that if you put it in an
insulated tray you have hours--you don't! Remember the
patients told us that they were more worried about cold
food temperatures--40°F to 55°F is only 15° difference.
That isn't much to play with.

QUESTION: Why did you pick the cook-freeze system
over the cook-chill?

GOODWIN: The cost advantage was not that much. It is
only about 8 cents per meal. We judge the quality to be
comparable, so what we did was look at the military mission. The military has to be able to answer in an emergency; they have to be able to double or triple their
capacity. If you are getting there with 42 days of inventory, you can double or triple capacity and it gives you
a week or so to react to start to increase your food
production. That is what we are talking about--42 days
versus about 4 days in the chill system--so we felt that
the frozen food system fit the military task a little
better than chill system. One other factor that comes in
here too is that when you do chilled food, there is an
awful lot of room for error. The military is noted for
personnel turnover. The military is not used to handling
this situation. If something is frozen, they think they
can let it sit at room temperature forever--if something
is chilled, that it will stay at that temperature even
sitting at room temperature.

QUESTION: Cost versus acceptability?

GOODWIN: Why do we only use food cost and not labor
cost? I don't know. Food cost is easier to arrive at.
What we were looking for is a ranking system. Most of
the items that we freeze are labor-intensive, anyway.
Yes, we did put labor in lasagne. That would be more
expensive than roast beef.

QUESTION: Do you consider your pop-out containers and
repackaging labor-effective as opposed to complete use of
disposables?

BUSTEAD: The cost of an aluminum disposable bottom is
25 cents. The cost of an aluminum disposable top is 17
cents. Some of you may remember the cook-freeze experiment in the regular dining hall at Fort Lee. I happened
to do the cost analysis on it. The one thing that defeated that, costwise, was the aluminum disposable container. So we went to the cheapest method. This par-

ticular container that we are using is a high-density
polythylene. You can't heat in it, but you can freeze in
it. Its thickness is 50 mil; its cost is $1.08 per con-
tainer. Packaging people estimated 20-200 uses. I don't
think any have been thrown away in 2 years. So, the point
is that it's working. It may stain a little bit, but it's
working and it's cheap. Now why do we pop it and repackage it? We are trying to hold this food for roughly 42
days. Sometimes we have to go as high as 60-80 days on a
certain item. You have to get the oxygen out of there or
you're going to start to get oxidation, or you are going
to start to get freezer burns. The containers we have
are not air-tight. The DuPont Clysife is 1 mm thick and
is air-tight and does a beautiful job. It will give us
over a year of shelf life if we need it. But that's why
we do it: It is cost-effective.

QUESTION: Is there any real advantage gained by quick-
chilling prior to blast freezing. Would it be better to
go blast freezing immediately?

BUSTEAD: There are mixed feelings on this as far as
"Do you need the chiller if you are going to freeze?" I
think you all know if you go directly into a freezer with
150°F food you're going to have evaporation and that darn
coil is going to freeze up and you're going to go through
a thaw cycle every 4 hours. A blast chiller is designed
to handle that capacity to get down and keep your equipment running. In chilling or freezing longer plus one
other thing, the heat transfer, the first thing you do
when you go into a blast freezer is freeze the skin around
it. Ice doesn't transmit heat very fast; the core temperature actually stays higher when you go directly into
a freezer than if you go through a chiller first. So,
yes, you can get by without a freezer--many do--but we
like to do things in a professional manner.

We only lease this equipment from Aladdin with an
option to renew for one year, or to buy at the end of
first year. At the end of the second year, if we choose
to lease for another year, it's buy or return. We went
into an agreement that we are trying some equipment; we
didn't commit the Army or Montcrief Hospital to this
system from here to eternity. All of the hot/cold carts
are in storage. We can go back to them at any time if
for any reason were unhappy with the system.

QUESTION: Since the Aladdin cycle has 36 minutes,
what do you do to prevent some things from overcooking
while some things don't get heated enough?

BUSTEAD: There are three different slots on that shelf. Each has a different wattage. The one for soup has a higher wattage; the one for vegetables has a lower wattage. Toast is a good example. If you don't want to heat it too much or it gets hard you can put it in the vegetable side, which has the lowest heat. You pick a slot and if you're afraid it's going to overheat you put an extra dish in and it is designed to get the thing that is the hardest with contact up to at least 160°F. Now, obviously, some things won't make good enough contact.

QUESTION: What is the change of the full-time equivalents? Are the 55 positions on the staff full-time equivalents?

BUSTEAD: Yes, the military has not made extensive use of part-timers at this time. Everybody is full-time. We're not prepared to talk about the change yet. The frozen food cart had allowed for the original staffing that we agreed to use, which is 63. The 55 full-time equivalents right now is 8 below that, and we feel this is largely due to the frozen food part of the system. We cannot estimate the full-time equivalents when this is over because we're still in the learning stage. We are now trying to change assembly to see if we can change a little bit more.

QUESTION: Are there any advantages to rapid thawing as opposed to just thawing in the refrigerator or at room temperature?

GOODWIN: If we thaw food under controlled conditions and we don't use it, then we can refreeze it or save it. If we set it at room temperature and we don't use it, we had better dump it. So, again, we want to do it in the professional way and leave the least room for mistakes.

QUESTION: What size batches do you use?

GOODWIN: We are trying to set up in a production mode. In a production mode, when you have a 60-gallon kettle you fill it up because the clean-up time and the set-up time is the same whether you half fill it or completely fill it. That is why I mentioned that we're aiming for a 42-day storage that is twice our cycle. However, we have to make 500 quarts, which is going to last 60 days, to fill the kettle because that is the only way that we're going to save in production.

QUESTION: Are we back to rapid thaw rather than refrigerator thawing?

GOODWIN: Incidentally, this rapid thaw unit has a heater in it. It likes to hold the temperature in it between 45°F and 50°F during the thaw cycle that is shown

on the dial in front. Then, after that, it reverts to
being a refrigerator. The reason we use rapid thawing is
because it allows us to save and carry over the food.
The other thing is that in a refrigerator it would take
about three times as long; we just don't have that kind
of refrigeration space.

QUESTION: In your project did you utilize any of the
information developed through the Walter Reed experiment?

GOODWIN: We have learned a lot from Walter Reed and
what occurred there. I think one of the things we picked
out of that is all the production guides. We have developed some of the things that Carol Dahl talked about
on the modified diets. We are going to be able to utilize
some of the work done on those and some of the work that
was done on the dental liquids. We are not yet using it
fully, but we will be. In terms of research into food
products, we got a lot out of that. You could talk all
day, I guess, about the things that we learned. One of
them is "keep it simple." I think we realized in a lot
of ways that simplicity is the key for what we do or what
we need to be doing. Other than that it is just a
combination of things. We have a lot more people in the
Army that have a lot more experience with this kind of
thing than we used to have. I think that a combined
effort of all those folks is going to contribute to more
success in the future.

QUESTION: In goal setting for this project did you
limit yourselves to a single system for all military
hospitals? Is this vein a bit narrow? Is it not true
that some systems adapt themselves to certain conditions?
Conditions must vary from one military hospital to the
next.

BREWER: Yes, that's true, and no, we're not looking
at this as a decision-maker for going into all of our
hospitals. We have 48 military hospitals around the
world. Obviously they have different requirements and
different needs. They range anywhere from 25 beds to
1,000 to 1,200 beds. So, whether this system fits each
hospital--I don't think that this study, at this particular point, is going to give us that answer. I would
certainly not be willing to step out on the limb and say
that if this study proves that this is the way that we
ought to go, then we go that way for every hospital that
we have. I would hope that we would take each hospital
and its needs separately. What we do hope to find out is
if there is a better way to serve our patients.

We do have to keep in mind that we have personnel eating in our dining facilities that lie in the barracks; they do not have another place to eat, other than McDonalds or other places just off post, and we have to keep in mind that they are going to be there three or four years. We don't want to drive them into monotony. So, if this system, say Aladdin, is determined to be a tight system that would work in this situation, then I don't see that we're necessarily deciding that Aladdin is the system we're going to. The criteria that are important to us, that we want to establish to stay when we put out bids, are that "This is the type of system that we want; and these are the criteria to meet." If you have four other people who will come up with systems that will meet these criteria, that's great for us because we get much criticism for going for single sources. It is almost an impossible task. So, we hope to get lots of answers. We have a lot of hospitals. When we have a post that has a division on it, or a training post such as Fort Jackson--this is where similar hospitals are in a similar construction phase, same chassis built--then we could utilize the information very readily to make a lot of decisions. Certainly there would be an analysis, more decision points in making that decision. We have not made our minds up about any decision at this point.

Optimizing Spontaneous Intake: A Challenge for the Hospital Food Service

George L. Blackburn, Joyce B. Tower, Nathaniel G. Clark,
Irene Borghi, and Joanne E. Wade

The challenges confronting a hospital dietetics department in attempting to meet the needs of its patients
clinically, emotionally, and economically are great. In
this paper, four major challenges will be discussed:
those facing (1) the patient, (2) the clinical dietitian,
(3) the food service area, and (4) the dietetics department in having to integrate the clinical and food service
areas. Each of these challenges will be discussed in general, and then the New England Deaconess Hospital, Department of Dietetics, will be presented as a case study for
how the aforementioned challenges are being successfully
met.

CHALLENGES TO THE PATIENT

The challenges facing the patient stem from the effects
of the patient's illness and/or therapeutic regimen.
Answers to these challenges must take into account the
reality that illness takes away appetite and meal satisfaction. The evolution of man has depended on the availability and use of body stores of nutrients. Mobilization
of these nutrients from adipose tissue, muscle, connective
tissue, and gastrointestinal mucosa requires a hormonal
shift consistent with starvation (e.g., anorexia during
illness). Basically the patient has a decline in insulin
and thyroid hormone and a rise in catecholamines, gluca-
gon, and glucocorticoids to mobilize fatty acids, glucose,
and amino acids from labile reserves.
   Adequacy of the patient's nutriture can be lost by
inadequate intake or changes in digestion or absorption.
Factors that can lead to decreased intake include: the
anorexia (lack of appetite) that often accompanies

disease; the side effects of antibiotics, steroids, and other medications used; and the more general effect of lack of taste appeal of diets necessarily controlled in sodium, potassium, protein, and fluid, among other components. Finally, a patient's intakes are often adversely affected by mealtime interruptions in the nature of diagnostic tests, physical exams, routine blood collections, etc. Each patient, as well, by his/her background limits the intake of specific foods based on individual food preferences, religious/ethnic food modifications, and response to the more general effects on spontaneous food intake of fear, apprehension, depression, and confusion.

Even if food intake is adequate, its nutritional adequacy can be influenced by maldigestion and/or malabsorption. Patients who have had surgery to the gastrointestinal tract often suffer from decreased ability to digest foods taken in. Whether it is a decreased gastric reservoir (as often occurs in stomach surgery), altered motility of the small bowel, or the lack of the digestive factors (bile and pancreatic enzymes), maldigestion can occur.

In addition to adequate intake and digestion, adequate absorption must also be present. Patients who have dramatically decreased small bowel absorptive surface, whether due to a surgical shortening of the bowel or decreased absorptive surface (decreased number or height of villi), may fail to thrive even with adequate intake. This decrease can accompany radiation treatments and some food allergies.

CHALLENGES TO THE CLINICAL DIETITIAN

Clinical dietitians face the major challenge of having to construct a nutritional care plan with food that the patient can (and will) tolerate, that meets his/her clinical needs, and that can be provided by the food service portion of the dietetics department. By a thorough assessment of the patient's case, they must make certain that what the medical team has ordered for the patient is appropriate. They must see that the diet order is communicated to the food service area and ascertain that the patient's intake is maximized. All of this must be accomplished within the reality that, because there is no standard patient, there can be no standard meal plan/formula. The broad variety of patients' clinical conditions thereby necessitates a large variety of food service products and flexibility of delivery systems.

CHALLENGES TO THE FOOD SERVICE AREA

The challenges inherent in the provision of appetizing, nutritious, and economical meals to large numbers of patients with widely different clinical conditions are tremendous. In this context the major challenges are: (1) the rising cost of food and labor, (2) the availability of preparation facilities and personnel, (3) government regulations, and (4) recent technology. The food service area must carefully balance the demands of the clinical staff as to which foods are necessary clinically with the requirement of fiscal responsibility/cost containment.

The greatest factor in any food service budget is the rapidly rising cost of food and labor. In addition, with any increase in menu diversity comes a requirement for specialized preparation facilities and personnel. Any food service operation must concern itself as well with the requirement imposed on it by government regulations. Both state and federal governments set standards for sanitation, quality control, and employee health and welfare. Finally, the incredible rise in food service technology creates new challenges in assuring that the processes in use are maximally efficient and produce a consistently high-quality product.

CHALLENGES OF CLINICAL/FOOD SERVICE INTEGRATION

Despite the fact that the primary goal of a dietetics department as a whole is the provision of meals that meet the patients' needs and that this goal is shared by both the clinical and food service areas, the food service and clinical areas often appear to have different sets of competing priorities. Unity of purpose is a workable goal, however, in the presence of high-quality management.

THE NEW ENGLAND DEACONESS HOSPITAL: A CASE STUDY

The New England Deaconess Hospital (NEDH) is the third largest hospital in Boston, a 489-bed, 14-building complex. The Deaconess is a specialty referral hospital

serving the medical and surgical needs of the general
public, as well as patients from the Joslin Diabetes
Center and the Overholt Thoracic and Lahey clinics with
which it is associated. A teaching affiliate of Harvard
Medical School, the Deaconess is known nationally and
internationally for the high quality of its patient care
and is particularly distinguished for its work in brain
and chest surgery and for diagnosis, treatment, and
research in cancer, diabetes, cardiac and renal disease,
and general medicine. The Nutrition/Metabolism Laboratory in the Cancer Research Institute and the Department
of Surgery were responsible for developing the first com-
prehensive Nutrition Support Service with primary focus
on the activity of the clinical dietitian specialist in
hyperalimentation.

The primary goal of the Department of Dietetics is to
provide nutritional care of the highest quality to the
hospital's patient population, which is made up predom-
inantly of acutely ill individuals. Because of the
specialty nature of the hospital, most patients are at
significant nutritional risk, and approximately 85
percent of all patients require a therapeutic diet,
frequently involving multiple restrictions. Moreover,
the two predominant groups of patients, oncology and
diabetes, which together may generally occupy as many as
6 percent of the nearly 500 beds, have quite divergent
menu requirements. The typical diabetic diet is low in
concentrated sources of simple carbohydrates and high in
a variety of low-caloric-density, high-nutrient-density
foods such as greens, fruits, and vegetables, which also
tend to be high in fiber and less easily digestible. The
oncology patient, on the other hand, undergoing extensive
diagnostic examination or surgical, radiologic, or chemo-
therapeutic treatment related to this disease, requires
increased calorie intake at a time when his appetite is
minimal and eating is an additional, unwanted burden. In
direct contrast to the needs of patients with diabetes,
the menu needs of oncology patients are for easily
swallowed and digested foods with maximum caloric density.

Diet Technician at the Bedside

The clinical dietetics team that responds to the patient's
nutritional needs is managed by clinical dietitians, who
coordinate all aspects of dietary care. Diet technicians
play a key role in the implementation of both clinical

and food service responsibilities. For example, they
assist dietitians in assessing the nutritional status of
patients, provide diet education for identified patients,
and document nutritional care in the medical record.
Technicians also work closely with food service personnel
to ensure effective implementation of nutrition
prescriptions.

Hot Meals at Most Times

The patient food service system employed at the New
England Deaconess utilizes a cook-chill concept. Food is
prepared in quantity 12 to 24 hours in advance of the
meal at which it is to be served, cooked to a degree
slightly less than fully done, and then refrigerated.
Immediately prior to meal time, individual items, still
in a chilled state, are portioned, which includes precise
weighing via gram scales of individual items for all
patients on diabetic diets. Trays are assembled according to each menu as they proceed along a motorized
assembly line. Trays are then placed, depending on
destination, either in carts cooled to 38°-45°F with dry
ice or on standard, unrefrigerated carts that are transported immediately to "roll-in" refrigerators located on
patient units. Only when the tray is ready to be served
is the chilled food rethermalized in microwave ovens
located in nourishment kitchens on each patient floor,
and in the process the final phase of cooking is completed. Since food service procedures include a
preliminary check with each patient to ascertain his
readiness to receive his meal, the system potentially
allows not only accommodation to the patient's schedule,
but also to his personal preference and immediate health
status as well.

Alternatives to Depending on Advanced
Hardware Technology

Thus far we have resisted, to a large degree, much of the
trend toward space age technology. Our system continues
to utilize conventional china, stainless steel flatware,
and a minimum of paper and plastic. The importance of
both aesthetic appearance and ease of access in placement
of items on the tray is still emphasized in in-service
training and orientation programs.

Role of the Selective Menu

In spite of the complexity of the dietary therapy demands, however, it has been the long-standing policy of the Department of Dietetics to offer all patients a selective menu. Each patient, no matter what or how many restrictions are imposed, has menu alternatives from which to choose. The current menu combines aspects of a restaurant style with the traditional cycle menu by providing five to six entrees at each of the luncheon and dinner meals, rotating through a one-week cycle. Based on data indicating an 11-day average length of stay, a 1-week, widely varied cycle avoids the visual monotony and repetition of the purely restaurant style menu, yet allows the most popular items to be featured frequently.

In addition to a master menu that includes lamb chops, roast sirloin, and seafood newburg, a variety of the most popular items, such as steak, breast of chicken, and macaroni and cheese, is available on any day upon request. An extensive selection of snacks is available three times a day between meals. These provide additional variety and permit the frequent small feedings often necessary to increase the intake of patients restricted to liquid foods or who have vastly increased caloric requirements but severe anorexia. The selection of snacks ranges from sandwiches, frappes, ice cream, and fresh fruit to crackers, cheese, peanut butter, and commercially prepared products of highly concentrated nutritive value.

Quality Control Measured by Patient Satisfaction

The technology today associated with food service delivery systems is impressive. Space constraints as well as rapidly escalating labor costs have spurred development of increasingly streamlined and automated equipment and delivery systems. What is often lost in this emphasis on efficiency, however, is the warmth and individualized attention essential to humanized patient care. The service concept can easily be lost from food service.

The large ratio of labor to other costs characteristic of health care delivery is also reflected in food service, where roughly two-thirds of the total operating budget represents labor costs. In spite of this, the majority of patients at the New England Deaconess are still assisted with menu selection prior to luncheon and

dinner. Though necessitating some adjustment to the
typical tally system for production planning, this has
been found to be the most expedient method of planning
meals with patients as acutely ill as our patients tend
to be.

In addition, menu assistance within 2 to 3 hours of
the meal's being ordered (1) reduces the chances of the
patient forgetting what he ordered due to apprehension,
confusion, or medication, which frequently occurs when
menus are planned 24 hours in advance; (2) eliminates
surprise trays to patients who may have selected a menu
but require a special test meal because of a last-minute
order by a physician; and (3) provides the patient the
opportunity to request a guest tray at a nominal fee for
a relative or friend, if desired.

Dietitians' Role in Patient Recovery

There continues to exist at the Deaconess Hospital strong
support for and commitment to standards of quality and
aesthetics related to food and food service. There is
pride as well as dedication in the responsibilities shared
by department personnel. Pressures, however, to go with
the tide are great and continue to grow.

Simple economic realities cannot be ignored. It becomes more difficult to justify additional costs simply
for aesthetics, or, when faced with the burgeoning growth
of labor costs, to justify personnel to provide assistance
in interpreting and selecting a menu or to spend the extra
time required to cut a patient's food or fetch a second
pot of coffee. Yet, all of these can be crucial in maximizing the patient's food intake.

Department Organization

The fourth challenge noted above was based on the need to
integrate the clinical and food service areas in ensuring
that the patient's needs are met. Primarily, as can be
seen from the Dietetics Department organization chart
(Figure 1), both areas report ultimately to the same person. The director is a clinical dietitian with extensive
experience in administrative principles, food service systems, and education and training of clinical dietitians.

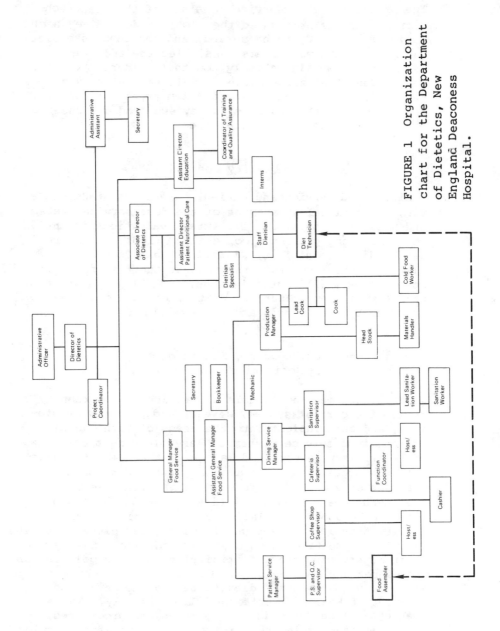

FIGURE 1 Organization chart for the Department of Dietetics, New England Deaconess Hospital.

Integration of Food Handler and Diet Technician

The process of meal service consists of the diet technician, who has prerounded the floor to determine which patients are ready to be served, and the food assembler, who reheats the meal items, assembles the tray, and delivers it, working closely together (Figure 2). At the completion of a meal service as well, a meal service report is written noting any problem areas (including patient comments), and this is reviewed and discussed in the food service and clinical areas.

Quality Control

Quality food service and patient care cannot take place without continual assessment of the food service system and patient needs (Table 1). Tray evaluations are held on a different patient floor daily. Floor nurses, residents, diet technicians, dietitians, and food service quality control supervisors evaluate the tray for: (1) completeness, (2) attractiveness, and (3) preparation of food (taste, temperature). Written evaluations are compiled by each member and reviewed.

Meetings: Reports, Education, Feedback, Motivation, and Morale

Departmental meetings (Table 2) provide an opportunity to review the current system, develop and plan new strategies, and gain insight into the needs of both the clinical and food service systems. Assemblers meet every two weeks with supervisors and managers at assemblers' meetings to discuss tray assembly, microwaving techniques, delivery service, etc. Team meetings with assemblers, diet technicians, and dietitians are held monthly to discuss the above in relation to the clinical perspective.

Diet technicians meet weekly with staff dietitians (in addition to meeting throughout each day individually with their supervising staff dietitian) to discuss policies and procedures and food service. Clinical management meetings are held with the staff dietitians and the Assistant Director of Patient Nutritional Care biweekly. These meetings are held to discuss policies and procedures, potential changes in the clinical areas, and food service. Staff at this point comment on overall functioning of the

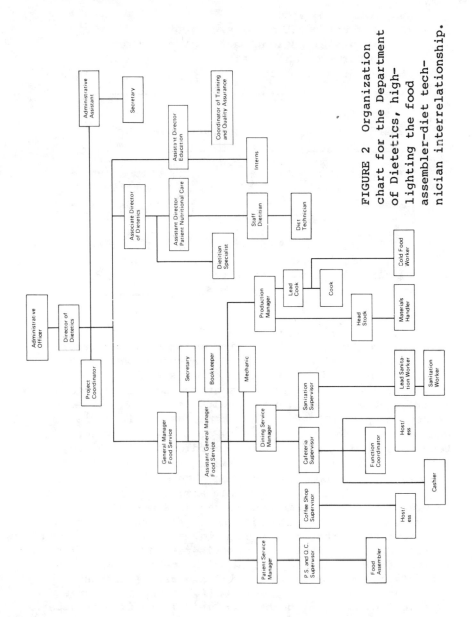

FIGURE 2 Organization chart for the Department of Dietetics, high-lighting the food assembler-diet technician interrelationship.

TABLE 1 Data Sources for Quality Control

1. Tray evaluations
2. Patient questionnaire/comments
3. Review of patient meal service reports
4. Supervisor checklists
5. Incident reports

TABLE 2 Frequency of Committee Meetings

Assemblers' meetings	Biweekly
Team meetings	Monthly
Diet technicians' meetings	Weekly
Clinical management meetings	Biweekly
Clinical staff meetings	Weekly
Administrative Committee	Biweekly
Standards Committee	Monthly
Quality Assurance Committee	Monthly

clinical and food service areas. Clinical staff meetings
are held weekly with all members of the clinical service.
Updates in general are discussed, in-service education
provided, and studies and protocols presented.

The standards and quality assurance committees meet
monthly. Quality assurance develops standards for all
aspects of patient care. The standards committee is
composed of technicians, quality control, supervisors,
food service managers, and the coordinator of teaching
and quality control. This committee tests new products
and evaluates recommendations for changes in portion
sizes, menu selections, etc. The administrative meeting
is biweekly. It is composed of the director of the
department, the associate director, assistant directors,
the Assistant Director of Education, and the General Food
Service Manager. This committee is responsible for the
general focus of the Department of Dietetics. All other
committees (standards and quality assurance) are sub-
committees of this committee. Policies and procedures
emanate from here for both the clinical and food service
systems.

CONCLUSION

The challenges for the clinical and food service systems are many, and in an era in which cost containment is necessary, quality nutritional care is difficult to achieve. However, when the clinical and food service areas work together, communicate openly regarding intradepartmental needs, and have the patient's nutritional needs as the focus of attention, optimizing spontaneous oral intakes no longer becomes a change but a choice for quality support.

A

APPENDIX

Advisory Board on Military Personnel Supplies

Ludwig Rebenfeld, President, Textile Research Institute, Princeton, New Jersey

Linda Bartoshuk, Associate Fellow, Pierce Foundation, and Associate Professor, Department of Epidemiology and Psychology, Yale School of Medicine

Harold A. Dewhurst, Director, Scientific Affairs, Owens Corning Fiberglas, Granville, Ohio

Daniel F. Farkas, Professor and Chairperson, Department of Food Science and Human Nutrition, University of Delaware

Enio Feliciotti, Senior Vice President, Research, Development & Quality Assurance, Thomas J. Lipton, Inc., Englewood Cliffs, New Jersey

Dee McDonald Graham, Director, Central Research, Del Monte Corporation, Walnut Creek, California

Theodore P. Labuza, Professor of Food Science and Technology, University of Minnesota

Reiner G. Stoll, Celanese Science and Technology Advisory Board, Celanese Corporation, New York, New York.

Frank R. Fisher, Executive Director, Advisory Board on Military Personnel Supplies, National Research Council

B
APPENDIX

Symposium on Hospital Patient Feeding Systems

STEERING COMMITTEE

Charnette Norton (Chairman) Director of Food and Nutrition
    Services, University of Chicago Hospitals and Clinics,
    Chicago, Illinois

Mary R. DeMarco (Vice Chairman) Senior Staff Specialist,
    Food Service Management, American Hospital
    Association, Chicago, Illinois

Paul W. Blackmon, Manager, Health Systems Statistics, and
    Evaluation Division, Analytical Services, Inc.,
    Arlington, Virginia

Colonel Jessie S. Brewer, Chief, Dietition Section, Office
    of the Surgeon General, Department of the Army

M. Eileen Matthews, Professor, Foodservice Administration,
    Department of Food Science, University of
    Wisconsin-Madison

Justin M. Tuomy, Chief, Food Technology Division, Food
    Engineering Laboratory, U.S. Army Natick Research and
    Development Laboratories

Liaison Member

Mary Lou South, President, American Dietetic Association

Symposium Staff

Frank R. Fisher, Executive Director, Advisory Board on
    Military Personnel Supplies, National Research Council

Virginia White, Staff Associate for Symposium, Research
Home Economist, U.S. Army Natick Research and
Development Laboratories

PROGRAM COMMITTEE

M. Eileen Matthews, Professor, Foodservice Administration,
Department of Food Science, University of
Wisconsin-Madison

Barbara J. Bobeng, Assistant Director, Dietary Department,
Massachusetts General Hospital

Major William L. Goodwin, Jr., Chief, Food Service
Division, Moncrief Army Hospital, Fort Jackson, South
Carolina

PUBLICATIONS COMMITTEE

Charles E. Eshbach, Chairman, Department of Hotel,
Restaurant, and Travel Administration, University of
Massachusetts

Raymond B. Peddersen, Director of Dietetics, LDS Hospital,
Salt Lake City, Utah

C

APPENDIX

Biographical Sketches of Symposium Committee Members

PAUL W. BLACKMON holds a B.S. degree in mathematics from The Citadel, an M.S. in statistics from the University of Chicago, and Ph.D. in statistics from Virginia Polytechnic Institute and State University. As Manager of Health Systems Statistics and Evaluation Division, Analytic Services, Inc., since 1975 he has been involved in many hospital-selected projects, including evaluation of the impact on personnel utilization of the application of an array of advanced technologies to a hospital food service, and assessment of a computerized medical information system at a major clinical center.

BARBARA J. BOBENG is Assistant Director of the Dietary Department and Assistant Professor of the Massachusetts General Hospital Institute of Health Professions in Boston. She has management responsibility for food service systems and plans for future facilities and services, is active in the selection and education of 26 dietetic interns, and is a member of the MGH Infection Control Committee. As Assistant Professor, MGH Institute of Health Professions, she is involved in planning for the Graduate Program in Dietetics and participates in the activities of the Institute's Course and Curriculum Committee and Program Admissions Committees in Dietetic and Social Work. She earned B.S. and M.S. degrees in Institutional Management from Iowa State University and a Ph.D. from the University of Wisconsin-Madison. The author of numerous publications, she is a member of the American Dietetic Association, the American School Food Service Association, the American Society for Hospital Food Service Administrators, Food Service Systems Management Education, the Institute of Food Technologists, and other professional associations. Dr. Bobeng was awarded the American Dietetic Association Mead Johnson Scholarship in 1975.

COLONEL JESSIE S. BREWER received a B.S. degree in foods and nutrition from Mississippi State College for Women and an M.S. degree in foods, nutrition, and institution administration from Oklahoma State University. She is a member of the American Dietetic Association, American Society for Hospital Food Service Administration, and Military Surgeons Association. She has been Chief of Dietitian Section, Office of the Surgeon General, Department of the Army, since 1978.

MARY R. DEMARCO is Director, American Society for Hospital Food Service Administrators and Senior Staff Specialist, Hospital Food Service Management, at the American Hospital Association in Chicago, Illinois. She earned an M.S. degree at Case Western Reserve University and was Director of Nutrition Services at Cleveland Metropolitan General Hospital for 23 years. Her numerous professional activities include serving as a consultant for the U.S. Department of Education and the Pan American Health Organization of the United Nations. She was Secretary-Treasurer of the American Dietetic Association, 1977-1979. She received the International Foodservice Manufacturers' Association (IFMA) Silver Plate Award in 1975 and in 1979 was named Notre Dame College Alumnae's "Woman of the Year." She has lectured throughout the United States and in China, New Zealand, and Germany.

CHARLES E. ESHBACH received B.S. and M.S. degrees from the University of Massachusetts an M.B.A. from Harvard University. He has authored or coauthored over 100 publications, including books on food service management and food service trends. As a professor at the University of Massachusetts, his teachings include food service management, purchasing, hospital and school food service administration, marketing, food service sanitation, and food handling. His research focus is on operational efficiency studies and economic and marketing surveys of food service operations in restaurants, hospitals, nursing homes, and schools.

MAJOR WILLIAM GOODWIN, JR., Chief, Food Service Division of the Moncrief Army Hospital, Fort Jackson, South Carolina, received a B.S. degree in institution management at Berry College, Mt. Berry, Georgia, and after Dietetic Internship at Brooke Army Medical Center earned an M.S. degree in Food Systems Administration at the University of Tennessee. Major Goodwin has worked largely as an administrative dietitian and special projects officer during the past 12 years in a variety of posts in Army medical treatment facilities. Assignments include Brooke Army Medical Center; Fitzsimons Army Medical Center; Walter Reed Army Medical Center; and the U.S. Army Hospital, Ft. Campbell, Kentucky. From 1976 to 1979 Major Goodwin served as consultant to the Army Surgeon General on hospital service systems design and analysis. He is a member of the American Dietetic Association and the American Society for Hospital Food Service Administrators.

M. EILEEN MATTHEWS is Professor, Department of Food Science, University of Wisconsin-Madison, where she has taught graduate and undergraduate courses in food service administration and conducted research since 1970. She earned a B.S. from Drexel University in Philadelphia in 1960 and an M.S. at Oklahoma State University with majors in food, nutrition, and institution management. Following an administrative dietetic internship at Oklahoma State University, she worked as an assistant nutritionist with the National Diet-Heart Study at the Johns Hopkins Hospital. Dr. Matthews earned a Ph.D. from the University of Wisconsin-Madison in 1970 with a major in food administration in the Department of Food Science and a minor in management in the School of Business. Her research interests include quality and safety of food during processing stages in quantity food production systems and the optimal use of management resources in food services. Dr. Matthews has authored or coauthored more than 60 publications on applications of management or food science to food service systems. Her publications have appeared in Journal of The American Dietetic Association, Journal of Food Protection, Journal of Food Science, Journal of Microwave Power, Hospitals, J.A.H.A., School Food Service Research Review, and others. In October 1980 Dr. Matthews received a Medallion Award for leadership in dietetics from the American Dietetic Association. She participated by invitation in the Catering/Foodservice Workshop of the International Symposium on Role and Application of Food Science and Technology in Industrialized Nations in Helsinki, Finland, September 15-17, 1981. Dr. Matthews is a member of numerous professional organizations in the food service industry and serves on several committees involving research and community service.

CHARNETTE NORTON is Director of Food and Nutrition Services, University of Chicago Hospitals and Clinics in

Chicago, Illinois. She has a B.S. in food and nutrition
and an M.S. in food systems management from the University
of Missouri-Columbia. Ms. Norton is Region 3 Director of
the American Society of Hospital Food Service Administrators and a member of the American Dietetic Association.
She has been affiliated with industrial organizations
providing food and feeding systems for hospitals and has
managed dietary services at other hospitals.

RAYMOND B. PEDDERSON is Director of Food Service at
LDS Hospital in Salt Lake City. He earned a B.S. degree
in behavioral science from Westminister College and
attended the School of Hotel Administration at Cornell
University. He received the 1980 Foodservice Operator of
the Year Award From the International Foodservice
Manufacturers Association. He is a member of the American
Society for Hospital Food Service Administrators and the
International Food Service Executives Association. He is
the author of many journal articles and several books
related to food service administration and systems for
schools and hospitals.

JUSTIN M. TUOMY is Chief of Food Technology Division,
Food Engineering Laboratory, U.S. Army Natick Research and
Development Laboratories, Natick, Massachusetts. He
received a B.S. degree in chemical engineering from the
University of Minnesota. In 1958 Mr. Tuomy started
working as a food technologist at the Food and Container
Institute, Chicago, predecessor organization of the Food
Engineering Laboratory; later he became Head, Dairy and
Dehydrated Products Section, and then Chief, Animal
Products Group. He spent 10 years in industry as Head,
Product Control, Oscar Mayer & Co., Chicago; Plant
Manager, Dry Sausage Plant, Oscar Mayer & Co.; Technical
Sales Manager, L. C. Spiehs Co., Chicago; and Plant
Manager, Horton Fruit Co., Louisville, Kentucky. Mr.
Tuomy spent four years on active duty as a U.S. Army
officer in World War II with antiaircraft and combat
engineers. He is a member of a number of technical
societies, author of numerous scientific papers, and holds
several patents.